BEGINNING
VISUAL STUDIO® LIGHTSWITCH DEVELOPMENT

BEGINNING

Visual Studio® LightSwitch Development

BEGINNING

Visual Studio® LightSwitch Development

István Novák

Wiley Publishing, Inc.

Beginning Visual Studio® LightSwitch Development

Published by
Wiley Publishing, Inc.
10475 Crosspoint Boulevard
Indianapolis, IN 46256
www.wiley.com

Copyright © 2011 by Wiley Publishing, Inc., Indianapolis, Indiana

Published simultaneously in Canada

ISBN: 978-1-118-02195-8
ISBN: 978-1-118-14851-8 (ebk.)
ISBN: 978-1-118-14850-1 (ebk.)
ISBN: 978-1-118-14854-9 (ebk.)

Manufactured in the United States of America

10 9 8 7 6 5 4 3 2 1

For general information on our other products and services please contact our Customer Care Department within the United States at (877) 762-2974, outside the United States at (317) 572-3993 or fax (317) 572-4002.

Wiley also publishes its books in a variety of electronic formats. Some content that appears in print may not be available in electronic books.

Library of Congress Control Number: 2011930875

To Henriett, Eszter, and Reka. I owe you many hours for the missed weekends.

ABOUT THE AUTHOR

 **ISTVÁN NOVÁK** is an associate and the chief technology consultant of SoftwArt, a small Hungarian IT consulting company. He works as a software architect and community evangelist. In the last 20 years, he participated in more than 50 enterprise software development projects. In 2002, he co-authored the first Hungarian book about .NET development. In 2007, he was awarded with the Microsoft Most Valuable Professional (MVP) title, and in 2011 he became a Microsoft Regional Director. As the main author, he contributed in writing the *Visual Studio 2010 and .NET 4 Six-In-One* book (Indianapolis: Wiley, 2010). He holds master's degree from the Technical University of Budapest, Hungary, and also has a doctoral degree in software technology. He lives in Dunakeszi, Hungary, with his wife and two teenage daughters. He is a passionate scuba diver. You may have a good chance of meeting him underwater at the Red Sea in any season of the year.

ABOUT THE TECHNICAL EDITORS

RITA RUBAN is a writer of educational material in computing (specifically, Visual Basic, Visual Basic for Applications, HTML, Excel, and various art software applications), mathematics, and biology, having been a teacher/lecturer for these subjects. She is also an artist and designer. Visit her page on LinkedIn for further information and web links, or e-mail her at ritaruban@yahoo.co.uk.

DIANNE SIEBOLD is a software developer and writer specializing in Visual Basic, C#, .NET Framework, Windows Communications Foundation, ActiveX Data Objects, and SQL Server. She has worked for a number of Microsoft partners writing enterprise applications, with an emphasis on services and data access. Reach her by e-mail at dsiebold@earthlink.net.

CREDITS

ACQUISITIONS EDITOR
Paul Reese

PROJECT EDITOR
Kevin Shafer

TECHNICAL EDITORS
Rita Ruban
Dianne Seybold

PRODUCTION EDITORS
Debra Banninger
Nick Moran

COPY EDITOR
Luann Rouff

EDITORIAL DIRECTOR
Robyn B. Siesky

EDITORIAL MANAGER
Mary Beth Wakefield

FREELANCER EDITORIAL MANAGER
Rosemarie Graham

ASSOCIATE DIRECTOR OF MARKETING
David Mayhew

PRODUCTION MANAGER
Tim Tate

VICE PRESIDENT AND EXECUTIVE GROUP PUBLISHER
Richard Swadley

VICE PRESIDENT AND EXECUTIVE PUBLISHER
Barry Pruett

ASSOCIATE PUBLISHER
Jim Minatel

PROJECT COORDINATOR, COVER
Katie Crocker

PROOFREADER
Nancy Carrasco

INDEXER
Robert Swanson

COVER DESIGNER
LeAndra Young

COVER IMAGE
© iStock / Pamela Moore

ACKNOWLEDGMENTS

I REALLY ENJOYED WRITING THIS BOOK. The idea started at the beginning of August, 2010 when Microsoft announced Visual Studio LightSwitch. A few weeks later, after trying the first Beta, I imagined an idea about how this great product could be evangelized. I'm happy that Acquisitions Editor Paul Reese supported my idea and helped to form this book.

In addition to my readers, I owe a lot to other great people who helped me with the writing of this book and ensured that my imagination became reality.

First of all, I'd like to thank Kevin Shafer for his amazing editorial work. This is my second book working together with Kevin, and I really appreciated how he carried the whole book writing process on his shoulders, and ironed my sentences. I hope I can meet Kevin personally in the near future, and shake his hand.

I'd also like to thank Luann Rouff for thoroughly reading the manuscript and translating my originally complex paragraphs to simple and tangle-free sentences. Dianne Siebold and Rita Ruban, the Technical Editors, raked over my submitted chapters and suggested many changes that made this writing much more accurate than it was before their reviews. I'm very grateful for their help.

The Hungarian Silverlight User Group and the Hungarian Windows Azure User Group provided me with several opportunities to speak about LightSwitch. They also gave me valuable feedback about positioning the product. Thanks for their support.

Finally, I owe many kisses to my wife and daughters for letting me spend so many hours away from them — in my study, working with the book. Now, they get their evenings and weekends back.

CONTENTS

PART IV: APPENDIX

APPENDIX: ANSWERS TO EXERCISES   401

INTRODUCTION

TO THOSE OF US WHO PAY ATTENTION to such things, the world of software development has changed a lot in the last few years. In the .NET world, Microsoft's Visual Studio 2010 is undoubtedly the most successful development environment. Since the release of the first .NET version in February 2002, this product has undergone dramatic changes. Currently, it encapsulates three languages (Visual Basic, C#, and F#) and many tools that support the entire life cycle of software development.

It provides great freedom for developers to create virtually any type of application for many devices, including desktops, portable devices, and phones; and now it supports cloud applications. Given the globalization of business and rapid changes in the world economy, the importance of fast time-to-market requirements continuously affects how software products — and especially line-of-business (LOB) applications — are developed.

While Visual Studio supports development teams, it still requires jumping over a relatively high entry barrier. Writing versatile business applications with this tool definitely requires deep software development knowledge — in exchange for the freedom it offers.

Visual Studio LightSwitch is a new member of the Visual Studio family. It was designed and developed with rapid data-centric LOB application development in mind. It targets primarily consultants and business analysts who are far removed from everyday programming — and not just experienced developers.

This book serves as a foundation for learning the basics of creating useful business applications with LightSwitch — using only minimal coding.

WHO THIS BOOK IS FOR

This book was written with IT consultants and business analysts in mind — those who have a deep understanding of business processes, and have specific business domain experience. With LightSwitch, they can independently materialize their LOB application prototype ideas — and implement productive applications — without the continuous help of developers and other IT experts. The book also helps those developers, consultants, and experts who want to rapidly achieve success in defining requirements and functional prototypes to accelerate the specification phase of their business application development projects.

The LightSwitch IDE also supports creating and deploying applications for the Windows Azure platform. No Azure-specific development knowledge is assumed to create cloud applications. Readers who plan to develop business applications for the cloud will benefit from LightSwitch, which makes it easy to deploy newly created LightSwitch applications without any additional coding or reconfiguring.

WHAT THIS BOOK COVERS

This book focuses on the features of Visual Studio LightSwitch, which enable you to write data-centric LOB applications in a very short time. Rather than going into subtle feature details in an attempt to teach you everything about LightSwitch, this book explains and demonstrates how to *utilize* this great product in business application development.

Most of the chapters follow the creation of a new project-tracking application (ProjectTrek) for a fictitious IT consulting company, ConsulArt. The discussions address not only LightSwitch, but also the context of ProjectTrek. Thus, you will learn how LightSwitch answers the challenges of LOB application development.

Of course, this book cannot show you every aspect of business application development; it just scratches the surface of things you can do with LightSwitch. Although it treats all important features, and provides you with a few recipes, there are many tasks it does not show you exactly.

This book is full of exercises that guide you through certain tasks. Rather than rushing through the exercise steps, try to do something a bit different (such as selecting an option other than the one suggested, changing a setting, adding a few more elements to a screen, and so on) and see the effect. This is the best way to discover many small details about LightSwitch that are not explicitly treated in this book.

HOW THIS BOOK IS STRUCTURED

This book is divided into three sections that will help you understand the concepts behind LightSwitch and become familiar with this great tool. The first part provides a quick overview that establishes the context of business application development, which will help you understand how LightSwitch responds to real-world challenges.

In the second part, the numerous hands-on exercises will enable you to learn the main concepts as you create the sample application, while the third part introduces a few advanced topics that are also important parts of the LightSwitch application development.

Most chapters first establish a context and treat the most important concepts, and then you learn how to use them through exercises. Each exercise concludes with a "How it Works" section that explains how (including all important details) the exercise achieves its objective.

Part I: An Introduction to Visual Studio LightSwitch

This section provides a context for Visual Studio LightSwitch and its approach to LOB application development — what it is and why it is an important addition to the Visual Studio family. It also provides an overview of the technologies that enable you to build a LightSwitch application.

> ➤ *Chapter 1: "Prototyping and Rapid Application Development"* — This chapter provides an overview of application prototyping and rapid application development (RAD) techniques.

Here you will learn how these techniques can answer LOB software development challenges, and learn how Visual Studio LightSwitch does it.

➤ *Chapter 2: "Getting Started with Visual Studio LightSwitch"* — This hands-on chapter enables you to form your first impressions of Visual Studio LightSwitch. By the time you finish this chapter, you will have installed LightSwitch and created your very first application with it — all without writing a single line of code.

➤ *Chapter 3: "Technologies behind a LightSwitch Application"* — This chapter provides an overview of the foundational technologies behind a LightSwitch application. It will help you understand the main concepts of the technologies, as well as the roles they play in LightSwitch applications.

➤ *Chapter 4: "Customizing LightSwitch Applications"* — The architectural and technological constraints provided by LightSwitch may seem too rigid. However, they actually help you to be productive, because the template-driven framework enables you to focus on your solutions, rather than the underlying design pattern. In addition, LightSwitch provides a full-featured set of customization features, which this chapter describes and demonstrates through examples.

Part II: Creating Applications with Visual Studio LightSwitch

The second section of the book treats the most important aspects of creating a fully functional LightSwitch application from scratch. Using the fictitious ConsulArt Company, you build a business application that helps the company control its projects.

➤ *Chapter 5: "Preparing to Develop a LightSwitch Application"* — To understand the functionality of the LightSwitch integrated development environment (IDE) and its development approach, you will create a new sample application from scratch. This chapter describes the application and prepares you for implementing it.

➤ *Chapter 6: "Working with Simple Data Screens"* — In this chapter, you will learn about the basics of creating tables and screens. Although you start with very simple tasks, they will help you understand LightSwitch's flexible and extensible approach, and the useful tools that it provides.

➤ *Chapter 7: "Working with Master-Detail Data Screens"* — Real applications contain data tables that have relationships between them. In this chapter, you will learn how to manage tables with relationships, and how you can build master-detail screens with them.

➤ *Chapter 8: "Using Existing SQL Server Data"* — When you develop LOB applications, you often must access and use data stored in existing back-end systems. Visual Studio LightSwitch has been designed with this functionality in mind. In this chapter, you learn how to use data stored in existing SQL Server databases.

➤ *Chapter 9: "Building and Customizing Screens"* — There are many opportunities in LightSwitch to build application screens. In this chapter, you learn the most important concepts and the basic architecture of screens. The step-by-step exercises will give you a clear understanding of each important element used to build and customize your screens.

➤ *Chapter 10: "Validation and Business Rules"* — All LOB applications must have associated rules that characterize the business. In this chapter, you will learn about the concept of data validation, and learn about the tools LightSwitch provides for creating compound business operations.

➤ *Chapter 11: "Authentication and Access Control"* — A real LOB application includes the capability of authenticating users and restricting them to using only functions they are permitted to carry out. In this chapter, you will learn the authentication and access control concepts of LightSwitch, and, of course, how to use them in your applications.

➤ *Chapter 12: "Microsoft Office Integration"* — Visual Studio LightSwitch has been designed with Microsoft Office integration in mind. The automation features of Office applications make it easy to use Word, Excel, Outlook, or even PowerPoint from LightSwitch, as you learn in this chapter.

Part III: Advanced LightSwitch Application Development

The last portion of the book is dedicated to two advanced topics. It helps you understand the options LightSwitch offers for deploying an application, and teaches you about information stored in SharePoint 2010 lists.

➤ *Chapter 13: "Deploying LightSwitch Applications"* — In general, application deployment is easy, but occasionally it can be a nightmare because of difficulties that result from creating setup kits and installation manuals. With LightSwitch, the whole process is straightforward. In this chapter, you learn about the options provided by the LightSwitch IDE, and you are guided through several deployment types.

➤ *Chapter 14: "Using SharePoint 2010 Lists"* — LightSwitch enables you to utilize the information stored in SharePoint 2010. In this chapter, you learn how to access SharePoint 2010 lists and use them in your applications — with the same ease that you experience while building SQL Server–based solutions.

WHAT YOU NEED TO USE THIS BOOK

This book assumes you have a system that meets the following requirements:

➤ You are running Windows Vista or Windows 7 (both require at least the Home Premium edition), or one of the Windows Server 2008 (or Windows Server 2008 R2) editions.

➤ You have at least 8GB of free hard disk space to install Visual Studio LightSwitch and use the samples with their databases.

You will need access to Visual Studio LightSwitch installation files. Those who already have Visual Studio 2010 with a Microsoft Developer Network (MSDN) subscription can find the online installation media among their downloadable items. A free trial version of Visual Studio LightSwitch is also available through the www.microsoft.com/visualstudio/lightswitch web page.

To go through the exercises in Chapter 14, you also must create a SharePoint site. You must access an existing SharePoint 2010 server. Chapter 14 describes all the required steps to prepare the environment required for the exercises.

CONVENTIONS

To help you get the most from the text and keep track of what's happening, we've used a number of conventions throughout the book.

TRY IT OUT

The *Try It Out* section is an exercise you should work through, following the text in the book. Some exercises use prepared samples. When you need to start with a prepared sample, you'll always be instructed where you can find the related files in the online source code that accompanies this book.

1. The exercises consist of a set of steps.

2. Each step has a number.

3. Follow the steps.

How It Works

After each *Try It Out*, the steps you've executed and the code you've typed are explained in detail.

 WARNING *Boxes with a warning icon like this one hold important, not-to-be-forgotten information that is directly relevant to the surrounding text.*

 NOTE *The pencil icon indicates notes, tips, hints, tricks, or asides to the current discussion.*

As for styles in the text:

➤ We *highlight* new terms and important words when we introduce them.

➤ We show keyboard strokes like this: Ctrl+A.

➤ We show filenames, URLs, and code within the text like so: `Application.User.HasPermission`.

➤ We present code in two different ways:

```
We use a monofont type with no highlighting for most code examples.
```

```
We use bold to emphasize code that is particularly important in the
    present context or to show changes from a previous code snippet.
```

Also, Visual Studio's Code Editor provides a rich color scheme to indicate various parts of code syntax. That's a great tool to help you learn language features in the editor, and to help prevent mistakes as you code. To reinforce Visual Studio's colors, the code listings in this book are colorized using colors similar to what you would see on screen in Visual Studio working with the book's code. In order to optimize print clarity, some colors have a slightly different hue in print than what you see on screen; but all the colors for the code in this book should be close enough to the default Visual Studio colors to give you an accurate representation.

SOURCE CODE

As you work through the examples in this book, you may choose either to type in all the code manually, or to use the source code files that accompany the book. All source code samples used in this book are available for download at www.wrox.com. When at the site, simply locate the book's title (use the Search box or one of the title lists) and click the Download Code link on the book's detail page to obtain the source code for the book.

 NOTE *Because many books have similar titles, you may find it easiest to search by ISBN; this book's ISBN is 978-1-118-02195-8.*

Once you download the code, just decompress it with your favorite compression tool. Alternately, you can go to the main Wrox code download page at www.wrox.com/dynamic/books/download.aspx to see the code available for this book and all other Wrox books.

This book contains code samples both in Visual Basic and in C#, available as separate downloads. Both downloads use the same two-level folder structure to help you locate the source code for a specific exercise. The first-level folder refers to the chapter, such as `Chapter 2`, `Chapter 4`, and so on. Within these folders are subfolders representing a specific phase of the application you will complete in the corresponding chapter.

Most exercises simply continue with the result of the previous one. However, a few start with a prepared LightSwitch project. In the latter case, the exercise explicitly tells you the folder of the project (for example, `Chapter 4\Sample 2 - Customizing Screens`), and instructs you when you need to open it. Exercises that complete a series of tasks also name the folder where you can find the completed sample code.

ERRATA

We make every effort to ensure that there are no errors in the text or in the code. However, no one is perfect, and mistakes do occur. If you find an error in one of our books, such as a spelling mistake or a faulty piece of code, we would be very grateful for your feedback. By sending in errata, you may save another reader hours of frustration, and at the same time you will be helping us provide even higher quality information.

To find the errata page for this book, go to www.wrox.com and locate the title using the Search box or one of the title lists. Then, on the book details page, click the Book Errata link. On this page, you can view all errata that has been submitted for this book and posted by Wrox editors.

 NOTE *A complete book list, including links to each book's errata, is also available at* www.wrox.com/misc-pages/booklist.shtml.

If you don't spot "your" error on the Book Errata page, go to www.wrox.com/contact/techsupport .shtml and complete the form there to send us the error you have found. We'll check the information and, if appropriate, post a message to the book's errata page and fix the problem in subsequent editions of the book.

P2P.WROX.COM

For author and peer discussion, join the P2P forums at p2p.wrox.com. The forums are a web-based system for you to post messages relating to Wrox books and related technologies, and interact with other readers and technology users. The forums offer a subscription feature to e-mail you topics of interest of your choosing when new posts are made to the forums. Wrox authors, editors, other industry experts, and your fellow readers are present on these forums.

At p2p.wrox.com, you will find a number of different forums that will help you, not only as you read this book, but also as you develop your own applications. To join the forums, just follow these steps:

1. Go to p2p.wrox.com and click the Register link.

2. Read the terms of use and click Agree.

3. Complete the required information to join, as well as any optional information you wish to provide, and click Submit.

4. You will receive an e-mail with information describing how to verify your account and complete the joining process.

NOTE *You can read messages in the forums without joining P2P, but in order to post your own messages, you must join.*

Once you join, you can post new messages and respond to messages other users post. You can read messages at any time on the web. If you would like to have new messages from a particular forum e-mailed to you, click the "Subscribe to this Forum" icon by the forum name in the forum listing.

For more information about how to use the Wrox P2P, be sure to read the P2P FAQs for answers to questions about how the forum software works, as well as many common questions specific to P2P and Wrox books. To read the FAQs, click the FAQ link on any P2P page.

PART I
An Introduction to Visual Studio LightSwitch

1

Prototyping and Rapid Application Development

WHAT YOU WILL LEARN IN THIS CHAPTER

➤   Coping with the main challenges of line-of-business software development

➤   Understanding how application prototyping can help you cope with those challenges

➤   Understanding rapid application development, and how it is related to Visual Studio LightSwitch

Microsoft is known as a company delivering great development tools. To create data-centric applications, for a long time, Microsoft has been offering only two tools that target separate audiences:

➤   Visual Studio is to be used by a wide range of developers from students and hobbyists, to enterprise developers and architects.

➤   Microsoft Access (a part of the Office Plus bundle) provides an easy-to-use approach to create data-centric applications for users with very basic development skills.

With Visual Studio, a wide range of applications can be created from the smallest console utilities to highly scalable web applications. The price of this freedom and scalability is that developers must invest a relatively high amount of work to create their applications. Although Visual Studio provides a number of productivity enhancement functions to create data-centric applications, using them requires advanced programming knowledge.

In contrast to Visual Studio, Microsoft Access requires only basic development skills. The simplicity of Access allows users without strong development backgrounds to create their database tables, forms, and reports. However, the price of this simplicity is that Microsoft Access has strong architecture limitations — it supports only monolith or traditional client-server application architectures. Creating a bit more complex user interface (UI) logic or data validation with Access than the default one requires advanced programming skills.

As a member of the Visual Studio family, Visual Studio LightSwitch is a great new development tool. Microsoft developed this product especially to support rapid application development (RAD) techniques in line-of-business (LOB) application development.

LightSwitch is the golden mean between the simplicity of Access and the flexibility of Visual Studio. With LightSwitch, you can easily create data-centric applications by simply designing data structure and the related UI. To create your own data validation or UI logic requires writing only a few lines of code — and most importantly, you not need to have advanced programming skills. Without any change in your application's structure, you can deploy it either as a desktop application or a scalable web application in the cloud.

When you need to extend an existing LightSwitch application, you can load it into the Professional, Premium, or Ultimate editions of Visual Studio 2010, and extend it with pretty complex business logic, UI behavior, or integrate it with your own back-end systems. Of course, it requires advanced software development knowledge. But you can use the existing LightSwitch application as a springboard, and do not have to create a new one from scratch.

This chapter provides overview about application prototyping and RAD techniques. Here you will learn how these techniques can answer LOB software development challenges, and also understand how Visual Studio LightSwitch does it.

LINE-OF-BUSINESS SOFTWARE DEVELOPMENT CHALLENGES

Today, most companies cannot survive without IT infrastructure supporting their operations. For a long time, *infrastructure* meant only hardware, operating system, and database management systems. Later, other services such as e-mail, collaboration platforms, and systems management services became standard parts of the IT infrastructure. Today, enterprise resource planning (ERP) and customer relationship management (CRM) systems are also part of the IT infrastructure in small and medium businesses.

Although many companies use almost the same IT infrastructure in terms of operating system, database and communication platforms, ERP, CRM, and so on, they still work in different ways with those systems. They all have some unique factors that differentiate them — and their businesses — from competitors on the same market segment. To be unique in this sense, they often need specific software tailored to their requirements and imaginations.

Because of these differences in how businesses use and think about their IT infrastructures, they also need to consider what kind of software to develop to best support their specific business processes. These management applications are often called *line-of-business (LOB) applications*, or *LOB software*.

LOB Software Development

There are many reasons why companies may need to develop LOB software, including the following:

➤ To create an application that meets business needs not currently met by existing systems

➤ To develop satellite applications to support existing systems

➤ To establish an ergonomic user interface (UI) for a legacy system

Traditionally, software development projects involve team members and stakeholders both from the business side and from the IT side. Generally, the business side is responsible for defining the business context and the issues (tasks) to be solved by the LOB application. Also, the business side undertakes managing user acceptance tests — and related quality tests — that validate the solution. The IT side is generally responsible for implementation of the LOB application, including system design, infrastructure, coding, testing, and deployment.

For some activities this division of labor is not so clear-cut. For example, in some companies web design is controlled by business stakeholders, while other companies delegate it to the IT side.

Developing LOB applications is a challenging task. Some of these challenges arise from technical or functional complexity, but the toughest ones reflect the different mindsets of the people involved. In this chapter, you will learn ways to meet many of these challenges.

NOTE *It would be far beyond the scope of one chapter, and indeed one book, to treat all of the LOB application development challenges. This chapter addresses the most significant ones you are likely to experience when working within a LOB application development team — representing either the business side or the IT side.*

Changing Project Environment

The traditional software development life cycle known as the *waterfall model* — whereby the design, implementation, test, and deployment phases follow each other without overlapping — does not work well in today's LOB application projects. Any project that takes more than one day — and most projects (if not all) belong in this category — must meet the challenges of the continuously changing environment surrounding the project. Accordingly, the original requirements, goals, and (at the end of the day) application features change, too. These changes can be legal, political, economic, technological, human, and so on. LOB applications are similarly affected by such changes, because the business environment also undergoes continual, and often rapid, change.

Creating a Requirements Specification

New LOB applications, or functional extensions of existing LOB systems, generally begin their lives with a requirement specification. This document summarizes all functional requirements (what the system is expected to do) and all quality requirements (performance, service level, UI, robustness, security, and so on), which form the basis for the detailed system specification or system design.

> **NOTE** *Many software development methodologies and frameworks do not use the term* requirement specification. *However, each has some artifact that outlines and describes what the sponsors and users want — whatever that artifact is called. What they share in common is the translation of a "wish list" into a detailed document or prioritized list of required features as agreed upon by members of the project team.*

Creating a clear requirements specification is an integral part of developing a LOB application. If this specification fails to mirror the real-world expectations and uses of the application to be implemented, the result may be a poor or even useless system. In some cases, it may conform to the specification but key users won't like it. Keep in mind that stakeholders from both sides of the aisle (business and IT) generally speak separate languages. Whereas some people quickly grasp a few simple sentences, others process information using screenshots and storyboards, and still others prefer formal descriptions, such as Universal Modeling Language (UML) use cases or activity diagrams.

> **NOTE** Unified Modeling Language *(UML) is a general-purpose modeling language that uses a visual model to describe a system. This model is built up from several types of diagrams that define the structure and the behavior of the system. For example, the* use case diagram *describes the functionality (called* use cases *in UML) of the system by means of how users (called* actors *in UML) interact with them. UML was elaborated by James Rumbaugh, Grady Booch, and Ivar Jacobson. It was standardized in 1997 by the Object Management Group (OMG) consortium, and is still managed by this group.*

Very often, a requirements specification is presented to stakeholders as one long document, and the stakeholders must weed through numerous details to find the information they are seeking. These documents typically use the language style of legal contracts, and digesting them is extremely laborious. The best requirements specifications are simple documents, but they can be anything that unambiguously communicates to stakeholders the LOB system to be developed.

NOTE *Not the range, but the content of a requirement specification makes it useful or useless. A good specification describes both* functional requirements *(what functions the system has) and* quality requirements *(how the function should work by means of performance, reliability, user friendliness, and so on). Defining requirements with measurable expectations (". . . this function must retrieve the results in 2 seconds . . .") and using prioritization to separate critical functionality from nice-to-have also adds value to the specification.*

Feedback Frequency

While a LOB application is under development, feedback from key users and business stakeholders about the burgeoning system is critical. If users see the new system only at the very end of the implementation phase, any issues or problems that are found can be time-consuming and expensive to fix, in some cases requiring expenditures that exceed the planned budget. Conversely, if key users want to see the new system's progress every day, that can cause a lot of overhead for development and support.

 NOTE *Problems found after the implementation phases of a project often reflect an ambiguous requirements specification and/or false assumptions regarding the application's usability.*

Finding the right balance for feedback frequency is a challenge whose solution will vary according to the project. For some projects, three days or a week might be fine, whereas several weeks might be optimal for others.

For example, while you are in the UI design phase of the project, having two feedback meetings in a week can help you to progress faster. Later, when you are about to elaborate specific business modules, having a review meeting every two weeks could be enough.

 NOTE *Don't underestimate the importance of finding the right feedback frequency, which can be a lifesaver. Especially for long and complex projects, using Visual Studio LightSwitch can significantly help you to communicate your ideas and understanding of LOB application requirements — as you will see after completing Part I of this book.*

You can even vary how often you provide feedback to your users. At the beginning (during the conception phase or while designing the application), it might be appropriate to communicate progress every few days. In some cases, you can even carry out a feedback cycle within one day.

For example, in a morning meeting, you might ask key users for feedback about a new screen issued the previous day. In the afternoon, you could present how you plan to address that feedback. Later, after implementing the desired feature(s), you could ease the initial frequency. When you are about to prepare for a pilot deployment or the production deployment, feedback frequency should again be increased.

APPLICATION PROTOTYPING

There are many ways to manage the challenges mentioned previously and mitigate the risks associated with them. The goal is to prevent risks that result from wrong information or insufficient information. For example, if an order management process is not entirely clear because you do not know the CRM system that stores customer information, the lack of this information is a risk. Similarly, not knowing all the attributes that should be entered for a new order is also a risk.

Application prototyping is a tool for managing such situations — and many challenges related to the human factor — as well as mitigating associated risks. While it is not the only tool, it is one of the best.

Prototyping, and the resulting application prototype, is defined in various ways. The essence of prototyping is the creation of a functional, and perhaps somewhat limited, model of the final application. Unlike specification and design documents that use literal or formal descriptions, this working model can be readily understood by key users.

For example, try to explain a UML user activity diagram to key users! Even if they understand it, they cannot truly appreciate how it will be implemented. Conversely, if you create a prototype of the activity, such as an order process, using a storyboard that represents the same UML diagram, users will have a greater level of confidence that the final product will be the right one.

You can also use application prototyping to obtain required information from users in an indirect way. If users are unable to clearly explain exactly what they want — which is not uncommon — you can create a prototype that implements an incomplete, or even obviously inferior, model. When you present such a prototype to key users, they can usually tell you what's wrong with it immediately, or what's missing.

The rest of this section describes the various kinds of prototypes you can use. Depending on your goals — that is, what you want to communicate — you might use one or more on a single LOB project.

Wireframe Models

The term *wireframe* has been used in three-dimensional (3D) modeling for a long time, especially in 3D computer graphics. This term is also used to describe UI prototypes, mainly for presenting website illustrations. A "wireframe" in this context depicts the layout of the fundamental elements in the user interface. Figure 1-1 shows an example of a wireframe describing the home page of a fictional company.

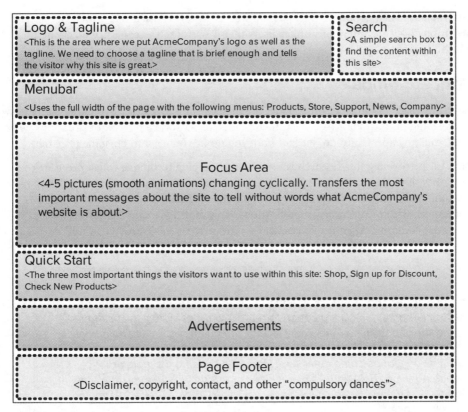

FIGURE 1-1: A wireframe example describing a home page

Note the simplicity of this wireframe. It does not contain a high-level, sophisticated design because its aim is not to present the graphical look of the home page but rather to enable key users to focus on its structure and elements. The colors used in this wireframe are just for separating layout segments visually; they are not the real colors to be used in the final design.

You may be wondering why it is useful to create a wireframe instead of a model that more closely resembles the final state of the home page. Wireframe models offer a few advantages over more detailed prototypes, including the following:

➤ They are relatively cheap to create. Even a whiteboard can be used to create them. Using wireframes, you can save time and the expense of creating possible unsuitable UI models.

➤ You can give a wireframe to key users and they will quickly have a basic understanding of your intention. If something is wrong, it can be corrected instantly.

➤ When you present a graphically designed home page prototype to users, their attention is focused on the *style* of the page — the logo used, the font type, and so on — instead of the *structure* of the page. Of course, later you must present them with the graphical design. But first the structure should be grabbed.

➤ A wireframe is also a good start for the final web design, because it relays a lot of information about the intentions of key users that is useful to the experts who create the graphical design.

Proof-of-Concept Models

For any project, any piece of information you are lacking is a source of risk. If you are unsure how to carry out any of the tasks in your to-do list, then that is also a source of risk. In situations where you know *what* you are expected to do, but not *how* you do it, you need to do some research.

A great method for performing this research is to use a prototyping technique called *proof-of-concept modeling*. Instead of thinking and making plans about how to solve a specific issue, you build a very simplified working model to prove the feasibility of your idea. If that is usable, you can use this model later, of course, with the necessary modifications. This model is called "proof-of-concept" because it can either confirm that your hypothetical solution works or disprove its viability.

NOTE *Let's assume you need to implement rapid search functionality for customers. Instead of the traditional approach whereby users type a part of the customer name and click a button to retrieve a list of matching customers, you need the capability to repeatedly reduce the number of matching names as users enter additional letters in the search box. You may assume you can do this but you cannot be completely sure. However, building a simple proof-of-concept model may help you. This precludes guessing whether you can meet this challenge, and it provides the information you need to plan how you'll implement the final function.*

Low-Fidelity Prototypes

In some situations, you cannot avoid implementing parts of the growing application in order to communicate how they work and what they do. Wireframes can indicate the layout of a particular UI, and proof-of-concept models implement a very simple (and probably only technical) aspect of the same UI.

If key users need more information to understand the solution you plan to provide them, you may need to create working prototypes that can be used to demonstrate and test your ideas. These working parts are not simple models, but real applications. In many cases, you can create a *low-fidelity prototype* that is sketchy and incomplete but represents the main characteristics of the target function.

For example, suppose you are required to demonstrate an order entry function implemented as a four-step process emulating the access to several back-end systems. You can create a low-fidelity prototype that leads the user through this process. Instead of just modeling the workflow, the prototype really implements it, but it omits parts that retrieve data from the CRM at the back end and write orders back in the ERP.

Because this prototype focuses on the process, you can create only a sketchy UI with a very basic design and a draft layout. Moreover, it does not have to deal with authentication, business logic parameterization, or any other things that are not closely related to the workflow.

High-Fidelity Prototypes

In some situations, you must create a *high-fidelity prototype* that provides much more detail about the intended functionality, and serves as evidence that the functionality can be carried out in the outlined way.

Returning to the low-fidelity order entry example, you may be asked to demonstrate this function in more detail. In this case, your prototype should not only mimic accessing the back-end systems, but also use them to retrieve and check customers from the CRM, and return the entered order to the queue of the ERP system. In addition, the sales department would like to ensure that the UI of the workflow is intuitive and provides a great user experience.

In this case, you could implement a high-fidelity prototype that is very close to the final solution.

> **NOTE** With the help of Visual Studio LightSwitch, you can create both low-fidelity and high-fidelity models easily.

RAPID APPLICATION DEVELOPMENT

Rapid application development (RAD) is a software development methodology that uses minimal planning and rapid prototyping, rather than thorough application design and waterfall-like models. The planning of the software using the RAD approach is generally interleaved with the coding — or implementation — phase of the software. This approach is very useful, because it enables software to be developed much faster — and makes it easier to accommodate the continuously changing project environment than waterfall-like models do.

The term "rapid application development" was introduced in 1991 by James Martin, who used it to describe a software development process that emphasizes an iterative approach to the whole construction phase, and handles prototypes as first-class citizens of the implementation process.

RAD is not a single, particular software development methodology. Rather, it is a generic name for concrete methodologies that primarily rely on iterations and prototypes in contrast to the traditional waterfall methodologies. RAD has many flavors, including generic agile software development methods, as well as Scrum, Extreme Programming (XP), Lean Software Development (LD), or Joint Application Development (JAD).

> **NOTE** This book does not cover individual software development methodologies, so if you want more details about these RAD technologies, use your search engine of choice to search online for more information.

The main strength of the RAD approach is that you can avoid a vast amount of rework in your software development projects. Rework most often occurs in the following two cases:

➤ You implement a piece of software in a wrong way, or with poor quality. In this case, you must spend resources to fix development issues.

➤ You implement a wrong piece of software — not the one expected by its key users, but something else. In this case, you must recreate the particular piece from the beginning.

Of course, RAD and other agile software development methodologies do not prevent you from making poor quality (or buggy) software. However, they can help you mitigate the risk of constructing a wrong piece of software. By building a prototype, you can verify that you are building the right functionality according to the right quality expectations — in other words, the product your key users want. While some rework may be required when you need to prepare a new prototype to replace a faulty one, this rework still costs less than recreating from scratch a software module that is intended to be a final product.

In some situations the RAD approach of making prototypes does not add much value to your development process. When your specification is very detailed, and you do not have significant technology risks (because you can handle them routinely), you can start implementing final products instead of prototypes.

RAD Tools

Today, practically all development tools and environments support the RAD approach. All tools promise to provide functions that help you to be agile and productive. Some of them add new visual design features to enhance manual code writing. Others use code libraries that dramatically reduce the length of source code. Several tools use wizards that lead you through a complex process. As technology evolves, developers expect increasingly sophisticated features from a RAD tool. While today the expectations are very high, this has not always been the case.

The following sections look at a few tools that are good examples of how RAD was implemented a few years ago.

Visual Basic

Visual Basic 1.0 (released in May 1991) was the first RAD tool for the Windows platform. For a long time, Windows development was a field on which only C and C++ programmers could play. The smallest "Hello, World" program for Windows was about 100 lines of code, whereas the statements to actually print out the "Hello, World" text required only about a dozen lines.

Visual Basic 1.0 took the development community by storm, and totally changed the programming model from code-oriented development to UI-oriented development. Whereas C and C++ programmers used resource files to describe the UI, Visual Basic invented the concepts of forms, controls, and visual GUI construction. The reusability and extensibility of forms and controls was a main design goal in Visual Basic. Developers could create their own custom controls using generic — or, conversely, application specific — properties and methods.

From a developer's point of view, Visual Basic was a real RAD tool. Developers could drag components and controls from a toolbox onto the surface of forms, and place them into the desired position. The behavior of controls could be changed by setting up the properties of visual elements. Forms and their controls had events represented by methods, with which programmers could code the logic of the application.

Visual Basic has evolved a lot since then, but using current development tools (such as Visual Studio), you can recognize that the elements of the integrated development environment (IDE) still resemble those used in the old versions. Figure 1-2 shows a screenshot from an old Visual Basic version running under Windows 95.

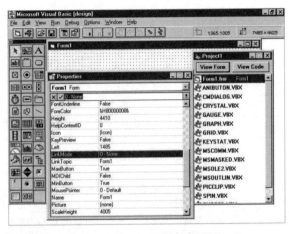

FIGURE 1-2: An old Visual Basic IDE running under Windows 95

Microsoft Access

Microsoft Access 1.0 was released in November 1992. It offered a relational database management system (RDBMS) for desktop applications — combined with a graphical user interface (GUI) and great visual tools. Developers could easily design database schemas, enter data with simple forms, and create reports. They could use the Visual Basic programming language (VBA, which was included with the product) to add code and create real applications for end-users.

Figure 1-3 shows the database window of the Northwind sample application in Microsoft Access 97.

FIGURE 1-3: Microsoft Access form objects in the design environment

Originally, Access used its own database engine — called Microsoft Jet Database Engine — but after the release of version 2.0, it could use external database tables. Microsoft Access 2000 allowed developers to work directly with SQL Server databases.

Access was — and still is — a great RAD tool. It lowered the entry barrier to relational database programming. While creating applications for most RDBMSs required a set of applications using several tools and programming languages, with Access it was much simpler and quicker.

Delphi

Delphi was originally developed by Borland, and its first version was released in 1995. This tool had an IDE that was very similar to the Visual Basic IDE. Delphi was designed to be a RAD tool that supported developing database applications, including simple ones and even enterprise applications.

It used the Object Pascal language — a successor of Turbo Pascal — which provided full object-oriented programming (OOP) capabilities, in contrast to Visual Basic.

The product evolved very fast with five versions released in the first five years of its life. Delphi was the first RAD tool capable of compiling 32-bit applications for Windows. It became very popular among enterprise developers because of its RAD features. It provided more than 100 components (elements of the Delphi Visual Component Library) that developers could immediately drop onto the Designer surface. In addition, developers could easily create their own visual components, and add them to the existing library.

 NOTE *At the time, Visual Basic also provided a separate control development SDK that made it possible to create additional components called* custom controls. *However, Delphi offered a very intuitive and much faster way to develop controls, because the IDE was designed with component reusability in mind.*

Figure 1-4 shows the Delphi 7 IDE. The largest part of the toolbar at the top of the IDE contains component category tabs and components.

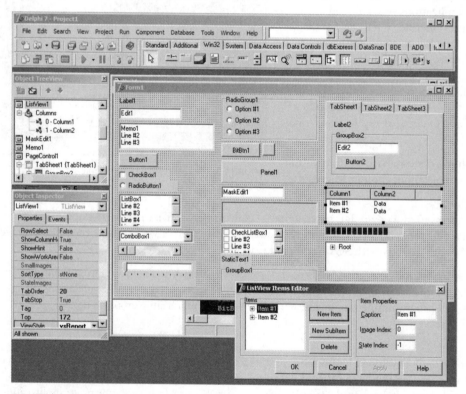

FIGURE 1-4: Delphi 7 IDE

Visual Studio LightSwitch and RAD

Visual Studio LightSwitch is the newest member of the Visual Studio family. Like Visual Basic, Microsoft Access, and Delphi, it is a RAD tool; but as its name suggests, it aims to make the development of LOB applications as easy as flipping a switch.

Most RAD tools are development environments made for programmers, and they provide productivity tools that enable the faster creation of applications. Visual Basic and Delphi are definitely such tools. Microsoft Access is a bit different in that it is not a generic development tool, but rather is intended for creating database applications for the desktop.

Visual Studio LightSwitch is a RAD tool that makes data-centric LOB application development available not only for developers, but also for business analysts, consultants, and IT experts working on business projects. As suggested earlier, "LightSwitch" in the name of the new product symbolizes how easy it is to create LOB applications.

In contrast to RAD tools like Visual Studio or Delphi, LightSwitch is designed to support prototyping with a minimal amount of coding — or no coding at all. Compared to the data-centric RAD style offered by Microsoft Access, which supports the traditional client-server separation of application layers, LightSwitch provides a clean and very sophisticated three-tier application architecture, and takes care of all the plumbing that binds the layers into a working application. With Visual Studio LightSwitch, you can create complete LOB applications, as well as low-fidelity or high-fidelity application prototypes.

In the following three chapters, you will learn about the fundamentals of LightSwitch and get a taste of this great tool. Chapter 2 focuses on the first steps to getting started with the product, while Chapter 3 treats the key technologies behind LightSwitch. You have several ways to customize your prototypes built with LightSwitch, as Chapter 4 demonstrates.

SUMMARY

Writing LOB applications has many challenges — mostly related to specifications and communication among the members of the development team. Projects that cannot meet these challenges can easily fail.

One of the main development challenges is addressing the often unclear or unspoken expectations of key users. Key users can rarely tell you their exact expectations, either because they are unable to communicate exactly what kind of functionality they expect or they are unsure how to use a certain business function.

Prototyping (that is, developing a working model to test ideas and feasibility) is a great technique to overcome these situations. Depending on your particular scenario, you can use several kinds of prototypes, including wireframes, low-fidelity and high-fidelity prototypes, or proof-of-concept models, to bridge the sea of missing information or clear communication between key users and the software construction team.

Most RAD tools — including Visual Studio LightSwitch — have robust features to support you in the creation of communicable prototypes.

In Chapter 2, you'll extend your knowledge about the role of LightSwitch among the members of the Visual Studio family. You will learn both how to install LightSwitch and how to create your first application — without writing any lines of code.

EXERCISES

1. Enumerate and explain a few challenges of LOB application development with regard to the human factor.

2. Explain what a wireframe is.

3. Explain what a proof-of-concept model is.

4. What is the fundamental principle of rapid application development (RAD)?

5. List a few methodologies that are based on the RAD principle.

 NOTE *Answers to the Exercises can be found in the Appendix.*

▶ **WHAT YOU LEARNED IN THIS CHAPTER**

TOPIC	KEY CONCEPTS
Line-of-business (LOB) application	A LOB application participates in managing the business processes of an organization.
Challenge of changing project environment	The environment of a project (one with the duration of several weeks, months, or even years) changes. Project planning must be undertaken with possible changes (legal, political, economic, human, technological, and so on) kept in mind.
Challenge of feedback frequency	Both developers and key users need feedback from each other during a LOB development project to mutually confirm that the right functionality is about to be implemented in the right way. Finding the optimal frequency for this feedback is essential to the project's success.
Wireframe	A wireframe is a prototype that depicts the layout of the fundamental elements in the user interface (UI). It emphasizes structure over graphical design.
Proof-of-concept model	A proof-of-concept model is a working prototype that can be used to check the feasibility of an idea. It focuses on the technical details to be checked, without implementing other application details.
Rapid application development (RAD)	Rapid application development (RAD) is a software development methodology that uses minimal planning and rapid prototyping, rather than thorough application design and waterfall-like models.

Getting Started with Visual Studio LightSwitch

➤ Key facts about Visual Studio LightSwitch and the types of applications you can develop with it

➤ Understanding the relationship between LightSwitch and Visual Studio 2010

➤ Installing Visual Studio LightSwitch

➤ Creating a new project in Visual Basic or C#

➤ Using the built-in Designers to create a simple application

In Chapter 1, you learned about the significant challenges you face in line-of-business (LOB) application development, and about why application prototyping is a great tool to handle those challenges.

This chapter introduces you to a new member of the Visual Studio family, Visual Studio LightSwitch. By the time you finish this chapter, you will have installed LightSwitch and created your very first application with it — all without writing a single line of code.

GETTING TO KNOW VISUAL STUDIO

Visual Studio is an integrated development environment (IDE) from Microsoft. Its newest version, Visual Studio 2010, can be used to develop applications for all Microsoft platforms, including Windows, .NET Framework, Windows Mobile, Windows Phone, Silverlight, and Azure. It has several editions, ranging from the free Express editions to the Professional, Premier, and Ultimate editions that are especially tailored for the needs of professional software developers.

INTEGRATED DEVELOPMENT ENVIRONMENT

When creating line-of-business applications, developers use several tools to ship their solution. They need an editor to create the source code of the application. Generally, these applications use database management systems, so tools to design the database schema are also indispensable. The source code must be compiled and deployed to test it, and in case of bugs, a debugger is a must-have element of the toolset.

Traditionally, these tools were separated from each other, and very often several different vendors used to provide them. An integrated development environment (IDE) provides this plethora of tools as a comprehensive set, in order to make developers more productive. Using an IDE frees developers from continuously changing tools depending on their current activities, and provides a smoother cooperation among tools.

Visual Studio supports different programming languages that target one or more underlying platforms. The built-in languages include Visual C++ (mainly used for native Windows application development), Visual C#, Visual Basic .NET, and F# (a relatively new functional programming language).

In addition to the built-in languages, you can install languages such as IronPython, IronRuby, or other supported languages. Some third parties offer Visual Studio integrated languages such as FORTRAN or COBOL, which you can purchase if you find these to be the best tools for your particular software development projects.

A Short History of Visual Studio

Microsoft continuously develops not only its operating systems and IT infrastructure products, but also the tools developers can use to create new applications for the server and desktop platform, as well as for mobile devices. Visual Studio editions are the most popular development environment for the Windows platform. The roots of this great product date back 20 years, and a bright future seems assured.

Roots

In the first couple of years of the Windows operating system, application development was a privilege of developers familiar with the C programming language. At that time, creating an application meant writing source code in a text editor, running a batch file that compiled the application, and linking the resulted binaries into an executable file — so it was free of any tools we use today with the epithet "visual."

Not only were graphical user interface (GUI) tools missing, but the simplest "Hello, World" program for Windows was almost 100 lines of code. About 80 percent of this code handled the Windows message loop, and even the remaining code to write out the "Hello, World" text was more than 10 lines of code.

Visual Basic dramatically changed the Windows development landscape when version 1.0 was released in May 1991. The concepts of forms, controls, modules, classes, and code-behind files that this tool introduced (or, perhaps, invented) as the modular way of developing code revolutionized application development. Instead of manually writing the message-loop-handling code, and writing more than 10 lines to express the intention to display the "Hello, World" text, the essence of the application was the following single code line:

```
MsgBox("Hello, World!")
```

Not only was the compactness of the Visual Basic code new, but also the way the code was created. Instead of using the text editor as the only coding tool, a visual form Designer was provided in the integrated development environment (IDE).

Visual Basic 1.0 made Windows programming available for the masses.

Other Visual Languages and Tools

Microsoft did not rest on its laurels after releasing Visual Basic, the first language to provide this new type of development experience. In a couple of years following the release of Visual Basic 1.0, a plethora of tools and languages were equipped with a visual composition feature.

In February 1993, Visual C++ was released, which provided a simple library called Microsoft Foundation Classes (MFC). This product proved that a language intended to provide full and granular control over the operating system can be used as a productive tool for creating great user interfaces in a simple way, too.

The year 1995 was full of exciting news about the new Java programming language. In response, Microsoft created the Visual J++ language, with its own Java Virtual Machine (JVM), which conformed to the original Sun specification.

Microsoft already had the FoxPro database programming product for its MS-DOS operating system. This tool was totally rewritten for the Windows platform, and at the end of 1995 it was released as Visual FoxPro 3.0.

Integrating Languages into Visual Studio

The architect team at Microsoft recognized that the visual aspect of an application can be totally separated from the programming language used to create it. They refactored the tools created separately for each language, and created a new, common IDE capable of hosting several programming languages. This product was released as Visual Studio 97.

The bundle contained Visual Basic 5.0, Visual C++ 5.0, Visual FoxPro 5.0, and Visual J++ 1.1 from the set of existing tools, and it was also extended with Visual InterDev, a new tool for developing dynamically generated websites. A snapshot of the Microsoft Developer Network (MSDN) Library was also a part of the package, but Visual Basic and Visual FoxPro still had their own IDE.

Visual Studio 97 was packaged with a new logo that has since become famous. This logo resembled the sign for infinity (or the Möbius strip), symbolizing the synergy among the constituent parts, as shown in Figure 2-1.

Unfortunately, Visual Studio 97 suffered from many subtle integration issues. The next version of the IDE, named Visual Studio 6.0, was released in June 1998. Although the version numbers of all programming languages were moved to 6.0, the level of integration increased only virtually, because Visual C++ was moved into its own separate IDE.

Moving to .NET

The success of the Java platform challenged Microsoft's dominance in the market. Their answer was the .NET Framework, which had been in development under another name since the late

FIGURE 2-1: The Visual Studio 97 package

1990s. In February 2002, .NET Framework 1.0 was released as part of a pair with Visual Studio.NET (the latter of which is often referred to as Visual Studio .NET 2002).

This new Visual Studio version achieved the original vision — the integration of several programming languages and tools into the same IDE. Developers could use four languages out-of-the-box: Visual Basic.NET, Visual C# (pronounced "C sharp"), Visual C++, and Visual J# (pronounced "J sharp"). Except for J#, these languages are still available in Visual Studio 2010.

Visual Basic also changed the programming landscape. Formerly a language that supported only object-based programming, it now became a fully object-oriented language — a consequence of the need to support the .NET Framework.

Visual C# was born as a new programming language based on the best traditions of other "curly-braced languages" such as Java, C, and C++. It was used extensively — and still is — within Microsoft itself to develop the Base Class Library (BCL) of the Framework.

Visual J# was considered a replacement for Visual J++. Although it had a Java syntax, it could build applications targeted for the .NET Framework common language runtime (CLR).

The .NET Framework has evolved a lot since its first version was released. In 2003, the 1.1 version was released in tandem with Visual Studio 2003. Two years later, .NET Framework 2.0 and Visual Studio 2005 was the next tandem released, with great new features.

Visual Studio 2008 and .NET 3.0 were shipped in November 2007. While the previous Visual Studio versions were compatible with the Framework version, Visual Studio 2008 targeted multiple frameworks simultaneously.

Visual Studio Editions

Microsoft has always endeavored to build a large developer community around its tools. To attract a wide range of developers — including hobbyists, students, as well as professional and enterprise developers — Microsoft wisely created specialized editions targeting certain audiences. The first of these were released a few months after Visual Studio 2005. Each new release of Visual Studio still provides the new versions of these editions, too:

➤ The Express Editions (such as Visual Basic Express, Visual C# Express, Visual Web Developer Express) are created primarily for developers who code for fun. These tools are available as free downloads.

➤ The Enterprise Editions target participants in enterprise development projects. Team System Editions provide out-of-the-box integration with Microsoft's Team Foundation Server, and add powerful productivity tools for specific development project roles.

Visual Studio 2010

Visual Studio 2010 is the newest version of Visual Studio. It is the first big leap toward the goal of basing the IDE itself on the .NET Framework. The development team implemented the shell of Visual Studio using Windows Presentation Foundation (WPF), which is a part of the .NET Framework, and rewrote the Code Editor using clean, managed code.

Microsoft's vision of even tighter integration among the parts and building blocks of Visual Studio is beautifully symbolized by its new logo, as shown in Figure 2-2.

FIGURE 2-2: The new logo of Visual Studio 2010

GETTING TO KNOW VISUAL STUDIO LIGHTSWITCH

Visual Studio LightSwitch is a rapid application development (RAD) tool designed to help write data-centric LOB applications. Unlike previous Visual Studio products, LightSwitch emphasizes minimizing the amount of code that must be explicitly written in order to develop an application.

Simply speaking, LightSwitch provides a few intuitive and easy-to-use GUI Designers to design data structures and the user interface (UI) for working with that data. Explicit coding is rarely required.

Just imagine, how quicker and easier it is, unlike the traditional application development with manually written source code! As you will learn in this chapter, you can create data-centric applications with LightSwitch in a few minutes — even without explicitly taking care of the suitable LOB solution architecture.

Business Code versus Plumbing Code

LOB applications generally follow the three-tier application pattern, whereby the three layers of an application (data, business logic, and presentation) are clearly separated from each other.

 NOTE *Chapter 3 treats the three-tier application pattern in more detail, and details the responsibilities of the data, business logic, and Presentation tiers.*

When developers create LOB applications, their everyday activities can be separated into two groups:

➤ Activities focused on writing business code (code that delivers explicit business functions to the user), such as the checkout process in an e-commerce site.

➤ Activities to create the plumbing code that binds tiers and components together in order to establish the flow from the UI to the data back end, and vice versa. This plumbing code includes the creation of interfaces that the layers use to communicate, the handling of transactions, the forwarding of error messages from the data back end to the UI, and so on.

In many LOB development projects, the effort spent on writing plumbing code can exceed the amount of time spent writing real (or valuable) business functions. Visual Studio LightSwitch decreases the amount of time spent on creating plumbing code. Actually, LightSwitch developers do not have to deal with plumbing code at all; rather, they can focus on delivering business functionality.

In addition to eliminating the need to write plumbing code manually, LightSwitch helps you to be more productive when developing business functions. The lion's share of the work — on the data and Presentation tiers — can be done with the GUI designers in the IDE. You only need to explicitly code for activities — such as writing business rules and other operation logic — for which coding is probably the best way to express your intention.

LOB Applications and LightSwitch

Microsoft describes Visual Studio LightSwitch as "the simplest way to create business applications for the desktop or the cloud." However, this assertion does not enable you to determine in which situations LightSwitch would be the best tool for the job, versus when you need to use other tools.

Because LightSwitch is a very new product, there are not enough case studies and concrete developer experiences yet to help you decide whether you should use it in your LOB projects. After reading this book and going through the concrete examples, however, you'll be equipped to make such decisions.

In terms of LightSwitch applicability, the following three groups, or zones, describe the degree to which this new member of the Visual Studio family applies to a LOB project:

➤ **White zone** — LightSwitch would be a great tool for these kinds of projects.

➤ **Black zone** — LightSwitch cannot be used as the main tool for projects in this zone.

➤ **Grey zone** — Certain parts (or phases) of your LOB project can be implemented with LightSwitch, but you definitely need other tools to complete it.

Table 2-1 describes a few stereotypical projects in each zone. (Keep in mind that this list is by no means complete.)

TABLE 2-1: Applicability of Visual Studio LightSwitch

ZONE	EXAMPLES
White	Your business application is implemented as a set of Excel worksheets right now, but you would like something more professional-looking and less susceptible to user errors.
	Your application has a small amount of data (for example, measurable in several thousands of records) with a simple structure (for example, a dozen or more entity types). Most operations create, edit, remove, and list data.
	You have an existing application and you must create a few new functions for a small group of users — for example, administering data dictionaries for a large system.
Black	Your project handles a massive amount of data (millions of entries), and, based on your experience, this data has proven to be challenging with other projects. These kinds of applications may require an architecture tuned especially for handling specific performance issues, so LightSwitch would not be a good choice.
	You already have a database and you must primarily create listings and reports. This is not the functionality LightSwitch is tuned for. You should use other products that are especially strong in reporting (such as Microsoft Access or SQL Server Reporting Services).
	You have some technology requirements that cannot be matched with LightSwitch. (Chapter 3 provides more information about the technologies behind LightSwitch.) For example, if you must create applications with a Windows Forms UI, then LightSwitch shouldn't be your tool of choice.
Grey	Your application handles a large amount of data, but the structure is simple, and the number of users is relatively small (for example, one or two dozen).
	Your application has a relatively small amount of data, but a lot of people use that data concurrently.
	Your application's business functions are complex, and most of them cannot be described as simple read, list, insert, modify, or remove operations.

You should use Table 2-1 only as a starting point when analyzing whether your task or your project can be built on LightSwitch. Note that even if your project falls into the grey zone, that does not mean you cannot use LightSwitch. It simply means that you must carefully consider whether LightSwitch is appropriate, and you should not step outside of the boundaries of its reasonable usability.

Even if you are sure that LightSwitch cannot be the ultimate tool for an entire project, you might be able to use it as a rapid prototyping tool. For most projects, creating a good prototype that can be used to communicate with business stakeholders can save you a lot of time and money, even if you must rebuild the final application totally from scratch. You'll save effort by having a clear — and readily communicated — view of what the project is about. Thus, you can avoid a lot of rework that would otherwise result from a fuzzy or incomplete view.

INSTALLING VISUAL STUDIO LIGHTSWITCH

Learning Visual Studio LightSwitch without using it is like taking a swimming lesson without getting into the water. To discover the benefits of this great product, you must first install it. This section provides a step-by-step overview of how to install LightSwitch.

> **NOTE** There are several sources from which you can obtain Visual Studio LightSwitch. If you or your company has an appropriate MSDN subscription, you can download the product as part of your subscription. You can also visit www.microsoft.com/visualstudio/lightswitch to get information about purchasing and using the product.

Types of Installation

Visual Studio LightSwitch uses *integrated shell mode*. That means LightSwitch integrates into the shell of an existing Visual Studio 2010 installation — assuming that Visual Studio has previously been installed on your computer. After the installation, when you start Visual Studio, you'll be able to use the Visual Studio functionality that was available before the LightSwitch installation, and the LightSwitch project types will be added by the set-up process.

If you do not have a previous installation of Visual Studio, the set-up process installs a Visual Studio shell to your machine with all of the LightSwitch features.

TRY IT OUT Installing Visual Studio LightSwitch

The installation steps of LightSwitch are the same regardless of whether you have Visual Studio 2010 already installed on your machine. However, a fresh installation (that is, when you do not already have Visual Studio 2010 on your computer) takes a bit more time because more components must be installed on your machine.

To install Visual Studio LightSwitch, follow these steps:

1. Read the installation notes in the Readme.html file that you find in the root directory of the installation media (or in the virtual device mapped upon the .iso file representing the setup

media). This file may contain information about prerequisites, such as service packs or other components, depending on your operating system (Windows Vista, Windows 7, Windows Server 2008, and so on).

2. Start the `setup.exe` in the root directory of the installation media. The set up program reads the installation components from the media and prepares the set-up process — it takes about 30 seconds.

3. Accept the License Terms, shown in Figure 2-3, by clicking the Accept button.

4. On the Welcome to Setup page that appears (see Figure 2-4), you have two installation options from which to choose. You can either continue with the predefined options by clicking the Install Now button or you can choose specific

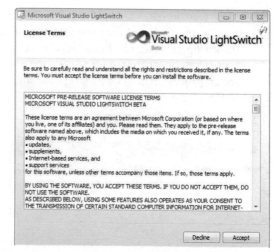

FIGURE 2-3: Visual Studio LightSwitch License Terms

LightSwitch options by clicking the Customize button. When you select the Customize option, the only setting you can control is the location of the installation folder, as shown in Figure 2-5. Do not modify the default location unless you have a real reason to change it. For computers with Visual Studio 2010 already installed, the default location is set to the current installation folder of Visual Studio.

FIGURE 2-4: The Welcome to Setup page, where you can select the installation mode

FIGURE 2-5: The Destination Folder page

5. Click Customize to set up the installation folder manually — just to see the Destination Folder page — but do not change the folder name. Simply click the Install button to carry on with the set-up process. The installation takes about 10–20 minutes, depending on the installation type (fresh or integrated into an existing Visual Studio 2010 shell). During this time, the set-up process displays a progress bar and status text about the current activity, as shown in Figure 2-6.

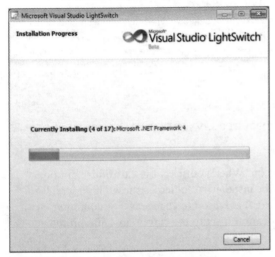

FIGURE 2-6: The Installation Progress page

 NOTE *The total number of components to install may be different on your machine, because other programs might have already installed a few prerequisite components (for example, when you already have Visual Studio 2010 on your computer). In several situations, when another application has already installed the .NET Framework 4 component on your machine, the set-up process will stop and ask you to restart your machine. Don't be surprised if this happens to you. As soon as you restart your computer and log in, the installation will continue.*

6. When all components are installed correctly, the "Setup complete" page is displayed, as shown in Figure 2-7. You can immediately start LightSwitch by clicking the Run the Product now button.

You can also click the Go to Our Online Development Center link to be taken to the MSDN home page of Visual Studio LightSwitch.

FIGURE 2-7: The "Setup complete" page

7. Click Exit to close the installation program.

Running LightSwitch for the First Time

After a successful installation, you should take a moment to familiarize yourself with the Visual Studio LightSwitch IDE — especially if you have never used Visual Studio before. You can start the IDE from the "Setup complete" page by clicking the Run the Product Now button, or you can start it from your Start menu under the Microsoft Visual Studio 2010 folder. If you plan to use the IDE frequently (and the fact that you're reading this book suggests that you are), create a shortcut to Visual Studio 2010 on your desktop, or use the Pin to Taskbar command available in Windows 7 to create a launch icon on your taskbar.

Start Visual Studio LightSwitch either from the Start menu, from the shortcut you have placed on your desktop, or from the taskbar. The first time you run Visual Studio, it configures user settings associated with your account. After about 30 seconds, the IDE is loaded and ready for you to begin work. You will see the Start Page, shown in Figure 2-8.

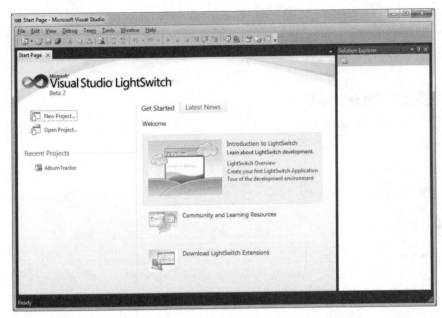

FIGURE 2-8: The Start Page of Visual Studio LightSwitch

NOTE *If you have Visual Studio 2010 already installed on your machine, you won't see any changes to your startup environment after LightSwitch setup. The Start Page, the main menu, toolbars, and window layout will be different from what is shown in Figure 2-8. If you are not sure whether LightSwitch is installed and integrated within the existing Visual Studio 2010 IDE, check the Help ⇨ About Visual Studio dialog. If you find Microsoft Visual Studio LightSwitch in the list of installed products integrated into the IDE, you can use it to follow the examples and exercises in this book.*

CREATING YOUR FIRST LIGHTSWITCH APPLICATION

The best way to demonstrate the RAD capabilities of Visual Studio LightSwitch is to create a small program. Generally, programming language courses begin teaching language features by creating a "Hello, World" application and sending this welcome message to the output, in order to get a sense of the language structure. Visual Studio LightSwitch application development is not about writing code, but creating a business application also requires writing business rule code. It is necessary to design data utilized in the program you create, and design screens that display data to the end-user, thereby enabling interaction with the application.

You do not need extensive experience in programming to be able to develop small business applications or prototypes. The first example you will create in this section is a simple program that enables you to keep track of your music collection.

WHAT LEVEL OF PROGRAMMING EXPERIENCE DO YOU NEED TO WORK WITH LIGHTSWITCH?

Most tasks can be carried out with LightSwitch in a declarative way using the GUI and the standard tool windows of the IDE (such as the Property window). However, a few things (for example, creating business rules) can be done only by imperative programming — that is, writing code.

Altogether, the number of code lines you need to write is an order of magnitude less than the traditional way, where every intention is expressed by code. You can choose from the Visual Basic or C# programming languages in LightSwitch.

You do not need extensive programming experience. If you have used macros in Microsoft Office products, you'll easily catch up with the programming knowledge base required — you can use Visual Basic when creating a LightSwitch application.

If you have ever used the C# language with the .NET Framework, or if this is your preferred language, select this language for LightSwitch applications.

If you need some external help from experienced developers, you can ask fellow developers who have more .NET experience to help you. When you can define business rules in a few sentences, and show the data structures you've created declaratively in the LightSwitch IDE, your fellow developers will be able to help you with programming questions.

Creating a Project

Just like the other members of the Visual Studio family or other IDEs like Eclipse, Visual Studio LightSwitch bundles all files and information related to an application (or to an independent component) into a container called a *project*. When you solve a certain business problem, generally you compose a *solution* from one or more projects.

Therefore, this section provides detailed instructions for creating a new project using Visual Studio LightSwitch. There are subtle differences between the menu structures and dialogs of Visual Studio LightSwitch and Visual Studio 2010. Notes included with the instructions will help you carry out the development steps in Visual Studio 2010 as well.

TRY IT OUT Creating a New Visual Studio LightSwitch Project

To create a new Visual Studio LightSwitch project, follow these steps:

1. Click File ⇨ New Project. (Alternatively, press Ctrl+Shift+N, or click New Project in the Start Page, which you can find directly beneath the program logo.)

2. In the New Project dialog that appears, select the type of project you intend to work with, as shown in Figure 2-9. Change the name to **AlbumTracker** and select a location for your project files (or you can accept the default location under your Documents folder).

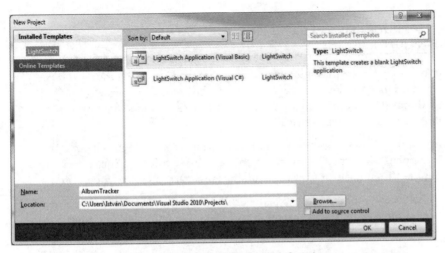

FIGURE 2-9: The New Project dialog in Visual Studio LightSwitch

As shown in Figure 2-9, LightSwitch offers only two options, which differ only in the programming language used for writing code. In this example, you will create an application without writing a single line of code, so it does not matter which project type (Visual Basic or Visual C#) you select. For the sake of simplicity, choose LightSwitch Application (Visual Basic).

In Visual Studio 2010, you can still use the Ctrl+Shift+N shortcut keys to create a new project. However, in this case, you find the related command under File ➪ New ➪ Project, not in File ➪ New Project. The New Project dialog in this case will list many project types displayed in several categories. You can find LightSwitch project types within the LightSwitch category, as shown in Figure 2-10.

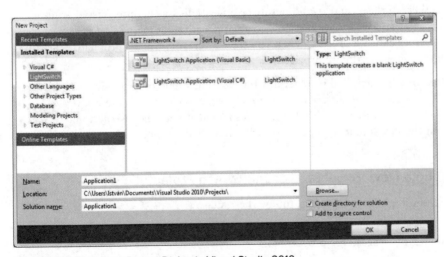

FIGURE 2-10: The New Project Dialog in Visual Studio 2010

3. Click OK in the New Project dialog. LightSwitch will create the project for you. In the background, the IDE creates dozens of files to describe your project and prepare the environment for building the application. However, you do not have to worry about these files. The structure of the project from your point of view is very simple, as shown in Figure 2-11.

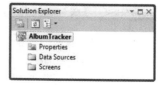

The root node of the hierarchy is the `AlbumTracker` node representing the project. The `Data Sources` and `Screens` folders are empty now, but as you continue with the application's development, they will be filled with the artifacts you create.

FIGURE 2-11: The solution structure in Solution Explorer

Creating a Table

At this point, the application you created can be built and run. However, it does not have any functionality yet. The largest part of the workspace in the IDE displays the Designer surface, which initially contains two task links, as shown in Figure 2-12.

These tasks suggest that you should first define the data your application needs to work with. You can either create a new table to be used by the application or attach an already existing (and, thus, external) database to create a UI interacting with the data stored there.

FIGURE 2-12: The Designer surface with the initial task links

---

WHAT ARE TABLES AND FIELDS?

Although a discussion of database design principles is beyond the scope of this book, at a minimum you should understand what tables and fields are.

You have probably worked with tabular data in Excel sheets. The set of tabular data represented by an Excel worksheet is called a *table* in database terms. Each row of the Excel worksheet represents a data entry called a *record* (or sometimes a *data row* or *row*). Each record is constituted from one or more *field*s that are the columns in the Excel worksheet.

When you define the structure of the table, you define the fields (that is, the columns in your Excel worksheet) by naming them and describing their most important properties. For example, you specify the type of data a field may contain (text, number, flag, money, date, and so on); whether it is required to contain data or can be left empty; and so on.

To be able to find and manipulate a record in a table (that is, a row in your Excel worksheet), each record should have a *primary key* that is a unique identifier and enables addressing the record unambiguously within the table.

TRY IT OUT | **Creating a New Table**

To create a new table, follow these steps:

1. Click the "Create new table" task (refer to Figure 2-12) to define the table that `AlbumTracker` will work on. If you do not see the Designer surface — or you see something very different from what is shown in Figure 2-12 — right-click the `Data Sources` node in Solution Explorer and select Add Table from the context menu that appears. An empty table definition is shown in the Designer, with `Table1Item` highlighted in its header, which is the default name of the newly generated table.

2. Change the name by entering **Album** and pressing Enter. The grid with the three columns represents the editor you use to design the structure of your table, as shown in Figure 2-13. The first predefined row contains the `Id` field, which serves as the unique identifier for each entry in the table.

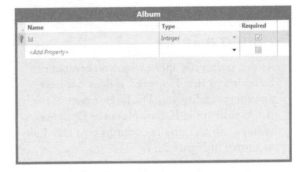

FIGURE 2-13: The Designer grid of the Album table

3. Click the empty cell below `Id` in the `Name` column to enter the field name. Type **Artist** in the `Name` column, and press the Tab key to move to the `Type` cell, which, by default, is set to String. You can use the drop-down arrow within the `Type` cell to change this setting, but keep String for now. Press the Tab key again to move to the `Required` cell, where you can use the space key to set or clear the check box. (Of course, you can also click the check box with the mouse to change its state.) Ensure that the `Required` box has a check in it.

4. Add a few new fields to the table, as shown in Table 2-2.

TABLE 2-2: New Fields of the Album Table

NAME	TYPE	REQUIRED
Artist	String	Yes
Title	String	Yes
Published	Short Integer	No
NumTracks	Short Integer	Yes
Description	String	No
Rating	Short Integer	No

When you have finished adding these new fields, your `Album` table structure should look similar to that shown in Figure 2-14.

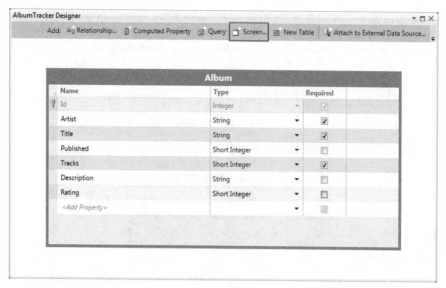

FIGURE 2-14: Album table fields in the Designer and the Screen button

5. Use the File ⇨ Save All command (or press Ctrl+Shift+S) to save the table definition in the project.

How It Works

Each row in the grid describes a field of the table, including a Name, a Type (the type of data stored in the field), and a flag indicating if the value of the field is Required (that is, the field must have a non-empty value).

You can also use the Enter key to move down from the current cell in the grid, and you can use the arrow keys to navigate around the cells as expected. Anytime you make a mistake, you can move to the faulty cell to fix its content, or click the row header and remove the row with the Delete key.

Creating a Screen to List Album Information

At this point, you have defined the structure for storing album information, but you still need a screen that enables users to edit its content. The following "Try It Out" exercise demonstrates how to create one.

TRY IT OUT Creating a New Screen

To create a new screen, follow these steps:

1. In the toolbar at the top of the Designer window, locate and click the Screen button (as highlighted in Figure 2-14) to display the Add New Screen dialog, shown in Figure 2-15. If you have already closed the Album Designer, you can open it again by double-clicking the `Albums` node under the `ApplicationData` folder in the Solution Explorer. Alternatively, you can right-click the `Screens` folder in Solution Explorer and select the Add Screen command from the context menu.

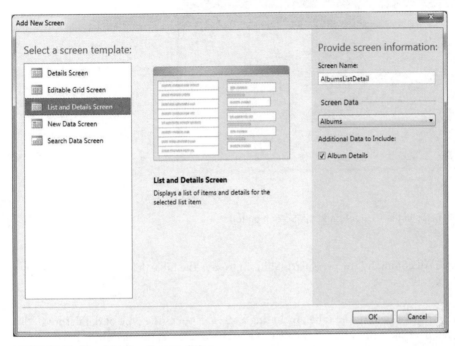

FIGURE 2-15: The Add New Screen dialog

2. From the list on the left side of the dialog, select the List and Details Screen option, which specifies the type (template) of screen you are going to create. The image in the middle of the dialog shows a draft, indicating the structure of this screen type. Below this image is a short description of the new screen when created with the specified template. The Screen Name field is set to `ListDetail` by default.

3. Select Albums from the Screen Data drop-down menu to indicate that your screen should be created with album information. When you select Albums from the drop-down menu, the screen name changes to `AlbumListDetail`.

4. Click OK to create the screen. Its structure is displayed in the AlbumTracker Designer window.

How It Works

If you have ever worked with application-generating screens (for example, Microsoft Access), you may expect a screen whose labels and controls are carefully positioned and assigned to the data they will display. LightSwitch is different. Instead of a WYSIWYG (what-you-see-is-what-you-get) view of the screen, you have a layout structure, as shown in Figure 2-16.

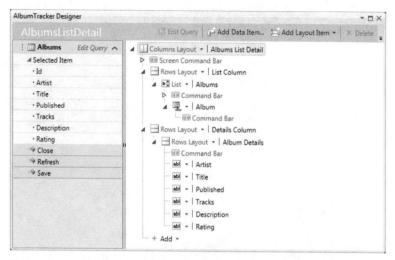

FIGURE 2-16: The SearchAlbum screen's Designer surface

Here, elements of the screen (called *controls*) are organized into a hierarchy. You can use the design surface to customize the screen (Chapter 9 covers screen customization in detail), or you can accept the layout as generated by default, as you do here.

TRY IT OUT   Running the Application

To run the application, follow these steps:

1. Use the Debug ➪ Start Without Debugging menu command (Ctrl+F5) to build and start the application. The IDE handles numerous details to prepare your application to run, including creating the database, generating application artifacts, and locally deploying the application. The application starts in a new window that has a ribbon-like panel at the top, and a tasks menu at the left. The largest part of the window is occupied by the Albums list and the text boxes representing the columns of the Album table. At this point the table is empty.

2. Click the Add button in the command bar of the grid to display a modal dialog, where you can enter a new album, as shown in Figure 2-17.

3. Fill these fields with valid data as shown in Figure 2-17, and click OK. The application closes the data entry window and displays the new album in the Album List Detail tab.

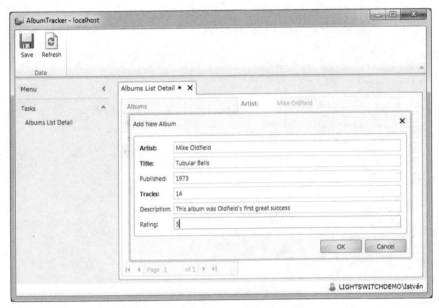

FIGURE 2-17: Modal dialog for adding a new album

4. Click the Add button again. This time, enter some invalid information (for example, leave the Title field empty, or enter letters where numbers are expected), and click OK. The invalid data items are visually highlighted on the user interface, as shown in Figure 2-18. Correct the invalid data (for example, by specifying the missing title).

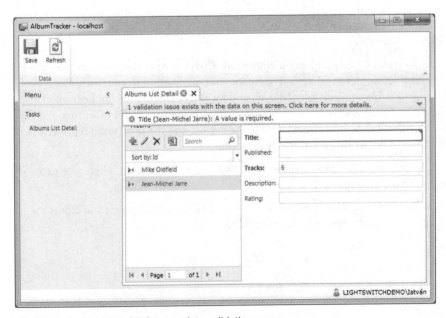

FIGURE 2-18: The UI highlights any data validation errors

Records you enter are not saved immediately into the database; they are stored only in the client application's memory. The unsaved records are marked with an asterisk, and the tab of the screen indicates that there is "dirty" (unsaved) data, as shown in Figure 2-19. In this case, the `Albums` list contains two dirty records (Jean-Michel Jarre and Vangelis), indicated by the asterisks to the left of the names.

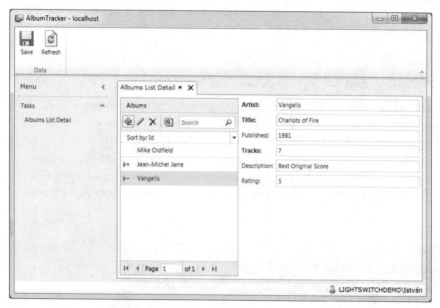

FIGURE 2-19: Unsaved data is marked with an asterisk.

5. Click the Save button in the toolbar. The data will be immediately persisted to the database.

6. Select an album and modify one of its attributes. For example, change the title of the first album and press Tab.

7. Click the Close button in the window's top-right corner. Because you are trying to close the application with unsaved data, you get a message telling you that you will lose the unsaved information if you continue to close the application. Click OK to confirm that you know the changes will be lost.

How It Works

Any data modifications you make, such as adding new records, deleting existing ones, or altering record attributes, are first saved into memory but left intact in the database. LightSwitch keeps track of all changes you've made. You must use the Save button to write all modifications into the database. LightSwitch uses its tracking list to send the modified records to the database as a single batch.

Making Runtime Customizations

As shown in Figure 2-17 and Figure 2-18, the UI automatically generated by LightSwitch may not be as nice as you would like it to be. Of course, you can customize all these properties in the IDE. However, the traditional customization cycle (that is, stop the application, modify visual properties, and restart the application to check changes) can be slow.

LightSwitch allows you to customize your application's screens while it runs in Debug mode, and it saves your changes in the open project in the IDE. This feature enables you to try several settings and immediately see the results without stopping and restarting the application.

TRY IT OUT   Customizing the Application's UI during Runtime

1.   Start the application in Debug mode by selecting Debug ➪ Start Debugging, or by pressing F5. When the application starts, you'll see a Design Screen button in the rightmost position of the toolbar. You can click this button to customize the layout properties of the current screen.

2.   Click the Design Screen button, which takes you to the Customization Mode screen, shown in Figure 2-20. The left panel shows the layout hierarchy of the screen, similar to how it appeared in Figure 2-16. The bottom-right panel shows the properties of the selected element in the layout hierarchy.

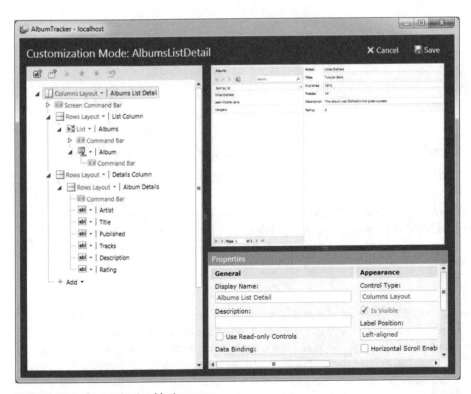

FIGURE 2-20: Customization Mode screen

3. Select the root node (Albums List Detail) in the layout hierarchy, and change its Display Name property in the Properties pane to Albums List. As you change the layout properties, you can see a preview of the changes.

4. Click the Save button at the top of the Customization Mode screen. This returns you to the runtime view of the application. Now you can see that the Albums List Detail title is changed to Albums List.

5. Click the Design Screen button again. In the Customization Mode screen, select the Published text box and change the Display Name property to "Published (year)." Scroll to the right of the Properties windows and set the sizing options as highlighted in Figure 2-21.

7. Click the Save Button to store the changes. You can immediately see how they affect your screen, as shown in Figure 2-22. The label of the Published field in the Album table has been changed to Published (year), and the width of the related text box has become narrower.

8. Close the AlbumTracker application.

9. In the LightSwitch IDE, open the AlbumsListDetail screen (double-click the AlbumsListDetail node underneath Screens). In the layout hierarchy, you can immediately see that runtime changes have been saved to your development environment. The name of the Published text box is now set to Published (year).

FIGURE 2-21: Changing the size properties of the Published text box

FIGURE 2-22: Result of Published text box changes

> **NOTE** *You may find complete code to download for this exercise on this book's companion website at* www.wrox.com *in the folder* Chapter 02\AlbumTracker.

How It Works

If you are not satisfied with the appearance of the generated UI, you can access the Customization Mode dialog anytime you run the application in Debug mode (start it by pressing F5) and modify the settings there in real time until you like the result.

SUMMARY

Visual Studio LightSwitch is a new member of the Visual Studio family that you can use as a RAD tool for data-centric applications. Instead of writing a large amount of code, you can use the graphical Designers that LightSwitch provides to define the data you intend to work with, and to create the UI that interacts with the data.

The plumbing code to bind the tiers of a LightSwitch application is automatically handled by the IDE behind the scenes. You only need to create code for the business logic (rules and validation code) of your application.

You can install Visual Studio LightSwitch as a standalone product or integrate it into your existing Visual Studio 2010 installation. When creating a new project, you just select your preferred programming language — either Visual Basic or Visual C#.

Whereas other RAD tools generate a UI layout that you can use to position UI elements one by one, LightSwitch creates a layout definition and renders it on-the-fly during runtime. You can customize the layout of your application by running it in Debug mode — and, of course, save this modified layout.

Chapter 3 takes a look at the technologies behind a LightSwitch application. You'll take a closer look at the three-tier application architecture pattern, and learn how these layers are represented in LightSwitch projects.

EXERCISES

1. Explain how Visual Studio and Visual Studio LightSwitch are related.

2. List some scenarios or software development project types for which LightSwitch can enhance your productivity.

3. List some scenarios or software development project types for which LightSwitch cannot be used as the main tool.

4. Which programming languages are supported in Visual Studio LightSwitch out-of-the-box?

5. What kind of information should you provide when editing a field of a table?

6. How would you describe a screen layout generated by LightSwitch?

7. What is an alternative to customizing a screen within the LightSwitch IDE?

 NOTE *Answers to the Exercises can be found in the Appendix.*

▶ **WHAT YOU LEARNED IN THIS CHAPTER**

TOPIC	KEY CONCEPTS
Visual Studio LightSwitch	Visual Studio LightSwitch is a new member of the Visual Studio family. It is a rapid application development (RAD) tool designed to help write data-centric line-of-business (LOB) applications.
Business code	Code that delivers explicit business functionality to the user.
Plumbing code	Code that creates programming infrastructure-related functions, such as binding tiers and components, establishing the flow from the UI to the data back end, and vice versa.
Integrated shell mode	Visual Studio LightSwitch integrates into the shell of an existing Visual Studio 2010 installation.
Creating a project	Use the File ⇨ New Project command (or pressing Ctrl+Shift+N), or click the New Project link in the Start Page (directly beneath the program logo).
Creating a table	Use the "Create new table" task shown in the Application Designer right after you create a new project; or right-click the Data Sources node in Solution Explorer and Select Add Table from the context menu that appears.
Creating a screen	Click the Screen button in the toolbar while you display a table in the Designer; or right-click the `Screens` folder in Solution Explorer and select the Add Screen command from the context menu.
Customizing a screen at runtime	Start the Application by selecting Debug ⇨ Start Debugging, or press F5. Select the screen from the Task menu you intend to modify; and when it is displayed, click the Customize Screen button to access the Customization Mode screen.

Technologies behind a LightSwitch Application

WHAT YOU WILL LEARN IN THIS CHAPTER

- ➤ Getting to know the three-tier application architecture pattern, and how it is used in LightSwitch

- ➤ Understanding how the .NET Framework is used in LightSwitch applications

- ➤ Getting to know Silverlight 4, and how LightSwitch uses this technology

- ➤ Understanding the role of SQL Server Express when developing applications

- ➤ Understanding how LightSwitch uses data stored in SharePoint 2010 lists

- ➤ Getting to know Windows Azure, and how LightSwitch supports using it

This chapter provides an overview of the technologies behind a LightSwitch application. This chapter will help you to understand the main concepts of the technologies, as well as the roles they play in LightSwitch applications. Also contained in this chapter are hints about sites and books that you can use to obtain more information.

THE THREE-TIER APPLICATION ARCHITECTURE PATTERN

In the "ancient times" of software development, most problems were caused by an error in the implementation of an algorithm. Today's line-of-business (LOB) applications, however, face architectural challenges. In a world where applications are increasingly accessible through the Web, regardless of geographical location or time of the day, several architectural aspects of applications have significant importance:

➤ *Variety of user interface technologies* — An application must provide many types of user interfaces (UIs) to enable end-users to interact with the system (such as desktop applications, thin clients running in browsers, or a UI tailored to mobile devices).

➤ *Scalability* — Applications (and services behind them) must be able to scale well. This means that as the load increases (for example, the number of transactions in a unit of time increases), applications must be capable of responding accordingly, without loss of performance. Similarly, with a decreased load, applications should release unused resources.

➤ *Security* — Applications must be able to authenticate users and allow them to carry out only operations for which they are authorized.

➤ *Testability* — Different aspects of an application (functionality, performance, UI responsiveness, and so on) must be carefully tested. Finding and fixing bugs after an application has been deployed is more expensive than handling them during the implementation phase.

 NOTE *Of course, other important aspects of LOB applications influence the ultimate architecture, such as operability, deployment, maintainability, and so on.*

For a long time, these architectural issues were handled with the concept of *separating concerns*. In this context, a *concern* is a piece of interest or focus in an application. There are many concrete ways of understanding and interpreting what separation of concerns means, and how it can be implemented. When developing LOB applications, the most popular practice is the use of the three-tier application architecture pattern. Figure 3-1 shows an overview of this pattern.

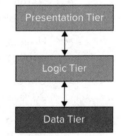

FIGURE 3-1: The three-tier architecture pattern

Each tier — Presentation, Logic, and Data — is a separate concern. As shown in the figure, the arrows between layers represent the information flow.

When the user initiates a request (for example, quarterly sales information about a specific product) from the UI of a three-tier application, the request is assembled in the Presentation tier. From there it goes to the Logic tier, which receives the request and carries out several checks, including permissions of the user to execute such a query. The Logic tier passes the query to the Data tier, which runs a query (for example, an SQL query) against the database server. The result of the database query is passed back to the Logic tier, which makes a few adjustments to the data (for example, adding a column qualifying the sales amount, such as Low, Normal, or High). The Logic tier sends the data to the Presentation tier, which displays it in the UI.

The Presentation Tier

The Presentation tier is the top-most level of an application and provides the UI. Its main responsibility is to translate user interactions to tasks that can be sent to the Logic layer, and to present the results returned from the Logic layer in a form that the user can understand (for example, tables, charts, and so on). A command-line console interface and a GUI are two examples of the Presentation tier.

Generally, the Presentation tier checks the input parameters of a task (for example, whether the format of an e-mail address is valid), and sends the request to the Logic tier only when the parameters are valid; otherwise, the user is asked to fix any invalid values.

The Logic Tier

This tier (sometimes called the Business Logic tier) is responsible for executing tasks (business functions) of the application. It may be as simple as forwarding a data-modification request to the Data tier; or as complex as a thorough check of a large set of *business rules* (for example, the cancellation of a booked trip).

In a well-architected application, the Logic tier never assumes the validity of requests received from the Presentation tier. It checks the identity of the user initiating the task from the UI, and confirms whether the user has the required permissions for the concrete task. Even when the UI is designed to check the input parameters of an operation, the Logic tier checks them again.

> **NOTE** *In current LOB applications, the Logic tier exposes operations through interfaces that are often open to external systems. The Logic tier does not have control over these external systems, so it cannot assume that they will provide only validated input parameters. Therefore, input parameter validation is a healthy paranoia. It makes the application secure and more robust; and, most importantly, it can guarantee that the business logic works according to the specification.*

The Logic tier has a significant role in the scalability of an application, too. This tier can use techniques such as asynchronous operations to improve the responsiveness of the UI, or caching to save the Data tier from superfluous work.

Asynchronous operations enable the running of multiple tasks when one of the tasks may take a long time, immediately returning control to the Presentation tier (UI). This way, users can carry on with their activities, rather than being forced to endure potentially long wait times until the long-running operation completes. When the task has been processed, the Presentation tier is notified, and it can render the results of the asynchronously executed task in the UI.

Caching is a great practice to avoid unnecessary communication with the Data tier. The results of queries about data that changes very infrequently (for example, attributes of a certain customer) can be stored in the cache (for example, the physical memory of the server) assigned to the Logic tier. When a subsequent request arrives from the Presentation tier with the same operation parameters, results can be retrieved from the cache, without communicating with the Data tier.

The Data Tier

The information used by an application is stored and retrieved through the Data tier. Most people think of database management systems (DBMSs) primarily, but the physical store behind a Data tier can be many other things, including the file system, an e-mail system, an enterprise directory, a remote system accessed through the Web, and much more.

The Data tier understands the requests coming from the Logic layer, and translates them to a protocol (or language) that is suitable to communicate with the data store. One real-world example is the SQL language used by relational database management systems (RDBMSs) to query underlying data. The results of these requests are converted to a form understood by the Logic layer before sending them back.

Generally, the information in the data store is represented with a different structure than in the Logic layer. For example, the Logic layer may work with Invoice documents, where each is treated as a single object holding all information about an invoice. However, at the data-store level, the documents can be stored as four related data tables, such as, Customer, Invoice Header, Invoice Detail, and Product. When the Logic layer creates an Invoice document, it might need to invoke Data tier operations four times — once for each data table — or might use a compound query joining the four tables to retrieve the result in one operation. The data flow shown in Figure 3-2 depicts the latter scenario.

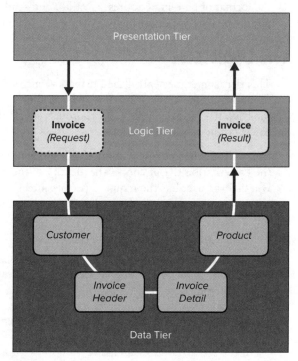

FIGURE 3-2: The request for an Invoice combines four tables in the Data tier to produce the result

LightSwitch and the Three-Tier Architecture Pattern

Implementing these three tiers introduces a lot of technological options, and this freedom is often coupled with complexity. In many cases, you must write plumbing code to bind the pieces (components) of the architecture together, and to handle aspects such as security, exception handling, data flow, and many more. Sometimes, writing plumbing code requires a lot of effort, which distracts developers from writing business code — the code that delivers value to customers.

As a RAD tool, Visual Studio LightSwitch creates applications that truly support the three-tier architecture. It removes the complexity of building a three-tier application by making specific technological choices for you. This enables you to focus on the business logic, not the plumbing.

A LightSwitch application's Presentation tier manages all human interactions. It is responsible for providing for data entry and visualizing information coming from the database. Although users may think of the Presentation tier as the entire application, this layer does not process the information. It simply passes data to the Logic tier and displays the result retrieved from there.

LightSwitch uses Silverlight 4 as the technology for the Presentation tier. This choice is very beneficial, because Silverlight applications can be either hosted in a web browser — including not only Internet Explorer, but also Firefox, Safari, and Google Chrome — or run in their own separate windows just like any other Windows desktop application. Silverlight also supports rich user interfaces and asynchronous technologies that allow smooth integration with the Logic tier.

> **NOTE** *You shouldn't feel embarrassed or intimidated by technologies you are unfamiliar with, such as "Silverlight 4." This chapter provides a short overview of all the technologies mentioned here — constrained to the most important things you need to understand about their roles and characteristics.*

The Logic tier of a LightSwitch application is responsible for processing data queries and data update requests coming from the Presentation tier. As an organic part of servicing queries and requests, the Logic tier validates the data before processing it. The data within this tier is represented as entities, which provide an intuitive programming interface to leverage when writing business rules or data processing code.

A component of the .NET Framework 4 Entity Framework (EF) is used to access data stored in back-end databases. A new protocol named OData is used to obtain and manipulate data accessible through standard HTTP web requests. WCF Rich Internet Application (RIA) Services is a component that binds the Silverlight 4 client with the Logic tier. It is a relatively new technology that simplifies the work of developers.

The Data tier is called the Storage tier in LightSwitch, emphasizing that the Logic tier is responsible for requesting the data, and the Storage tier is responsible for retrieving and persisting it. LightSwitch supports three kinds of data storage components out-of-the-box:

➤ SQL Server 2008 (that is, an RDBMS)

➤ SharePoint 2010 lists

➤ Other storage services that provide an OData interface

For developers who want to create cloud applications, LightSwitch can also work with SQL Azure, which stores databases in the cloud.

CLOUD APPLICATIONS

With LightSwitch, you can create applications that users can access over the Internet, eliminating the need to install and run the application on the user's own computer. From the user's point of view, these applications are implemented somewhere in the Internet, hence the term *cloud applications.*

One option for providing the infrastructure for web applications is to deploy them to your company's dedicated servers, or to servers operated by an Internet Service Provider (ISP). These can be either physical servers or virtual servers.

Some companies provide infrastructure accessible though the web that you can use as a development platform. This is called *Platform-as-a-Service (PaaS).* Such a company is Microsoft, which provides Windows Azure as a PaaS. Generally, when you deploy an application to a PaaS infrastructure, you are not working with physical computers. Instead, you perceive a transparent platform that is capable of hosting your application. The term "cloud application" often means that the application is deployed to a PaaS infrastructure.

Figure 3-3 shows the stack of technologies used in a LightSwitch application. Don't worry about the boxes containing technologies not mentioned yet; all of them are explained in more detail later in this chapter.

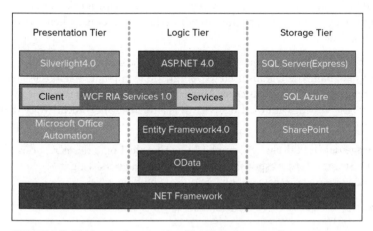

FIGURE 3-3: Technologies used in a LightSwitch application

As you can see in the figure, the .NET Framework is the backbone of LightSwitch applications, and it is utilized in all tiers. Let's take a look at what the .NET Framework is all about.

THE .NET FRAMEWORK

The Microsoft .NET Framework is a runtime environment that sits between the operating system and the applications. Its main role is to provide access to all services of the underlying operating system in a managed way that enables developers to be productive. .NET adds several fundamental benefits to software development:

> ➤ *Uniform runtime* — Before the .NET era, each Windows application development tool used a separate runtime environment. For example, Visual Basic had the VB runtime, Delphi utilized the Visual Component Library (VCL), and Visual C++ developers could select between Microsoft Foundation Classes (MFC) and Active Template Library (ATL). When developers had to change a programming language, it was not enough to learn a new language; they also needed to learn a new runtime library. With .NET, developers can utilize the same runtime regardless of the specific programming language used.

> ➤ *Patterns to prevent common errors* — Developers tend to make similar errors, such as using already released objects in the memory, creating memory leak issues and type-unsafe conversions, and so on. The .NET Framework has a component called the common language runtime (CLR) that provides an infrastructure to prevent such problems. For example, developers can allocate memory for objects without explicitly recycling it. If the amount of memory gets low, the garbage-collector mechanism automatically frees the unused (but explicitly not released) memory.

> ➤ *Making complex things simple* — Many complicated tasks must be carried out through the operating system application programming interfaces (APIs). For example, most simple tasks may require several subsequent API calls, as well as extra care for checking and handling exceptional situations. The .NET Base Class Library (BCL) provides thousands of objects that translate complicated tasks into very simple operations.

The first version of the .NET Framework was released in February 2002 (in tandem with Visual Studio.NET). During the more than ten years since the first announcement, seven main versions were released. The latest is .NET Framework 4.0, which was released in March 2010. Visual Studio LightSwitch uses this version.

The .NET Runtime

All software products do essentially the same thing: execute machine instructions on the CPU of a computer. These instructions are very low-level ones, manipulating memory and bits in the registers of the CPU. Because software applications are traditionally developed with a programming language that is much closer to human (developer) thinking than CPU instructions, compilers parse these programming languages into machine-readable executable files that contain instructions capable of running directly on the CPU.

With the .NET Framework, this is different. The source code described in the programming language (you can use several programming languages with .NET) is compiled into an intermediate code called *Intermediate Language (IL)*, often referred to as *Microsoft Intermediate Language (MSIL)*. When an application runs, the IL code is loaded into memory. When it is time to run the code related to an object (in .NET, all executable elements belong to an object), a Just-In-Time (JIT) compiler translates the IL code to machine-specific code that can directly run on the CPU. Figure 3-4 shows the steps of this code-execution mechanism.

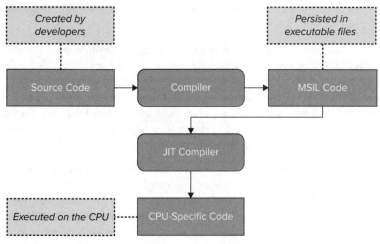

FIGURE 3-4: Overview of the .NET code-execution mechanism

Following are some of the advantages of compiling source code into an IL instead of machine instructions:

➤ The IL is CPU-independent. With the appropriate JIT compilers, the IL code can run on different CPU types, even with different CPU architectures.

➤ The JIT compiler can generate different machine-specific code according to the status of the execution environment. For example, it may take the number of CPUs and the amount of free memory into account.

.NET Languages

The .NET Framework is a language-independent framework. Developers can use several languages to write their programs. They can even work on projects for which several languages are used together — according to their strengths. The languages supporting the .NET runtime are called *managed languages*.

Microsoft ships three managed languages in Visual Studio 2010:

➤ *Visual Basic* — Today, Visual Basic is fundamentally an object-oriented programming (OOP) language. However, the new functional language features to be introduced in the forthcoming versions shift Visual Basic toward being a multi-paradigm programming language. It started its life in the mid-1960s as a high-level language that enabled the general user to program computers. For users familiar with Microsoft Word or Excel, Visual Basic is also known as the language for writing macros.

➤ *Visual C# (pronounced "C sharp")* — C# is a new multi-paradigm programming language that began its life as an object-oriented language. The development team of the C# language was led by Anders Hejlsberg, who joined Microsoft in 1996 after being exceptionally successful with Turbo Pascal and Delphi at Borland. The first version of C# was released together with the .NET Framework 1.0, and it is often referred to as the native language of .NET.

➤ *Visual F# (pronounced "F sharp")* — This is a multi-paradigm programming language that embraces functional programming, as well as imperative object-oriented programming, disciplines. The language grew out of the work of Don Syme and his team at Microsoft Research (MSR) in Cambridge, Great Britain.

 NOTE Although Microsoft ships only Visual Basic, C#, and F# with Visual Studio 2010, the company also encourages third parties and communities to create their own languages supporting the .NET Framework. The IronPython (www.ironpython.net) and IronRuby (www.ironruby.net) language communities are patronized by Microsoft.

You can use Visual Basic and Visual C# when writing code in LightSwitch. There are no essential differences between these languages from a usability point of view. Both are equally suitable for solving tasks that require you to create code. Following are a few points to help you make your choice:

➤ If you have concrete experience with one of the languages, or you prefer one of them, choose that language.

➤ If you have written Microsoft Office macros or used them before, Visual Basic might be your best choice, because you'll be able to use familiar syntax and language constructs.

➤ If you have used C, C++, Java, or JavaScript before, it's much easier to start with C#, because the syntax of the language and the main semantics are much closer to those languages than to Visual Basic.

 WARNING While most Visual Studio project types support mixing languages in a solution, LightSwitch does not. When you start a new LightSwitch project, you must select a programming language; and after the project skeleton is created, this language cannot be changed.

.NET Framework and LightSwitch

The .NET Framework is presented in every tier of a LightSwitch application. The Logic tier uses .NET 4.0, where the Entity Framework 4.0 is the cornerstone of managing data. ASP.NET and WCF are responsible for hosting the Logic tier components within Internet Information Services

(IIS) and providing web-service protocol-based communication with the Presentation tier. Most data access operations use LINQ, which you'll find especially useful and efficient when you are creating business rules within your LightSwitch application.

On the client side, Silverlight 4 also uses its own CLR to execute applications.

Sources for More Information about the .NET Framework

If you are interested in getting closer to .NET, the best place to start is the .NET Framework Developer Center on MSDN (`http://msdn.microsoft.com/netframework`). If you prefer books (either printed or eBooks editions), visit `wrox.com`. On the home page, select the .NET topics to browse related books. It is faster and easier to get experience with .NET if you do it in parallel with learning the basics of Visual Basic or C#. Start with one of the following books:

> ➤ *Beginning Visual Basic 2010* by Thearon Willis and Bryan Newsome (Wiley, 2010)

> ➤ *Beginning Visual C# 2010* by Karli Watson, Christian Nagel, Jacob Hammer Pedersen, Jon D. Reid, and Morgan Skinner (Wiley, 2010)

SILVERLIGHT 4

Silverlight is an emerging UI platform that represents a revolutionary change from the UI technologies that ruled Windows development for almost 20 years.

In 2001, Microsoft founder Bill Gates created a new team tasked with researching and developing a new presentation layer, one that would shift the different, but overlapping, UI technologies to a new and unified engine. At the time, the technology under development by the new group was code-named "Avalon." It was later renamed Windows Presentation Foundation (WPF), which first appeared in version 3.0 of the .NET Framework.

In the meantime, WPF's cousin, Silverlight (originally called WPF Everywhere, or WPF/E), began to take shape. The goal was to create a trimmed-down version of the Windows-only WPF, and apply the same key principles to the Web, other operating systems, and other devices.

Silverlight 1.0 was released in September 2007, and focused on media playback. It was programmable via the browser's JavaScript engine. The real revolution occurred with Silverlight 2.0, which launched one year later, in October 2008. In a mere 4MB download, Silverlight 2.0 included a trimmed-down version of the full .NET Framework with dozens of controls and media support.

Silverlight 3 was released only nine months later, with fantastic new features, including H.264 video codec support, pixel shaders, limited GPU acceleration, out-of-browser support, and much more. Silverlight 4 launched in April 2010 (exactly three years after Silverlight 1 was introduced), and focuses on LOB applications, media, and advanced out-of-browser scenarios. Silverlight 5 contains numerous great features, including full three-dimensional graphics support, text clarity enhancements, and improved media support.

Silverlight is officially supported on Windows and Intel-based Mac OS X computers, and in Firefox, Internet Explorer (IE), and Safari. This technology is free, and can be used together with Microsoft's free Visual Studio Express editions as well.

A New UI Concept

Silverlight is all about a rich UI. It is designed and tailored so that you can create rich, powerful Internet applications that offer users a superior experience. In addition to providing simple UI elements such as text boxes, buttons, lists, combo boxes, images, and so on, it gives you the freedom to create content with animation and media elements. In contrast to the traditional — you may even say boring — UI approach (with rectangular UI elements repeating from application to application), Silverlight enables you to change the entire face of an application, thus enabling it to be part of today's web application variegation.

Animations and transitions help direct the attention of the user, explain why things happen, and generally make the virtual experience feel smoother and better by bringing it closer to the real world. Silverlight animations are time-based, rather than frame-based. This means that if an animation is set to last two seconds, it will take exactly two seconds, even if the computer is very busy and can only display a few frames while the animation runs. Not only is a time-based animation more predictable, it enables the Silverlight runtime to continuously adapt to the computer's performance by skipping or interpolating animation frames.

Transformations enable the moving, rotating, scaling (changing the size), and skewing of UI elements. Media in Silverlight includes playing back audio and video files, as well as providing access to the microphone and the web cam on the computer.

Layout

In contrast to traditional Windows applications, whereby UI elements such as text boxes, buttons, lists, and combo boxes were exactly positioned on the screen, Silverlight provides a very flexible layout system that makes it easy to create layouts, which automatically adapt to the following factors:

➤ Available screen size

➤ Number of items displayed

➤ Size of the displayed elements

➤ Magnification factor

Silverlight's layout strategy is different from what you may be used to in Windows Forms or ASP.NET. The layout system allows nesting UI elements into other UI elements (called *content controls*), and it provides layout controls that can automatically position their child elements. LightSwitch also utilizes this strategy to trust the Silverlight layout engine to render complex master-detail forms. Figure 3-5 shows an example of this layout.

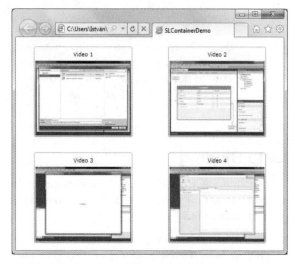

FIGURE 3-5: Example of Silverlight's layout strategy

Here you can see four panels with titles. However, those titles are actually buttons that you can click to play the video. What's nice is that the videos and the title texts are embedded into the button, because the button is a content control. The four buttons are aligned with a grid layout control.

DECLARING THE USER INTERFACE IN SILVERLIGHT

Silverlight uses a declarative approach to describe the UI element with a language called Extensible Application Markup Language (XAML, pronounced "zamel"). The nature of XAML allows an easy description of the layout strategy used by Silverlight. The following code snippet gives you a taste:

```
<Button HorizontalAlignment="Center" VerticalAlignment="Center"
    Margin=" 8">
  <StackPanel Orientation="Vertical">
    <TextBlock Text="Video 1" HorizontalAlignment="Center"
        VerticalAlignment="Center"
      Margin="5" />
    <MediaElement Width="200" Height="150" Source=
        "file:///H:/video1.wmv"
      AutoPlay="True" />
  </StackPanel>
</Button>
```

The `Button` tag declares the properties of the button you can see in the top-left position in Figure 3-5. It embeds a `StackPanel` tag that automatically places its two children (a `TextBlock` and a `MediaElement`) vertically because the `Orientation` attribute is set to `Vertical`. The `TextBlock` represents the title of the button, while `MediaElement` describes a video that automatically starts when the button is clicked.

The UI described by XAML can be created dynamically, too. LightSwitch uses this latter approach, so you do not have to know the XAML syntax to create LightSwitch applications. However, when you become a LightSwitch expert and you want to develop LightSwitch extensions — you can read more about this topic in Chapter 15 — XAML is an indispensable tool.

Data Binding

Data binding is a technology used to connect elements of the UI to data, or other UI elements, declaratively. Silverlight's data binding works in cooperation with styles, templates, layouts, and even animations.

This mechanism is especially useful in LOB applications. With the help of data-binding information coming from the database and processed by the Logic tier, elements can be declaratively bound — without writing code — to the UI elements.

Figure 3-6 shows a screen from the `AlbumTracker` application you created in Chapter 2. The list on the left side of the screen is bound to the list of albums retrieved from the Logic tier of the application. The text boxes at the right such as Artist, Title, Publication (year), and the others, are bound to the object representing the selected line in the list.

FIGURE 3-6: A simple screen in the AlbumTracker application

Data binding allows for two-way synchronization and validation, and automatically ensures that the UI and the underlying data are consistent. You can use data-binding techniques for displaying and editing data entry as well. When you use two-way binding, not only is the data arriving from the Logic tier shown in the UI, but the data changed by the user is written back to its source object. Data binding is a key element in making possible the separation between the UI and the logic.

Without this mechanism, developers would have to write code that populates UI elements with the data coming from the back end, and would have to provide code that collects data from the screen after the user modified it — in other words, they would have to write plumbing code. Having complex data structures and many fields, it would be very laborious and detract developers from writing valuable business functions.

LightSwitch does a good job with data binding, and makes unnecessary many activities that would require some time with other tools.

Styles and Templates

Keeping the look of UI elements consistent within an application adds great value, makes the application easier to use, and helps users intuitively find screen elements for carrying out their tasks.

Separating logic and presentation is a key design principle for Silverlight. Logic is to be implemented by developers, while presentation belongs to designers. In traditional web design projects, the inability of developers and designers to cooperate seamlessly is typically a source of conflict, because the interests of developers are often at odds with the interests of designers.

Silverlight's features (especially styles and templates) contribute to a smooth cooperation between developers and designers. Developers implement the logic of the application, so they never set the visual properties of the UI directly. Instead, they signal programmatically that the state of the UI is changed. Designers create the visuals of the UI, taking into account the possible states of the UI.

For example, an operation cannot be executed when the data provided in the UI is not valid. Using the traditional approach, developers disable a button associated with the operation when the application perceives that the parameters are invalid.

In Silverlight, however, developers signal that the state of the UI does not allow that specific operation. It's the responsibility of the designer to represent this state visually. The designer can disable the button, hide it, or even display a big blinking warning — whatever they deem useful for signaling this state — without modifying the logic at all.

THE ROLE OF THE DESIGNER

The freedom of the designer is very important in Silverlight — and in all applications with a rich UI. The designer is more than someone who creates only nice graphics; the designer also creates the interaction used in an application.

Let's return to the example of disabling a button when the related operation is not allowed because of invalid parameters. This example explicitly assumes that a button is added to the UI to represent the operation, and it ties the hands of the designer. What if the interaction designer thinks that a task link would be better to start the operation than a button? The designer would need the help of the developer to change this model — so they would need to work together in tandem.

Using states, the designer's freedom remains intact. The developer signals the new state of the UI — let's say, "operation is invalid" — and the designer represents the state (in this case, with a disabled task link). The only thing the designer and the developer must agree on is the list of states and what they mean.

Styles and templates in Silverlight are key features for separating the logic and the presentation. *Styles* are simple constructs that enable you to define a consistent set of properties, and you can apply them to UI elements. For example, you can create a style for buttons that defines the color and width of the border, the brush object to fill the background, or even animations for events such as when the mouse hovers over the button or leaves it.

Rather than set each button's properties separately, you can assign the appropriate style to all buttons. That way, when you want to change the look of the buttons, you do not need to change them individually. You only change the style, which is immediately reflected in each button's visual properties.

 NOTE *Although the analogy is not perfect, styles in Silverlight serve a very similar purpose to Cascading Style Sheets (CSS) in web pages. Both are important tools for "skinning" the UI.*

The separation of logic and design in Silverlight is often described as "controls are lookless." That means that a control is nothing more than the definition of its behavior. For example, a button is an element the user can click to initiate an action. The definition of the button does not specify anything about its design! It is not carved in stone anywhere that a button must be rectangular with rounded corners and center-aligned text. Of course, when you design the UI and place a button on the screen, it must be somehow visually represented, so Silverlight uses a default design.

Templates in Silverlight provide a mechanism to replace the visual look of a control entirely or change how data is displayed or laid out in a list box.

Figure 3-7 demonstrates why templates are useful. In this case, the data template of list box items has been changed, and a button that uses a custom template replaces the default one. These templates are resources in a Silverlight project, so you can use the same template for several list boxes and buttons to provide a consistent visual style. Changing the template will cause the layout of all controls that use it to change.

Sources for More Information about Silverlight 4

Silverlight is an exciting, quickly evolving technology. The best place to get started with it is `http://silverlight.net`. Here you'll find a lot of helpful materials to get you started with Silverlight. Following are two books on Silverlight that will help to deepen your knowledge after getting experience with the basics:

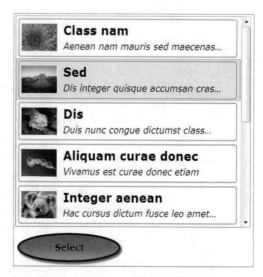

FIGURE 3-7: This UI uses Silverlight templates to change the outlook of the list and the button

➤ *Professional Silverlight 4* by Jason Beres, Bill Evjen, and Devin Rader (Wiley, 2010)

➤ *Silverlight 4: Problem-Design-Solution* by Nick Lecrenski (Wiley, 2010)

These books are also available in Adobe e-book formats.

SQL SERVER 2008

SQL Server 2008 is a relational database management system (RDBMS) designed to store information represented in the form of related tables. Although you can represent data tables and relations even in an Excel workbook, an RDBMS (such as SQL Server, Oracle, or MySQL) must be used to provide a more robust solution. Visual Studio LightSwitch uses SQL Server 2008 as one of its primary data source types for applications.

SQL Server Features

SQL Server 2008 has several important features that keep your data safe and consistent, several of which are summarized in Table 3-1.

TABLE 3-1: Essential SQL Server Features

FEATURE	DESCRIPTION
Scalability	SQL Server is designed to be able to serve a large number of users (even several thousand) simultaneously. It can utilize all CPUs in a computer to provide the best throughput, and may use the physical memory in the computer to cache data and results of often-used queries to prevent loading the data from the hard disk every time.
Handling transactions	Data-manipulation operations can be organized into transactions. A transaction may modify several records, or even a large amount of data stored in one or more tables. Transactions are atomic, which means either all operations involved in a transaction are carried out, or none of them is executed. If a transaction is interrupted by hardware issues, software discrepancies, or errors in the transaction logic, the changes are automatically rolled back — as if they had never happened, preserving the state at the beginning of the transaction.
Logging	Each data-manipulation operation is logged in a separate database log file. If a transaction is interrupted by a system shutdown, or by a serious event that would stop the database management system, the next time the system is started, the log files are used to preserve the consistency of the database. With the help of the information stored in the log file, the system can roll back the database to the last known consistent state — or, in a few cases, roll forward (complete) the interrupted transactions.
Referential integrity constraints	You can define *referential integrity constraints* among the tables of a database. These constraints can prevent you (or any application) from making changes in the database that would make its state inconsistent.
	For example, assume your application manages `Customer` and `Order` instances, where each `Order` contains a reference to a `Customer` by storing the identifier of the related `Customer` record. If you save an `Order` with an identifier of a non-existing customer, it would hurt your system's consistency. To avoid this situation, you can define a referential integrity constraint that allows you to save `Order` instances only if they provide an identifier for an existing `Customer`. If you try to insert or save an `Order` with an invalid `Customer` identifier, SQL Server would refuse the change, indicating that it negates the referential integrity constraint between `Order` and `Customer`.
Indexes	Most manipulations require filtering data according to specific conditions. If you have a large amount of data (for example, several million records), it can take a long time to find among them those that match your criteria.
	For example, if you have a million customers, it could take some time to find the one named "William Bartalome" if you had to weed through each customer record one by one. Indexes are special utility structures that help you easily find records by using the value of a certain field (or a set of fields). For example, you can add an index for customer names to find them by their names. If a telephone book represents your database table, the book's table of contents is the index. If you search for "William Bartalome" in the table of contents, you can find the page number where names starting with "W" begins, which makes it easier to find your customer.

FEATURE	DESCRIPTION
	Indexes are special storage structures — using binary trees — organized so that you only need a relatively small number of lookups to find records you're searching for. For example, you need about 10 lookups to find a customer among 1,000 records, and about 20 lookups to find him among 1 million other customers. You can imagine how much quicker this is than scanning through 1 million of them.
Stored procedures	Often-used operations can be given to SQL Server in the form of stored procedures, which are described in Transact-SQL (T-SQL) language. These procedures are compiled when they are used, and their execution plan is saved. Stored procedures are blackboxes to their users. Developers can change them without bothering users (for example, to tune performance), unless their parameters and semantics are not altered.
	Stored procedures can also provide a security barrier. Users can be granted access to well-defined operations through stored procedures that use tables, with no direct user access.

SQL Server 2008 Express

You do not have to worry about how you can install SQL Server in your development environment, because Visual Studio LightSwitch installs SQL Server 2008 Express on your machine. SQL Server 2008 Express is a lightweight (and free) version of SQL Server that you can definitely use for small applications. From the developer's point of view, the Express edition provides all the functionality of the non-free editions. It uses only one CPU, even if you have more CPUs in your machine. The maximum size of a database can be up to 10GB.

TRY IT OUT **Looking at SQL Server 2008 Express Data**

As mentioned, Visual Studio LightSwitch installs SQL Server 2008 Express. When you created the `AlbumTracker` application in Chapter 2, the data was stored in a SQL Server data file.

To have a look at the content of this data file, follow these steps:

1. Start Visual Studio LightSwitch.

2. Open the `AlbumTracker` project. You have several ways to do this. After Visual Studio starts, you can find `AlbumTracker` under the Recent Projects section of the Start page. A second option is to select File ➪ Recent Projects and Solutions. Finally, you can use the File ➪ Open Project command and select your project from the location where you added it when you created it.

3. Select Build ➪ Rebuild AlbumTracker to build the application.

4. Select View ➪ Server Explorer to display the Server Explorer window. By default, this window is docked to the left edge of the main window. When you use it for the first time, it contains only a single `Data Connections` node, as shown in Figure 3-8.

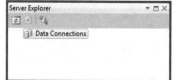

FIGURE 3-8: Data Connections node in the Server Explorer window

5. Right-click `Data Connections` and Select the Add Connection command from the context menu. When you use this command for the first time, the Change Data Source dialog appears (shown in Figure 3-9); otherwise, the Add Connection dialog appears (shown in Figure 3-10). Your dialog might look different from Figure 3-10, depending on the most recently used data source type. If you see the Add Connection dialog, click the Change button to the right of the Data Source text box, and the Change Data Source dialog will appear.

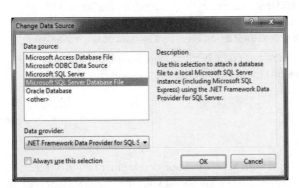

FIGURE 3-9: The Change Data Source dialog

FIGURE 3-10: The Add Connection dialog

6. Select the Microsoft SQL Server Database File in the Change Data Source Dialog and click OK. The Add Connection dialog will be shown with the focus set to the "Database file name (new or existing)" text box.

7. Use the Browse button to select the SQL Server database file. Navigate to the folder where you put the `AlbumTracker` project when you created it, and find the `AlbumTracker\bin\Data` folder under it. Select the `ApplicationDatabase.mdf` file (the file extension may be hidden), and click Open. Figure 3-11 shows the dialog from which you can select this database file.

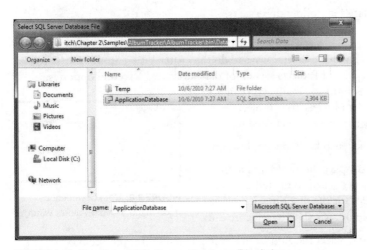

FIGURE 3-11: The Select SQL Server Database File dialog

8. In the Add Connection dialog, be sure that the Use Windows Authentication option is selected, and see if the database file is accessible by clicking the Test Connection button. If it is accessible, it will pop up a simple "Test connection succeeded" message on the screen. Close it, and then close the Add Connection dialog by clicking the OK button.

9. A new `ApplicationDatabase.mdf` node is added to the `Data Connections` node in Server Explorer. Expand this node by clicking the little triangle to the left of the node. Then, expand the `Tables` and then the `Albums` nodes, as shown in Figure 3-12. Here you can see the fields you defined in Chapter 2 when you designed the structure of the `Albums` table.

10. Right-click the `Albums` node and select Show Table Data from the context menu. A new window appears with a grid displaying the album data you entered earlier into this table, as shown in Figure 3-13.

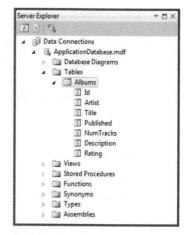

FIGURE 3-12: Fields of the Albums table in Server Explorer

	Id	Artist	Title	Published	NumTracks	Description	Rating
▶	2	Mike Oldfield	Tubular Bells	1973	14	This was Oldfield's first great succe...	5
	3	Jean-Michel Jarre	Oxygen	1976	6	A great synthesizer album	4
	4	Vangelis	Chariots of Fire	1982	12	Won the Best Original Score Acade...	5
*	NULL	NULL	NULL	NULL	NULL	NULL	NULL

Albums: Query(lightswitchb1\36ad3b78-78a3-43.F484FBF42FDBB10F44BD45BA80A6C75D_BOX\VS LIGHTSWITCH\CHAPTER 2\...

◄◄ ◄ | 1   of 3 | ► ►► ►⁎ | ⊕ |

FIGURE 3-13: Data in the Albums table

11. Close the window with the table data.

12. Right-click the `ApplicationDatabase.mdf` node in Sever Explorer and select Delete from the context menu. When the message box pops up, confirm that you want to delete the connection. This command will remove your database from the data connections, but will not delete the file containing your database.

How It Works

When you displayed the data in the `Albums` table, Visual Studio created a T-SQL query — if you are familiar with the SQL language, you'll understand it — that looks like this:

```
SELECT Id, Artist, Title, Published, NumTracks, Description, Rating
FROM Albums
```

The IDE sent this query to the SQL Server Express database engine. The database engine used the `ApplicationDatabase.mdf` file as the database, and retrieved the data from the server. It was then displayed in the window shown in Figure 3-13. With LightSwitch, you do not have to deal with SQL queries. Those are created and executed in the background. Moreover, you cannot execute your own SQL commands; LightSwitch does not allow you to do that.

This short exercise only scratched the surface of SQL Server Express's functionality. Using Visual Studio LightSwitch, you do not need to know very much about how SQL Server works behind the scenes. However, in many cases, when you are examining issues or application bugs, it is valuable to know how you can look at the data stored in SQL Server Express.

Sources for More Information about SQL Server

SQL Server is a huge server product available in many editions. The SQL Server Developer Center on MSDN is the one-stop shop for developers working with this DBMS, but it assumes you already possess the basics of the SQL language and have had some practice working with databases.

Wrox has published great books about SQL Server 2008. The following books are useful if you want to familiarize yourself with database programming:

➤ *Beginning T-SQL with Microsoft SQL Server 2005 and 2008* by Paul Turley and Dan Wood (Wiley, 2008)

➤ *Beginning Microsoft SQL Server 2008 Programming* by Robert Vieira (Wiley, 2009)

SHAREPOINT 2010

Microsoft SharePoint 2010 is a collaboration platform that integrates web content management, document management, enterprise search, and Web 2.0 features in a single product. Both enterprises and communities can use SharePoint to facilitate cooperation among individuals, groups, and organizations.

SharePoint 2010 Features

Although most users interact only with the web portal UI of SharePoint, the product involves much more functionality than perceived through the UI. Table 3-2 summarizes the most significant features of this great collaboration platform. Of course, this table is by no means complete.

TABLE 3-2: Essential SharePoint 2010 Features

FEATURE	DESCRIPTION
Sharing information with sites	SharePoint 2010 serves as a great platform for creating sites that can function as a one-stop shop for publishing information related to the user's business, daily work, or community activities. The product provides a vast set of tools for creating virtually any kind of site to share information, and a single infrastructure that simplifies site management. Novice or expert, anyone can quickly create, customize, and publish a site that looks great and meets a specific business or community need. SharePoint prides itself on delivering a personalized experience with its robust features, such as audience targeting, multilingual interface support, and user tagging.

FEATURE	DESCRIPTION
Collaboration platform	The most significant feature that distinguishes SharePoint from other collaboration portals is the wide variety of tools it provides to enable information workers, business partners, community members, and other groups to work together. In addition to the well-known collaboration tools such as blogs, wikis, tags, and ratings, users can navigate their organizational structure, recognize each other with photos, change e-mails and instant messages, or call someone. Just like social portals, SharePoint enables users to manage their own home page — integrating photos, personal blogs, and links.
Managing content	In SharePoint, content is king. Because SharePoint is closely integrated with Microsoft Office products, most users find it familiar and easy to use. Most documents opened in the portal are shown in the appropriate Office application, and SharePoint makes simultaneous editing by multiple users simple. SharePoint 2010 takes compliance seriously. In addition to managing versions, it also applies retention schedules, declares records, and places legal holds in order to reduce the risk of mistakes that result from improper information archiving or disposal procedures.
Enhanced search	Working with a huge amount of content is practically impossible without useful and sophisticated search opportunities. SharePoint 2010 provides an interactive and visual search experience to help users quickly find what they need among a vast number of documents in multiple formats. With the help of metadata assigned to content, search results can be refined. The relevance model can be tuned, too. In addition to searching the content, People Search enables users to easily find one another.

SharePoint 2010 Lists and LightSwitch

Most of the information that SharePoint 2010 stores is represented as *lists*, including document libraries, contacts, events, links, announcements, tasks, and more. Users can also create custom lists with their own structures. Figure 3-14 shows a custom list named My Favorite Albums that contains information similar to the AlbumTracker application. Visual Studio LightSwitch can access SharePoint lists, and utilize their content just like any other table you create — with subtle constraints.

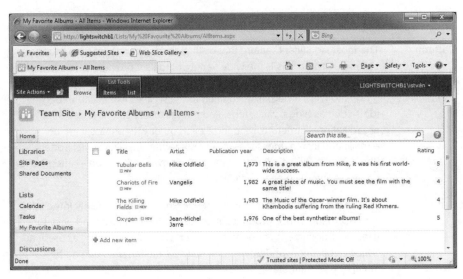

FIGURE 3-14: A custom list in SharePoint 2010

At first glance, it may not be very obvious why accessing SharePoint lists is really beneficial. However, retrieving those lists and handling them as if they were database tables allows you to leverage the information stored there.

For example, a SharePoint list managed by the Human Resources division of your company may contain a description and schedule of courses. If you implemented an application to manage enrollments, you had to create data tables and functions in your application to administer the list of courses — duplicating the job the Human Resources department also did for you. By connecting to the SharePoint list, you simply use the information without duplicating it. As soon as the list of courses is altered, your LightSwitch application immediately sees the changes.

Using SharePoint lists requires access to a SharePoint site. If you want to use it on your own computer, you must install SharePoint 2010. Chapter 14 provides details about using lists, and offers examples demonstrating how to link your LightSwitch application with SharePoint 2010.

MICROSOFT OFFICE

It would probably be hard to find anyone using the Windows platform who isn't also familiar with Microsoft Office. These products are so closely integrated that users who work with Outlook, Word, Excel, or PowerPoint often forget that these applications are not part of the operating system.

LightSwitch was designed with the idea of Office integration in mind, so that your application can leverage the existing functionality of Office components. For example, you can easily create invitation letters with Word using the contact and event information stored in your application's database, or you can create a presentation with charts about the current sales reports based on your application's data.

Microsoft Office Application Features

Each Microsoft Office application has a wide variety of functions, although 90 percent of them are not used by the typical user, including the author of this book. The full Office system actually provides a dozen applications — not merely the four mentioned earlier. Table 3-3 offers a very brief description of each.

TABLE 3-3: Microsoft Office 2010 Applications

APPLICATION	DESCRIPTION
Word	Document editor application used to create professional-looking documents and manage their full authoring life cycle
Excel	Professional spreadsheet management application with easy-to-use programming capabilities, analysis, and business-intelligence functionality
Outlook	Application used to access your vital information — business or social — including e-mail, calendar, tasks, and notes
PowerPoint	A tool for creating, rehearsing, showing, printing, and distributing professional presentations
Visio	Diagramming tool with a diverse set of built-in stencils, drawing blocks, and connectors — especially useful for flowchart creation.
Access	A simple database management tool used to access data locally and remotely — with easy and effective forms and reports creation
OneNote	A professional note-management tool that aids in making and organizing plans, notes, and minutes
InfoPath	An application used to quickly design and build forms and workflows connecting to LOB systems
Project	A professional tool used to plan, manage, and track tasks, schedules, and resources of a simple project or a group of related projects
Publisher	An intuitive application used to create impressive publications (for example, letters, invitations, business cards, covers, and more) in a few simple steps
SharePoint Workspace	A desktop application used to support small collaborative teams with managing and synchronizing their information stored in SharePoint libraries
Lync	A real-time collaboration tool for people working together — including features such as instant messaging, screen sharing, and live meeting

Applications within the Office bundle are well integrated with each other — and with other products such as SharePoint, Visual Studio, and Visual Studio LightSwitch.

The functionality of these components can be accessed in external applications by using the Office Automation Model. The applications you can create with Visual Studio LightSwitch also can leverage this functionality.

Exporting Information to Microsoft Excel

Visual Studio LightSwitch is designed with Microsoft Office integration in mind. You can easily export data to Microsoft Excel — without writing any code. The following "Try It Out" exercise demonstrates how.

TRY IT OUT　**Exporting Information to Microsoft Excel**

To export the album information used in previous examples to Microsoft Excel, follow these steps:

1.　Start Visual Studio LightSwitch.

2.　Open the `AlbumTracker` project. You can click the `AlbumTracker` link under the Recent Projects section of the Start page.

> **NOTE** *You may find the* `AlbumTracker` *project's code to download for this exercise on this book's companion website at* www.wrox.com *in the folder* `Chapter 02\AlbumTracker`.

3.　Select Debug ➪ Start Debugging (or press F5) to start the application. After your application starts, the Album List screen is displayed.

4.　Click the "Export to Excel" button on the toolbar of the Album List screen, as highlighted in Figure 3-15. In a few seconds, Microsoft Excel will open with the list of albums, as shown in Figure 3-16.

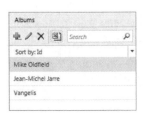

FIGURE 3-15: The "Export to Excel" button on the toolbar

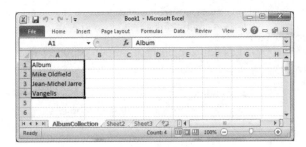

FIGURE 3-16: Artist names exported to Excel

As shown in Figure 3-16, only the artist names have been exported to the Excel worksheet, because the current view of the list displays only artists. However, you can change this view.

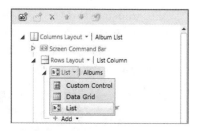

5. Click the Design Screen button (at the top-right corner of the `AlbumTracker` application window). When the Customization Mode screen appears, click the drop-down arrow of the fourth node, as shown in Figure 3-17.

FIGURE 3-17: Changing the layout of the Album list

6. From the drop-down list, select the Data Grid item, and click Save to close Customization Mode. Instead of single artist names, you can now see a grid with all album fields.

7. Click the "Export to Excel" button. Unlike Figure 3-16, the newly created export will contain all album fields, as shown in Figure 3-18. The "Export to Excel" button passes all data to Excel which is displayed in the UI control.

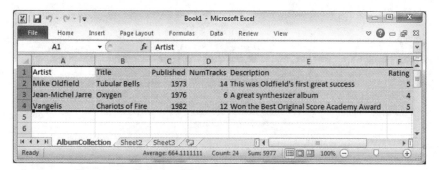

FIGURE 3-18: Album list exported to Excel

You can use the Microsoft Office Automation Model to communicate with Office applications (such as Word, Excel, and PowerPoint), and carry out more complex tasks with them (such as generating documents, creating charts and reports, or even building presentations programmatically). Chapter 12 covers this topic in more detail.

WINDOWS AZURE

Windows Azure is Microsoft's cloud computing platform, or a PaaS — Platform as a Service. Simply said, cloud computing is an approach to information technology whereby resources, computing capacity, software, and services are provided to computers and other devices on-demand through the Internet. Users generally pay according to their usage of the related resources, such as computing capacity, storage, network throughput, and so on.

Cloud computing can be an effective solution in scenarios where the amount of resources used by a system or application varies. Figure 3-19 shows several situations for which the on-demand resource allocation model is very useful. All scenarios depict situations where the computing capacity required by the specific business system changes over time.

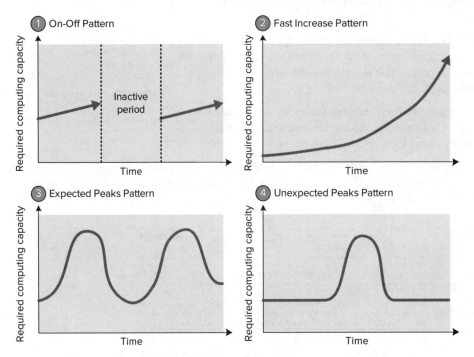

FIGURE 3-19: Scenarios with dynamic computing resource requirements

If your system's infrastructure had a fixed number of physical server machines and you required a computing capacity similar to one of the patterns in Figure 3-19, it would be very difficult to set up the right hardware resources. That's because if you plan those resources for peak load, you will waste resources when the load is much lower. In the case of the second pattern, it's difficult to guess in advance what the maximum load will be in the future. If you underestimate your resources or allocate them for average use, users will suffer during peak usage. In the worst-case scenario, your system will collapse — and you'll lose business.

A cloud computing platform such as Windows Azure enables you to avoid these problems. The following sections describe how Windows Azure works with Visual Studio LightSwitch to deliver the computing capacity you need.

Dynamic Resource Allocation

Using Windows Azure, you can dynamically adjust computing resources to your needs. When you allocate resources, you can use several virtual machines with different computing capacity. Your application can be split into several pieces such as *web roles* (front-end modules that service web pages and web services) and *worker roles* (modules for background processing). These pieces can be assigned to separate virtual machines — with separate processing capacities.

For example, let's assume that your system comprises exactly one web role and one worker role, and initially you allocate a virtual machine with two CPUs for each role. As Christmas approaches, your system gets slower. Using monitoring tools, you observe that the load on the worker role increases by 30 percent, but the load of the web role increases by 80 percent. To cope with this situation, you assign a virtual machine to the worker role with four CPUs, and two more virtual machines — each with two CPUs — to the web role. The new resources solve your load issue. As soon as the system load gets back to its normal mid-year state, you can release the newly allocated virtual machines and use the original capacity.

Upsizing and downsizing your system running in Windows Azure takes about 10–15 minutes each time, so it's faster and much more flexible than using physical hardware. Of course, you have to pay proportionally more when using more resources. But as soon as you downsize the system, you revert back to your original fee. If you have unexpected peaks, you can respond to them in a very short time.

Application Development with Windows Azure

Teaching you Windows Azure development is beyond the scope of this book; but with Visual Studio LightSwitch, you have a tool that can be used to develop simple business applications that run in the cloud — on Windows Azure.

If you are an experienced Visual Studio developer — and you do not know LightSwitch — you can still easily develop applications for the cloud. You can download development tools that integrate with Visual Studio, and start developing your applications.

The tools — including the Windows Azure SDK — enable you to create applications on your machine that run in a development *fabric* that emulates Windows Azure. You can implement, test, and debug your software in the context of the fabric, using the Azure features just as if everything were running from the cloud. When an application is ready for upload to the Azure environment, it can be easily deployed to the cloud using your Azure subscription.

Windows Azure and LightSwitch

Visual Studio LightSwitch provides a jumpstart for Azure development! Without using the development fabric for software development, testing, and debugging, with LightSwitch you can create Azure applications. Moreover, you do not need to decide at the beginning of your projects to host the system in the cloud; you can move to the cloud model later when the application is ready and works as expected. LightSwitch has a deployment option that uploads the application directly to Windows Azure. You can find more details about this sort of deployment in Chapter 13.

 WARNING *In order to deploy your applications to Windows Azure, you must subscribe to the services you intend to use. If you are an MSDN subscriber or attend certain academic programs, you may have free subscriptions that include a limited set of free resources. These are generally more than enough to weed through the initial learning curve. However, when your free resources are entirely consumed, you must pay for additional use.*

Sources for More Information about Windows Azure

Windows Azure and cloud computing are relatively new topics for almost all developers, IT pros, and business decision makers. However, as the whole IT industry moves toward the "Information-Technology-as-a-Service" vision, you can benefit from becoming familiar with this field.

The best place to start is the "Learn Cloud Development" page on MSDN at `http://msdn .microsoft.com/en-us/ff380142.aspx`. A great book titled *Cloud Computing with the Windows Azure Platform* by Roger Jennings (Wiley, 2009) also provides a great overview from the business perspective as well.

SUMMARY

LightSwitch uses a well-defined set of design patterns and technologies in the applications you can create with it.

The three-tier application architecture pattern implements an important principle — the separation of concerns — by dividing your application into three independent layers: the Data, Logic, and Presentation tiers.

The backbone of LightSwitch development is the .NET Framework, a managed runtime environment sitting between the operating system and your application. The common language runtime (CLR) of the Framework is responsible for providing most of the features, such as the flexible type system and just-in-time (JIT) compilation. With the help of the Base Class Library (BCL) and infrastructure services, you can solve tasks that would be rather difficult using the operating system's API directly.

Silverlight is a new and modern UI platform that provides great freedom in establishing the application's UI, and helping with developer-designer collaboration. The layout strategy, data binding, styles, and templates help you implement your own new UI approaches. LightSwitch uses Silverlight as the core of its Presentation tier.

The new data you create with a LightSwitch application is stored in a SQL Server 2008 Express database. The Express Edition of SQL Server supports all important relational database management features, such as referential integrity constraints, indexing, server-side programming, transaction management, and much more. LightSwitch can also access data stored in SharePoint 2010 lists.

LightSwitch applications can export lists and tables to Microsoft Excel without writing any code. With code, your application can interoperate with other Office applications through their automation interface.

LightSwitch can deploy your application directly to Windows Azure, enabling you to enter the exciting arena of cloud application development.

EXERCISES

1. What are the names and responsibilities of tiers in the three-tier application architecture pattern?

2. How would you define the main role of the .NET Framework in regard to LightSwitch applications?

3. What is the Base Class Library in the .NET Framework?

4. How would you describe the layout strategy of Silverlight?

5. Why is Silverlight data binding an important feature?

6. Which tool window can be used in Visual Studio LightSwitch to look at SQL Server 2008 databases?

7. How can LightSwitch use data in a SharePoint 2010 site?

8. Why is it worthwhile to deploy a LightSwitch application to Windows Azure?

 NOTE *Answers to the Exercises can be found in the Appendix.*

▶ **WHAT YOU LEARNED IN THIS CHAPTER**

TOPIC	KEY CONCEPTS
Three-tier application architecture pattern	This architecture pattern is used in LightSwitch applications to separate the Data, Logic, and Presentation tiers. The Data tier is called the Storage tier in LightSwitch terminology.
.NET Framework	The Microsoft .NET Framework is a runtime environment that sits between the operating system and the applications. Its main role is to provide access to all services of the underlying operating system in a managed way that enables developers to be productive.
Common language runtime (CLR)	The layer of the .NET Framework that provides an abstraction layer over the operating system.
Base Class Library (BCL)	The Base Class Library (BCL) provides a large number of objects that make complex tasks simple and intuitive — by using the operating system's application programming interface (API.
Infrastructure services	These services provide object types, tools, and patterns to develop .NET applications in a consistent way. Examples of these services are Windows Communication Foundation (WCF), Workflow Foundation (WF), ASP.NET, and the Entity Framework (EF).
Silverlight	Silverlight is a new and sophisticated UI platform that enables you to create applications with a rich UI, including flexible layout, multimedia elements, and animation. Silverlight applications can run in the major web browsers such as Internet Explorer, Firefox, Safari, or Google Chrome.
Data binding	Data binding is a technology used to connect elements of the UI to data or other UI elements declaratively. Silverlight's data binding works in cooperation with styles, templates, layouts, and even animations.
Styles and templates	Separating logic and presentation is a key design principle for Silverlight. Styles and templates are tools for implementing this principle.
	Styles are simple constructs that enable you to define a consistent set of properties, and you can apply them to user interface elements. Templates provide a mechanism to globally replace the visual look of a control.
SQL Server 2008 Express	SQL Server 2008 Express is a relational database management tool, a lightweight version of SQL Server 2008 that can be scaled to serve a huge enterprise. The data created in your LightSwitch applications is stored by default in the SQL Server 2008 Express instance installed with Visual Studio LightSwitch.

TOPIC	KEY CONCEPTS
SharePoint 2010 lists	Most information SharePoint 2010 can store is represented as lists, including document libraries, contacts, events, links, announcements, tasks, and much more. Visual Studio LightSwitch can access SharePoint lists and utilize their content just like any other table you create.
Exporting to Excel	With Visual Studio LightSwitch, you can export the contents of lists and data grids in your applications without writing code.
Deploying applications to Windows Azure	Windows Azure is Microsoft's cloud computing platform (it is a PaaS — Platform as a Service). LightSwitch has a deployment option that uploads the application directly to Windows Azure.

Customizing LightSwitch Applications

WHAT YOU WILL LEARN IN THIS CHAPTER

➤ Changing table and field names

➤ Customizing the data structure by creating a relationship between tables

➤ Creating a new search screen and changing its layout from a grid to a list

➤ Creating an editable grid and using a drop-down list

➤ Writing code to set up the default value of an entity

➤ Setting the startup screen of your LightSwitch application

In Chapter 3, you learned that LightSwitch provides you with a framework based on the three-tier application architecture pattern. This pattern separates the data, logic, and Presentation tiers. LightSwitch also utilizes preselected technologies to implement these tiers, and provides the plumbing that binds communicating components to ensure the right information flow among application tiers.

These architectural and technological constraints may seem too rigid. However, they actually help you to be productive, because the template-driven framework enables you to focus on your solutions, rather than the underlying design pattern. In addition, LightSwitch provides a great set of customization features, so you aren't limited by the templates offered.

This chapter provides a brief overview of those features. You will learn about several customization features through examples. What you find here is intended to be an appetizer, enabling you to taste only a small variety of the rich set of customizations available in LightSwitch.

Later, in Part II of this book (Chapters 5 through 13), you will learn about more features and subtleties for each customization technique. Part III (Chapters 14 and 15) covers advanced LightSwitch topics. Chapter 15 in particular examines LightSwitch extensibility, and provides an overview of several advanced customization features.

CUSTOMIZING DATA

In Chapter 2, you created a simple application named `AlbumTracker` that used a single database table created in the LightSwitch IDE. In real life, you often create applications that use an already existing database. Instead of duplicating the data from the database, your application must connect to that database and utilize the information stored there.

In many cases you have more than one back-end database, and you need to access the information stored in all of them. For example, your customer data might be stored in the CRM system's SQL Server database, while account information about those customers is stored in a separate database of a web portal. When you are requested to create a new application, you might want to use the customer information from both the CRM system and the web portal database.

Using LightSwitch, you can connect to existing databases and create relations among the data tables (entities) — even if they belong to separate databases. You can extend the existing databases with your own tables — created in LightSwitch — and use them just as if they were located in the back-end systems.

 NOTE *With regard to data-centric applications, the "table" and "entity" terms are different. A table is an object in a database management system (DBMS). An entity is a conceptual object that sometimes involves more than one table from the underlying database. In LightSwitch, you can use both terms. For the sake of simplicity, this chapter uses the "table" term. In Chapter 5, you will learn more about the relationship between tables and entities.*

In some situations, you might like to change the names of existing tables and fields, or sometimes even field data types. LightSwitch allows you to perform this kind of database customization.

Creating the Aquarium Database

In this chapter, you will create a sample application demonstrating the data customization features described in the preceding section. Following is the scenario for this sample:

➤ You work for the Pacific Sea Shop, a company that has a SQL Server back-end database named `Aquarium`.

➤ The database has a data table named `Sea_Creature` that contains data about sea-living animals sold by the shop.

➤ Your task is to create a small application that enables managing a product catalog and a simple shopping cart. The cart functionality should be implemented such that the contents of the cart may be stored in the application's own database.

TRY IT OUT   Creating a Simple SQL Server Database

In this exercise, you create a simple database outside of LightSwitch. This database will represent the back-end data used by Pacific Sea Shop. The database is created with a script (CreateAquarium.sql) that you can download from the wrox.com website.

To create the database, follow these steps:

1.   Save the CreateAquarium.sql file into a temporary folder and note the name of this folder.

2.   Start a command prompt by typing **cmd** in the "Search Programs and Files" box of the Start menu and pressing the Enter key, or by selecting Command Prompt from the All Programs ➪ Accessories folder of the Start menu.

3.   Type the following line into the command window and replace *<folder>* with the name of the folder that you noted in Step 1:

```
sqlcmd -S .\SQLEXPRESS -i "<folder>\CreateAquarium.sql"
```

For example, if your folder is C:\Temp, use the following command line:

```
sqlcmd -S .\SQLEXPRESS -i "C:\Temp\CreateAquarium.sql"
```

This will create the Aquarium database in a few seconds. Once the database is created, the command prompt window displays the simple message shown in Figure 4-1.

FIGURE 4-1: The SQLCMD command-line utility creates the Aquarium database

How It Works

The sqlcmd utility can execute the specified commands on SQL Server. The -S .\SQLEXPRESS command-line argument tells the utility that it must connect to the SQL Server Express instance installed on your computer together with Visual Studio LightSwitch. The -i "<folder>\ CreateAquarium.sql" argument specifies the name of the file that contains the commands to be executed on SQL Server. This file creates the database, then the Sea_Creature table, and fills it with sample data.

You can open the CreateAquarium.sql file with Notepad to see the table creation and data insert statements.

WARNING *This activity assumes that you are logged into your computer with administrative privileges — with a user account that is a member of the Administrators group. Otherwise, running the database creation script may fail. If you run the creation script more than once, the subsequent runs will fail. However, this does not affect the database created in the first successful run.*

Connecting to an Existing Database

Visual Studio LightSwitch makes it very easy to use an existing database. You can simply attach existing tables and use them as if you had created them with LightSwitch. The following activity demonstrates how.

TRY IT OUT **Connecting to an Existing Database**

The `Aquarium` database you just created will serve as Pacific Sea Shop's back-end database. You are going to connect to this database and use the `Sea_Creature` table.

To connect to the Aquarium database, follow these steps:

1. Open LightSwitch and create a new LightSwitch project with the File ⇨ New Project command. Select the LightSwitch Application (Visual Basic) template from the New Project dialog, as shown in Figure 4-2, and name it `Aquarium`. Click OK and the project will be created.

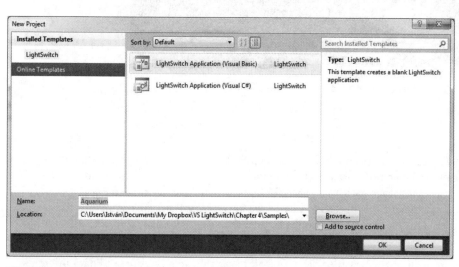

FIGURE 4-2: Selecting the LightSwitch Application (Visual Basic) template in the New Project dialog

2. Visual Studio displays the application Designer surface in the middle of the workspace. You can either create a new table or attach to an external database, as shown in Figure 4-3. Because you intend to use the existing `Aquarium` database, select the "Attach to external Data Source" option.

Create new table
Attach to external Data Source

FIGURE 4-3: From the Designer surface, select the "Attach to external Data Source" link

3. The Attach Data Source wizard starts and shows you the types of data sources to which you can connect. Select Database, as shown in Figure 4-4. This option enables you to access an existing SQL Server database. Click Next.

4. The Connection Properties dialog appears. This is where you can select the database to which to connect. Use the "Server name" text box to type `.\SQLEXPRESS` and also type **Aquarium** in the "Select or enter a database name" combo box, as shown in Figure 4-5. You can verify the connection by clicking the Test Connection button. This will display either a message confirming the successful connection or, if you have mistyped something, an error message. If the test confirms that your settings are correct, click OK.

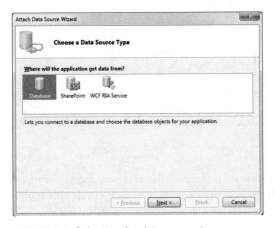

FIGURE 4-4: Selecting the data source type

FIGURE 4-5: Setting connection properties

WARNING *If your computer hangs for about 30 seconds (or sometimes more) after clicking the Test Connection button, you probably mistyped the* `.\SQLEXPRESS` *server name, and, therefore, LightSwitch is unable to find the server you've specified. If so, you'll receive a message indicating a network-related error. If you get a message that the specified database does not exist, you mistyped the name* `Aquarium`. *If you click OK without testing the database connection, the mistyped database name displays a confirmation dialog asking whether you would like to attempt to create the database. Cancel the confirmation dialog and correct the database name.*

5. After the Attach Data Source wizard retrieves the list of database objects, you can select the ones you'd like to use within the LightSwitch project. Expand the `Tables` node and select the `Sea_Creature` table by clicking the check box to the left of the name, as shown in Figure 4-6. Click Finish.

The wizard adds the `Sea_Creature` table to your project, which LightSwitch displays on the Designer surface. You can also find it by using Solution Explorer and looking under the `AquariumData` node, which represents the database connection you have built in this activity, as shown in Figure 4-7.

FIGURE 4-6: Selecting the Sea_Creature table

FIGURE 4-7: The Sea_Creature table in Solution Explorer

How It Works

LightSwitch stores the connection properties of the SQL Server database. Whenever you access data in the `Sea_Creature` table, LightSwitch will use these properties. From now on, you can handle this table as if it were manually created in your LightSwitch project.

Changing Names and Types in the Existing Table

The newly attached `Sea_Creature` table represents an old back-end system using legacy naming conventions. As shown in the Designer surface in Figure 4-8, these names contain underscores and "C" prefixes from the old convention. You can also see that the type of the `C_Picture` field is `Binary` (that is, it is stored as a `varbinary` field in the SQL Server database). This field stores the photo of the related record.

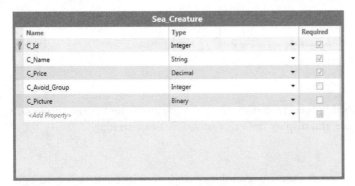

FIGURE 4-8: The Sea_Creature table on the Designer surface

In your LightSwitch project, you need to get rid of the old naming style, and let LightSwitch know that the `C_Picture` field contains photos that can be displayed in the UI. The type of the `C_Price` field is `Decimal`, so it is handled as a number. However, it would be better if LightSwitch used and displayed it as a currency value. In the following "Try It Out" exercise, you will resolve these issues.

TRY IT OUT Changing Names and Types in an Attached Table

To change the table names and types for use with LightSwitch, follow these steps:

1. Double-click the `Sea_Creature` text in the header of the table within the Designer. When the `Sea_Creature` text is highlighted, you can change it. Type **Creature** and press Enter to change the name of the table.

2. Click the `C_Name` field (in the Name column). The `C_Name` text becomes highlighted, indicating that you can edit it. Type **Name** and press Enter.

3. The focus moves automatically to the `C_Price` field. Enter the name **Price**. Pressing Enter moves the focus to the `C_Avoid_Group` field.

4. Change `C_Avoid_Group` to **AvoidGroup** and `C_Picture` to **Picture**.

5. Click the drop-down arrow of the `Picture` field's Type column (as shown in Figure 4-9), and click the `Image` option to change the type of this field to Image.

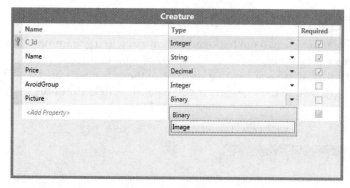

FIGURE 4-9: The customized fields of the Creature table

6. Using the same technique described in Step 5, change the type of Price from Decimal to Money. From now on, LightSwitch will use and display the value of Price as a currency.

How It Works

The changes you've made leave the original Sea_Creature table — and all of its fields — intact. You have not changed the name of the C_Id field, because it is the primary key field of Sea_Creature, and LightSwitch does not allow renaming it. Also, you cannot change field types arbitrarily (for example, from Decimal to String). In Chapter 8 you will learn more about restrictions.

LightSwitch does not change the existing database, which could lead to unexpected, and unwelcome, failures in the existing systems. Instead, LightSwitch creates mappings between the existing data table and its representation used within LightSwitch. These mappings are used with all database operations. For example, when you query the content of the Price field, LightSwitch takes care of using the C_Price name when communicating with the remote database.

Creating the Cart Table

At this point, you have customized the table describing the sea creatures available for purchase from the Pacific Sea Shop. Although you have changed the names and types of fields, the data is still stored in the Aquarium database — representing the shop's back-end system.

Your next task, demonstrated in the following "Try It Out" exercise, is to create a table representing the items stored in a shopping cart. This table will be stored separately from the Aquarium database.

TRY IT OUT   Creating a New Table Related to an Existing One

In this example, you create a table named Cart. Each row of this table represents one item in the shopping cart. To create the Cart table, follow these steps:

1. In Solution Explorer, right-click the Data Sources node and select the Add Table command from the context menu. In the Designer, a new table appears with Table1Item text highlighted in its header.

2. Type **Cart** to rename this new table. If the header of the table is not highlighted, double-click it before typing its new name. LightSwitch automatically creates one property for this table named Id. As its name suggests, this property uniquely identifies records in this table, and you cannot change or delete it.

3. Click the <Add Property> cell in the Designer and type **Quantity** to set the name of a new field. Press Tab to move to the Type column and set it to Short Integer — either by using the drop-down menu or by typing **Short Integer.**

4. Add another property named Price, and set its type to Money.

Now the Cart table has a property for the quantity and price of a shopping cart entry, but it does not have information about the product — in this case, a sea creature — belonging to the cart item. Information about the sea creatures is stored in the existing Aquarium database in the Sea_Creature table (renamed in the application to Creature). You are going to create a relationship to use the Creature information within the Cart table.

5. Click the Relationship button in the toolbar of the Designer. The Add New Relationship dialog appears. The upper part of the dialog contains a table with columns, From and To, representing the source and the destination of the relationship, respectively. The source is filled with Cart, as the Name row of the table shows. Use the drop-down arrow of the To column in the Name row to select the Creature table. This action specifies that the destination of this relationship is Creature. The dialog updates its contents, as shown in Figure 4-10.

These settings describe a one-to-many relationship from Creature to Cart. This means that an item in the Cart table has exactly one related item in Creature, while a Creature item can have zero, one, or more related Cart items.

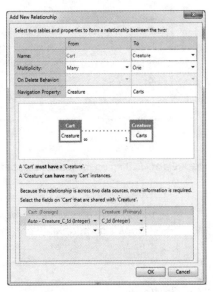

FIGURE 4-10: Setting up the relationship between the Cart and Creature tables

 NOTE *In Chapter 7 you will learn more about relationship types and the Add New Relationship dialog.*

6. Click OK to set up the relationship. Two new properties are added to the Cart table. Creature represents the row of the related Creature table, and Creature_C_Id is the identifier of the

related `Creature` item. The one-to-many relationship is indicated in the Designer, as shown in Figure 4-11. Click the Save icon in the main toolbar — or press Ctrl+S — to save the modified table definition.

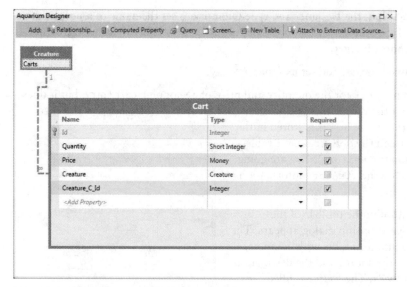

FIGURE 4-11: Setting up the relationship between the Cart and Creature tables

> **NOTE** *You may find complete code to download for this exercise on this book's companion website at* www.wrox.com *in the folder* Chapter 04\
> Sample 1 - Customizing Data.

How It Works

LightSwitch created a relationship that enables you to navigate between the related tables. From a `Cart` item, you can access the related `Creature` item through the `Creature` property; similarly, with the `Carts` property of a `Creature` item, you can access the collection of `Cart` entries that refer to the specific `Creature`.

Many database tools allow defining relationships only between tables in the same database. As you can see, LightSwitch allows you to create a relationship between separate databases.

> **NOTE** *The preceding design does not allow using separate shopping carts for each potential customer; it can store only a single cart. Of course, in real life that has no purpose, but it is useful for demonstrating a simple example.*

CUSTOMIZING SCREENS

At this point, you've set up a database with the `Creature` and `Cart` tables, which have a one-to-many relationship. However, your users cannot work with the data without screens.

LightSwitch makes it extremely easy to create a new screen based on templates that ship with the product. If you aren't satisfied with any of the default template layouts, a few clicks enable you to tailor the generated screens to fit your needs.

In this section, you will create a couple of screens and learn how easy it is to customize them.

Creating a Creature Catalog

The Pacific Sea Shop needs a system that enables users to view a product catalog. In this case, the catalog is actually the content of the `Creature` table you created earlier. Because users typically expect to locate items in the catalog by using search functionality, you will create a search screen.

TRY IT OUT Creating a New Search Screen

To create a search screen for the sea creatures sold by the Pacific Sea Shop, follow these steps:

1. Right-click the `Screens` nodes in Solution Explorer and select the Add Screen command from the context menu. The Add New Screen dialog opens.

2. Select the Search Data Screen template from the list and set the Screen name to `ListCreatures`. From the Screen Data combo box, select `AquariumData.Creatures`, as shown in Figure 4-12. Click OK.

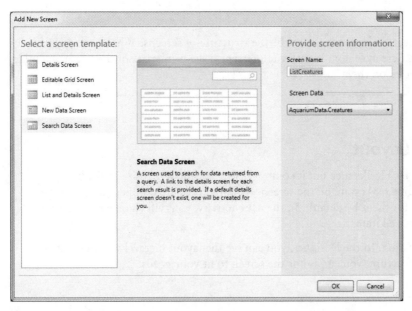

FIGURE 4-12: Use the Add New Screen dialog to create a search screen for the Creature table

3. A simple search screen in generated. Press F5 to start your application. In a few seconds, the Aquarium application starts and displays the ListCreatures screen. Figure 4-13 shows the properties of each record in the grid, including the picture.

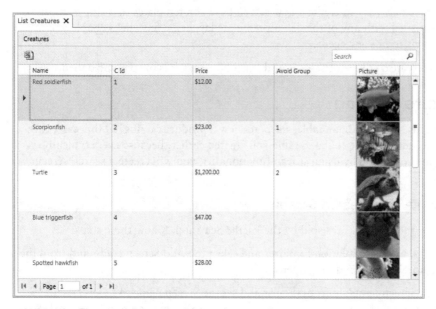

FIGURE 4-13: The search screen in action

How It Works

LightSwitch uses hierarchical screen layouts to describe the structure of screens. When you specified the table type in the Add New Screen dialog, LightSwitch retrieved the properties of the Creature table and generated a grid layout based on them.

Changing the Grid Layout

The grid shown in Figure 4-13 looks nice but it contains the C_Id and AvoidGroup fields, which unnecessarily consume real estate on the screen. Also, pictures are cropped to fit into the rectangular area provided for them by default. In the next activity, you will change the default grid layout to a list with customized items.

Close the Aquarium application. In the Designer, you can see the layout hierarchy of the search screen. By changing this structure, you can tailor the screen to fit your needs.

TRY IT OUT Changing the Screen Layout

In this activity, you are going to modify the layout hierarchy of the ListCreatures screen. This hierarchy contains a data grid bound to the Creatures table, and you change it to a list layout to provide a friendlier view.

To change the layout of the search screen, follow these steps:

1. Click the drop-down arrow of the Creatures Data Grid node in the Designer, and select List from the options displayed, as shown in Figure 4-14. This changes the grid layout to a list layout.

2. Click the drop-down arrow of the Creature Summary node, and select the Picture and Text layout, as shown in Figure 4-15. This sets up the items of the list layout so that they will contain a picture and a few text elements describing a Creature record.

3. Expand the Creature node to view the layout elements of an item (see Figure 4-16). The small X icon and the *Choose Content* text indicate that you must specify the fields to display.

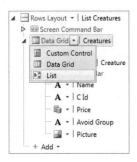

FIGURE 4-14: Changing the grid layout to a list layout

FIGURE 4-15: Changing the list item layout to Picture and Text

FIGURE 4-16: Item layout elements to specify

4. Click the Choose Content text of the (PICTURE) node and select Picture from the list, as shown in Figure 4-17. Repeat this simple step to set the content of (TITLE) and (SUBTITLE) to Name and Price, respectively. Figure 4-18 shows the result.

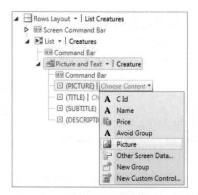

FIGURE 4-17: Selecting the field for the item's picture

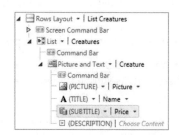

FIGURE 4-18: All items are set up

5. Click the `Picture` node you set up in Step 4, and go to the Properties window (select View ⇨ Properties). Use the scroll bar of the window to reach the properties at the bottom. Change the `MaxWidth` and `MaxHeight` properties to 80 and 60, respectively, and the `Stretch` property from `UniformToFill` to `Uniform`, as shown in Figure 4-19.

6. All layout changes are done. Press F5 to see how these changes affect the screen layout. When the application starts, you can immediately recognize the result, as shown in Figure 4-20.

FIGURE 4-19: Changing picture properties

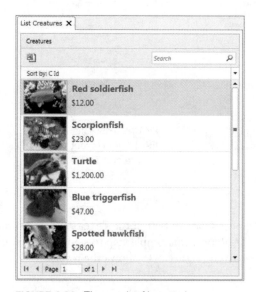

FIGURE 4-20: The result of layout changes

7. Close the `Aquarium` application.

How It Works

LightSwitch uses the layout hierarchy (the elements of the UI as depicted by the Designer) to render screens during runtime. The relationship of elements and their properties drives the rendering engine to display your imagined layout.

The changes you've done in this exercise altered the layout hierarchy. When you start the application, the rendering engine uses the new layout information, and that's how it shows a list with customized items instead of a grid.

Creating a Shopping Cart Screen

The `ListCreatures` screen is a very simple product catalog. To enable users to put items into the shopping cart, you will create a new screen that represents the cart. In the following "Try It Out" exercise, you will create an editable grid for this purpose.

TRY IT OUT Creating a Shopping Cart Screen with an Editable Grid

To create the shopping cart screen, follow these steps:

1. Double-click the `Carts` node in Solution Explorer to display the `Cart` table in the Designer. Click the Screen button in the Designer toolbar to launch the Add New Screen dialog. This is an alternative way to create a new screen; you can still use the context menu of the `Screens` node in Solution Explorer to add a new screen.

2. When the dialog appears, select the Editable Grid Screen template. Set the name to `ShoppingCart` and select `Carts` from the Screen Data combo box. Click OK.

3. Press F5 to view this new screen. When the `Aquarium` application starts, it displays the `ListCreatures` screen (you will change this behavior later). Click `Shopping Cart` in the Tasks menu on the left of the screen and the new screen will be immediately displayed.

4. The shopping cart is empty. Double-click the empty cell below the `Creature` column. The row representing the shopping cart item will be filled with default values. Note the drop-down arrow within the `Creature` cell, as shown in Figure 4-21. Click this arrow to display the list from which you can select a `Creature`. As an alternative, you can select an item from the list without dropping it down, but just typing a few characters. For example, when you press the M key in the Creature cell, a list pops up with all items beginning with "M," as shown in Figure 4-22. The text box is automatically completed with the remaining characters of the first matching item ("Moray eel"). You can either type more letters to tighten the list of selectable items, or click with the mouse to select a listed item.

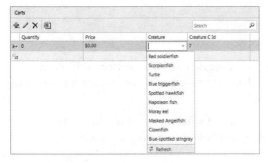

FIGURE 4-21: The grid layout of the Shopping Cart screen with the list of Creatures

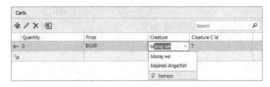

FIGURE 4-22: The list of Creatures beginning with "M"

This grid could be nicer if the `Creature_C_Id` column would be removed. Also, a column order of Creature, Quantity, Price seems better. You can alter the layout accordingly in a few steps.

5. Close the application. If you are asked, confirm that you want to discard changes. If you cannot see the `ShoppingCart` screen layout in the Designer, double-click the `ShoppingCart` node in Solution Explorer.

6. Expand the Cart `Data Grid Row` node, right-click the Creature C Id item, and select the Delete command to remove this field from the layout, as shown in Figure 4-23.

7. Click the `Creature` node, but before releasing the mouse button, drag it before `Quantity`, as shown in Figure 4-24. With this operation, you set the column order to `Quantity`, `Price`, and `Creature`.

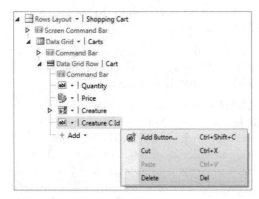

FIGURE 4-23: The layout hierarchy of the ShoppingCart screen

FIGURE 4-24: Changing the display order of columns

8. Press F5 to start the application and select the `ShoppingCart` screen. Edit it by adding a few items, and use the drop-down list of the Creature column, as shown in Figure 4-25.

FIGURE 4-25: The altered ShoppingCart screen in action

9. Click the Save button in the main toolbar to store the shopping cart and close the application.

 NOTE *You may find complete code to download for this exercise on this book's companion website at* www.wrox.com *in the folder* Chapter 04\ Sample 2 - Customizing Screens.

How It Works

Just as you did earlier when you added the ShoppingCart screen, the changes here are interpreted by the LightSwitch rendering engine, which displays the screen according to the altered layout structure.

This simple shopping cart screen seems to work, but it doesn't handle the Price and Quantity fields correctly. Each Creature in the product catalog has a Price value, and you expect this grid to take this Price field by default when selecting (or changing) the Creature field. The Quantity field has a default value of 0, but it should be 1. Similarly, it would be great to see the total price of a cart item (multiplying Quantity by Price).

It is time to write a few lines of code.

WRITING CODE

At this point, you have created a couple of samples: the AlbumTracker example in Chapter 2, and the Aquarium example in this chapter. These simple examples did not require writing any code.

In most cases, you can establish your data structures and screens with LightSwitch, and you can handle CRUD (Create, Retrieve, Update, and Delete) operations without writing any code. However, when you must use a formula, define a business rule, or extend an operation, some formal description — a programming language — is the best way to declare your intention. LightSwitch was designed with this requirement in mind, and it fully supports writing code.

In this section, you will extend the logic behind the ShoppingCart screen so that it handles the Quantity and Price of cart items as expected.

Setting a Default Property Value in Code

When you put a new item into the shopping cart, it is inserted there with a Quantity value set to 0. It would be a better user experience if Quantity were 1 by default. The following "Try It Out" exercise demonstrates how to change this.

TRY IT OUT **Handling the Default Price**

To set the default quantity for a cart item, follow these steps:

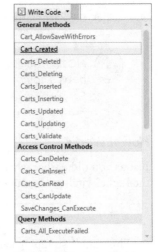

1. Double-click the Carts node in Solution Explorer. The Cart table will be displayed in the Designer.

2. The rightmost command in the Designer toolbar is Write Code. Click its drop-down arrow. In the list that appears are several methods triggered by an event. Select Cart_Created, as shown in Figure 4-26.

3. The Cart.vb (Cart.cs, if you use C#) file is opened in the IDE and an empty Cart_Created method is generated:

VB
```vb
Namespace Aquarium

  Public Class Cart

    Private Sub Cart_Created()

    End Sub
  End Class

End Namespace
```

FIGURE 4-26: Selecting the Cart_Created method

C#
```csharp
namespace LightSwitchApplication
{
    public partial class Cart
    {
        partial void Cart_Created()
        {

        }
    }
}
```

 WARNING *If you accidentally click the Write Code text instead of the drop-down arrow in Step 2, the* Cart.vb *file will be opened and no method skeleton is created. In this case, close the file and go back to Step 2, or type in the* Cart_ Created *method manually.*

4. Put the `Quantity = 1` statement into the method body:

VB
```vb
Namespace Aquarium

  Public Class Cart

    Private Sub Cart_Created()
      Quantity = 1
    End Sub
  End Class

End Namespace
```

C#
```csharp
namespace LightSwitchApplication
{
  public partial class Cart
  {
    partial void Cart_Created()
    {
      Quantity = 1;
    }
  }
}
```

5. Press F5 to run the application. Select the `ShoppingCart` screen and add a new entry by double-clicking the Price cell in the last (empty) row. A new record is added and the Quantity field is immediately set to 1.

6. Close the application and click Discard when the confirmation dialog appears, asking whether you want to save the changes.

How It Works

Any time a new `Cart` instance is created, the runtime engine checks whether a `Cart_Created` method is defined. If so, it is invoked, and it has the opportunity to set up the properties of the `Cart` instance. The method you wrote simply sets the `Quantity` property to 1.

Setting the Startup Screen

Whenever you start the `Aquarium` application, it automatically shows the `ListCreature` screen. Generally, however, users want to use the `ShoppingCart` screen more often, so in this section you will change the configuration to show `ShoppingCart` by default when the application starts.

TRY IT OUT Setting the Startup Screen

To set `ShoppingCart` as the startup screen, follow these steps:

1. Click the `Aquarium` in Solution Explorer and press Alt+Enter. Alternatively, you can right-click the `Aquarium` node and select Properties from the context menu.

2. The properties of the project are displayed in the Designer. You can see that this dialog has a few tabs. Select Screen Navigation, as shown in Figure 4-27. The `List Creatures` item under Tasks is highlighted in bold. This indicates that `List Creatures` is the startup screen. The label right below the navigation structure also explicitly names the startup screen.

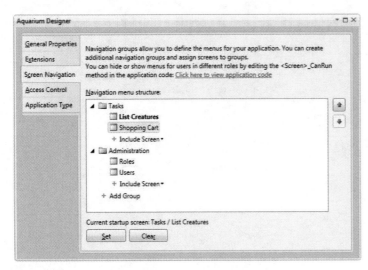

FIGURE 4-27: Screen navigation properties

3. Click `Shopping Cart` and then the Set button. This action changes the startup screen from `List Creatures` to `Shopping Cart`.

4. Start the application by pressing F5 and check that the `Shopping Cart` screen is displayed after startup. Close `Aquarium`.

Managing Price Information

Cart entries still contain no price information after a `Creature` has been selected. However, users expect to see the price of the selected item in the cart. They also expect to see a total price based on the quantity selected. With a few lines of code you can solve these issues, as shown in the following "Try It Out" exercise.

TRY IT OUT Setting the Price When Creature Changes

Follow these steps to set the value of the `Price` field as expected:

1. Double-click the `Carts` node in Solution Explorer to display it in the Designer. On the left side, select the `Creature` field, as shown in Figure 4-28.

2. In the Designer toolbar, click the drop-down arrow of the Write Code command, and select the `Creature_Changed` property method, as shown in Figure 4-29. The Designer opens the `Cart.vb` (`Cart.cs`) file, where you can see the `Cart_Created` method you added earlier. The Designer creates the skeleton of the `Creature_Changed` method, too:

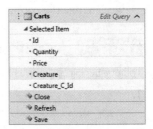

FIGURE 4-28: Selecting the Creature field

VB

```vb
Namespace Aquarium

    Public Class Cart

        Private Sub Cart_Created()
            Quantity = 1
        End Sub

        Private Sub Creature_Changed()

        End Sub
    End Class

End Namespace
```

C#

```csharp
namespace LightSwitchApplication
{
    public partial class Cart
    {
        partial void Cart_Created()
        {
            Quantity = 1;
        }

        partial void Creature_Changed()
        {

        }
    }
}
```

FIGURE 4-29: Selecting the Creature_Changed method

3. Add the following highlighted statement to the body of Creature_Changed:

VB

```vb
Private Sub Creature_Changed()
    Price = Creature.Price
End Sub
```

C#

```csharp
partial void Creature_Changed()
{
    Price = Creature.Price;
}
```

4. In Solution Explorer, double-click the Carts node. When the Cart table opens in the Designer, add a new property to the table named Subtotal, and set its type to Money. While this new property is selected in the Designer, in the Properties window, click the Is Computed check box, as shown in Figure 4-30.

5. In the Properties window, click the Edit Method task link. The Cart.vb (Cart.cs) file is opened again, and a new method named Subtotal_Compute is generated with a comment in its body:

FIGURE 4-30: Setting the Is Computed flag

VB
```vb
Private Sub Subtotal_Compute(ByRef result As Decimal)
    ' Set result to the desired field value

End Sub
```

C#
```csharp
partial void Subtotal_Compute(ref decimal result)
{
    // Set result to the desired field value

}
```

6. Type the highlighted code into the method body:

VB
```vb
Private Sub Subtotal_Compute(ByRef result As Decimal)
    ' Set result to the desired field value
    result = Quantity * Price
End Sub
```

C#
```csharp
partial void Subtotal_Compute(ref decimal result)
{
    // Set result to the desired field value
    result = Quantity * Price;
}
```

7. In Solution Explorer, double-click the ShoppingCart node. In the layout hierarchy, expand the Cart Data Grid Row, click the Add button, and select Subtotal from the list, as shown in Figure 4-31. This action adds a new column to the shopping cart grid that displays the full price of the cart item. A Money Viewer control is added to the layout.

8. Press F5 to run the application. In a few seconds, the Shopping Cart screen is displayed. Add a few items to the cart, and confirm that the Price field is automatically set to the default price of the Creature you select from the drop-down list. Also, when you modify either the Quantity or the Price value, the Subtotal value is recalculated. Figure 4-32 shows the shopping cart in action.

FIGURE 4-31: Adding the Subtotal column to the grid

Carts			
Creature	Quantity	Price	Subtotal
Scorpionfish	2	$23.00	$46.00
Turtle	1	$1,200.00	$1,200.00
Napoleon fish	4	$680.00	$2,720.00
Spotted hawkfish	3	$28.00	$84.00

FIGURE 4-32: Shopping Cart now displays the full price

NOTE *You may find the complete code to download for this exercise on this book's companion website at* www.wrox.com *in the folder* Chapter 04\ Sample 3 - Writing Code.

How It Works

The LightSwitch runtime takes care of calling the methods you defined in this activity. It recognizes when a `Creature` is selected from the list, and it uses the `Price = Creature.Price` expression to set the cart item price to the price of the creature in the Creature table. The runtime engine also knows that the `Subtotal_Compute` method should be invoked when either the `Price` or the `Quantity` properties change, and recalculates the full item price.

Other Points Where Code Is Used

Of course, in the activities of this section you've only scratched the surface of opportunities available by writing code. You can intercept many operations with your code, which means that you can customize the behavior of the UI and influence the application logic. Here is a small sample of what you can do in LightSwitch by writing code:

➤ You can intercept operations that modify tables, such as insert, update, and delete. You can define code to be executed before these operations run — this code can even prevent them from being carried out — and code to run when these operations have completed. This feature enables you to create business rules.

➤ You can define code to check security permissions related to tables, and determine whether the current user is authorized to carry out data modifications.

➤ You can validate data before you add it to a table — or modify the content of data already in a table — to ensure that it's correct or that it meets particular criteria. For example, you can check that an order has at least one item.

➤ You can intercept data-retrieval operations in order to customize queries before they run.

➤ You can also write code that runs when your data-modification operations succeed or fail. This kind of code can be very helpful for writing robust business logic.

➤ You can handle events related to the UI, such as when a screen is loaded, its data is initialized, it is about to save the modified information, and so on.

The forthcoming chapters of Part II will examine all these features in more detail.

SUMMARY

LightSwitch is a rapid application development (RAD) tool that enables you to create data-centric applications with a few clicks. It provides customization features that are available for the data, logic, and Presentation tiers, so you can easily customize your data — regardless of whether it is defined in your application or an external database. You can change table and field names, customize field types, and create new relationships.

Screens — the fundamental components of the UI — are described by a layout hierarchy, whereby each element has several properties that influence its visual appearance and behavior. By changing the layout structure and element properties, you can create totally new layouts in minutes.

LightSwitch generates the plumbing code for you, so you never have to deal with binding application tiers together. The runtime engine also provides default table operations with simple logic. You can write your own code to intercept operations and events, enabling you to define complex business logic and UI behavior.

In Chapter 5, you will learn about the LightSwitch application development life cycle, and prepare to implement a new compound sample named `ProjectTrek`.

EXERCISES

1. Which utility can be used to execute a script directly on the SQL Server Express instance installed on your computer?

2. What happens when you change table and field names of an external table in LightSwitch?

3. Can you create relationships between tables declared in LightSwitch and external SQL Server databases?

4. How can you customize a screen in LightSwitch?

5. Do you need to write code if you want to allow retrieving values for a field from another table?

6. List a few instances when writing code is required.

 NOTE *Answers to the Exercises can be found in the Appendix.*

▶ WHAT YOU LEARNED IN THIS CHAPTER

TOPIC	KEY CONCEPTS
Using external entities	LightSwitch makes is possible to use entities referencing tables stored in an external database.
Mapping field names and field types	You can change the names of tables and their properties based on tables stored in an external database. LightSwitch does not (and cannot) change the original names. It uses mappings between the new names and the original ones to access data.
Relationships between multiple databases	LightSwitch allows you to create relationships between the tables defined in separate databases. For example, you can create a relationship between a table defined in your application and another table in an existing back-end database.
Screen layout hierarchy	Each screen has a layout hierarchy that defines the elements of the screen. By changing this hierarchy (including the template, order, and properties of elements), you can alter the visual appearance and behavior of the screen.
Changing the startup screen	In Solution Explorer, select the node representing your project and press Alt+Enter. When the project properties are opened, select the Screen Navigation tab. Choose the screen you want to display at application startup, and click the Set button.
Setting the default value of an entity	Open the entity definition in the Designer and select its `Created` method from the Write Code drop-down list. In the method body, write an initialization statement that sets default property values.

PART II
Creating Applications with Visual Studio LightSwitch

5

Preparing to Develop a LightSwitch Application

WHAT YOU WILL LEARN IN THIS CHAPTER

➤ Grasping the functionality of the `ProjectTrek` sample application

➤ Understanding the most important elements of the LightSwitch application development life cycle

➤ Using the LightSwitch integrated development environment (IDE) to establish your workspace

In this part of the book, you will learn the most important aspects of using Visual Studio LightSwitch. To understand the functionality of the LightSwitch IDE and its development approach, you will create a new sample application from scratch.

This chapter describes the sample application and prepares you for implementing it. Subsequent chapters lead you through the development process, from the first steps to the deployment of the sample, while teaching you the fundamental LightSwitch techniques.

THE PROJECTTREK SAMPLE

A fictitious company named ConsulArt employs about 30 software technology consultants and business advisors who work for several dozen customers. ConsulArt has many small consulting projects, ranging from one week to three months. These projects sometimes involve only a single consultant, but occasionally a team of three to five experts. For a long time, ConsulArt used to plan and track projects, and schedule and assign employees, using Excel worksheets. However, using Excel worksheets has several issues ConsulArt would like to avoid:

➤ An Excel worksheet can be used only by one user at a time.

➤ Creating company-wide reports requires merging data in several Excel worksheets.

➤ It is difficult to manage user permissions.

ConsulArt is a successful and growing business, and plans a rapid expansion in the next two years, so management decided to create a new application to replace the currently used Excel worksheets. Internally, ConsulArt's IT specialist named the new application `ProjectTrek`.

ConsulArt needed an application that could be developed in a fairly short time frame and could support its ambition to enhance it with newer functions as the organization expands. It did not endeavor to build the ultimate application for its resource management. The management of ConsulArt intended to use this application for an interim time period of one year before deciding whether to buy an enterprise resource planning (ERP) system, or build an ultimate version of `ProjectTrek`.

The experts of ConsulArt had been using Visual Studio LightSwitch for a long time. They tried its Beta versions, and they decided to use it as the main platform to develop `ProjectTrek`. Also, they intended to utilize the experiences gained in this project for their existing and new customers.

The Functionality of ProjectTrek

ConsulArt management provided only a few paragraphs about their hopes and requirements for the new system. Following is an extract from a conversation about `ProjectTrek` recorded during a management meeting:

> Jane (CEO): *Well, Joe, so you call this new app* `ProjectTrek`*. I like this name, and as I understand it, it will largely replace those old Excel worksheets we're using right now, yes? You know, I want to be sure that it'll manage all utilization information to measure the staff's personal performance.*

> Joe (CIO): *Yes, of course. About a week ago, you mentioned something about project planning — you know, recording additional costs such as component licenses, photocopying, and so on.*

> Jane: *Exactly! I want to track all costs on projects, including your employees, the utilities, books they buy for the projects, and any other things they spend money on. I want all project managers to set up any new projects with a plan for these additional costs. Without it, the project must not start. If we don't account for these expenses, we cannot expand! Currently, I see we spend thousands, but I can't tell whether that money goes to a specific customer, or is spent on training, or is just thrown out the window.*

> Joe: *I understand. You mean the project managers need to not only plan for these additional costs, but also be obliged to track them. So, Jane, do you need a report about these costs?*

> Jane: *Oh, yes. I would like to see it included with the others you send me before the weekly meeting. Just add the costs to a new Excel worksheet, you know, and I can create my charts and pivots myself . . ."*

NOTE *If you are wondering why this short transcript is included here, keep in mind that in real life, almost any requirement specification — or whatever you call the document that summarizes the expected features and quality requirements — starts its life in a meeting. Essentially, it represents a "wish list." Generally, it takes an intensive analysis to translate this wish list into solid specifications. Often, wish lists are scorned by analysts, because they are not accurate or detailed enough. However, they can contain especially useful information about the most wanted functions and features.*

Joe asks Mary, one of the experienced business analysts, to undertake the task of planning `ProjectTrek`'s functionality. Using her experiences with the Excel worksheets currently used, and the expectations of the CEO, Mary summarizes the functionality of `ProjectTrek` with the use case diagram shown in Figure 5-1.

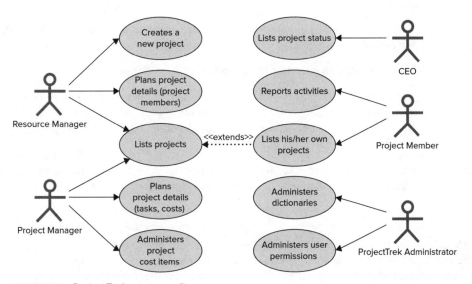

FIGURE 5-1: ProjectTrek use case diagram

This diagram follows the Universal Modeling Language (UML) conventions. It depicts the system's actors (users of the `ProjectTrek` system) and the functionality they use. Table 5-1 summarizes the roles of the actors shown in Figure 5-1.

UML AND USE CASES

Unified Modeling Language (UML) is a general-purpose modeling language created by James Rumbaugh, Grady Booch, and Ivar Jacobson. UML uses visual descriptions with its diagram types. One of them is the use case diagram type that is used to depict actors (users of a system) in tandem with the functions (use cases) they use in the system. Many software development methodologies (or frameworks) use this kind of diagram (or an equivalent) to help facilitate understanding of the functional scope of a system.

TABLE 5-1: Actors in the ProjectTrek System

ACTOR	ROLE
Resource Manager	This person is responsible for keeping track of projects and related resources within ConsulArt. Responsibilities include creating a new project and setting it up with the most important attributes (deadlines, planned revenues, project members, and so on).
Project Manager	Each project is led by a project manager who is responsible for planning the tasks and additional costs of the project, and keeping track of the project's status.
CEO	The CEO wants an overview of each project's overall status.
Project Member	Project members report their daily activities so that the project manager can follow that project's resource usage. Project members send invoices, bills, and notes of cost items (books, photocopying, and other expenses) to the project manager, who administers those items.
ProjectTrek Administrator	This person is responsible for setting up user rights for ProjectTrek and administering dictionary tables (for example, time categories) in the system.

NOTE *Of course, the functionality of* ProjectTrek *is intentionally kept simple in this book. In the real world, such a system would be more complex, including more use cases and even more actors. The functionality treated here is appropriate for learning about Visual Studio LightSwitch.*

In subsequent chapters of this book, you will implement the ProjectTrek application with this functionality.

The ProjectTrek Application Database

According to the use cases composed by Mary, Bob (a data modeling expert) designed the higher-level data model — called *entity model* — of ProjectTrek. He analyzed the structure of the currently used Excel worksheets and the functional requirements, and then prepared the entity model. In this section, you learn about the model designed by Bob.

> ### DATA MODELS
>
> The data model of a system describes the tables of a system and the relationship between them.
>
> This book cannot undertake the mission of teaching you all about database design. However, without knowing the basics, you won't understand the data model of the `ProjectTrek` application that you will create in subsequent chapters. If you have some experience with creating simple data models, you can skip this section; otherwise, here you can learn the basics that will help you understand entities and how they are related to tables.
>
> Wrox published a great book, *Beginning Database Design Solutions* by Rod Stephens (Indianapolis: Wiley, 2008) that is a good source to use to learn data modeling.

Understanding Tables and Entities

Your line-of-business (LOB) application — as with all data-centric applications — works with *entities* that describe objects in the real world. An example for an object might be a customer, an order, a time category, or many other things you can describe with properties and behavior. A customer can have a name, a business address and a shipping address, a discount category, and so on. These are the *properties* of a customer entity.

The data describing entities is stored in a database management system (DBMS). An entity is represented as one or more related *tables* in the database. While entities are used to describe a model at a higher (often referred to as *logical)* level, tables describe the same model at the database (often referred to as *physical)* level. Generally, the physical level description is more detailed than the logical one.

For example, a set of customers stored in a database can be represented as shown in Table 5-2. Each row represents a separate customer.

TABLE 5-2: Customers Stored in a Database Table

ID#	NAME	BUSINESS ADDRESS
1001	Geller, Wilhelm	21 Kurfürstendamm, Berlin, 12345-Germany
1002	Tschekashev, Boris	124 Uljica Gorkova , Moscow, 56789-Russia
1003	Dickinson, Terry	12 NE 4th Avenue, Seattle, WA, 98005
1004	Horvath, Gabor	116 Kossuth utca, Budapest, 1116-Hungary
. . .	. . .	. . .
42135	McDonald, James	910 Wilshire Boulevard, Los Angeles, CA, 90017
42136	Wagner, Bill	480 N 8th Street, Renton, WA, 98057

Table Structure

Each column in Table 5-2 describes a property of a customer. As you can see, a customer has an ID#, a Name, and a Business Address, as reflected in the column heads of Table 5-2. In database terms, the columns are called *field*s.

When you work with a customer (for example, displaying their orders or updating their data), you must tell the system which customer you intend to deal with. To do that, you must provide the system with the information it needs to select a specific customer (that is, row) from the table.

Tables contain a special field that has a unique value for each row within the table. This property is called a *primary key* (or often simply *key*). DBMSs are careful about managing this key. They do not allow the insertion of more than one row having the same key value. In Table 5-2, the ID# field is the primary key, and each customer has its own unique ID#.

> **NOTE** *In most DBMSs, a primary key can be composed from multiple fields. This kind of key is called a* compound primary key. *Of course, in such a case, the combination of values comprising the compound key must be unique in the table.*

Related Entities

In data-centric applications, entities have relationships among themselves — generally based on natural relationships and business processes. For example, customers have zero, one, or more orders; orders have one or more items.

In relational database management systems (RDBMSs), these kinds of associations are implemented as relationships between tables. For example, assume that you want to describe customers and their orders as shown in Table 5-3. The structure of this table is very similar to Table 5-2, but it has a new column named Orders that contains books ordered by the customer. (For the sake of simplicity, the address is represented only with a city, but this column would normally provide a complete address.)

TABLE 5-3: Customers and Their Orders

ID#	NAME	ADDRESS	ORDERS
1001	Geller, Wilhelm	Berlin	*Fireflies in December;* 12/20/2010; $11.40 *My Christmas Wish;* 12/18/2010; $6.28 *The Hunger Games;* 11/24/2010; $8.42
1002	Tschekashev, Boris	Moscow	*With God in Russia;* 09/17/2010; $16.25 *The Cossacks;* 08/22/2010; $8.45
1003	Dickinson, Terry	Seattle	*100 Ways to Cook Eggs;* 12/17/2010; $4.95
1004	Horvath, Gabor	Budapest	*Hunting with the Bow and Arrow;* 08/21/2010; $9.28 *The Hunger Games;* 12/11/2010; $8.55
. . .	. . .	. . .	

ID#	NAME	ADDRESS	ORDERS
42135	McDonald, James	Los Angeles	*My Christmas Wish;* 11/30/2010; $6.11
42136	Wagner, Bill	Renton	*The Cossacks;* 09/14/2010; $9.25 *100 Ways to Cook Eggs;* 11/26/2010; $4.95

As shown in Table 5-3, the `Orders` column provides customer data for not only one order, but possibly multiple orders for each customer. Also, a single order contains a book title, an order date, and a price. If an RDBMS stored entities in this way, it would be very difficult to process the orders and ensure consistency.

These issues can be solved by using a technique called *normalization*. Instead of storing compound data such as that shown in Table 5-3, information is divided into separate tables that have relationships between them. For example, the customers and their orders in Table 5-3 can be separated into three tables, as shown in Table 5-4 (`Customer`), Table 5-5 (`Book`), and Table 5-6 (`Order`).

TABLE 5-4: Customer Table

ID#	NAME	BUSINESS ADDRESS
1001	Geller, Wilhelm	Berlin
1002	Tschekashev, Boris	Moscow
1003	Dickinson, Terry	Seattle
1004	Horvath, Gabor	Budapest
...	...	...
42135	McDonald, James	Los Angeles
42136	Wagner, Bill	Renton

TABLE 5-5: Book Table

ID	TITLE	CURRENT PRICE
1	*The Hunger Games*	$8.20
2	*The Cossacks*	$8.55
3	*100 Ways to Cook Eggs*	$4.95
4	*My Christmas Wish*	$7.05

continues

TABLE 5-5 *(continued)*

ID	TITLE	CURRENT PRICE
5	*Fireflies in December*	$11.50
6	*With God in Russia*	$16.25
7	*Hunting with the Bow and Arrow*	$9.28
...	...	...

TABLE 5-6: Order Table

ID	CUSTOMER ID	BOOK ID	DATE	PRICE
100	1004	7	08/21/2010	$9.28
101	1002	2	08/22/2010	$8.45
102	42136	2	09/14/2010	$9.25
103	1002	6	09/17/2010	$16.25
104	1001	1	11/24/2010	$8.42
105	42136	3	11/26/2010	$4.95
106	42135	4	11/30/2010	$6.11
107	1004	1	12/11/2010	$8.55
108	1003	3	12/17/2010	$4.95
109	1001	4	12/18/2010	$6.28
110	1001	5	12/20/2010	$11.40

The structure of Customer (Table 5-4) and Book (Table 5-5) is pretty simple. However, Order (Table 5-6) has an unusual structure. Each entry describes an order for a concrete book belonging to a particular customer. The Book ID field is the identifier of the related book in the Book table, and Customer ID is the identifier of the related customer (who placed the order) in the Customer table. The Price field is simply copied from the Current Price field of the Book table at the time the order was placed.

The Book ID and Customer ID fields are called *foreign keys* in database terms, because they reference the primary key of another (foreign) table. The relationship between the Customer and Order tables is called a *one-to-many relationship*, because there can be zero, one, or more rows in the Order table belonging to a specific Customer row, and one Order row has exactly one related row in the Customer table. Similarly, you can see that there is a one-to-many relationship between

Book and Order. The relationships between these tables can be shown in a simple modeling diagram, as shown in Figure 5-2.

The boxes in Figure 5-2 represent the tables. (Note that, in database modeling, table names generally are singular.) The lines between the boxes depict the relationships between the tables. You can see that the ends of the line close to Order have an asterisk ("*") label. This indicates the "many" end in a one-to-many relationship.

Designing Databases

Database designers are the experts who understand the business issue to solve, and then design the structure of entities and the relationships between them to create a model that meets the functional requirements specified. This entity model is mapped (either manually or with appropriate tools) into relational database tables.

Other experts, who have experience with concrete DBMSs, can translate the table structure into physical tables. This mapping applies transformations that enable optimal performance of the back-end database of a business application. For example, they partition tables among physical devices, add indexes to tables, and fine-tune storage options.

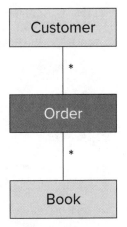

FIGURE 5-2: Sample diagram showing the relationships between Customer, Book, and Order tables

ProjectTrek Entities

According to the use cases composed by Mary, Bob designed the entity model shown in Figure 5-3.

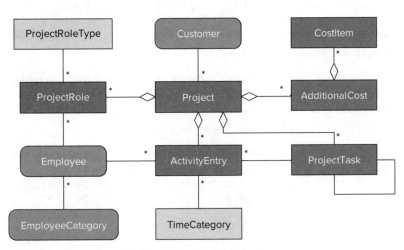

FIGURE 5-3: Entity model of the ProjectTrek application

Bob knew that ConsulArt had recently built a small SQL Server–based application containing useful data about customers and employees. As shown in Figure 5-3, he marked the entities stored in this already existing database with rounded corners. His design suggested that a few entities needed to be created in the LightSwitch project. Bob marked the lookup tables (that is, simple tables storing items used in lookups, mostly used in drop-down lists) with a light background. He added a dark shade to transactional tables, which contain data continuously changing as the application is used.

Table 5-7 summarizes the roles of the entities shown in Figure 5-3.

TABLE 5-7: The Roles of ProjectTrek Entities

ENTITY	ROLE
Customer	This entity contains the basic data of ConsulArt customers. It already exists in a SQL Server database.
Project	This is the main entity of the system. It holds the most important information about a project (such as its name, start and end dates, planned revenue, etc.). It has a reference to a Customer entity representing the customer this project is for.
ProjectTask	This represents a single task belonging to a project. As indicated in Figure 5-3 with a line starting from ProjectTask and returning to it, a task can contain child tasks. ProjectTask has a reference to Project.
ActivityEntry	This entity represents an entry in the personal activity reports of employees. At the end of each day, employees report their activities (the project and the task worked on). ActivityEntry has references to Project, ProjectTask, TimeCategory, and Employee.
TimeCategory	Sometimes employees must work overtime or on weekends. TimeCategory represents this information for each activity entry.
AdditionalCost	One of the most important requests from management was planning for additional project costs. This entity represents a single cost item planned for a project. It has a reference to Project, because a project can have zero, one, or more AdditionalCost items.
CostItem	A CostItem entity represents a concrete item that adds cost to a project. It has a reference to AdditionalCost. For example, AdditionalCost may allocate $1,000 for books, and a book bought for $35 represents a CostItem belonging to the $1,000 AdditionalCost entry.
ProjectRole	A project entails a team, with each member having his or her own dedicated role (such as project manager, architect, developer, tester, etc.). This entity defines the role of a project team member. It has references to Project, ProjectRoleType, and Employee.
ProjectRoleType	This entity represents lookup information for a project member's possible roles.
Employee	This defines an employee of ConsulArt who can be a member of a project team and can report activities and project costs. This entity already exists in a SQL Server database. An Employee has a reference to an EmployeeCategory.
EmployeeCategory	This entity represents lookup information describing a category to which the employee belongs. This entity already exists in a SQL Server database.

Bob made several modeling decisions when creating the entity data model diagram shown in Figure 5-3:

➤ The `ActivityEntry` entity contains a reference to both the `ProjectTask` and `Project` entities. It would be adequate to reference only `ProjectTask`, because it has a reference to `Project`, so the project to which an activity entry is reported can be obtained through `ProjectTask`. However, Bob decided to add another reference to `Project` for performance reasons.

➤ There is a similar situation with the `AdditionalCost` and `CostItem` entities. `CostItem` contains a reference only to `AdditionalCost`, not to `Project`. A project will contain many more tasks and activity entries than additional cost items. Bob did not expect significant performance penalties, and he did not add a reference from `CostItem` to `Project`.

Now that you understand the functionality and data model of `ProjectTrek`, let's take a look at the development life cycle of LightSwitch applications.

LIGHTSWITCH APPLICATION DEVELOPMENT LIFE CYCLE

There are many methodologies and best practices you can follow when developing a line-of-business (LOB) application. Visual Studio LightSwitch is especially great when you develop small applications, satellite applications for large back-end systems, or when you use it to create prototypes.

In the LightSwitch IDE, you can define new tables, or connect to existing databases with a few clicks. The built-in Designer helps you create new screens based on commonly used templates, and enables you to customize them without writing any lines of code. With a few lines, you can add simple business rules to your application, and your prototype is ready to work.

The rapid application development (RAD) approach to developing applications emphasizes the importance of prototypes and iterations. The traditional (you might say "older") methodologies used to follow a phase-to-phase development approach, whereby the phases (that is, design, implementation, test, deployment, and operation) followed each other sequentially without overlapping. These methodologies are often called *waterfall models*, because the phases follow each other just like cascades of a waterfall.

Waterfall models work very well in cases where requirements are clear, the project environment changes only slightly, and there are no significant risks. However, there are very few projects with these characteristics. Most projects have a fuzzy specification — at least at the beginning — and hide many risks. Often, the project environment — that is, the priority of certain requirements, scope, legal environment, project members, and so on — is in continuous change. This is where the iterative life cycle model offers significant advantages.

The Iterative Model

Unlike a simple sequential software development life cycle, iterative development refers to phases that are repeated with multiple cycles. Each cycle can have its own design, implementation, test, and deployment (or even other) phases. At the beginning of a project, the design may get more emphasis than implementation or test, whereas closer to the end of the project, deployment gets the focus.

The traditional phases may overlap each other. While you are implementing a certain feature set, another part of the team can work on the design of a separate set of functionality, and someone may focus on deployment tasks. Figure 5-4 shows how a cycle can be divided into phases.

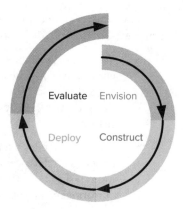

In Figure 5-4, the *Envision* phase is where the scope and features are established for the cycle. The *Construct* phase produces the features according to the imagined scope of the project, including the necessary design and tests. The *Deploy* phase delivers the features to end-users so that they can seize the product. During the *Evaluate* phase, wishes and future directions come to light, which can influence the scope and features in the next iteration.

FIGURE 5-4: Phases of a cycle

NOTE *Different methodologies use different names for the phases depicted in Figure 5-4, and some use more phases to describe a cycle. There are only slight differences among them; however, the primary approach is the same.*

LightSwitch encourages using iterations. You can create inexpensive prototypes in a very short time. This means that you can perform experiments that test several alternative ways to solve a problem. You do not need to make decisions in advance that may tie your hands in a future phase. Make several prototypes, evaluate them, and decide according to the results.

For example, if you must implement an order-creation process, you can make a few prototypes. Assume that you create a simple screen that asks for all order attributes, a wizard that guides the user through the process in three steps, and a third prototype that uses a purchased third-party component. When you elaborate them, you can present the process prototypes to your customers and let them pick the solution that best meets their needs.

A full cycle can take a few minutes or a few days. Deployment is often just a virtual phase, because by building the application (that is, by compiling it) you can evaluate it — at least on your own machine.

Construction: Design and Implementation

The use of prototype applications provides a very quick return on investment, so prototypes are especially useful during design and implementation. With LightSwitch, these two aspects of development often cannot be clearly separated. When you design a table and create a screen, LightSwitch can bind the design with the implementation.

Recall that when you created the `AlbumTracker` application in Chapter 2, you did not write any code. When you created the `Album` table and the `AlbumListDetails` screen in LightSwitch, did that effort represent design or implementation? Actually, it doesn't matter! The result of the RAD approach was the construction of a small application.

In Chapter 4, you created the `Aquarium` application, and you wrote a few lines of code that contained very simple initialization and interaction logic. Again, there is no reason to determine whether the code-writing activity belonged to design or implementation.

As you can see, it might be better to collectively call these phases *construction*.

> **NOTE** *"Construction" is another overloaded term. Some methodologies call the entire LOB software development life cycle (starting from when the project is approved in accordance with a set of business requirements) "construction." In some other contexts, "construction" means the collection of phases in which a team of software development experts create the application. In the case of LightSwitch, everything that's part of creating a prototype of a working application ready for deployment can be considered "construction."*

LightSwitch was designed with data-centric LOB applications in mind. In the construction phase, you can follow the activities shown in Figure 5-5.

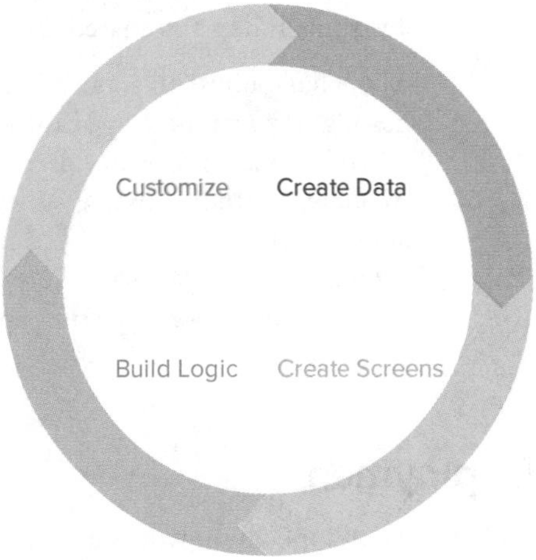

As you build an application, you repeat the steps depicted in Figure 5-5 until you reach your milestone, at which point the application is ready for deployment. Following are the steps:

1. *Create data* — Design and create your data structures, including new entities, and entities based on existing data. Then you establish the relationships between them.

2. *Create screens* — Create screens based on the data you've created, and establish their basic layout.

3. *Build logic* — Declare simple rules characterizing the business logic of your application, and write code for more complex business rules, and for user-interaction logic.

FIGURE 5-5: Construction phases in LightSwitch

4. *Customize* — Perform some visual tuning to enhance the user experience, and, if necessary, make slight modifications to data structures and related business logic.

Testing

Before deploying your application, you must ensure that it works according to the specification. This check should include both the expected functionality and other quality requirements, such as performance, user interface (UI) ergonomics, response times, and so on.

Visual Studio LightSwitch currently does not offer any tools for testing. Perhaps a future version will. Until then, you must test your applications manually. Because Visual Studio LightSwitch builds your application with a predefined and thoroughly tested architecture, you can be sure that it binds the application components (data, screens, business rules) correctly, so you do not need to manually test this.

Rather, you should focus on testing the business functionality of your application. The best way to do that is to create a list of manual test cases that can be replayed before each deployment. When you describe these cases, create several scenarios for each business function, including the normal execution scenario (assuming all input is correct) and exceptional scenarios (wrong input is provided). Also, test whether business rules work as expected.

TEST METHODOLOGIES

Using the appropriate testing approach in LOB application development is a key element of successful projects. Many methodologies describe how you should do that (including automated tests), but covering them all here is far beyond the scope of this book. Although Visual Studio LightSwitch does not provide test tools, you can load your LightSwitch project into the Professional, Premium, and Ultimate editions of Visual Studio 2010, all of which provide several tools for automated tests (including automated UI testing).

Wrox has published some great books that help you learn more about software testing. *Professional Application Lifecycle Management with Visual Studio 2010* by Mickey Gousset, Brian Keller, Ajoy Krishnamoorthy, and Martin Woodward (Indianapolis: Wiley, 2010) provides indispensable information about how to manage software testing in a team environment. *Testing ASP.NET Web Applications* by Jeff McWherter and Ben Hall (Indianapolis: Wiley, 2009) puts the emphasis on concrete testing approaches.

Deployment

When your application works as expected in the development environment (or the test environment), you can deploy it. As you have already learned, LightSwitch uses the three-tier application architecture pattern. That means each tier can be deployed onto separate computers. You can put your database on a specific server, the business logic on another one, and use the presentation layer on end-users' computers. Creating installation tools for such distributed systems can be a challenging task.

Fortunately, LightSwitch was designed with this in mind. You do not need to manually write installation tools or scripts. With the help of the deployment function built into the integrated development environment (IDE), you can choose from client and application server topology options, and the IDE will guide you through the whole deployment process.

You have two client topology options:

➤ *Desktop client* — The application runs on the end-user's desktop.

➤ *Browser client* — The application runs in the end-user's browser.

The following are application server topology options:

➤ *Client machine* — The application services run on the end-user's machine. The database can be put on any remote computer in the network, including the client machine.

➤ *Internet Information Services (IIS)* — The application services run on a separate server machine, hosted in IIS. The database can be put on any remote computer in the network, including the application server machine.

➤ *Windows Azure* — The application services and the database are hosted in Windows Azure.

Chapter 13 is entirely dedicated to deployment. There you will learn about using these options.

Extending a LightSwitch Application

One of the most irritating issues when developing LOB applications with Microsoft Access is that it works great only when you need the limited, simple features it offers. However, when you must make small customizations in the UI or in the business logic, it can be a nightmare to program — and not at all intuitive. Nor is adding extra functionality (such as using existing .NET assemblies) a trivial task with Access.

In contrast, LightSwitch provides a simple transition from a basic (or prototype) application to a complex one. You can install Visual Studio LightSwitch on a machine where any of the Professional, Premium, or Ultimate editions of Visual Studio 2010 have already been set up; in this case, LightSwitch runs within the Visual Studio 2010 IDE. You can open your LightSwitch solution in the Visual Studio IDE, and add any other kind of project types (mostly class libraries) to extend the LightSwitch application. You can also create extension components for LightSwitch in Visual Studio 2010, and install them on a computer equipped with Visual Studio LightSwitch only.

Figure 5-6 shows how this approach extends the LightSwitch application development life cycle.

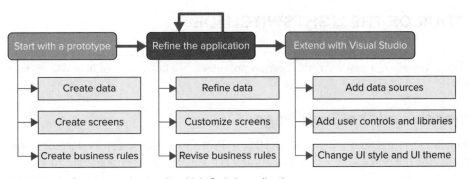

FIGURE 5-6: Creating and extending LightSwitch applications

Figure 5-6 solidifies the generic cycles and phases shown in Figure 5-4 and 5-5. Generally, in the first cycle you create a simple prototype with data and screens, to have a communicable application model. Later, you refine the LightSwitch application with data and business rule tuning, and screen customization.

Although LightSwitch provides you with a wide variety of UI elements, as well as APIs to implement more complex business scenarios, these tools cannot provide the flexibility accessible in Visual Studio. LightSwitch provides you with several extensibility options. For example, you can change the theme (skin) of your application, or alter its style (color scheme) without writing any code.

Although you cannot create these components within the LightSwitch IDE, you can install extensions implemented by Microsoft or third parties. With Visual Studio 2010, you can also create your own extensions.

Team Foundation Server Support

Visual Studio LightSwitch fully supports Microsoft Team Foundation Server (TFS) 2010 integration, just like other Visual Studio 2010 editions. You can store the source code of your solutions in a Team Foundation Server 2010 team project and use all the teamwork techniques that it offers, including source code control, work item management, automatic builds, and more.

Although LightSwitch development projects are generally smaller than other Visual Studio projects (less team members work together), that does not mean you must omit teamwork practices. Work item management can be especially useful. Even if you work on your own, LightSwitch enables you to manage your task lists related to the application under development.

It is far beyond the scope of this book to teach you how to use Team Foundation Server 2010 in tandem with Visual Studio LightSwitch. If you are interested in team techniques, see *Professional Application Lifecycle Management with Visual Studio 2010* by Mickey Gousset, Brian Keller, Ajoy Krishnamoorthy, and Martin Woodward (Indianapolis: Wiley, 2010).

By now, you have learned about the `ProjectTrek` application to be created, and have a good understanding of the LightSwitch application development life cycle. Before you dive into developing `ProjectTrek`, it is time to learn the basics of the LightSwitch IDE.

A SHORT TOUR OF THE LIGHTSWITCH IDE

If you have already used Visual Studio 2010 and know the basics of the IDE, you can skip this section. However, if you are a new user, this section provides a brief overview of how to use the LightSwitch IDE.

The Workbench and the Start Page

When you launch the Visual Studio LightSwitch IDE, it displays a splash screen as the tool starts up. In a few seconds, the IDE loads all the components and is ready to start creating applications.

> **NOTE** *If you already have Visual Studio 2010 on your computer before installing LightSwitch, all LightSwitch components will be integrated into the Visual Studio 2010 IDE. You won't find any separate menu item for LightSwitch. In the Visual Studio 2010 IDE, you can create LightSwitch projects, and when they are open, you can work them exactly the same way as if you are using the LightSwitch IDE.*

The structure of LightSwitch's main screen is similar to other Windows applications. At the top you find the main menu, with the toolbar beneath. The largest part of the screen is filled up with the Start Page, as shown in Figure 5-7.

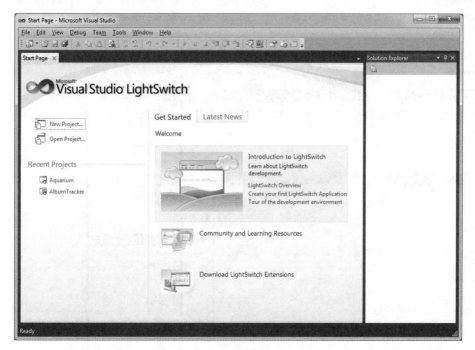

FIGURE 5-7: The Start Page of Visual Studio LightSwitch

As its name suggests, the Start Page contains task links for accessing the most frequently used commands or information you need to work with a LightSwitch project. You can click the New Project link to create a brand-new LightSwitch application, or select the Open Project link to browse for an existing project file. The Recent Projects section lists the most recently used projects. You can open the specific project in the IDE by clicking any of the listed project names.

The right side of the Start Page contains a couple of tabs with useful links to assist you while working with LightSwitch. The Get Started tab provides links to learn the fundamentals of using Visual Studio LightSwitch. The Latest News tab lists posts and articles related to LightSwitch. To list the posts on the Start Page, you must click the Enable RSS Feed button shown in Figure 5-8.

FIGURE 5-8: You must enable the RSS feed to access latest LightSwitch news

When you work with a project, the Start Page window is automatically closed. You can display it again by selecting View ⇨ Start Page from the main menu.

Solution Explorer

Most of the time, you work with a solution open in the IDE. A *solution* is a collection of projects each of which contains related items such as source files, resources, configuration information, and other artifacts that comprise your LightSwitch application. Solution Explorer is an important tool window that lists these items, as shown on the right side of the main window in Figure 5-9.

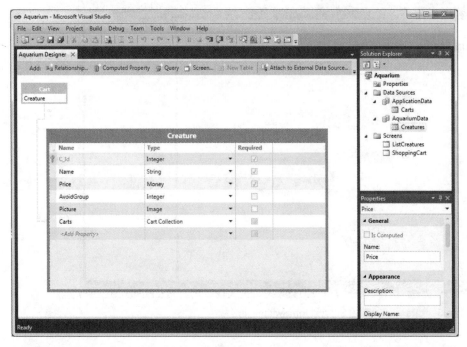

FIGURE 5-9: The main window displays the Application Designer (in the middle of the screen), Solution Explorer (on the right), and the Properties window (beneath Solution Explorer)

The items in Solution Explorer are logically organized into folders, with a little triangle icon to the left of them (such as `Data Sources` and `Screens` shown in Figure 5-9). When you click the triangles, you expand or collapse the related folder.

If Solution Explorer is not visible, you can display it with the View ⇨ Solution Explorer command, or by pressing the Ctrl+Alt+L keyboard shortcut. If you want to look at an item, double-click it to open it in the Application Designer.

The Application Designer

The largest part of the screen is used by the Application Designer while you work with tables or screens, which are the most important artifacts in LightSwitch. For example, as shown in Figure 5-9, the Creatures node is selected in Solution Explorer, so the related `Creature` table is shown in the design view. Because the project's name is `Aquarium`, the Application Designer window is titled "Aquarium Designer."

When you open another project item in Solution Explorer, only the new item is shown in the Designer.

The Properties Window

The constituent elements of a LightSwitch application (such as tables, fields, screens, layout items, resources, and many others) have properties that influence their visual appearance and behavior. You can use the Properties window to edit the properties of a selected element.

In Figure 5-9, the Aquarium Designer is displaying the `Creature` table with the `Price` field selected. The Properties window beneath Solution Explorer contains the properties of `Price`. These are grouped into categories such as General and Appearance, as shown in the figure. You can scroll the content of the window to find the property you intend to edit.

If the Properties window is not visible, press the F4 key, or use the View ➪ Properties command to display it.

The Code Editor Window

While you develop a LightSwitch application, you may need to write a few lines of code to create a validation rule or describe UI interaction. This is done in the Code Editor window belonging to the project artifacts. In contrast to the Application Designer, you can open several Code Editor windows at the same time, as shown by the tabs at the top of Figure 5-10.

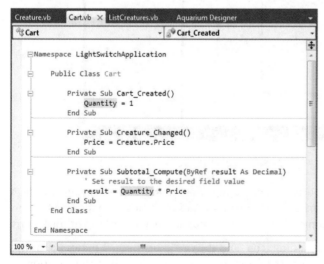

```vb
Namespace LightSwitchApplication

    Public Class Cart

        Private Sub Cart_Created()
            Quantity = 1
        End Sub

        Private Sub Creature_Changed()
            Price = Creature.Price
        End Sub

        Private Sub Subtotal_Compute(ByRef result As Decimal)
            ' Set result to the desired field value
            result = Quantity * Price
        End Sub
    End Class

End Namespace
```

FIGURE 5-10: The Code Editor window

As shown in the figure, the `Cart.vb` editor file is active. You can click any other tab to make the related document (code file or the Application Designer) active. Each tab can be separately closed by clicking the "X" to the right of the tab name.

Window Management

Visual Studio automatically arranges the windows you are working with, but you do not have to accept the default layout it offers. You can change your workspace completely.

The windows within the IDE can float or be docked to the edges of the main window or other windows. Drag any window by its caption and move it to another position. When you start to move a window, a guiding diamond appears in the middle of the frame to where the mouse is pointing, as shown in Figure 5-11.

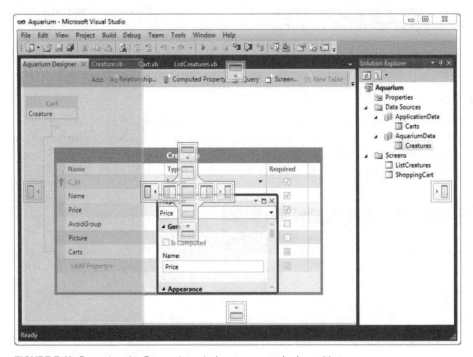

FIGURE 5-11: Dragging the Properties window to a new dock position

Each icon of the diamond represents a position. For example, the four arrows point toward the four sides of the editing pane. Four other icons point to the four edges of the main window. As you move the window over another frame, the diamond changes to represent dock positions within that frame.

You can move the mouse pointer over a guiding icon, and then a "ghost frame" shows up in the new dock position. If you release the left mouse button, the window is docked to this position. Figure 5-11 shows that the Properties window is dragged over the guiding icon that docks the window to the right edge of the editing pane. If you release the mouse button without pointing to any guiding icon, your window will float. If you have multiple monitors, you can drag a window to any of the available monitors.

You can also resize any window by dragging its border. When you double-click the caption of a docked window, it changes to a floating window. Double-clicking on a floating window's caption will maximize it.

SUMMARY

This chapter used a fictitious company, ConsulArt, to examine a few main concepts about designing an application to be implemented in LightSwitch. For ConsulArt's `ProjectTrek` application, two important design artifacts were utilized: a use case diagram that illustrates the functionality of the system, and an entity relationship diagram that provides an overview of the data's structure.

You can use several software development methodologies to create applications with LightSwitch, but iterative methods provide the best results. Iterations guide you closer and closer to the productive application. You can start with a simple prototype and customize it to fulfill all the requirements before you deploy it.

You can load a LightSwitch application project into Visual Studio 2010 and extend it with functions that you cannot develop directly in the LightSwitch IDE. With Visual Studio 2010, you can also create extensions for the LightSwitch IDE.

EXERCISES

1. How does the use case diagram in Figure 5-1 help you understand the functionality of the `ProjectTrek` application?

2. According to Figure 5-3 and Table 5-7, what is the purpose of the `Project`, `AdditionalCost`, and `CostItems` entities?

3. Does LightSwitch encourage you to use iterations during application development?

4. How can Visual Studio 2010 help to extend your LightSwitch applications?

NOTE *Answers to the Exercises can be found in the Appendix.*

▶ **WHAT YOU LEARNED IN THIS CHAPTER**

TOPIC	KEY CONCEPTS
Use case diagram	This diagram type is defined in the Universal Modeling Language (UML). It is used to depict actors (users of a system) in tandem with the functions (use cases) they use in the system. Many software development methodologies, or frameworks, use this kind of diagram (or an equivalent) to help facilitate understanding of the functional scope of a system.
Entity model	This depicts the entities (including the relationships between them) of a system in a visual form. This kind of representation is often called an *entity relationship diagram (ERD)*.
Waterfall model	This is the common name for traditional system design and development methods in which phases (for example, design, implementation, test, deployment, operation, and so on) follow each other sequentially, without overlapping — just like cascades of a waterfall.
Iterative model	This model uses system design and development methods that incorporate iterations of a few cycles and overlapping phases — in contrast to waterfall models, in which phases follow each other sequentially.
Construction phases in LightSwitch	LightSwitch encourages iterative development. You can establish a business solution starting from a very simple prototype. During the iterations, you continuously enhance this prototype until your application is ready to go live.
Testing in LightSwitch	LightSwitch does not provide any explicit test feature. You should manually test your application. As a best practice, create a document of test cases — ensuring that these cases are repeatable — and include both normal and exceptional scenarios.
Application deployment with LightSwitch	LightSwitch can create installation kits and deploy your application directly from the IDE. You can use either a desktop or browser client, and the application services can be hosted on the client machine, on a separate server running Internet Information Services (IIS), or in Windows Azure.

Working with Simple Data Screens

WHAT YOU WILL LEARN IN THIS CHAPTER

- ➤ Creating new tables with the LightSwitch Designer
- ➤ Setting up table and field properties
- ➤ Creating search, new data, and details screens with the Add New Screen dialog
- ➤ Understanding how data and layout items describe a screen
- ➤ Adding an editable grid screen to your project
- ➤ Modifying a screen by setting up layout item properties

In this chapter, you will learn the basics of creating tables and screens. You will start with very simple tasks to help you understand the powerful approach and tools that LightSwitch provides.

This chapter guides you through designing a simple table (TimeCategory) and several screens that enable you to search and edit the table's data. After going through all the exercises in this chapter, you'll be able to repeat what you have learned to create another table (ProjectRoleType) with a related screen.

CREATING NEW TABLES

For the example in this chapter, the scenario involves a fictitious company named ConsulArt that has designed the ProjectTrek application to enable project team members to report their activities. In addition to working normal daily business hours (for example, 9:00 A.M. to 5:00 P.M.), project team members sometimes need to put in overtime, and they probably have to work on weekends. The `TimeCategory` table represents a lookup table that defines these reporting categories. This table is simple, so it is a perfect example to use to learn the basics of creating tables.

Creating the ProjectTrek Project

Before you can create any tables or screens, you must create the project for the `ProjectTrek` code sample. You can decide whether you want to use Visual Basic or C# as the programming language. Most of the exercises in this book are totally independent from the language selected. The only exception is code. This book provides listings for both programming languages, so you can choose your preferred language.

While you work with the sample application, you cannot change your programming language. However, the sample code available from the Wrox website (`www.wrox.com`) contains all samples in both Visual Basic and C#.

TRY IT OUT Creating The ProjectTrek Project

To create the `ProjectTrek` sample application, follow these steps:

1. Start Visual Studio LightSwitch by clicking Start ⇨ All Programs ⇨ Microsoft Visual Studio 2010 ⇨ Microsoft Visual Studio LightSwitch.

2. Select File ⇨ New Project (or press Ctrl+Shift+N) to display the New Project dialog.

3. Select either the LightSwitch Application (Visual Basic) or the LightSwitch Application (C#) template, depending on your language preference. Set the name of the project to **ProjectTrek**, as shown in Figure 6-1. Click the Browse button to select the folder in which to store project files (or accept the default location).

FIGURE 6-1: The New Project dialog setup for creating the ProjectTrek sample application

4. Click OK. The IDE creates an empty project skeleton and opens the Designer, as shown in Figure 6-2. The Designer displays two task links, one for creating a new table, and one for attaching to an external database.

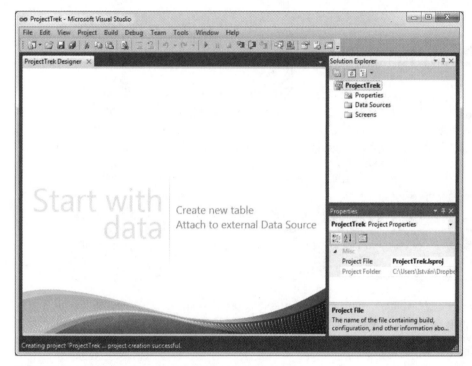

FIGURE 6-2: The ProjectTrek sample has been created

How It Works

According to the template you selected, the IDE generated an empty skeleton and prepared a large folder structure under your project folder to store the project files. The virtual folder structure (called the *logical view*) you see in Solution Explorer hides this complexity. It contains only three virtual folders:

➤ `Properties` — Stores the project settings

➤ `Data Sources` — Displays the hierarchy of databases, tables, and queries in the project

➤ `Screens` — Stores the project screens you add to the project

Although the skeleton is empty, it represents an application you can immediately start. Press F5 to build and start the project. As shown in Figure 6-3, your application is just a simple shell. It does not have any real functionality yet.

Designing the TimeCategory Table

Users can interact with a LightSwitch application through screens. To add functionality to screens, you need data to be displayed in the UI. The first step is to add your data tables to the project, and then you can create screens using the data you've added.

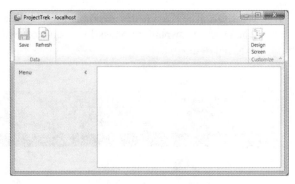

FIGURE 6-3: The empty application shell

 NOTE *LightSwitch allows you to create screens that are not bound to any data, but you rarely use them. Even if you have such screens in your application, it would be unlikely that you would start designing them at the very beginning of your project.*

The `TimeCategory` table is intended to be a lookup table. It will display time category entries to be shown in a drop-down list as team members report their activities. Such a lookup table should contain a displayable name, a short description, and a flag that indicates whether the specific item is to be displayed in the drop-down list.

This flag is important because as time reporting policies change at ConsulArt, some time categories might not be used any longer. For example, a time category named "Special" can be used for an interim period because of special project conditions. When this interim period is over, "Special" should be deprecated so that ConsulArt employees cannot report to this time category any more.

These items cannot simply be deleted, because there might be activity items related to those categories. However, you want to avoid selecting an obsolete (no longer used) time category when adding a new activity item. Adding a flag to each `TimeCategory` entry will help you keep things straight. With this flag, "Special" can be marked as obsolete.

TRY IT OUT Creating the TimeCategory Table

To create the `TimeCategory` table, follow these steps:

1. Click the "Create new table" task link in the Designer. A new table appears with `Table1Item` text highlighted in its header. The highlighting indicates that this text has the focus, and that you can edit it.

2. Without clicking the mouse anywhere, type **TimeCategory** to change the highlighted text. `TimeCategory` will be the name of the new table. This table has one field named `Id`, and it

cannot be changed — it is dimmed out, as shown in Figure 6-4. `Id` represents the primary key of `TimeCategory`. Its name and type are fixed, so you cannot alter those properties.

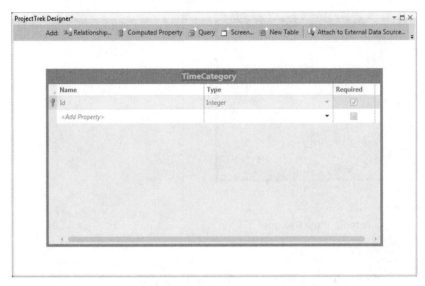

FIGURE 6-4: The empty TimeCategory table

3. Click the <Add Property> cell and type **DisplayName**. The typed text appears in the Name column, indicating the name of the field.

4. Press Tab to move the focus to the Type column, where `String` is automatically selected. This means that the `DisplayName` column is a textual field that can contain arbitrary text.

5. Press Tab again. Now the Required column has the focus. The check box indicates that this field must have a value; it cannot be left empty.

6. Press Tab to add a new row to the table, enabling you to define a new field. Name it **Description** and then press Tab twice. The focus is now on the Required column. Press the spacebar to clear the check box. You can press the spacebar again to enable the check box, and again to clear it. This field contains an optional description of a time category entry, so it can have empty value — and that is what the unchecked box indicates.

7. Press Tab again to add the last field to `TimeCategory`. This field will be a flag (that is, it can have only Yes or No values). It indicates whether the corresponding item can be used with a new activity report item. Type **Active** into the Name column and press Tab to select its type. The default `String` type is not appropriate for storing a flag because a `String` type can contain any text. The correct type for a flag is the `Boolean` type, so start typing **Boolean**. As you type "B" and then "o," Boolean is selected. Alternatively, you can click the drop-down arrow of the Type cell and select Boolean from the list.

8. The Required field is set for the `Active` field. Leave the `Required` property checked for the `Active` field. This signifies that the `Active` field must contain a value.

9. The `TimeCategory` table is ready. Save it by pressing Ctrl+S. Figure 6-5 shows the Designer with the completed table.

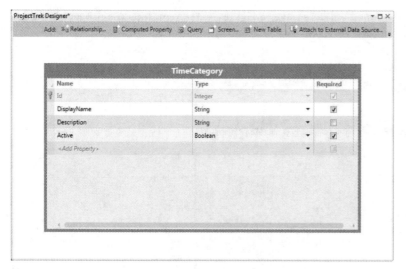

FIGURE 6-5: The completed TimeCategory table in the Designer

 NOTE *You have several ways to save the modifications in the LightSwitch IDE. The easiest is to press Ctrl+S, which is the shortcut of the File ⇨ Save command. You can also use the File ⇨ Save All command (its shortcut is Ctrl+Shift+S), or click any of the floppy disk icons in the Standard toolbar, which is located beneath the IDE's menu bar.*

How It Works

The IDE stores the table definition you created. When you build the application, the build process automatically creates a database with the specified table structure, and generates all plumbing code needed to bind the `TimeCategory` table with screens and other programming artifacts.

The `Id` is a required field, so its value cannot be empty. Its type is `Integer`, which represents a 32-bit integer that can have a value between -2,147,483,648 and 2,147,483,647. In the database, `Id` is defined (it is an `Identity` field in SQL Server terms) so that it is filled with an automatically incremented value every time a new record is inserted into the table. This behavior ensures that each `TimeCategory` item will have a unique `Id` value.

Table Fields and Properties

As you just saw in the last "Try It Out" exercise, creating a new table is very simple. You assign a name to the table, and then add fields to it by specifying a field name, a field type, and a flag indicating whether the field must contain a value. Of course, the Designer offers you many more options when you create or modify a table.

Naming Tables and Fields

You cannot give an arbitrary name to a field, because names must satisfy a few conditions. These names are used in the physical databases to name tables and fields, and internally in the entity model of the application.

When writing code, you can use the names to program the behavior of the entities wrapping tables and fields. For example, when you set the default value of the `Active` field of the `TimeCategory` table through the `myTable` variable, you use the following statement in Visual Basic:

```
myTable.Active = True
```

Or, you could use the following in C#:

```
myTable.Active = true;
```

This means that you must use table names that conform to the syntax rules of Visual Basic and C# identifiers. You can use field names that start with a letter or the underscore (_) character, followed by zero, one, or more alphanumerical characters or underscores. You can use either lowercase or uppercase letters.

> **CASE SENSITIVITY OF IDENTIFIERS**
>
> The C# programming language is case-sensitive — for example, the lowercase "a" character is differentiated from the uppercase "A" character, which means that the `alpha` and `Alpha` identifiers are different. In contrast, Visual Basic is a case-insensitive language that does not differentiate lowercase and uppercase letters, so `bravo` and `Bravo` are the same identifiers in Visual Basic.
>
> A good practice (and one this book follows) is to use *camel-case* names, whereby the elements of compound words or phrases are joined without spaces, with each element's initial letter capitalized within the compound — such as `TimeCategory`, `DisplayName`, `ProjectTask`, and so on.

Note that some reserved words cannot be used as identifiers. These are the keywords of the C# and Visual Basic languages, or entity and property names reserved by the LightSwitch entity model.

All field names in a table must be unique. This is a natural requirement; otherwise, you have no way to differentiate two fields that have the same name.

If you try to use an invalid name, such as a field name with a space in it, the Designer underlines the name with red squiggles, as shown in Figure 6-6.

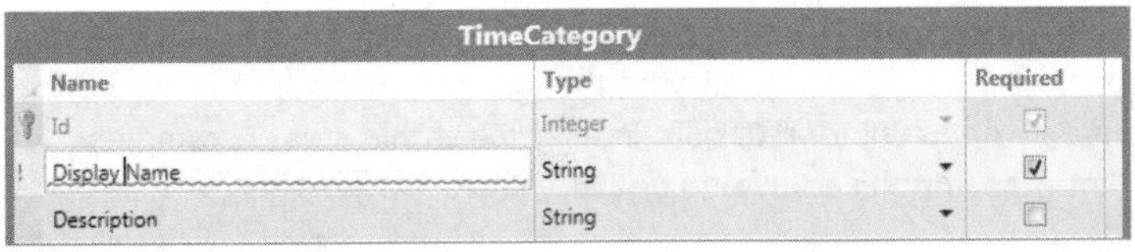

TimeCategory		
Name	Type	Required
Id	Integer	☑
Display Name	String	☑
Description	String	☐

FIGURE 6-6: Invalid name underlined with red squiggles

Field Types

LightSwitch allows you to select field types from *intrinsic types* or from *business types*. Intrinsic types represent physical storage types such as `Integer`, `String`, `Binary`, `Boolean`, and so on. When you assign one of these to a field, it guarantees that the field's value and basic behavior will conform to the specific type's definition. For example, an integer field allows storing only integer numbers between the minimum and maximum value of its range, but no text or arbitrary binary data.

Business types extend the behavior of storage types. You can think of them as wrappers around intrinsic types that provide extra behavior. For example, they can constrain the value set offered by the intrinsic type they extend. A good example is the `EmailAddress` business type, which is based on `String`. `EmailAddress` constrains the values you can specify for such a field to the strings that describe valid e-mail addresses. In addition to validation, business types can provide other features such as automatic conversion and masked editing.

 NOTE *Various LightSwitch documentation (mainly that which targets developers), contains different terminology. For example, business types are described as* semantic types *because they provide specific formatting, visualization, and validation for an existing intrinsic type — or, in other words, a* simple data type.

Table 6-1 summarizes the intrinsic field types you can use with your tables, and Table 6-2 describes the business types.

TABLE 6-1: Intrinsic Field Types

NAME	DESCRIPTION
Binary	This type allows you to store arbitrary binary data in the field. This data can be the content of (binary) files, bit arrays used for special purposes, security keys stored in binary format, and so on. If you plan to store photos or pictures in your database, use the `Image` type (see Table 6-2), which provides a better way of doing so.
Boolean	This type is ideal for storing flags, as it can have two values: `True` (Yes) or `False` (No). The value is generally used in business logic to branch execution flow according to the value of a `Boolean` field. Another frequent application is filtering — for example, how the `Active` field of the `TimeCategory` table will be used. This type of field is very often bound with a check box in the UI.
	Avoid using this field to represent any values that have only two states. For example, don't use it to represent a gender field with values such as Male or Female. Use this type where the True/False or Yes/No semantics describe the field's usage.
DateTime	This type stores a date and a time between 00:00:00 January 1, 0001 A.D. (C.E.) and 23:59:59 December 31, 9999 A.D. (C.E.), with the accuracy of about 1 millisecond (ms). Use this type when you need to handle the time within a day. Examples include login time, last modification, and delivery time.

NAME	DESCRIPTION
Decimal	This type stores a fixed decimal-point value with up to 38 significant digits. Such a value is stored with a specific precision (i.e., number of significant digits) and scale (i.e., number of digits after the decimal point). A Decimal value is suitable for financial and monetary operations because basic operations applied with it handle rounding rules according to the specified scale.
Double	A Double type stores a floating decimal-point value with about 15- to 16-digit precision. The values can be between ±1.0e−28 to ±7.9e28. Use this type for scientific calculations.
Short Integer	This type stores a 16-bit unsigned integer between -32,768 and 32,767.
Integer	This type stores a 32-bit unsigned integer between -2,147,483,648 and 2,147,483,647. This integer type is suitable for most purposes.
Long Integer	This type stores a 64-bit unsigned integer between -9,223,372,036,854,775,808 and 9,223,372,036,854,775,807. Use this type only when you need to work with extra-large integers.
String	A String type stores a variable-length character string, or a sequence of zero or more Unicode characters. You can use this type to store any kind of text — from a simple character to very long text (up to 2,147,483,647 characters in length).

TABLE 6-2: Business Field Types

NAME	DESCRIPTION
Date	This type stores a date between January 1, 0001 A.D. (C.E.) and December 31, 9999 A.D. (C.E.). Use this type where only a date is needed, not the specific time within a day. Examples include a shipping date, publication date, or birth date. This type is based on DateTime but is treated as a date only. LightSwitch truncates any time portion.
EmailAddress	This type represents a String treated as an e-mail address.
Image	This type represents a Binary treated as an image. The default output of this field is the image described by the binary data behind the field.
Money	Money is based on Decimal, and it is treated as a monetary value.
PhoneNumber	This type represents a String treated as a phone number.

You are not constrained to using only the business types listed in Table 6-2. LightSwitch provides an extensibility mechanism that makes it easy to add your own business types (for example, ISBN, Social Security Number, bank account number, and so on) to your applications.

Table and Field Properties

When designing a table, you have much more influence on the behavior of the table than simply setting field names and types, and declaring whether a certain field is required. Using the Properties window, you can set up several properties to define more sophisticated behavior of the business logic and screens based on your tables.

The `TimeCategory` table you designed earlier in this chapter has two string-typed fields, `DisplayName` and `Description`. In the real world, strings in a database usually have a maximum length defined to constrain the size of input that users can enter. Using the Properties window, you can set this length, as well as other important attributes of a table and its fields. The following "Try It Out" exercise demonstrates how.

TRY IT OUT Setting Up TimeCategory Properties

To change the properties of the `TimeCategory` table, follow these steps:

1. Double-click the `TimeCategories` node in Solution Explorer to display the `TimeCategory` table in the Designer. Click the header of the table. The Properties window (located beneath Solution Explorer) shows the properties of the `TimeCategory` table, as shown in Figure 6-7. If the Properties window is not visible, select View ⇨ Properties Window, or press F4 to display it.

2. Properties are organized into categories. Figure 6-7 shows that the `TimeCategory` table has two categories, General and Appearance. By clicking the small triangle to the left of the category names, you can collapse or expand category panels. The top of the Properties window contains a drop-down list of elements displayed in the Designer. Click the drop-down arrow of this list to view the entries for the `TimeCategory` table and its fields, as shown in Figure 6-8. Select the `DisplayName` field to set up its properties.

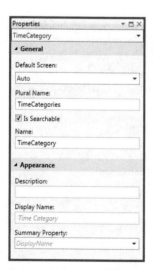

FIGURE 6-7: TimeCategory table properties displayed in the Properties window

FIGURE 6-8: List of TimeCategory table fields in the Properties window

3. Check the "Include in Unique Index" flag at the top of the Properties window. This flag signifies that the `DisplayName` field of a time category must be unique, so you cannot add two entries with the same `DisplayName` value.

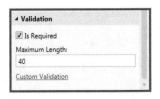

4. Scroll down to the Validation category in the Properties window. Change the Maximum Length property value from 255 (this is the default when you add a new string field) to 40, as shown in Figure 6-9. This change specifies that `DisplayName` cannot be longer than 40 characters.

FIGURE 6-9: Changing the Maximum Length property

5. In the Designer, click the small rectangular header of the `Description` row (to the left of the Description text). This is an alternative way to select the element in the Properties window. By doing this, you display the `Description` properties. Scroll down to the Validation category and set the Maximum Length property to 1000. This setting now specifies that the optional description of a time category entry can be up to 1,000 characters.

> **NOTE** *You may find the complete code to download for this exercise on this book's companion website at* www.wrox.com *in the folder* Chapter 06\ Sample 1 - Creating a Table.

How It Works

LightSwitch creates your database so that it will store the `DisplayName` and `Description` values with the specified maximum length. When you create screens, the related input fields won't let you type more characters than the number specified by these values. `DisplayName` is also marked as a unique field. If you enter two items with the same `DisplayName` value, LightSwitch won't save them.

You can set several properties of tables and fields. Table 6-3 describes table properties.

TABLE 6-3: Common Table Properties

PROPERTY	DESCRIPTION
Default Screen	Using the options available in this list, you can select the screen to be used as the default details screen for this table. When you click the summary links of a table, the default details screen is displayed.
Plural Name	Several objects related to the table (such as the object representing a query that retrieves all records from the table) use the plural form of the table name. LightSwitch automatically pluralizes the table name you specify; but if you don't like it, this property enables you to override that name.
Is Searchable	Setting this flag instructs LightSwitch that the table (and all its string fields by default) is searchable. It automatically provides a search box in list views.
Name	This is the name you assigned to the table.

continues

TABLE 6-3 *(continued)*

PROPERTY	DESCRIPTION
Description	You can assign a description to the table, helping you and the development team to remember the role of the table in the application.
Display Name	This is a user-friendly name for the table. When LightSwitch displays the table name in your application, this is the name that is used. It may contain spaces and other characters that are not allowed in table names.
Summary Property	You can select one of the fields of the property as a summary property, which is used to represent a record of the table when displaying its contents on the screen. For example, in the case of the `TimeCategory` table, the summary property is the `DisplayName` field.

Fields have several common properties, as summarized in Table 6-4. Some of them are available as values to set in the Properties window, while others are task links that display dialogs to set up the property value, or redirect you to code files to write code.

TABLE 6-4: Common Field Properties

PROPERTY	DESCRIPTION
Include in Unique Index	Signifies that the value of this field must be unique in the table. Setting this flag prevents you from entering more than one entry with the same field value.
Is Computed	LightSwitch allows you to create computed properties that are calculated from other fields. When this check box is set, the property is a computed one. For example, you can create a `FullName` computed property from `FirstName` and `LastName` fields.
Name	This is the name of the field, as set in the Name column of the table Designer.
Choice List	This task list activates a dialog in which you can create a list of options (generally represented as a drop-down list in screens) to use to select a value for the field. In this dialog, you can set up display names associated with values. When your application runs, the display names appear in a drop-down list. LightSwitch takes care of storing the associated value of the item selected by its display name.
	For example, instead of displaying values 1, 2, or 3, you can set up a choice list with display names "One," "Two," and "Three" associated with the numeric values, respectively.
Description	You can assign a description to the field, helping you and the development team to remember the role of the field in the application.
Display Name	This is a user-friendly name for the field. When LightSwitch displays the field name in your application, this is the name that is used. It may contain spaces and other characters that are not allowed in field names.

PROPERTY	DESCRIPTION
Display by Default	This flag indicates whether the field is visible on related screens by default. If this box is selected, any time you add a new screen, the field is added to the layout. Uncheck this flag for fields that are used as utility or status fields that you intend to conceal from users.
Is Required	This property is the same as the one you can set in the Required column of the table Designer. It defines whether the field must have a value.
Custom Validation	This task link redirects to the code file of the entity wrapping your table. In the code file, you can write your own custom validation code to check whether this field's value conforms to the application's rules.

Table 6-5 summarizes the specific properties of `String` fields.

TABLE 6-5: String Field Specific Properties

PROPERTY	DESCRIPTION
Is Searchable	Setting this flag instructs LightSwitch that the field is searchable. When information is entered in the search box of a screen, this field will be involved in the search.
Maximum Length	This property defines the maximum length of the string that can be stored in the field. Input controls associated with the field will not allow entering more characters than the value specified here. You can use values between 1 and 2,147,483,647.

There are many field types (such as `Date`, `DateTime`, `Decimal`, `Double`, `Short Integer`, `Integer`, `Long Integer`, and `Money`) that enable you to define the range of valid values. Table 6-6 describes the properties that define the valid range.

TABLE 6-6: Field Range Properties

PROPERTY	DESCRIPTION
Minimum Value	Defines the lower bound of the value range. The field's value must be greater than or equal to this value.
Maximum Value	Defines the upper bound of the value range. The field's value must be less than or equal to this value.

`Decimal` and `Money` types use fixed-point decimal numbers. You can configure their accuracy and number of significant digits with the properties summarized in Table 6-7.

TABLE 6-7: Decimal-Specific Properties

PROPERTY	DESCRIPTION
Precision	This property shows the number of significant decimal digits for the number stored by the field. The value must be between 1 and 38. The number of decimal digits is the number of digits preceding the decimal point, plus the number of digits following the decimal point.
Scale	This property specifies the number of digits after the decimal point. This value must be between 0 and 38, and cannot be greater than the Precision value.

For example, if Precision is 6 and Scale is 2, you can store values up to $999.99, and the value 87.128 is represented as $87.13.

Business types have several additional properties. These provide you with a range of customization options to set up the validation, conversion, and formatting behavior of fields. Table 6-8 summarizes these properties.

TABLE 6-8: Business Type Specific Properties

TYPE	PROPERTY	DESCRIPTION
EmailAddress	Default Email Domain	Specifies the default e-mail domain. It is used when the user does not provide a domain name. For example, if all employees have the same e-mail domain, you can specify that e-mail domain here.
	Require Email Domain	This check box specifies whether the e-mail address must have an e-mail domain. If this is not the case, deselect this check box. If you do not require an e-mail domain, then you must specify a default value in the Default Email Domain property.
Money	Currency Code	Specifies the currency code to be used. For example, if your currency is listed in United States dollars, enter USD here. For Euro, use EUR.
	Decimal Places	Specifies the number of decimal digits to display. For example, if you enter 2, two digits will be displayed after the decimal point. The Scale property determines how many decimal digits are used for money operations (such as rounding). Decimal Places is used only for displaying the value.

TYPE	PROPERTY	DESCRIPTION
	Is Formatted	Select this check box if you want to display the value as monetary value (using currency symbol, digit grouping separator, and custom decimal digits). In this case, modify the Symbol Mode, Is Grouped, and Decimal Digits properties to define the display format.
	Is Grouped	Select this check box if you want to display a digit grouping separator. For example, if this check box is selected, a monetary value will display as 1,234,567.89, rather than 1234567.89.
	Symbol Mode	This property specifies whether to display the currency symbol. You can select the available options from this drop-down list. To display the currency symbol, select either Currency Symbol or ISO Currency Symbol. To not display it, select No Currency Symbol.
PhoneNumber	Phone Number Formats	This task link opens the Phone Number Formats dialog. Here you can specify how you want to validate and display phone numbers. You specify the format for the phone number using the letter C for country code, A for area or city code, and N for local number, and any symbols that are currently used to display phone numbers, such as +, −, (,) , . , and spaces. The list allows you to add more than one format. When entering a phone number, LightSwitch first tries to validate against the first format in the list. If the digits match the format, then the phone number is displayed in that manner. Otherwise, LightSwitch tries to validate against the remaining formats in the list until a match is found.

CREATING SCREENS

Using traditional design tools, creating several screens to list, search, and modify data is a much more laborious and resource-consuming job than creating data tables. This is especially true when you follow the three-tier application architecture pattern — namely, you must create a large amount of plumbing code to bind the tiers. RAD tools make this process much easier and less time-consuming.

With Visual Studio LightSwitch, it's even simpler. LightSwitch utilizes the table and field properties you provided at design time, and enables you to create a set of screens in just a few minutes.

In this section, you add screens to the `TimeCategory` table and learn the basics of LightSwitch screen management.

The Add New Screen Dialog

You have several options when you decide to add screens to your project. You can start from Solution Explorer by right-clicking the `Screens` folder and selecting Add Screen from the context menu. Another option is to select Project ➪ Add Screen, or you can use the Screen toolbar button when a table is open in the Designer.

Whichever technique you use, the Add New Screen dialog appears, as shown in Figure 6-10. This simple dialog performs the lion's share of the work when you create a screen.

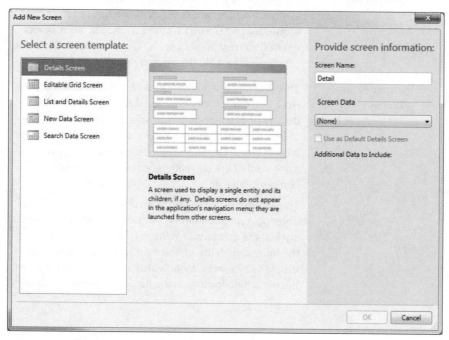

FIGURE 6-10: The Add New Screen dialog

The list on the left of the dialog displays the available screen templates from which you can choose. Your new screen will be based on this template. In the middle area of the dialog is a short description of the selected template, as well as a draft (wireframe) of the screen. In the panel on the right side of the dialog, you can provide information, such as the name of the screen and the data you intend to display or edit.

Predefined Screen Types

Several screen templates are installed with Visual Studio LightSwitch. These provide you with a great starting point for your simple applications. Table 6-9 summarizes the out-of-the-box templates provided with LightSwitch.

TABLE 6-9: LightSwitch Screen Templates

TEMPLATE	DESCRIPTION
New Data Screen	This type of screen is used to create a new data-entry UI.
Search Data Screen	This template enables you to search for data in a table (or return data from a query, as you will learn later).
Details Screen	This template is used to display a single entity. The Details screen does not appear in the application's navigation menu; it is launched from other screens.
Editable Grid Screen	This template provides you with a grid you can use to display and edit records.
List and Details Screen	This template displays a list of items and details for the item selected in the list.

TRY IT OUT   Creating a Search Screen for TimeCategory

To create a search screen for the `TimeCategory` table, follow these steps:

1. Use the Project ➪ Add Screen command to launch the Add New Screen dialog. Select the Search Data Screen template, and choose the `TimeCategories` item from the Screen Data drop-down list. The Screen Name is set to `SearchTimeCategories`. Click OK. LightSwitch generates the screen layout and displays it in the Designer.

2. Press F5 to start the application. When the `ProjectTrek` application starts, it shows the `SearchTimeCategories` screen using the Search Time Categories title. It's empty, so you cannot try the search functionality. Close the application.

   Somehow you need to add new records to this table. LightSwitch can generate default screens for adding a new item or editing an existing one on-the-fly. You can change the layout of the screen to make these default screens available.

3. Expand the Time Categories `Data Grid` node and select the `Command Bar` node; expand it. Using the Add button, extend the command bar with the `AddAndEditNew` button, as shown in Figure 6-11. When the button is added, its text changes to Add..., as shown in Figure 6-11.

4. Add two more buttons to `Command Bar`, `EditSelected`, and `DeleteSelected`. Figure 6-12 shows the layout with the three new buttons added.

5. Press F5 to launch `ProjectTrek`. When the Search Time Categories screen appears, you can see icons representing the new buttons in

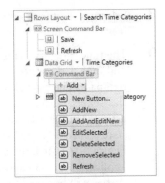

FIGURE 6-11: Adding the Save button to the screen command bar

FIGURE 6-12: The command bar of DataGrid after adding three new buttons

the command bar. Click the Add... button and a new pop-up dialog appears. Here you can add a new time category entry. Type **Normal** in the `DisplayName` field, as shown in Figure 6-13. Type **Working days, 9AM-5PM** in the `Description` field. Finally, click the `Active` check box and click OK.

FIGURE 6-13: LightSwitch generates a screen for adding new records

6. Add three more active time categories with the following display names and descriptions, respectively:

➤ *Overtime* — "Working days, out of the 9am-5pm window"

➤ *Weekend* — "Weekend, any time"

➤ *Test* — "Test"

7. Select the Weekend entry and click the pencil icon representing the Edit... button on the command bar. The application will display a default Edit dialog that has a similar layout as the default Add dialog. Change the description to "Weekend or holiday, any time."

8. Select the Test entry and click the X icon representing the Delete button on the command bar. The Test entry will be removed from the list.

9. The time category items you have added and modified are not yet saved to the database. The asterisk in the header tab of the `SearchTimeCategory` screen and the asterisks in the grid row headers signal this state (called a "dirty" state), as shown in Figure 6-14. Click the Save button in the application's command bar, and the new entries will be saved to the database.

FIGURE 6-14: The modified records have not yet been saved

10. Click the search box of the screen. Type **me** and press Enter. The list will be filtered to only those records that match the "me" criterion. Figure 6-15 shows that the Overtime and Weekend entries are matches. The first entry contains "me" in the `TimeCategory` column, and the second one in the `Description` column, as shown in Figure 6-15.

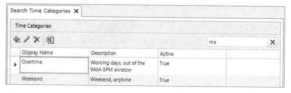

FIGURE 6-15: Search results

11. Close the application.

> **NOTE** *You may find the complete code to download for this exercise on this book's companion website at* www.wrox.com *in the folder* Chapter 06\ Sample 2 - Creating a Screen.

How It Works

The buttons you added in Steps 3 and 4 are associated with commands, as their names suggest. Because you didn't explicitly define screens for adding and editing records, LightSwitch generated these screens on-the-fly.

Modifications are first saved in the application's memory, and are persisted into the back-end database only when you explicitly save them.

The search for "me" looked for this pattern in both the `DisplayName` and `Description` fields because both of them were marked as searchable when you designed the `TimeCategory` table.

The Layout Structure of a Screen

In the previous "Try It Out" exercise, you modified the default search screen layout with a few clicks a couple of times. This section looks at how LightSwitch handles the layout of screens.

 NOTE *Most RAD tools can create screens for you, too. However, the majority of them create a layout with exactly positioned UI elements, including labels, controls, containers, and adornments. LightSwitch uses a totally separate — and more flexible — approach.*

The screen Designer displays two hierarchies when you edit the UI of a screen. On the left side is the hierarchy of *data item*s. On the right side, you can work with the hierarchy of *layout item*s, as shown in Figure 6-16.

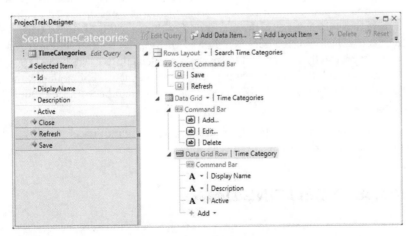

FIGURE 6-16: The structure of the screen Designer

These hierarchies represent the embedding or containment of elements. For example, the `DisplayName` data item is embedded in `Selected Item`, which is contained in the `TimeCategoryCollection` query. Similarly, the `Save` and `Refresh` Shell Button layout elements are embedded in the `Screen Command Bar` layout element.

Data elements describe those components that represent data — bound to either data in the database or data used locally in the screen. Layout elements describe the constituting parts of the UI. The header of the Designer contains the name of the screen (`SearchTimeCategories`, in the case of the example), and has a number of toolbar buttons, as summarized in Table 6-10.

TABLE 6-10: Screen Designer Toolbar Elements

TOOLBAR ELEMENT	DESCRIPTION
Edit Query	You can use this button to modify the default query behind the screen. For example, you can filter and sort records.
Add Data Item	With this command, you can add new items to the data item hierarchy.
Add Layout Item	This drop-down list contains the layout elements you can embed in the currently selected control of the layout hierarchy. Select one from the list to add it to the UI.
Delete	This deletes the selected data or layout item. If you click Delete by accident, you can select Edit ⇨ Undo, or press Ctrl+Z or Alt+Backspace to undo the delete.
Reset	This resets the layout elements to their default state, as determined by the screen template.
Write Code	This is a drop-down list of methods for which you can write custom code.

The Designer binds the elements of the data hierarchy with the elements of the layout hierarchy. At runtime, as a result of this binding, a data element retrieved from the database is displayed in all layout controls to which it is bound. Conversely, if the user modifies the data (for example, edits a text), the modified content is put back into the data item bound with the UI control. In Figure 6-16, you can see that the layout hierarchy elements indicate the data element they are bound to (that is, they are separated by a vertical line from the type of the layout element). For example, the `DisplayName` data item (on the left) is bound to the Display Name layout item beneath the Time Category `Data Grid Row` item.

Data elements can be bound to other data elements, too. Right now you might not see why this would be useful, but you will learn about this later in the chapter.

INSERTING, EDITING, AND DELETING DATA

As you learned earlier in this chapter, LightSwitch generates a screen to add and edit new `TimeCategory` items on-the-fly. While these defaults are a great feature, in many cases you may want to change the default screens. In this section, you learn how you can add your own screens to add and edit new items.

Creating a Details Screen

You might have noticed something interesting in the last "Try It Out" exercise. After you saved the `TimeCategory` modifications, the first column (Display Name) changed to a hyperlink, as shown in Figure 6-17.

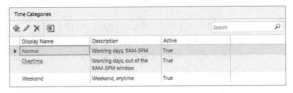

FIGURE 6-17: The summary column is represented as a link

When you click this link, a new screen pops up, where you can edit details for the `TimeCategory` entry. However, this screen is not the same as the one you access with the Edit... button in the toolbar. It is not a pop-up screen, as Figure 6-18 shows.

FIGURE 6-18: Default edit screen for a time category entry

Although it is great that LightSwitch creates this screen for you, it does have two issues to deal with. First, it displays the `Id` field, which is best hidden from users. Second, the `Description` field may contain up to 1,000 characters, so leaving a simple text box would not provide space to edit such a long entry.

Let's create a new edit screen that is free of these issues.

TRY IT OUT   Creating a New Details Screen for TimeCategory

To create the new details screen, follow these steps:

1. Right-click the `Screens` node in Solution Explorer and select Add Screen from the context menu. In the Add New Screen dialog, select the Details Screen template, and then select `TimeCategory` from the Screen Data drop-down list. The Screen Name changes to `TimeCategoryDetail`. The "Use as Default Details Screen" check box and the TimeCategory Details check box (located under the "Additional Data to Include" label) are checked. Click OK.

2. The screen is displayed in the Designer. Click the root `Rows Layout` node. Then, in the Properties window, scroll down to the bottom and change the Label Position property to Top, as shown in Figure 6-19.

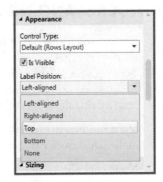

FIGURE 6-19: Changing the Label Position property

3. In the layout Designer, click the `Description` text box. Then, in the Properties window, scroll down to the bottom, click the Lines option and change its value from 1 to 5.

4. Press F5 to launch ProjectTrek. When the Search Time Categories screen is displayed, click the Overtime link in the first column. Your new detail screen is displayed, as shown in Figure 6-20.

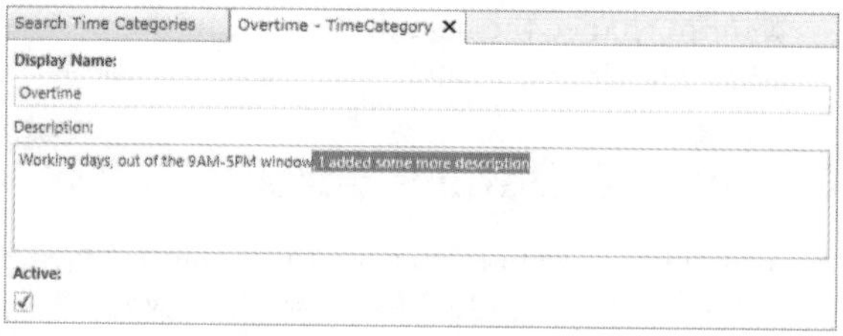

5. Edit the description of the entry. For example, add or remove some text. Press Tab and click Save on the application toolbar.

FIGURE 6-20: The new TimeCategory detail screen

6. Click the close (X) icon in the tab of the detail screen to close it. Note that the details of the Overtime entry in the Search Time Categories screen are not refreshed. Click the Refresh button on the application toolbar to see the modifications you've made in the detail screen.

7. Close the ProjectTrek application.

How It Works

Because you checked the "Use as Default Details Screen" option in Step 1, LightSwitch displays this screen when you click the link of any item in the SearchTimeCategories screen. The TimeCategoryDetail screen is autonomous; its state is totally independent from SearchTimeCategories. Therefore, when you change data in the details screen, it won't be refreshed in the list of the search screen. This is not a bug; it is by design.

You can still use the Edit... button in the toolbar of the search screen, and it still displays the modal details screen that is generated on-the-fly. This modal screen belongs to the search screen and shares its state, so changes made there are automatically refreshed in SearchTimeCategory.

UNDERSTANDING HOW THE DETAIL SCREEN WORKS

Earlier, you learned that screens have data and layout elements. In Figure 6-16, the root data element is TimeCategories, which is a query retrieving a set (zero, one, or more items) of TimeCategory data entities from the back-end database. The Edit Query task link to the right of TimeCategories indicates that you can modify this query to retrieve a constrained or ordered result set. (By default, it gets all TimeCategory records.)

Open the TimeCategoryDetail screen in the Designer, and click the Id element under Query Parameters in the data layout panel, as shown in Figure 6-21. An arrow points to another Id element.

Now, click the TimeCategoryId element to which the arrow points. This element is a parameter of the screen, as indicated by the checked Is Parameter check box in Figure 6-22. You can also see that its type is Integer, which allows the caller of the TimeCategoryDetail screen to pass a 32-bit integer when displaying this screen.

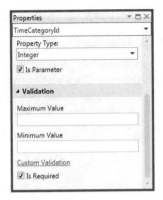

FIGURE 6-21: Default edit screen for a TimeCategory entry

FIGURE 6-22: Properties of the Id parameter

> **NOTE** *Here is a short explanation to help you understand how the parameterized query is used to obtain time category details from the database. Assume that, in the search screen, you click the "Overtime" item. The identifier of this item is 2 in the database. As you click "Overtime," the detail screen is started and 2 is passed as the* `TimeCategoryId` *parameter of the screen. When the screen opens, 2 is passed to the* `Id` *parameter of query behind the screen. The query uses 2 to read the details of the time category item with this identifier from the database, and it results in the details of "Overtime." In Chapter 7 you will learn more about queries and parameters.*

The binding between the `Id` query parameter and the `Id` screen parameter (represented by the arrow) means that the query uses the parameter passed to the screen. The detail screen works as follows:

1. The user selects an entity to edit. The unique identifier (primary key) of the entity is passed to the detail screen, which accepts it in its `Id` parameter.

2. The detail screen starts a parameterized query that retrieves a single record from the database. The query uses the parameter passed to the detail screen.

3. When the query retrieves the single record (assuming there is a record with the specified identifier at all), the entity data is bound to the visual elements of the screen.

4. The user modifies the data. Data binding enables the modifications to be saved to the entity behind the detail screen.

5. The Save command is invoked (either by the user or programmatically), and the entity behind the detail screen is saved back to the database.

Creating a New Data Screen

You can create your own screen for adding a new `TimeCategory` entry with a few steps, similar to how you created a detail screen.

Creating a New Data Screen for TimeCategory

To create the new data screen, follow these steps:

1. Right-click the `Screens` node in Solution Explorer and select Add Screen from the context menu. In the Add New Screen dialog, select the New Data Screen template, and then select `TimeCategory` from the Screen Data drop-down list. The Screen Name changes to `CreateNewTimeCategory`. Check the TimeCategory Details option, and then click OK.

2. The new data screen layout is displayed in the Designer. Press F5 to run the application. Click Create New Time Category in the Tasks menu. The new dialog to add a `TimeCategory` entry is displayed, as shown in Figure 6-23.

FIGURE 6-23: The new data screen to add a TimeCategory entry

3. Type some text into the `DisplayName` and `Description` text boxes, and then click Save in the application toolbar. The new `TimeCategory` data is immediately saved into the database and the `TimeCategoryDetail` screen is displayed so that you can edit the properties of the new `TimeCategory` entry you added.

4. Close the application.

How It Works

The new data screen has a very similar layout hierarchy as the detail screen. However, its data items are different, as shown in Figure 6-24.

The `TimeCategoryProperty` data item is a simple property holding the attributes of a `TimeCategory` entry, and each item is bound to the corresponding layout element. When you enter the data, input values are written back to the `TimeCategoryProperty` elements. When you click Save, the data is simply added to the database.

The new data screens are generated such that after the Save operation, they display the default detail screen. If you would like to change this behavior, you can do so by modifying the code behind the data screen — as you will learn later.

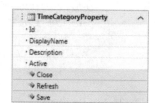

FIGURE 6-24: Data items of the CreateNewTimeCategory screen

Creating an Editable Grid Screen

Although you have created a search screen, a detail screen, and a new data screen, a few issues still need to be resolved:

➤ When you click the Add... or Edit... buttons in the `SearchTimeCategory` screen, they still display the default modal screens for adding or editing an entry, respectively.

➤ The Active field displays True and False text instead of a check box.

➤ `CreateNewTimeCategory` can be accessed in the Tasks menu, but it would be better to display it as a pop-up after the Add... toolbar button is clicked.

These issues can be fixed quite easily. The `TimeCategory` table can be maintained with a grid. The table has only three columns, and during the lifetime of `ProjectTrek`, it will contain only a few rows (probably less than a dozen). Instead of using several screens, you can create a single one — an editable grid screen, as demonstrated in the following activity.

TRY IT OUT Creating an Editable Grid Screen for the TimeCategory Table

To create an editable grid screen, follow these steps:

1. Click the `CreateNewTimeCategory` node in Solution Explorer and press Delete. Visual Studio pops up a confirmation screen asking whether you really want to remove all associated code with the screen to be deleted. Click OK. The screen will be immediately deleted from your project.

2. Repeat Step 1 to delete the `SearchTimeCategories` screen, and then delete `TimeCategoryDetail`.

3. The `ProjectTrek` application now has no screens. Right-click the `Screens` node in Solution Explorer and then click Add Screen in the context menu. When the Add New Screen dialog appears, choose the Editable Grid Screen template. Select `TimeCategories` from the Screen Data drop-down list and click OK.

4. After the IDE creates the screen layout, expand the command bar beneath the `Data Grid` node. Right-click the Add... button and choose Delete from the context menu to remove this button, as shown in Figure 6-25.

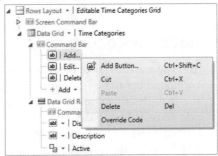

5. Repeat Step 4 to remove the Edit... button from the command bar.

6. Click the Description text box; and in the Properties window, set the Lines property (located at the bottom) to 3.

FIGURE 6-25: Removing the Add button from the command bar

7. Press F5 to run the application.

8. When the Editable Time Categories Grid screen is displayed, try to edit an existing record.

    You can click the Active check box to enable/disable its state, or double-click in text cells to modify their contents. Within the Description cells, you can use the Enter key to start a new line. Double-click any cell of the last row (it contains only empty cells) to add a new time category entry. Figure 6-26 shows this screen in action.

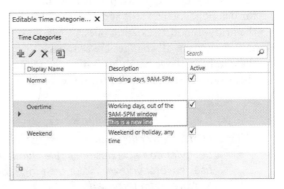

FIGURE 6-26: EditableTimeCategoryGrid in action

> **NOTE** *You may find the complete code to download for this exercise on this book's companion website at* www.wrox.com *in the folder* Chapter 06\ Sample 3 - Editable Grid Screen.

How It Works

The Add... and Edit... buttons added by default to the editable grid screen provide modal dialogs to add and modify records in the grid, respectively. You don't need these screens, however, which is why you deleted them here.

Setting the Rows property of Description to 3 lets you display three lines of text in the grid, and to use the Enter key when working within a cell.

Working with a separate search screen and detail screen to edit table data is not really straightforward, because you must use two screens simultaneously. With an editable data grid, you can work very similarly as with an Excel worksheet. You can use the mouse clicks, arrow keys, Tab, Enter, and Delete, just like you do when working with Excel.

Deleting a Record

You can use the Delete button on the command bar to delete any row from the grid. Deleting a row does not delete the related record from the database immediately; it only marks it on the client side for deletion. A small icon indicates that the record is to be removed, as shown in Figure 6-27 (to the left of the Special entry).

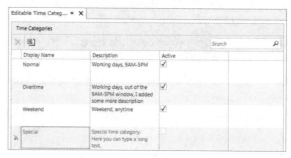

FIGURE 6-27: Deleted entry is marked with an icon

Although you cannot modify the row marked for deletion, you can still add new rows to the grid, or modify existing ones. When you save the screen, all changes are sent back to the database in one batch, including the new and modified records. The records you deleted on the client side are then removed from the database.

> **NOTE** *Currently, you can delete any time category entries from the grid. This behavior can hurt business rules (you may delete a time category entry still in use), so later you will make a change that restricts removal to only those entries that are not referenced.*

POLISHING

The `EditableTimeCategoriesGrid` screen seems like an appropriate one to use to maintain the time category entries in the `ProjectTrek` application. It works as expected, and changing a few field title would it make more intuitive.

Finalizing the EditableTimeCategeory Screen

With a few changes, you can alter the `EditableTimeCategoriesGrid` screen it so that it will take its final form.

TRY IT OUT   Finalizing the Editable Grid Screen

To establish the final form of the `EditableTimeCategory` screen, follow these steps:

1. Double-click `TimeCategories` in Solution Explorer to open this table in the Designer.

2. Select the `DisplayName` field and change its Display Name property to `Category`.

3. Select the `Active` field and change its Display Name property to `Active?` in the Properties window.

4. While the `Active` field is selected, click Choice List in the Properties window. The Choice List dialog opens. Click the Add Value cell and type **True**. Press Tab and type **Yes**. Then press Tab again. Similarly, add the "False" value with the "No" display name as the second row of the choice list, as shown in Figure 6-28. Click OK to close the dialog.

5. Save your changes by pressing Ctrl+S.

6. Double-click `EditableTimeCategoriesGrid` in Solution Explorer to open it in the Designer.

7. Change the Display Name of the root `Rows Layout` element layout item to `Maintain Time Categories`.

8. Change the Display Name of the `Data Grid` element layout item to `List of Time Categories`.

9. Press F5 to run the application. The effect of these changes is shown in Figure 6-29. As you see, the title (tab) of the screen is changed to Maintain Time Categories, and you can also see that the column headers are changed according to Step 2 and Step 3.

FIGURE 6-28: The Choice List dialog

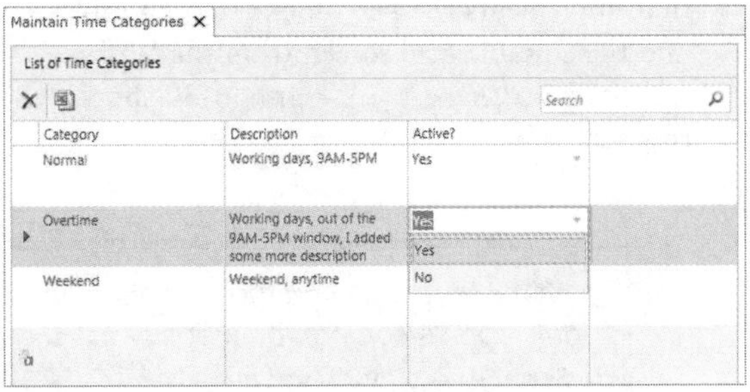

FIGURE 6-29: The final polished form of the EditableTimeCategoriesGrid

How It Works

The changes you made in the table Designer are automatically used in the screen layout. The layout items in the screen use the default control type. When you added a choice list to the `Active` field, the default control for the `Active` data grid item automatically changed to a combo box.

Implementing the ProjectRoleType Entity

The `ProjectTrek` application uses a table named `ProjectRoleType` to maintain the roles that team members can have in ConsulArt's projects. This table has exactly the same semantics as the `TimeCategory` table you worked with earlier in this chapter. By now, you have learned how to create a table and simple screens by yourself.

Use the knowledge you gained in this chapter to create the `ProjectRoleType` table and an editable grid screen to maintain it. You won't be provided with detailed step-by-step information to solve this task; instead, you can use what you learned in this chapter's exercises.

To create the table and the screen, follow these general steps:

1. Add the `ProjectRoleType` table to the project with the same fields as `TimeCategory`. Don't forget to set the maximum length of string fields.

2. Set up the Display Name properties of fields, and add a choice list to the `Active` field.

3. Create an editable grid for the `ProjectRoleType` table, and set up its layout elements.

4. Run the application and add several records to the grid.

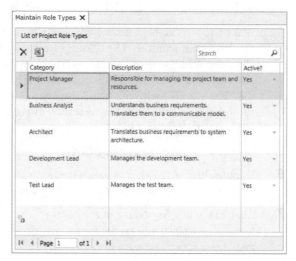

If you don't have time to carry out these tasks, you can download the source code that implements the `ProjectRoleType` table and the editable grid screen from the Wrox website (www.wrox.com). Figure 6-30 shows this screen in action.

FIGURE 6-30: The new screen maintaining project role types

 NOTE *You may find the complete code to download for this chapter on this book's companion website at* www.wrox.com *in the folder* Chapter 06\
Sample 4 - Polishing.

SUMMARY

With just a few clicks of your mouse, you can create new tables and add them to your LightSwitch project. In the table Designer, you can easily add fields by setting up their names and types, and specifying whether they require a value. LightSwitch provides a few simple types out-of-the-box (such as integers, decimals, floating-point numbers, strings, dates, Booleans, and so on). You can also use business types that wrap simple types to define additional behavior (such as the `EmailAddress`, `Money`, `Image`, and `PhoneNumber` types).

With the Add New Screen dialog, you can create screens in seconds. You select a screen template in the dialog (such as the New Data Screen, Search Data Screen, and so on), specify the data to be displayed, and LightSwitch creates the screen for you. Instead of creating a layout with exactly (absolutely) positioned UI elements, LightSwitch generates a data item hierarchy and a layout hierarchy to define the screen, and establishes bindings between data and layout items.

The table and screen Designers enable you to customize items with many attributes that you can set in the Properties window.

In Chapter 7 you take another a step. You will learn about creating tables with a master-detail relationship and creating screens built upon them.

EXERCISES

1. List several ways to start the process of creating a table.

2. Which field property influences the number of characters stored for `String` fields?

3. What is the difference between intrinsic field types and business field types?

4. Which ones of the following screen types have no query behind them?

➤ Details Screen

➤ Search Screen

➤ New Data Screen

➤ Editable Grid Screen

5. How can you define a layout element so that the user can select a value from a predefined list?

 NOTE *Answers to the Exercises can be found in the Appendix.*

▶ **WHAT YOU LEARNED IN THIS CHAPTER**

TOPIC	KEY CONCEPTS
Creating a project	Use the File ⇨ New Project command (also available by pressing the Ctrl+Shift+N shortcut key), or click the New Project link in the Start Page (found directly beneath the program logo).
Designing a table	Use the "Create new table" task in the application Designer right after you create a new project, or right-click the Data Sources node in Solution Explorer and select Add Table from the context menu that appears. Add fields to the table by specifying the name and type of the field. In the Designer, you can select the entire table or an individual field. In the Properties window, you can modify the attributes of the selected object.
Intrinsic field types	Intrinsic types (sometimes called simple data types) reflect physical storage types, such as `Integer`, `String`, `Binary`, `Boolean`, and so on.
Business field types	Business types (sometimes called *semantic types*) extend the behavior of intrinsic field types. They are wrappers around intrinsic types, and provide the capability for extra behavior, such as predefined validation, specialized data entry, and data formatting.
Creating a screen	Click the Screen button in the toolbar while you display a table in the Designer; or right-click the `Screens` folder in Solution Explorer and select the Add Screen command from the context menu.
Add New Screen dialog	You can use this dialog to create a new screen based on the template and data you select. LightSwitch ships with several screen templates (such as New Data Screen, Search Data Screen, Details Screen, Editable Grid Screen, List and Details Screen).
Screen data items	Data elements describe those components of screens that represent data — bound to either data in the database or data used locally in the screen.
Screen layout items	Layout elements describe the constituent parts of the UI. They can be bound to data items. At runtime, as a result of this binding, a data element retrieved from the database is displayed in all layout controls to which it is bound. Conversely, if the user modifies the data (for example, edits text), the modified content is written to the data item bound with the UI control.
Query	Screens that display data coming from the database use queries to retrieve the data, and these queries can have parameters. For example, in detail screens, the identifier of the record to be displayed is passed to the underlying query as a parameter.
Property data item	Screens can have properties that allow passing arguments to them. For example, detail screen receive the identifier of the record to be displayed through a property data item.
Choice list	A choice list allows the user to select a value for a field from a predefined list. In a choice list, values are associated with display names. When the application runs, users can see the display names in a drop-down list. LightSwitch takes care of storing the associated value of the selected item by its display name.

7

Working with Master-Detail Data Screens

WHAT YOU WILL LEARN IN THIS CHAPTER

➤ Understanding detail table relationships

➤ Grasping the essence of master-detail screens

➤ Understanding the role of data and layout items in master-detail screens

➤ Creating and using queries to filter and sort data

➤ Building master-detail screens manually from simple screens

Most data-centric applications work with more than one table, and those tables are related to each other. It is very common for a simple application screen to display data coming from multiple, and related, tables. For example, when you display order information, generally that screen contains an Order record (order date, shipping address, delivery method, and so on) and one or more related OrderDetail records (product, quantity, unit price, tax percentage, full price, and so on).

This kind of screen is called a *master-detail screen*. In this chapter, you will learn how you can manage master-detail screens with Visual Studio LightSwitch. Using the ProjectTrek application, you will create screens using the Project, ProjectTask, AdditionalCost, and CostItem entities, whose relationships are depicted in Figure 7-1.

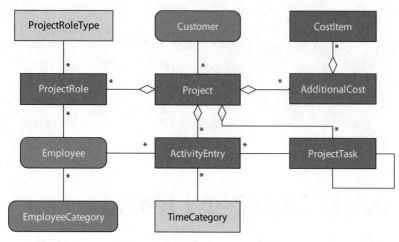

FIGURE 7-1: The entity-relationship diagram of ProjectTrek

The entities stored in this already existing `ConsulArtCRM` database are marked with orange background and rounded corners. The lookup tables (that is, simple tables storing items used in lookups, mostly used in drop-down lists) are shaded with a light blue background. The dark blue background signifies transactional tables containing data that is continuously changing as the application is used.

CREATING DETAIL TABLES

Following are the characteristics of a master-detail relationship (or parent-child relationship) among two tables:

➤ A record in the master (or parent) table has zero, one, or more related records in the detail (or child) table.

➤ Each record in the detail table has exactly one related record in the master table.

The relationship between the `Order` and `OrderDetail` tables is a master-detail relationship. The term *detail table* refers to a table that is on the detail side in a master-detail relationship, so (as its name suggests) `OrderDetail` is a detail table.

Generally, you can only say that a table is a master table or a detail table when you mention the table in the context of a relationship.

Relationships

A *relationship* is an essential concept in data modeling and data-centric applications. It describes how the rows in one table are related to the rows in another table. You can use this concept in regard to tables and entities. In Chapter 5, you learned a few of the basics about this idea, and here you will learn more.

One-to-Many Relationship

The most common type of relationship is the *one-to-many relationship.* This means that the table record on the "one" side has zero, one, or more related instances (or records) on the "many" side, while any record on the "many" side has exactly one record on the "one" side.

In databases, this kind of relationship between tables is implemented so that the table on the "many" side contains a field (called a *foreign key)* that stores the value of the related record's *primary key* (the field that is a unique identifier of the record) on the "one" side. Figure 7-2 shows this relationship between the `Order` and `OrderDetail` tables.

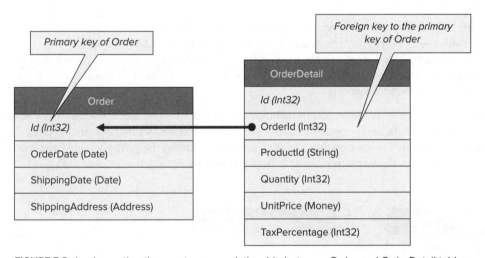

FIGURE 7-2: Implementing the one-to-many relationship between Order and OrderDetail tables

The `OrderId` field of the `OrderDetail` table is a foreign key that contains the `Id` of the `Order` record to which the specific `OrderDetail` belongs.

Many-to-Many Relationship

As its name suggests, in the *many-to-many relationship,* a table record on any side has zero, one, or more related records on the other side. For example, this kind of relationship could exist between `User` and `Group` tables. If a `Group` can involve many `Users`, and a `User` can be a member of more than one `Group`, this is a many-to-many relationship.

In databases, this relationship cannot be resolved with only the two related tables. Also required is a third utility table, which contains a *compound primary key* that is assembled from the two foreign keys that store the values of the primary keys of the related tables, respectively. Figure 7-3 shows the usage of this utility table to connect the `User` and `Group` tables.

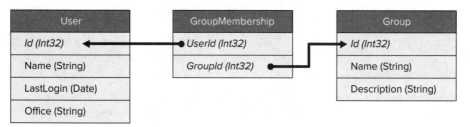

FIGURE 7-3: Implementing the many-to-many relationship between User and Group tables

One-to-One Relationship

A *one-to-one relationship* is most often used to describe an "is a" kind of connection between entities and tables — in other words, a generalization or specialization. For example, if you store Person records in a database, ContactPerson can be a specialized form of Person (for example, it has a phone number and e-mail address in addition to Person). In object-oriented terms, ContactPerson inherits from Person.

As the name suggests, in a one-to-one relationship, a table record on one side has zero or one related record on the other side. In databases, this relationship is implemented so that the primary key of the more-specific table is also a foreign key that stores the value of the primary key of the less-specific table. Figure 7-4 shows the relationship between Person and ContactPerson.

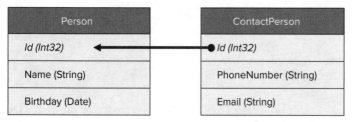

FIGURE 7-4: Implementing the one-to-one relationship between Person and ContactPerson tables

Hierarchies and Self-Referencing Relationships

You can create relationships where the same table is used at both ends of a relation. The most common application of a *self-referencing relationship* is to depict hierarchies, where a table is in a one-to-many relationship with itself. A good example of such a relationship is the ProjectTask table, which can contain child tasks, which also can contain other smaller child tasks, and so on. In databases, these relationships are implemented such that the table contains a foreign key to its own primary key. Figure 7-5 shows this solution for the ProjectTask table.

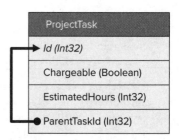

FIGURE 7-5: Implementing the self-referencing relationship of the ProjectTask table

A Few More Things about Relationships

There are more variations of the one-to-many, many-to-many, and one-to-one relationship types between two entities. They can be described formally with the $n_1..m_1:n_2..m_2$ expression. This expression indicates that there are a number of n_1 to m_1 entities on one side of the relationship, and from n_2 to m_2 entities on the other side. Table 7-1 describes a few of these variations, with examples to help you understand them.

TABLE 7-1: Frequently Used Relationships

RELATIONSHIP	EXAMPLE
1:1	For performance reasons, an entity holding information about persons is split into two tables. The `Person` table contains a few attributes of persons used to store search information. `PersonDetails` holds several dozen attributes that are not used in searches. These two tables are in a `1:1` relationship. This means that a `Person` record must have exactly one related record in `PersonDetails`.
1:0..1	The relationship shown in Figure 7-4 between `Person` and `ContactPerson` is such an example. There can be `Person` records that have no related `ContactPerson` records.
1:n	`User` and `EmailAddress` tables have this relationship. A user can have no e-mail address, but each e-mail address must belong to exactly one user.
0..1:n	The self-referencing relationship of the `ProjectTask` table is a good example. All child tasks have exactly one parent task, but there are root task items that do not have parent tasks at all.
1:1..n	`Order` and `OrderDetail` are in such a relationship. Each `OrderDetail` must have exactly one `Order` to which it belongs, and each `Order` must have at least one `OrderDetail` item.

 NOTE *Most relationships are supported by relational database engines declaratively through integrity constraints. However, for a few you must add business logic to constraint declarations to fully implement the relationship. For example, you can declare* 1:1, 1:0..1, 1:n, *and* 0..1:n *relationships, but not the* 1:1..n, *or the generic* $n_1..m_1:n_2..m_2$ *relationship. In these cases, you must declare a wider (more enabling) relationship at the database level, and tighten it with business rules implemented in your application.*

The Add New Relationship Dialog

LightSwitch makes it very easy to create relationships among tables. You have learned about the concept of a foreign key, which plays an essential role in connecting related tables. The LightSwitch table editor takes care of creating and using foreign keys, which makes relationship building a much more intuitive task.

Creating Project-Related Tables

In Chapter 6, you learned how to create tables with the LightSwitch table Designer. In this section, you will use what you learned to create four new tables (namely, `Project`, `ProjectTask`, `AdditionalCost`, and `CostItem`) in order to establish the relationships among them.

TRY IT OUT Creating Tables Related to a Project

 NOTE *In this exercise, you continue the sample that you finished in Chapter 6. You can find the starting sample on this book's companion website at* www .wrox.com *in the folder* Chapter 07\Start.

To create the new tables, follow these steps:

1. Start Visual Studio LightSwitch and open the `ProjectTrek` sample.

2. Add a new table and name it **Project**. Add the fields listed in Table 7-2 to `Project`. Use the number in braces trailing the `String` type to set up the Maximum Length property of the corresponding field. The last column of the table contains a short description about the field. If you want, you can type that text into the Description property of the field, but it isn't necessary. Save the table definition by pressing Ctrl+S.

TABLE 7-2: Fields of the Project Table

NAME	TYPE	REQUIRED	DESCRIPTION
Code	String [16]	Yes	Project code used in ConsulArt reports
Name	String [64]	Yes	Friendly name of the project
Description	String [1000]	No	Optional description of the project
StartDate	Date	Yes	Official date when the project is started
PlannedEndDate	Date	Yes	Planned date when the project is to be completed
PlannedRevenue	Money	Yes	Revenue planned for this project (in U.S. dollars)
Closed	Boolean	Yes	Set to True when the project is closed

3. In the Designer, select the `Code` field. In the Properties window, check the "Include in Unique Index" flag to ensure that each project's code is unique.

4. Add a new table and name it **ProjectTask**. Use the information in Table 7-3 to set up its fields. Save the table definition.

TABLE 7-3: Fields of the ProjectTask Table

NAME	TYPE	REQUIRED	DESCRIPTION
Name	String [64]	Yes	Friendly name of the task
Chargeable	Boolean	Yes	Whether this is a task that can be charged to the customer
EstimatedHours	Integer	Yes	Estimated number of hours to be spent on this task

5. Add the `AdditionalCost` table to the project, and use Table 7-4 to set up its fields. Save the table definition.

TABLE 7-4: Fields of the AdditionalCost Table

NAME	TYPE	REQUIRED	DESCRIPTION
Name	String [64]	Yes	Friendly name of the cost category
Description	String [1000]	No	Optional description of the cost category
Amount	Money	Yes	Money allocated for this cost category (in U.S. dollars)

6. Add the `CostItem` table to the project, and use Table 7-5 to set up its fields. Save the table definition.

TABLE 7-5: Fields of the CostItem Table

NAME	TYPE	REQUIRED	DESCRIPTION
Name	String [64]	Yes	Friendly name of the cost item
Amount	Money	Yes	Money spent for this cost item (in U.S. dollars)

 NOTE *You may find the complete code to download for this exercise on this book's companion website at* www.wrox.com *in the folder* Chapter 07\ Sample 1 - Creating Project Tables.

How It Works

Currently, these new tables have no relationships. Table 7-6 summarizes the roles of these tables.

TABLE 7-6: Table Roles Created in This Activity

TABLE	DESCRIPTION
Project	This is the main entity of the ProjectTrek system. It holds the most important information about a project.
ProjectTask	This represents a single task belonging to a project. As indicated in Figure 7-1, a task can contain child tasks. This fact is depicted by the self-reference (the line going from ProjectTask back to ProjectTask).
AdditionalCost	A record in this table represents a single cost container planned for a project. One of management's most important requests was allowing for additional project costs.
CostItem	A CostItem record represents a concrete item that adds cost to a project.

Creating Relationships

Now you must add the relationships between these tables. LightSwitch provides a great tool for that purpose, the Add New Relationship dialog, which makes it very simple to set up the necessary table relationships.

TRY IT OUT   **Creating a One-to-Many Relationship between the Project and ProjectTask Tables**

To create the relationship, follow these steps:

1. Open the ProjectTask table in the Designer (double-click the ProjectTasks node in Solution Explorer).

2. Click the Relationship button in the Designer's toolbar. The Add New Relationship dialog, shown in Figure 7-6, pops up.

3. The From column shows the relationship attributes for the source entity that is set to ProjectTask. Its Multiplicity is set to Many, indicating that ProjectTask is at the "many" side of the relationship. The To column displays the attributes of the target entity. Click the drop-down arrow of the To column in the Name row and select Project from the list, as shown in Figure 7-7.

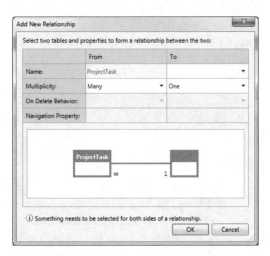

FIGURE 7-6: The Add New Relationship dialog

The Multiplicity in this relationship is set to One by default, indicating that this table is on the "one" side. As shown in Figure 7-8, other attributes are also filled with default values.

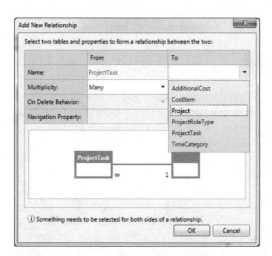

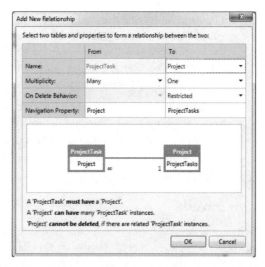

FIGURE 7-7: Selecting Project as the destination of the relationship

FIGURE 7-8: The relationship attributes in the dialog

The Restricted value in the On Delete Behavior row means that a `Project` record cannot be deleted unless there are no related `ProjectTask` records.

The Navigation Property values are set to Project for `ProjectTask` and ProjectTasks for `Project`.

Note that the dialog also provides a short explanation beneath the relationship diagram to clarify what the settings mean.

4. Click OK to create the relationship you've defined. As shown in Figure 7-9, the Designer shows the one-to-many relationship between `Project` and `ProjectTask`.

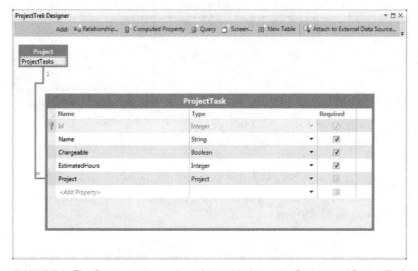

FIGURE 7-9: The Designer shows the relationship between Project and ProjectTask

The line connecting the two tables indicates the relationship between them. The small labels ("1" and the infinity sign) indicate the sides of the relationship. Notice that the `ProjectTask` table now has a property in its last row, named `Project`. Through this property — which is a *navigation property* — you can access the project of a specific task. The `Project` entity has a `ProjectTasks` property to access the collection of tasks that belong to a specific project.

Navigation properties are great programming tools. With the help of these tools, you can easily navigate from one object to a related one. For example, if you want to carry out a calculation with the tasks of a `Project` instance, you can use its `ProjectTasks` navigation property to process-related project tasks.

5. Press Ctrl+S to save the changes.

How It Works

Behind the scenes, LightSwitch created a foreign key field in the `ProjectTask` table that stores the `Id` of the related `Project` record. However, this field is not exposed to you. LightSwitch generates navigation properties both for the source and the target endpoints of the relationship. Assuming you have variables named `project` and `projectTask`, you can access related objects with code using the navigation properties such as `projectTask.Project` and `project.ProjectTasks`.

Because of the Restricted value of the On Delete Behavior, LightSwitch sets up the database so that deleting a `Project` record is refused by the SQL Server engine unless it has no related `ProjectTask` records. Practically speaking, this means that you must first delete all related tasks before you can delete a project.

Relationship Properties

You can edit the properties of a relationship. In the Designer, click the line representing the relationship. As shown in Figure 7-10, in the Properties window you can see the relationship's name and a task link to display the Edit Relationship window. You can change the Name to another one, as long as it conforms to the identifier syntax rules (the same syntax used for table and field names).

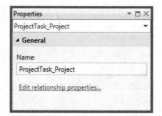

FIGURE 7-10: Properties of a relationship

The Edit Relationship dialog has the same layout as the Add New Relationship dialog, but it does not allow changing the tables participating in the relationship. You can still alter the Multiplicity and On Delete Behavior properties of the tables, as well as the name of navigation properties.

You can select from the "One," "Zero or one," and "Many" Multiplicity options for both the source (From column) and target (To column) tables. You cannot select the same multiplicity for both tables, but all the other variations are allowed.

With the On Delete Behavior property, you can specify what to do when a specific record is about to be deleted. You can specify it only for that table in a relationship that has the lower multiplicity value. In this sense, "Zero or one" is lower than "Many," and "One" is lower than "Zero or one." Therefore, if you have a "Many" side, you can set the delete behavior on the other side, because "Many" is higher than the other two multiplicity values. If you have "One" and "Zero to one," the "One" side wins, because it has a lower multiplicity value. The following delete behaviors are defined:

➤ *No Action* — The record is simply deleted without any previous checks or subsequent actions. This option is available only for the "Zero or one" multiplicity. For example, if you have a `Person` and a `ContactPerson` table (with a one-to-zero-or-one relationship among them), No Action means that you can delete a `Person` record, even if it has a related `ContactPerson`.

➤ *Cascade Delete* — The record at the "One" or "Zero or one" side is deleted together with the related records at the other side. In other words, you can delete a record and its related record in a single step. For example, if you delete a `Project` record, all related `ProjectTask` records will also be deleted.

➤ *Restricted* — This behavior is available only when there is a "many" side in the relationship. The record on the other side can be deleted if (and only if) there are no related records on the "many" side. For example, you cannot delete a `Project` record while it has any related `ProjectTask` records.

The navigation properties name the property of the entity that can be used to navigate to the entity or collection of entities at the other end of the relationship. LightSwitch uses the table names by default — it pluralizes them when navigating to the "many" end of the relationship. You can change them to other names that better describe the navigation role. Navigation property names have the same restrictions as table names, so they must conform to identifier syntax rules, and cannot have the same name as the entity holding them. The navigation property name must be different from any field name within the same entity, too.

Adding Other Relationships

You must add a few other relationships in order to establish all logical relations between the four tables you created earlier.

TRY IT OUT   **Building Other Relationships**

To establish the other relationships between the tables, follow these steps:

1. The `ProjectTask` table should be opened in the Designer, so if you have closed it, open it again.

2. Click the Relationship button in the Designer's toolbar, and when the Add New Relationship dialog opens, select the `ProjectTask` table as the target end. Because both the source and the target are the same table, this is a *self-referential relationship*, which allows a Multiplicity setting of only Zero or One-to-many ($0..1:n$). This fact is indicated at the bottom of the dialog, as shown in Figure 7-11.

3. Select the "Zero or one" option as the target Multiplicity (in the To column). The On Delete Behavior is set to Restricted, because this is the only one allowed for this kind of relationship.

4. The Navigation Property values are set to `ProjectTask1` and `ProjectTasks2`, respectively. Although these names are valid, and the plural `ProjectTasks2` indicates a collection, these names are not really helpful. Type **ParentTask** in the From column and **ChildTasks** in the To column. Click OK to create the self-referential relationship. On the right side of the table, the small U-shaped line with the multiplicity labels represents the new relationship, as shown in Figure 7-12.

FIGURE 7-11: The self-referential relationship cannot be many-to-one

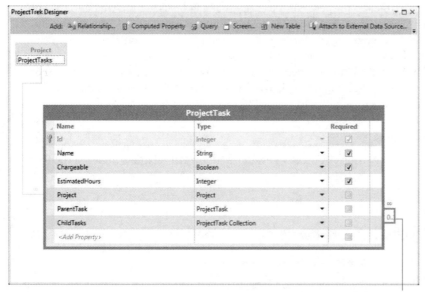

FIGURE 7-12: The new self-referential relationship

5. Double-click the header of the `Project` table in the Designer to show its details. (The table is in the top-left corner of the Designer, as shown in Figure 7-12.) Click the Relationship command on the toolbar.

6. When the Add New Relationship dialog opens, `Project` is set up to be on the "many" side of the relationship. However, it should be at the "one" side, so change the related Multiplicity value. Set the target to `AdditionalCost` and the target Multiplicity to `Many`. Leave the other attributes at their default value. The new relationship should have the attributes shown in Figure 7-13. Click OK to create it. The new relationship is immediately shown in the Designer.

7. Double-click `CostItems` in Solution Explorer to open the `CostItem` table. Click the Relationship command on the toolbar.

8. In the dialog, select `AdditionalCost` as the target of the relationship, and leave the other attributes unchanged, as shown in Figure 7-14. Click OK to create this new relationship.

FIGURE 7-13: The relationship between Project and AdditionalCost

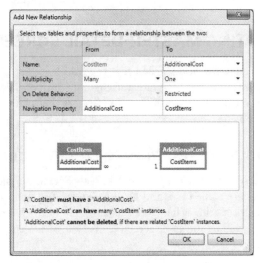

FIGURE 7-14: The relationship between AdditionalCost and CostItem

9. Press Ctrl+S to save the changes.

 NOTE *You may find the complete code to download for this exercise on this book's companion website at* `www.wrox.com` *in the folder* `Chapter 07\ Sample 2 - Creating Relationships`.

How It Works

In this exercise you have used the `Project`, `ProjectTask`, `AdditionalCost`, and `CostItem` tables. In the previous exercise, you established a relationship reflecting that projects can have zero, one, or more tasks. Here, you've added a self-referencing relationship to `ProjectTasks`, which describes that each task can be composed from smaller tasks. You have also defined that a project can have zero, one, or more additional cost items — as a kind of cost category. Each additional category item can have zero, one, or more cost items.

The self-referential relationship allows only the Zero or One-to-many (0..1:n) multiplicity settings because otherwise you wouldn't be able to add records without parents to the table. Just think about adding the very first record to the table. If a one-to-many relationship were allowed, the first `ProjectTask` record must have a reference to another `ProjectTask` record; but at the moment of this very first operation, there is no record in the table, so this insertion cannot be done!

The best practice is to set up a new relationship in the Designer starting from the "many" side. The Add New Relationship dialog's initial state is set up by this logic. However, as Step 6 shows, you can start from the "one" side as well. In this case, you need a few more clicks to complete your task.

CREATING MASTER-DETAIL SCREENS

In Chapter 6, you learned that the Add New Screen dialog generates a customizable screen layout according to the template and the data entity you select. LightSwitch goes beyond this, however. As you will learn in this section, it uses the relationship information to create master-detail screens for you.

Understanding Master-Detail Screens

When you worked with the Add New Screen dialog earlier, you may have noted that there is a template named List and Details Screen. With this template, you can generate screens that contain a list or a grid. When you select an item in the list or grid, the details of the selected items are displayed on the same screen. This type of screen is called a *master-detail screen*.

The following "Try It Out" exercise demonstrates how to create this screen.

TRY IT OUT   Creating a List and Details Screen

In this activity, you will create a new screen for the `Project` table. Follow these steps:

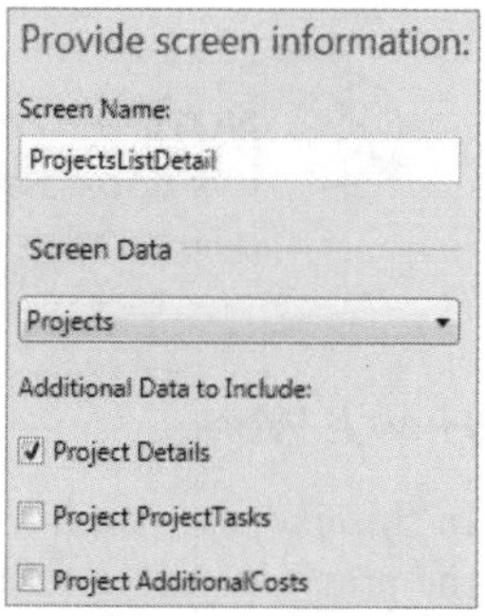

1.   Right-click Screens in Solution Explorer and use the Add Screen command. In the Add New Screen dialog, select the List and Details Screen template, and choose `Projects` from the Screen Data drop-down list. Leave the screen name and the options beneath the "Additional Data to Include" heading at their defaults (shown in Figure 7-15), and click OK.

2.   Press F5 to start the application. Click Projects List Detail in the Tasks menu to display the new screen. The left side of the screen contains the list of projects. The right side shows details about the project selected in the list.

FIGURE 7-15: Creating a List and Details Screen for the Project table

3. Right now, this list is empty. Use the Add button in the toolbar to display the default screen for adding a new project. Use the data shown in Figure 7-16 to add a new project, and click OK.

4. Add several more projects to the list.

5. Click Save to store the project information you added.

6. Click the PT-001 project in the list. The right panel of the screen now shows the details for this project. Alter its description, as shown in Figure 7-17. Click Save to store the changes.

7. Click any other project in the list and observe that now the selected project's details are shown on the right of the screen.

8. Close ProjectTrek.

How It Works

The structure and behavior of this screen is very simple. The left side is a list that behaves like a search screen; the right side allows editing the record selected in the list.

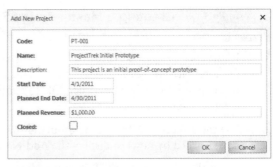

FIGURE 7-16: Adding a new project to the list

FIGURE 7-17: The ProjectsListDetail screen

The "List and Details Screen" name suggests that the screen created in this activity is a master-detail screen. From the perspective of screen layout, it really does have a "master" (the list on the left) and "details" (the record data on the right).

However, the concept of the master-detail screen is more generic. The "master-detail" epithet is generally used for screens that display records from two or more tables that have a net of master-detail relationships (in other words, variations of one-to-many relationships) among each other.

For example, there is a one-to-many relationship between the Project and ProjectTask tables. With LightSwitch, you can create a master-detail screen to display and edit not only the details of a specific project, but also the related project tasks.

Using the Add New Screen Dialog to Create Master-Detail Screens

Creating such a master-detail screen is fun with LightSwitch. In this section, you'll create a "List and Details Screen" for the Project table, but this time you'll also add the related ProjectTask information to the dialog.

TRY IT OUT **Creating a Master-Detail Screen, Including Project and ProjectTask Data**

1. Right-click `ProjectsListDetail` in Solution Explorer and click Delete. Or, alternatively, select `ProjectListDetail` and press the Delete key. In the pop-up message box, click OK to confirm that you really want to delete the screen object.

2. Use the Project ➪ Add Screen command (or use any alternatives you have learned by now) to display the Add New Screen dialog.

3. Select the List and Details Screen template, and choose `Projects` in the Screen Data drop-down list. Beneath the Additional Data to Include heading, check the Project ProjectTasks check box, as shown in Figure 7-18. Click OK.

4. Press F5 to run `ProjectTrek`.

> Provide screen information:
>
> Screen Name:
> ProjectsListDetail
>
> Screen Data
> Projects ▾
>
> Additional Data to Include:
> ☑ Project Details
> ☑ Project ProjectTasks
> ☐ Project AdditionalCosts

FIGURE 7-18: Adding ProjectTask details

5. When the application is started, click Projects List Detail to display the new screen. As shown in Figure 7-19, the right panel of the screen is divided horizontally. The upper part of the panel shows the project details; the bottom panel is a list (now empty) displaying related `Project Tasks` records.

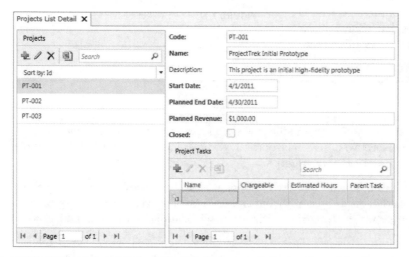

FIGURE 7-19: The new Projects List Detail screen with Project Tasks list

When you select a project in the `Projects` list (left panel), you can see and edit the related project details on the right — just as in the previous activity. Now you have the `Project Tasks`, where you can add tasks for the selected project.

6. Select the `PT-001` project in the list, and use the Add command in the `Project Tasks` toolbar to insert three or four new tasks for this project. Leave the `ParentTask` property empty. Figure 7-20 shows an example task to add.

FIGURE 7-20: Adding a new task to a project

7. Select another project in the list. You can see that the Project Tasks grid is updated to display the tasks that belong to the selected project. If you have not added tasks to the selected project, the list is empty. Add a few tasks to the newly selected project as well.

8. Click Save to store your changes.

9. Close ProjectTrek.

> **NOTE** *You may find the complete code to download for this exercise on this book's companion website at* www.wrox.com *in the folder* Chapter 07\
> Sample 3 - Master-Detail Screens.

How It Works

LightSwitch handles the relationship between the Project and ProjectTasks tables, and manages the navigation logic behind the scenes. When you select a project, LightSwitch displays only related tasks in the Project Tasks grid.

Also, when you add a new task, LightSwitch knows that the task is related to the currently selected project, and automatically creates the reference for you. As you learned, table records on the "many" side of a one-to-many relationship use foreign key fields to store the primary key of the table on the "one" side. LightSwitch takes care of implementing such plumbing, so you do not have to deal with it at all.

The Structure of Master-Detail Screens

Master-detail screens use exactly the same approach as simple screens. They have data items representing the information to be displayed on the screen, and use layout items to represent the constituent parts of the UI. Data items are bound with layout items.

Data Items, Layout Items, and Queries

The essence of the master-detail mechanism can be understood through the data items of a screen. The `ProjectsListDetail` screen has two queries, as shown in Figure 7-21.

The `Projects` query gets the list of projects from the database. This query retrieves `Project` records. The other query is `ProjectTasks`, which retrieves a list of `ProjectTask` records. The arrow pointing from `ProjectTasks` to the `Add ProjectTasks` item — embedded in the `Selected Item` node — indicates a binding, which means that the `ProjectTasks` query retrieves its result not from the database but from the `ProjectTasks` property of the selected `Project` item.

The structure of layout items adds more clues to help you understand how data items are visualized in the `ProjectsListDetail` screen. As shown in the hierarchy of layout items in Figure 7-22, the `List` item is bound to the `Projects` query, and the data grid in the bottom part of the right column gets its content from the `ProjectTask` query (displayed as Project Tasks).

FIGURE 7-21: Data items of the ProjectsListDetail screen

Understanding How Master-Detail Screens Work

You should now be able to assemble the pieces and understand how the `ProjectsListDetail` screen displays project and task data:

➤ When you open the screen, the `Projects` query runs and retrieves all `Project` entities from the database. The query is bound to the Projects `List`, so it displays the project data.

FIGURE 7-22: Layout items of ProjectsListDetail

➤ The Details Column `Rows Layout` provides a panel (Project Details `Rows Layout`) at the top with detailed project data. This part is bound to the `Projects.SelectedItem` property (check its Data Binding property in the Properties window), so it always shows the project selected in the list.

➤ The Project Tasks `Data Grid` is bound to the `ProjectTasks` query. The source of this query is the `ProjectTasks` property of the project selected in the list. As the selected item changes, the `ProjectTasks` property also changes. It triggers the `ProjectTaskCollection` query to be run, and the data is refreshed in the grid of project tasks.

As you learned in Chapter 6, the data binding mechanism collects the changes you made in the UI and stores the altered values back to the entities. When you click Save, the entities are persisted in the database.

However, one question remains unanswered. When you add a new `ProjectTask` record, which mechanism takes care of assigning this record to the currently selected project?

The new `ProjectTask` record you add is added to the `ProjectTasks` property of the currently selected project. Remember, this is the source of the `ProjectTasks` query. Behind the scenes, the Entity Framework component of .NET 4.0 is responsible for persisting entities to the database. The Entity Framework is designed so that its tracking mechanism knows that a `ProjectTask` entity added to the `ProjectTasks` property of a concrete `Project` entity belongs to that `Project`, and writes back the data to the database, thus preserving this relationship.

QUERIES

In this chapter, you have encountered the term "query" several times, and you already learned that data screens are based on queries. This section provides more details about queries and how you can use them in your LightSwitch applications.

Understanding Queries

Queries are operations that retrieve a single record or a collection of records according to specific criteria from a certain source. This means that the source of the query contains zero, one, or more records. With queries, you can select those records that have the focus — because you want to display them in the UI, or you want to carry out a specific operation with them.

When you create a table, LightSwitch creates a related item, and two queries:

➤ A query returning a collection of records (all of them) stored in the database. This query can return zero, one, or more records in the collection.

➤ A query returning a single record by its identifier. This query returns either no record (that is, the record with the specified identifier does not exist in the source), or exactly one record.

You can discover these queries in the `ProjectTrek` application, as shown in Figure 7-23. They appear in the Add Data Item dialog, which you will learn about later. As you see, the queries are in pairs. The pluralized forms of the entity name are those that retrieve all records from the database. For example, the Projects query retrieves all Project records displayed in the `ProjectsListDetail` screen. The queries with the `SingleOrDefault` suffix are those that retrieve only a single record by its identifier.

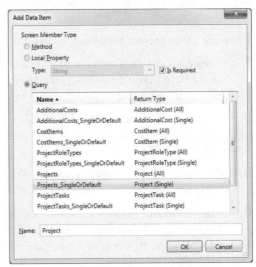

FIGURE 7-23: Queries used in ProjectTrek

NOTE *You may have noted that in Solution Explorer, you see pluralized names of tables under the `Data Sources` node. The node name represents the query returning a collection of entities — all entities — from the table behind, which is why a plural entity name is used there. When you open the table in the Designer, you can confirm that it still has the original — singular — name.*

Editing Queries

When you create a screen, the Add New Screen dialog enables you to select a table from the Select Data drop-down list. According to the template, the resulting screen uses either the query returning all entities from the table (*list screen*), or the query selecting a single record by its identifier (*details screen*).

When you work with a list screen, you can edit the query retrieving the screen data. Of course, you cannot entirely change it, but you can specify additional filter criteria and a sort order that are applied to the result of the original query. The following activity shows you how.

TRY IT OUT Changing the Query of a Screen

In this activity, you create a new screen that lists projects and related tasks.

 NOTE *By now, you have learned how to open tables or screens in the Designer, and how to create new ones. Hereinafter, the instructions do not contain the steps for finding a command in the menu system or in Solution Explorer. For example, instead of telling you to "right-click Screens in Solution Explorer and select Add Screen from the context menu," you will be instructed to "create a new screen." Of course, complete instructions are provided for any commands you have not learned yet.*

To create a new project list screen, follow these steps:

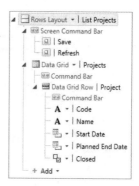

1. Create a new screen with the Search Data Screen template. Select Projects in the Screen Data drop-down menu of the Add New Screen dialog and change the screen name to `ListProjects`. Close the dialog by clicking OK.

2. In the screen layout, expand the Project `Data Grid Row` node and delete the `Description` and `PlannedRevenue` elements by clicking them and pressing the Delete key.

3. Change the Control Type property of the `Closed` element to Check Box. The layout of the screen should look like the one shown in Figure 7-24.

FIGURE 7-24: Layout of the ListProjects screen

4. Press F5 to run the application. Open the List Projects screen, and check whether any project records are closed. If any project contains a checked Closed property, uncheck it and save the changes. Figure 7-25 shows an example of this screen.

Projects					
				Search	
Code	Name	Start Date	Planned End Dat	Closed	
▶ PT-001	ProjectTrek Initial Prototype	4/1/2011	4/30/2011	☐	
PT-002	ProjectTrek Functional Prototype	5/1/2011	5/31/2011	☐	
PT-003	ProjectTrek Extended Prototype	6/1/2011	6/30/2011	☐	

FIGURE 7-25: The List Projects screen with no closed projects

5. Close the application.

6. In the Screen Designer, click the Edit Query task link near the `Projects` data item on the left side of the screen. The Designer opens the query, as shown in Figure 7-26.

7. Click Add Filter. A new Filter row appears with five drop-down list fields in which you can assemble a condition. In the first one, you can select the type of the condition (`Where` or `Where Not`). The second enables you to select the field to involve in the condition. Set this to `Closed`. The third list lets you select the comparison operator. Choose "= (equals)". Select Literal from the fourth list, and set the value in the last box to `False`. With this condition, you declare that the query should retrieve only the open projects (where the `Closed` property has a value of `False`).

FIGURE 7-26: The ListProjects query in the Designer

8. Click Add Sort, and a new sort order declaration appears with two drop-down lists. Select `StartDate` from the first one and Descending from the second one. You declared that the projects should be sorted by their start date, with the project with the latest date at the top. Figure 7-27 shows the query Designer with these changes.

FIGURE 7-27: The ListProjects query with a new filter condition and sort order definition

9. Click the Back to ListProjects link at the top of the query Designer to return to the screen layout. Save the changes (Ctrl+S) and start the application by pressing F5.

10. Open the List Projects screen. As shown in Figure 7-28, now projects are ordered according to the StartDate property, with the youngest project at the top.

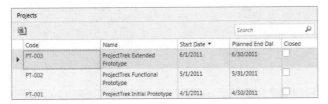

FIGURE 7-28: Project items are in descending order by StartDate

11. Check the Closed property of any project. Click Save in the application toolbar, and then click Refresh. The closed project is not in the list because of the filter condition you set up earlier.

NOTE *You may find the complete code to download for this exercise on this book's companion website at* www.wrox.com *in the folder* Chapter 07\ Sample 4 - Queries.

How It Works

LightSwitch composed the original query of the screen with the extra criteria you set up. As a result, only the data for open projects is retrieved, and the records are ordered as you declared in their sort order.

Creating New Queries

Often, you will want to use the same query in more than one screen. For example, you may need the list of active projects not only in the `ListProjects` screen, but also in other dialogs as well.

When you have multiple screens with the same queries behind them, it would not make sense to edit them individually in each screens. Not only is this laborious, it's also very prone to error. When you must modify the query, you want to ensure that it is correct for all related screens. The following activity demonstrates how, using what is called an *explicit query*.

TRY IT OUT Creating an Explicit Query

LightSwitch supports the creation of *explicit queries*, independent from the screens for which you intend to use them. In this activity, you create a new query to retrieve the list of active projects.

To create a new explicit query, follow these steps:

1. In Solution Explorer, right-click the `Projects` node and select the Add Query command. A new query opens in the Designer with the name `Query1` highlighted in its header, indicating that you can change this name. The design surface is the same as you have already seen in Figure 7-26 and Figure 7-27.

2. Type **ActiveProjects** and press Enter to rename the query.

3. Add a new filter condition to the query that states `Where Closed = False`, and a new sort order declaration `SortBy StartDate Descending`, exactly in the same manner as you did in Step 7 and Step 8 of the previous activity.

4. Save the query.

5. Add a new screen with the Search Data template and name it **ListActiveProjects**. When you select the source of the screen from the Screen Data drop-down list, you can see the new query right beneath `Projects`, indicating that `ActiveProjects` is based on `Projects`, as shown in Figure 7-29. Select `ActiveProjects` and click OK.

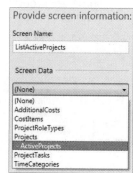

FIGURE 7-29: You can use the query as the screen data

6. Run the application and open the `ListActiveProjects` screen. You can confirm that it shows only the active projects (the same projects as shown in Figure 7-28).

How It Works

Instead of composing the set of records from the implicit query based on the table and filter conditions added to the screen, now the `ActiveProjects` query retrieves the record set to display. When the `ListActiveProjects` screen is displayed, instead of the `Project` table, the `ActiveProjects` query is used. Because this query retrieves only active projects, you won't see any closed projects in the screen. The logic of the screen remains unchanged.

Query Parameters

Queries provide great flexibility. They can accept parameters, which can be set dynamically through data binding between query parameters and other data elements of a screen, or they can be set up programmatically.

To understand the benefit and simplicity of a parameterized query, the next few activities build a new master-detail screen that makes use of them.

TRY IT OUT | **Creating a Parameterized Query**

In this activity, you change the `ActiveProjects` query so that it will accept an optional parameter indicating whether all or only active projects should be retrieved. You do not bind this parameter to any value in the `ProjectsListDetail` screen. You may expect that this query won't work because of its missing parameter value, but it will.

To create a screen with the parameterized `ActiveProjects` query, follow these steps:

1. Delete the `ProjectListDetail` and `ListProjects` screens. Right-click the `ListActiveProjects` screen in Solution Explorer and select Rename in the context menu. Type **ListProjects** and press Enter.

2. In Solution Explorer, open the `ActiveProjects` query by double-clicking it.

3. Click the Add Parameter command. A new parameter entry is displayed. Here you can name the parameter and select its type from a drop-down list. Type **ShowClosed** as the parameter name and set its type to `Boolean`, as shown in Figure 7-30.

FIGURE 7-30: Adding a new parameter to the query

4. While the parameter is selected, go to the Properties window and set the Is Optional property to `True`.

5. Click the `Where Closed = False` filter condition to edit it. Click the drop-down arrow of the fourth box, and select Parameter from the list. From the fifth box, select `ShowClosed` from the list of options. Now the filter condition should look as shown in Figure 7-31.

FIGURE 7-31: The altered filter condition

6. Save the query and start the application by pressing F5.

7. Open the `ListProjects` screen. The screen shows all projects — including the active and closed ones. These are the same projects, and in the same order, as those shown in Figure 7-28.

8. Close the application.

How It Works

The `ListProjects` screen still uses the `ActiveProject` query you changed in this activity. You added a new query parameter and set a filter condition using this parameter. You have not bound the query parameter to any value, so it might seem a bit weird that the screen works at this point.

The `ShowClosed` parameter you defined in Step 3 is set to be optional in Step 4. In LightSwitch, if an optional parameter is not bound to any value at runtime, any condition for which it is used is omitted from the query composition. In this case, because `ShowClosed` is not bound to a value, the `Where` condition set in Step 5 is omitted, and the query returned all projects.

If you defined `ShowClosed` as a required parameter, the query would not retrieve any projects, because this parameter's value is not specified.

Binding Query Parameters with Screen Data

To leverage a required query parameter, you must bind it to a screen data item. With LightSwitch, it is very easy, as you will learn through the following simple example. You are going to change the `ListProjects` screen so that it enables you to choose whether you want to see all projects or only active ones. Figure 7-32 shows the completed screen. When you uncheck the Display Closed check box, only active projects are listed; when you check it, all projects are displayed.

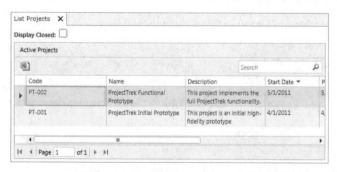

FIGURE 7-32: Using a query parameter in the ListProjects screen

TRY IT OUT | **Binding a Query Parameters with a Screen Property**

To implement the `ListProjects` screen to work as shown in Figure 7-32, follow these steps:

1. Open the `ActiveProjects` query and add a new filter condition. (Click the Add filter beneath the existing condition.) Use the input fields of the new condition to set it to `Or Closed = False`, as shown in Figure 7-33. Save the `ActiveProjects` query.

FIGURE 7-33: Adding a new filter condition

2. Open the `ListProjects` screen and click Add Data Item in the Designer's toolbar. In the Add Data Item dialog, select the Local property option, and then set the Type to `Boolean`. Type **DisplayClosed** in the Name box, as shown in Figure 7-34. Click OK.

3. On the left side of the Designer, select the `ShowClosed` data item node (beneath Query Parameters) and click the Parameter Value box in the Properties window. A few options are listed beneath the box, as shown in Figure 7-35. Double-click `DisplayClosed`. With this action, you bound the `ShowClosed` query parameter to the `DisplayClosed` screen property.

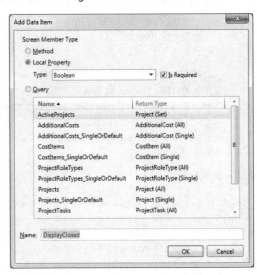

FIGURE 7-34: The Add Data Item dialog

4. Select the root layout item (the List Projects Rows Layout). Click Add Layout Item in the toolbar and select Group. A new `Rows Layout` item is appended to the layout. Click the Add button and choose Display Closed from the list, as shown in Figure 7-36.

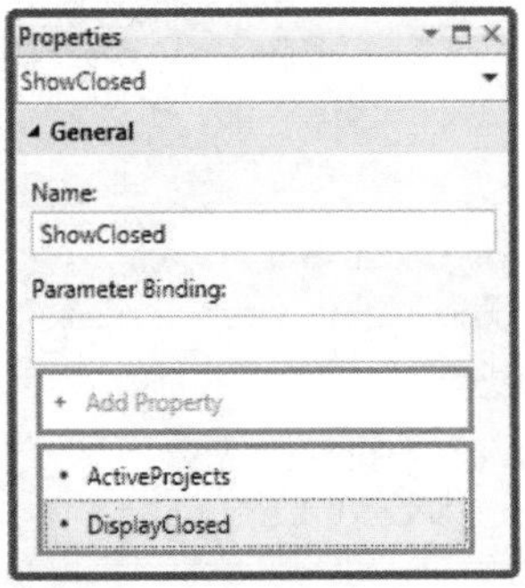

FIGURE 7-35: Binding the ShowClosed query parameter to the DisplayClosed screen property

FIGURE 7-36: A new group with the Display Closed property

5. Display Closed is added as a Label. In the Properties window change its Control Type property from Label to Check Box.

6. Click the Group text of the newly added group. Then, without releasing the mouse button, drag it before the Active Projects `Data Grid` item. Your completed layout is shown in Figure 7-37.

7. Start the application by pressing F5. Open the List Projects screen and note how it works as you check and uncheck the Display Closed check box at the top of the screen. You can see that when the box is unchecked, only open projects are displayed, but when you check the box, all projects are listed (refer to Figure 7-32). Close the application.

FIGURE 7-37: The completed layout of the ListProjects screen

NOTE *You may find the complete code to download for this exercise on this book's companion website at* www.wrox.com *in the folder* Chapter 07\ Sample 5 - Parameterized Query.

How It Works

You changed the `ActiveProjects` query so that it has two filter conditions connected with a logical OR operator. The first condition (`Where Closed = ShowClosed`) will filter out the projects according to the `ShowClosed` parameter. If `ShowClosed` is set to `False`, it will retrieve active projects; otherwise, it filters out the active ones. The second condition (`Or Closed = False`) retrieves active projects. The combination of the two conditions results in displaying all projects if `ShowClosed` is set to `True`.

The value of the `DisplayClosed` check box is bound to the `ShowClosed` query parameter. When the value of the check box changes — that is, it is checked or unchecked — the `ActiveProjects` query runs again with the updated value of the `ShowClosed` parameter, and the list of displayed projects is changed.

ADDING DETAILS TO SCREENS

It is very easy to build master-detail screens with the Add New Screen dialog because it allows adding detail data based on the relationships belonging to the main table. The LightSwitch Screen Designer enables you to easily add such details to a screen later.

In this section, you change the `ListProjects` screen so that it displays project task data and additional cost data as well. You also add a section to the screen to edit the selected project's attributes.

After you make these changes, the `ListProjects` screen will contain three details' areas — two embedded in a tabbed panel at the bottom — as shown in Figure 7-38.

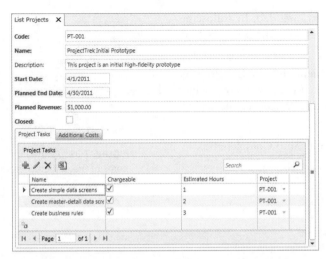

FIGURE 7-38: The ListProjects screen with project tasks and additional cost data

Adding Project Details to ListProjects

The data grid in the `ListProjects` screen now displays all project attributes, including the description, which is a wide field. Therefore, you must scroll the grid horizontally in order to examine all project details. The following activity demonstrates a better solution: removing a few attributes from the grid and putting them in a separate area on the screen. You can also add support to edit project details.

TRY IT OUT   Adding Project Details to the ListProjects screen

To change the `ListProjects` screen, follow these steps:

1. Open the `Project` table in the Designer. Select the `Closed` field and edit its choice list (click Choice List in the Properties window). Click the Add Value cell and type **True**. Press Tab and type **Yes**. Then press Tab again. Similarly, add the **False** value with the **No** display name as the second row of the choice list, and click OK to close the dialog.

2. Save the changes (by pressing Ctrl+S).

3. Open the `ListProjects` screen in the Designer.

4. Expand the Project `Data Grid Row` under the Active Projects `Data Grid` node, and delete the Description and Planned Revenue properties. Change the control type of `Closed` from the default Auto Complete Box to Label.

5. Select the Command Bar of the `Data Grid` and append the AddNew button to it. Take care not to select the AddAndEditNew instead of AddNew.

At this point, the DataGrid changes as intended. By following the next steps, you build an editable detail panel for `Project` properties.

6. Select the root element of the layout hierarchy (the List Projects Rows Layout) and use the Add button at the bottom of the hierarchy to append `SelectedItem` beneath Active Projects as shown in Figure 7-39.

7. Change the control type of Closed from Auto Complete Box to Check Box.

8. Start the application by pressing F5, and select the List Projects screen in the Tasks menu. Now you can see and modify the selected project's details, as shown in Figure 7-40.

9. Close the application.

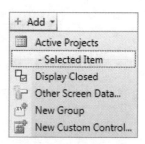

FIGURE 7-39: Adding the items of the selected Project to the screen

How It Works

In Step 1, you added a choice list to the Closed field so that Yes/No text could be displayed in the grid, rather than a check box representing a True/False option. The key action of this activity is performed in Step 8, where you added the details of the selected project.

FIGURE 7-40: Project details

Adding ProjectTask and AdditionalCost Details

The user administering projects would probably like to edit other project details in the planning, or setup, phase — such as the constituent tasks and the additional cost items planned for the project. When you designed the data model of the `ProjectTrek` application, you declared the relationship between `Project` and two detail tables such as `ProjectTask` and `AdditionalCost`. You saw earlier that the Add New Screen dialog uses this relationship information to create layout elements for detail tables.

When you have a screen, it takes only a few clicks to add related detail information. In the following activity, you add both project task and additional cost information to the existing `ListProjects` screen to see how easy it is. To demonstrate these LightSwitch features, you will create a tabbed view to display these details.

TRY IT OUT   Adding Task and Additional Cost Details to the ListProjects Screen

1. Open `ProjectTasks` in the Designer.

2. Select the `ParentTask` field of the table (either click it in the table or select it in the Properties window), and uncheck the Display by Default property.

3. Open the `ListProjects` screen in the Designer.

4. Select the List Projects `Rows Layout` and use the Add Layout Item button in the Designer's toolbar to append a new group to the bottom of the hierarchy. The new group is represented with a Vertical Stack control, and its name is Group1.

5. Change the control type of Group1 from Rows Layout to Tabs Layout. Every group you add to Group1 will be represented as a separate tabbed panel.

6. Under the `Projects` data item, on the left side of the screen, are two task links (`Add ProjectTasks` and `Add AdditionalCosts`). Click each of them to add data items representing the tasks and costs related to a project. These data items are automatically bound to `Projects` as details, as the arrow starting from `AdditionalCosts` in Figure 7-41 indicates.

7. Select the Group1 node in the layout hierarchy. Click the Add button and select the Project Tasks data item from the drop-down list. As a result of this operation, a new data grid is added to the layout. Its data source is bound to the `ProjectTasks` item.

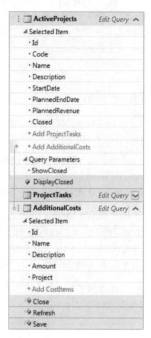

FIGURE 7-41: Task and cost details of a project added as data items

8. Select the Group1 node in the layout hierarchy, click the Add button again, and this time select the `AdditionalCosts` data item from the list. A new data grid is added, bound to `AdditionalCosts`.

9. Start the application by pressing F5, and open the List Projects screen. Maximize the application window or scroll down until you can see the Project Tasks and Additional Costs tabs. Using the Add, Edit, and Delete buttons, you can edit the content of data grids. You can confirm that you can add or edit project details, tasks, and additional costs, and send them to the database in a single batch by clicking the Save button. Whereas Figure 7-38 showed the tab with tasks data, Figure 7-42 shows the tab with a few sample cost items.

FIGURE 7-42: Additional cost details of a project shown in a tab

10. Close the application.

NOTE *You may find the complete code to download for this exercise on this book's companion website at* www.wrox.com *in the folder* Chapter 07\ Sample 6 - Adding Details.

How It Works

This activity demonstrated how easy it is to add new layout and data items to any LightSwitch screens. In Step 4 and Step 5, you created a new area at the bottom of the screen for a tabbed view.

LightSwitch knows that the Project table has a one-to-many relationship with the ProjectTasks and AdditionalCost tables, and therefore provides the task links you used in Step 6 to add new data items for related project tasks and additional costs.

When you added a new layout item for the project tasks in Step 7, you actually selected the related data item (ProjectTasks), and the Designer created a grid representing this data item. The properties of a project task were automatically mapped to data grid columns. In Step 8, you used the same procedure to add a new tab for the additional cost items.

You already learned that LightSwitch generates pop-up screens to add and edit data, and that is how you could add new task and cost details in Step 9.

As you have seen in the last two activities, it is easy to add details to screens, based on existing relationships. You are not limited to adding details only to the base entity of the screen, however. You can also add additional details to detail tables, and create "master-detail-more-detail" screens.

Aggregations

When working with master-detail screens, you often need to display aggregated detail data at the master level. For example, the ProjectTrek application stores an EstimatedHours property in a ProjectTask entity that shows the estimated effort, in hours, planned for a certain task. It would be nice to see at the project level the total hours planned. Similarly, each AdditionalCost entity stores an Amount property. Summing it at the project level would show the total additional costs planned.

As you learned in Chapter 6, LightSwitch supports adding computed properties to a table. Using this feature, you can easily display aggregated data.

In the next activity, you add two computed properties to the Project table to represent these aggregations, and then modify the ListProjects screen to display them.

TRY IT OUT **Displaying Aggregated Data with Computed Properties**

To create and display aggregated properties, follow these steps:

1. Open the `Project` table in the Designer.

2. Click the Computed Property button in the Designer's toolbar. A new row is added to the table with a small icon in the row header, indicating that you are going to define a computed property.

3. Name this new property **TotalTaskHours** and set its type to `Integer`.

4. While the `TotalTaskHours` row is selected in the table, click the Edit Method link in the Properties window. The `Project.vb` (`Project.cs`) file opens, and the `TotalTaskHours_Compute` method's skeleton is created:

VB
```vb
Namespace ProjectTrek

    Public Class Project

        Private Sub TotalTaskHours_Compute(ByRef result As Integer)
            ' Set result to the desired field value

        End Sub
    End Class

End Namespace
```

C#
```csharp
namespace LightSwitchApplication
{
    public partial class Project
    {
        partial void TotalTaskHours_Compute(ref int result)
        {
            // Set result to the desired field value

        }
    }
}
```

In the body of this method, you can define the computation that calculates the value of the property.

5. Add the following boldfaced code to the method body:

VB
```vb
        Private Sub TotalTaskHours_Compute(ByRef result As Integer)
            ' Set result to the desired field value
            result = Me.ProjectTasks.Sum(Function(t) t.EstimatedHours)
        End Sub
```

C#
```csharp
        partial void TotalTaskHours_Compute(ref int result)
        {
            // Set result to the desired field value
            result = this.ProjectTasks.Sum(t => t.EstimatedHours);
        }
```

6. Save the changes by pressing Ctrl+S and close the file.

7. Add a new computed property to the `Project` table, name it **TotalAdditionalCosts**, and set its type to Money. Click Edit Method in the Properties window (make sure that the `TotalAdditionalCost` row is selected). Now the `TotalAdditionalCosts_Compute` method is prepared to add the calculation:

VB
```vb
Private Sub TotalAdditionalCosts_Compute(ByRef result As Decimal)
    ' Set result to the desired field value

End Sub
```

C#
```csharp
partial void TotalAdditionalCosts_Compute(ref decimal result)
{
    // Set result to the desired field value

}
```

8. Type the following boldfaced code into the method body:

VB
```vb
Private Sub TotalAdditionalCosts_Compute(ByRef result As Decimal)
    ' Set result to the desired field value
    result = Me.AdditionalCosts.Sum(Function(c) c.Amount)
End Sub
```

C#
```csharp
partial void TotalAdditionalCosts_Compute(ref decimal result)
{
    // Set result to the desired field value
    result = this.AdditionalCosts.Sum(c => c.Amount);
}
```

9. Save the changes and close the file.

10. Open the `ListProjects` screen in the Designer and click the `SelectedItem` Vertical Stack in the layout hierarchy. With the Add button beneath the `Closed` check box, append the `TotalTaskHours` and `TotalAdditionalCosts` properties to the screen.

11. Run the application by pressing F5. Open the `ListProjects` screen and select a project that has task and cost items. As shown in Figure 7-43, now aggregated properties are displayed.

12. Close the application.

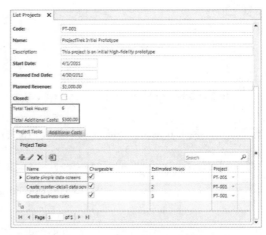

FIGURE 7-43: New aggregated fields are added to the screen

> **NOTE** You may find the complete code to download for this exercise on this book's companion website at www.wrox.com in the folder `Chapter 07\ Sample 7 - Aggregations`.

How It Works

Computed properties are just like any other properties of an entity, but of course they are read-only. You cannot change their values. You must define the calculation method. The code you wrote in Step 5 and Step 8 was responsible for carrying out the aggregations.

In Step 10, you added layout items that reference the computed properties. When they are about to be displayed, the compute methods are called, and they calculate the value to display. LightSwitch is very smart in managing computed properties. It invokes a compute method in a "lazy" way only when it is really needed.

> **NOTE** Both computation methods use LINQ (a component of .NET Framework 4.0) and lambda expressions (a feature of Visual Basic and C# languages). For example, the total additional cost of a project was computed with the following expression:

```
Me.AdditionalCosts.Sum(Function(c) c.Amount)
```

> Here, `Me` represents a project, and `Me.AdditonalCosts` is a collection of cost items belonging to this project. The `Sum` function — defined in LINQ — is a so-called *extension function* that operates on an object — in this case, this object is the `Me.AdditionalCosts` collection. It sums a collection of values. The argument of `Sum` is a function — called a *lambda function* — that indicates how the items of `Me.AdditionalCosts` take part in the operation. The `Function(c) c.Amount` expression specifies that each `AdditionalCost` item in the collection (represented by `c`) should be projected to its `Amount` property. As a result, the expression sums the `Amount` properties of additional cost items belonging to a project.
>
> With the same semantics, C# has a different syntax for describing a lambda expression:

```
this.AdditionalCosts.Sum(c => c.Amount);
```

POLISHING

The `ListProjects` screen is very close to its final form. It's time to apply the final touches. By now, you have learned all the details, so you can carry out the last few changes by yourself without any click-by-click instructions.

Change the display names of the `Project` and `ProjectTask` entities as shown in Table 7-7 and Table 7-8, respectively.

TABLE 7-7: New Display Names of Project Properties

PROPERTY	DISPLAY NAME
StartDate	Start
PlannedEndDate	Planned Completion
Closed	Is Closed?
ProjectTasks	Tasks
TotalTaskHours	Total Hours Planned

TABLE 7-8: New Display Names of ProjectTask Properties

PROPERTY	DISPLAY NAME
Chargeable	Chargeable?
EstimatedHours	Hours

Change the display names of `ListProjects` screen elements as shown in Table 7-9.

TABLE 7-9: New Display Names in the ListProjects Screen

OLD DISPLAY NAME	NEW DISPLAY NAME
Display Closed	Display Closed Projects
List Projects	List of Projects
Project Tasks	Tasks

NOTE *You may find the complete code to download for this chapter on this book's companion website at* `www.wrox.com` *in the folder* `Chapter 07\ Sample 8 - Polishing`.

SUMMARY

With LightSwitch, you can easily establish relationships among entities. The Add New Relationship dialog is the key tool to manage them. Although at the database level you must create foreign keys, LightSwitch manages the relationships at the entity level and hides the foreign keys from you. With the entities created in the IDE you can navigate among the relationships.

The concept of relationships is visible at the level of the user interface. The Add New Screen dialog recognizes that your base entity has other related entities, and you can easily create master-detail screens. The Designer takes care of binding the master entity instances with their details; and as the selected master instance changes, the appropriate details are displayed.

Behind the scenes, LightSwitch uses queries to retrieve entities from the underlying database tables or entity models. You can customize these queries by adding filter criteria and sort order declarations. You can also create explicit queries that are reusable in your screens. Queries can have parameters that are bound to screen data items.

The LightSwitch data model supports the concept of computed properties. With very concise code (generally in one line), you can easily add aggregation data to master entities.

In Chapter 8, you will learn how to attach to external SQL Server databases and use tables with already existing data.

EXERCISES

1. Explain what a one-to-many relationship between two entities means.

2. How does the Add New Screen dialog help you create master-detail screens?

3. Explain the difference between explicit and implicit queries.

4. How can you pass parameters to a query?

5. Explain what a computed property is.

6. How would you create a `TaskCount` property (representing the number of tasks belonging to a project) for the `Project` table?

 NOTE *Answers to the Exercises can be found in the Appendix.*

▶ WHAT YOU LEARNED IN THIS CHAPTER

TOPIC	KEY CONCEPTS
One-to-many relationship	A kind of relationship between two entities or tables whereby the entity instance (or table record) at the "one" side has zero, one, or more related instances (or records) at the "many" side, while any record at the "many" side has exactly one record at the "one" side.
Many-to-many relationship	A kind of relationship between two entities or tables whereby an entity instance (or table record) at any side has zero, one, or more related instances (or records) at the other side.
One-to-one relationship	A kind of relationship between two entities or tables whereby an entity instance (or table record) at one side has zero or one related entity (record) at the other side.
Creating a new relationship	Open the table (at the "many" side) of the relationship in the Designer and click the Relationship button in the toolbar. Using the Add New Relationship dialog, you can set up the target entity, multiplicity type, and delete behavior, and you can name the navigation properties.
Creating a master-detail screen	Use the Add New Screen dialog and select a table (or query) as the screen data source. LightSwitch knows which related tables can be details on your screen, and displays them beneath the Additional Data to Include label. Select the entities you intend to include in your screen.
Query	A query is an operation that retrieves a single entity or a collection of entities according to specific criteria from a certain source — generally from the database.
Creating a query	In Solution Explorer, select the table you want to use as the source (base) of the query and select the Add Query command from the context menu. You can add filter conditions, sort order declarations, and parameters to the queries. The parameters can be optional. If an optional parameter does not have a value, all filter conditions using this parameter are omitted from the composition of the query.
Editing a query in a screen	You can edit a query behind a data screen by selecting the data item and clicking the Edit Query task link.
Query parameters	A query can accept parameters. These can be set either dynamically with data binding or programmatically.
Binding a query parameter to a screen data item	Select the data item representing the query parameter. In the Properties window, click the text box of the Parameter Value property, and select the appropriate data item from the list by double-clicking it.

TOPIC	KEY CONCEPTS
Computed property	A computed property is a read-only property that is calculated during runtime. When defining a computed property, you must define a calculation method to produce the value of the computed property. In the application, it behaves just like any other property, except that it cannot be modified.
Creating a computed property	Open the table in the Designer, and use the Computed Property button in the Designer's toolbar to add a new property. Specify its name and type, and then click the Edit Method link in the Properties windows. Write the calculation code that computes the property value.

8

Using Existing SQL Server Data

WHAT YOU WILL LEARN IN THIS CHAPTER

➤ Using the Server Explorer tool to connect to LightSwitch databases and to explore external databases

➤ Understanding how external SQL Server databases are accessed from LightSwitch applications

➤ Learning how to use external databases

➤ Using LightSwitch to customize external tables

➤ Creating relationships between LightSwitch tables and external tables

When you develop line-of-business (LOB) applications, you often must access and use data stored in existing back-end systems. Even if an application's functionality is new and requires new data structures, the information stored in existing databases might be very valuable, and also allows you to reuse information you already created. In many cases, you create applications that work with already existing data. For example, you might need to implement an application that enables administering dictionary tables of a large banking system.

Visual Studio LightSwitch has been designed with this functionality in mind. As you have learned, the LightSwitch IDE offers you two options for performing tasks right after creating a new project: creating a new table or connecting to an existing database.

Out-of-the-box, LightSwitch provides access to three kinds of data sources:

➤ *SQL Server 2008* — This is data stored in SQL Server 2008 and 2008 R2 databases. Most database editions are supported, including SQL Server Express, Standard, Developer, Enterprise, and even SQL Server Azure.

➤ *SharePoint 2010* — LightSwitch can access and modify list objects used in SharePoint 2010, similar to how SQL Server tables are handled. Chapter 14 is entirely dedicated to this topic.

➤ *Other data sources (through WCF RIA Services)* — LightSwitch supports accessing data through the OData protocol using standard HTTP web requests. It is a relatively simple task to create an OData adapter for databases with Windows Communication Foundation (WCF) Rich Internet Application (RIA) Services. With such an adapter, you can directly access databases that are not supported by LightSwitch This is an advanced topic beyond the scope of this book.

 NOTE *You can visit* http://odata.org *to obtain more information about OData. With the Professional, Premium, or Ultimate editions of Visual Studio 2010, you can create OData adapters for databases.*

In this chapter you will learn how to use data stored in existing SQL Server databases.

CONNECTING TO SQL SERVER DATABASES

The tables you create in a LightSwitch project are put into a SQL Server database file. When you run the application, it uses a connection to the SQL Server Express instance installed on your computer. The connection is established so that the SQL Server instance receives the name of the file storing the data, and it uses this file to retrieve and save the information your application works with.

This is a very convenient solution for application developers because the data is in your project folder structure. When you move the project folder, the data also moves with it. You can copy it to another machine and continue with the development there.

The situation is a bit different with existing data. Of course, for security reasons, in many cases you cannot copy the data to your development machine. Databases can also be so huge that you can't place them on your machine.

When accessing such databases, you establish a connection to a SQL Server instance running on a separate machine over the network, and name the database you want to access. That remote SQL Server instance uses the database name in the connection information to process data retrieval and modification requests sent by the LightSwitch application.

WORKING WITH EXISTING DATA

Enterprises' databases (or even databases used by small companies) may contain sensitive data that should be hidden from the eyes of developers. To protect this information, many companies use a policy whereby only fake data is visible to developers.

The original data is copied to a temporary (development-time) database, and the sensitive information is changed to fake data that mimics the behavior of the real data. For example, personal information (such as original names, phone numbers, or e-mail addresses) or sensitive information is obfuscated. It is very important to leave the structure of the original database intact.

When the application is tested and deployed for production, the SQL connection is changed so that it points to the real, productive database.

In many cases, you can learn more about databases that have been created by LightSwitch or external databases if you examine their structure. Server Explorer in the Visual Studio LightSwitch IDE is a great tool to use for such examinations.

Using Server Explorer

As you have learned throughout this book, you can display Server Explorer with the View ⇨ Server Explorer menu command, or by pressing Ctrl+Alt+S. This tool window is generally docked on the left edge of the main screen. If you have not used it before, it contains a single `Data Connections` node, as shown in Figure 8-1.

This node is a container that lists the connections you have added to external database instances — including SQL Server, Oracle, Microsoft Access, ODBC, and so on.

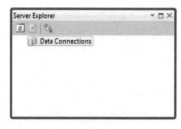

FIGURE 8-1: The Server Explorer tool window

 NOTE *Open Database Connectivity (ODBC) is a technology that provides a standard interface for accessing database management systems (DBMSs). With ODBC applications, you can access any type of database that has an ODBC provider. First released in September 1992, ODBC is an old technology. It is still used today, mostly for accessing legacy DBMSs.*

Connecting to LightSwitch Databases

You can easily add a connection to an existing LightSwitch database, as demonstrated in the following activity.

TRY IT OUT   **Connecting to a LightSwitch Database in Server Explorer**

To connect to a database created by LightSwitch, follow these steps:

1. Start Visual Studio LightSwitch and open the `ProjectTrek` project.

2. Click the root node (`ProjectTrek`) in Solution Explorer and go to the Properties Window. Click the Project Folder property. Press Tab and then Ctrl+C to copy the folder path of the project.

3. Use the View ⇨ Server Explorer command (or press Ctrl+Alt+S) to display the tool window.

4. Right-click the `Data Connections` node and select Add Connection from the context menu (or, alternatively, click the rightmost icon, which depicts a database with a plus sign) in the Server Explorer toolbar.

5. The Add Connection dialog, shown in Figure 8-2, appears.

6. Click the Change button to the right of the "Data source" box. The Change Data Source dialog will open. Select Microsoft SQL Server Database File from the "Data source" list, as shown in Figure 8-3. Click OK.

FIGURE 8-2: The Add Connection dialog

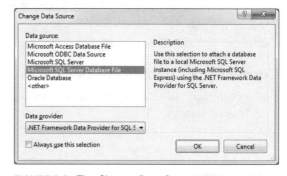

FIGURE 8-3: The Change Data Source dialog

7. The Add Connection dialog is displayed again, but now it differs from the one shown in Figure 8-2 because it displays the connection parameters for a SQL Server database file. Click the Browse button to open the Select SQL Server Database File dialog. Press Ctrl+V to paste the folder information you copied in Step 2 into the "File name" box, and then press Enter.

8. The dialog lists the contents of the project folder. Double-click the `bin` folder, and then the `Data` folder. Select the `ApplicationDatabase` file, as shown in Figure 8-4, and then click Open.

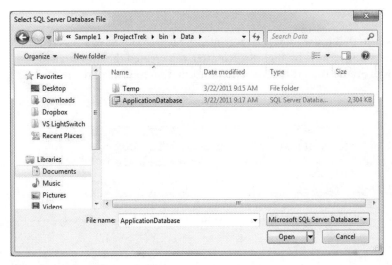

FIGURE 8-4: The Select SQL Server Database File dialog

9. You are taken back to the Add Connection dialog. The file you selected appears in the "Database file name" box, and the Use Windows Authentication option is selected, as shown in Figure 8-5. Click OK.

10. Visual Studio adds a new connection node to Server Explorer named `ApplicationDatabase.mdf`. You can expand this node to explore the structure of the database. For example, when you expand the `Tables` node, you can see a list of tables, as shown in Figure 8-6.

FIGURE 8-5: The Add Connection dialog with the selected SQL Server file

FIGURE 8-6: Tables of the ApplicationDatabase.mdf connection

How It Works

In Step 6, you set up the connection so that it uses a SQL Server file. In Steps 7 and 8, you selected the `ApplicationDatabase.mdf` file that was created by LightSwitch after you created the first table of the `ProjectTrek` application. Visual Studio used this connection information to display the related data in Server Explorer.

 NOTE *SQL Server uses data files to store database objects such as tables, views, indices, stored procedures, and so on. The* `ApplicationDatabase.mdf` *file is such a data file.*

Connecting to Existing Databases

In Chapter 4, you worked with the `Aquarium` database and learned a few things about customizing data. This database was created externally (that is, not from within a LightSwitch project). You will use this database in the following exercise to learn how to connect to an existing SQL Server database with Server Explorer.

TRY IT OUT   **Adding an Existing SQL Server Database Connection to Server Explorer**

To connect to the `Aquarium` database in Server Explorer, follow these steps:

1. In Server Explorer right-click the `Database Connections` node and run the Add Connection command from the context menu. The Add Connection dialog opens (refer to Figure 8-2), displaying Microsoft SQL Server (SqlClient) in the "Data source" box. If you see another data source type, click Change, select the Microsoft SQL Server item in the Change Data Source dialog, and click OK.

2. Type **.\SQLExpress** in the "Server name" box. This name represents the SQL Server Express instance running on your local machine. Click Test Connection at the bottom of the dialog.

3. A message box should pop up with the "Test connection succeeded" message, confirming that the local server is available. If the dialog seems frozen instead of displaying the success message, you probably mistyped the server name. In this case, after about a half minute, you'll get a message mentioning a network-related or instance-specific error. Fix the mistyped server name and click the Test Connection button again.

4. When the connection succeeds, select the `Aquarium` database from the combo box beneath the "Select or enter a database name" option, and click OK.

5. A second connection is added to Server Explorer, as shown in Figure 8-7. You can use the hierarchy of objects beneath this new node to explore the details of the `Aquarium` database.

How It Works

In this activity, you specified the name of the SQL Server instance and the database to use on that instance before connecting it. Using this type of connection, you can access remote SQL Server instances.

FIGURE 8-7: The object of the Aquarium database

The database connection information you see in Server Explorer is saved when you close Visual Studio. Therefore, when you start the IDE the next time, you don't have to recreate your connections. Simply open Server Explorer to immediately work with them.

> **NOTE** *You can also remove existing database connections from Server Explorer. Select the connection to remove and press the Delete key. Or, alternatively, right-click the connection and select Delete from the context menu. A confirmation dialog pops up asking whether you really want to delete the connection. Click OK. Only the connection is removed; your database is left intact. Later, you can reconnect to it again.*

Server Explorer provides a convenient way to discover the structure of a database. Moreover, you can change both the data and the data structure. There are many tools and commands available in Server Explorer to manage the connected database. The following exercise shows you how to use a few of them.

TRY IT OUT   Exploring the Project and ProjectTask Relationship

In Chapter 7, you created a relationship between the `Project` and `ProjectTask` tables of the `ProjectTrek` database. You learned that foreign keys are used at the "many" side of one-to-many relationships to store the primary key value on the "one" side. This activity demonstrates how LightSwitch implements the connection between a project and its related tasks.

To explore this structure, follow these steps:

1. Expand the `ApplicationDatabase.mdf` node in Server Explorer. Then expand the `Tables` node and right-click `ProjectTasks`. Select the Open Table Definition command, as shown in Figure 8-8.

2. The `ProjectTasks` table structure is displayed in the IDE. In addition to the `Id`, `Name`, `Chargeable`, and `EstimatedHours` fields, this structure contains two other fields: `ProjectTask_Project` and `ProjectTask_ProjectTask`, as shown in Figure 8-9. These are foreign key fields generated by LightSwitch behind the scenes. `ProjectTask_Project` stores the identifier of the project encapsulating the task. `ProjectTask_ProjectTask` is the foreign key of the self-referential relationship that describes the hierarchy of project tasks.

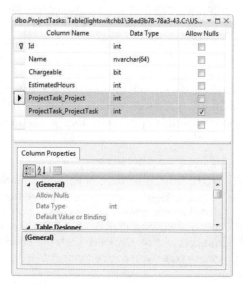

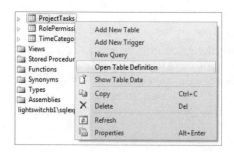

FIGURE 8-8: Database table commands in the context menu

FIGURE 8-9: Fields of the ProjectTasks table, including the highlighted foreign key fields

3. When the table structure is displayed, you can access several more table-related functions. Right-click in the table Designer; the context menu displays several commands, as shown in Figure 8-10. Select the Relationships command.

4. The Foreign Key Relationships dialog appears. Here, you can explore the details of a relationship, as shown in Figure 8-11.

FIGURE 8-10: The database table's context menu

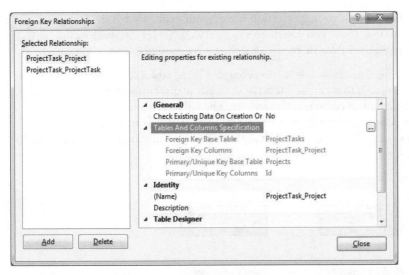

FIGURE 8-11: The Foreign Key Relationships dialog

5. Click Close.

With the database management tools built into Server Explorer, you can look at almost all of the details for a database. Of course, you do not need to manage these details here, because the Designers in the LightSwitch IDE provide you with everything you need to create and handle tables and relationships. However, as shown later in this chapter, SQL Server offers additional tools for sophisticated table design that are not available in LightSwitch. For example, you cannot create indexes or unique key constraints in LightSwitch, but you can in Server Explorer.

 WARNING *Although it is possible to modify the database structure with Server Explorer tools, you should avoid such modifications. Changing the database created by LightSwitch may cause your application to stop working correctly. It's very difficult to fix such errors. Use Server Explorer only to* view *what's in the database.*

Establishing a Connection to a SQL Server Database

You don't need to open a project in order to discover database structures in Server Explorer. However, when you want to use databases in your LightSwitch applications, Server Explorer doesn't help you.

You must connect to a database within your application project and explicitly tell the Designer which tables you would like to use. Once you attach an external SQL Server database to the LightSwitch project, you can use the tables there just as if they were created within LightSwitch.

As shown in Figure 8-12, the `ProjectTrek` application contains three tables (`Customer`, `Employee`, and `EmployeeCategory`) that can be found in the customer relationship management (CRM) system of this book's example company, ConsulArt. The CRM is a simple system developed in-house by a few ConsulArt developers a few years ago, and it is still used as a productive application. This is the database where the authentic and up-to-date list of customers and employees can be found.

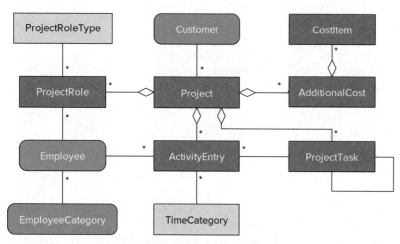

FIGURE 8-12: The entity-relationship diagram of ProjectTrek; Entities with orange backgrounds are being stored in the CRM

Creating the ConsulArtCRM Database

Of course, before you can use the CRM database for adding tables, you must create a copy that can be used at development time. As you learned earlier, generally a copy of the production database is used by developers and testers. This copy has exactly the same structure as the original database, but sensitive data is changed to fake data.

TRY IT OUT Creating the ConsulArtCRM SQL Server Database

In this exercise, you create the `ConsulArtCRM` database in the SQL Server Express instance of your computer, and use it as the development-time snapshot of the production CRM database. The database is created with a script (`CreateConsulArtCRM.sql`) that you can download from this book's companion website (www.wrox.com). The script file is located in the `Chapter 08\ConsulArtCRM` folder.

To create the development-time database, follow these steps:

1. Download and save the `CreateConsulArtCRM.sql` file into a temporary folder. Note the name of this folder.

2. Start a command prompt by typing **cmd** in the Search Programs and Files box of the Start menu, and press the Enter key. If you are used to any other way to run the command prompt, do as you like to start it.

3. Type the following line into the command window, replacing *<folder>* with the name of the folder you noted in Step 1:

    ```
    sqlcmd -S .\SQLEXPRESS -i "<folder>\CreateConsulArtCRM.sql"
    ```

    For example, if your folder is `C:\Chapter8`, use the following command line:

    ```
    sqlcmd -S .\SQLEXPRESS -i "C:\Chapter8\CreateConsulArtCRM.sql"
    ```

This will create the `ConsulArtCRM` database in your local SQL Express instance in a few seconds. Once the database is created, the command prompt window displays the simple message shown in Figure 8-13.

How It Works

The `sqlcmd` utility executed the commands in the `CreateConsulArtCRM.sql` file on the SQL Server Express instance on your machine. The `-S .\SQLEXPRESS` command-line argument tells the utility that it must connect to the SQL Server Express instance, and the `-i "<folder>\CreateConsulArtCRM.sql"` argument specifies the name of the script file.

FIGURE 8-13: The sqlcmd command-line utility created the ConsulArt database

This script file first creates the database, then three tables, and fills them with sample data. Using Server Explorer, you can connect to the `ConsulArtCRM` database and explore the new tables there, as shown in Figure 8-14.

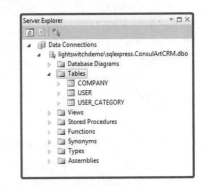

FIGURE 8-14: The ConsulArtCRM database in Server Explorer

Attaching to Tables in External Databases

In the previous exercise, you successfully installed the development-time `ConsulArtCRM` database. You must attach to the tables in `ConsulArtCRM` to use them in the `ProjectTrek` application. With LightSwitch, this is an easy task, as shown in the following exercise.

TRY IT OUT | **Adding the ConsulArtCRM Database as a Data Source**

NOTE *In this exercise, you continue the sample that you finished in Chapter 7. You can find the starting sample on this book's companion website at* `www.wrox.com` *in the folder* `Chapter 08\Start`*.*

To use the tables in the `ConsulArtCRM` database, follow these steps:

1. Start Visual Studio LightSwitch and open `ProjectTrek`.

2. Right-click the `ProjectTrek` node in Solution Explorer and select Add Data Source from the context menu. (Alternatively, you can select the `Data Sources` project node and use the Add Data Source command from its context menu.)

3. The Attach Data Source Wizard appears and asks you to select a data source type, as shown in Figure 8-15. Choose the Database option to connect to a SQL Server instance.

4. Click Next. The Connection Properties dialog appears, where you must specify the connection information. Type **.\SQLExpress** in the "Server name" box (the dot character is needed before the backslash), and then click Test Connection at the bottom of the dialog.

5. A message box pops up with the "Test connection succeeded" message, confirming that the local server is available.

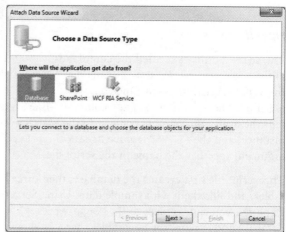

FIGURE 8-15: The Attach Data Source Wizard asks you to choose a data source type

6. Select the `ConsulArtCRM` database from the combo box beneath the "Select or enter a database name" option, as shown in Figure 8-16. Click OK.

7. The wizard displays the objects in the `ConsulArtCRM` database. Expand the `Tables` node and select the `USER` and `USER_CATEGORY` tables, as shown in Figure 8-17. The Data Source Name text box is set to `ConsulArtCRMData`. Click Finish.

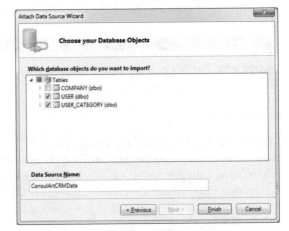

FIGURE 8-16: Connection properties to access ConsulArtCRM

FIGURE 8-17: The USER and USER_CATEGORY tables are selected for import

8. The new data source and the selected tables are added to the project, as shown in Figure 8-18, and the USER table is displayed in the Designer. There is a one-to-many relationship between USER_CATEGORY and USER. The Designer shows this relationship with a line binding these tables.

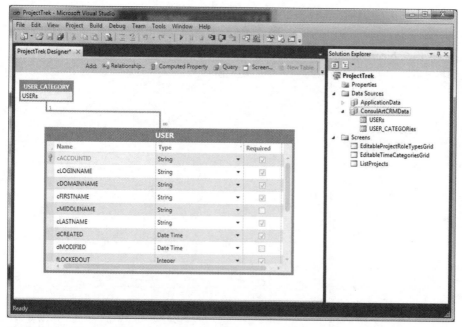

FIGURE 8-18: The new data source and its tables in Solution Explorer

How It Works

With the help of the Attach Data Source Wizard, you specified a database connection (Steps 4 through 6) and selected the data tables to attach (Step 7). LightSwitch stored the database connection information with the ConsulArtCRMData, as the highlighted node in Figure 8-18 shows. This connection information is especially important for LightSwitch, because it provides a way to access the information about the data structure — during both design time and runtime.

The ConsulArtCRM database contains a relationship between the USER and USER_CATEGORY tables. LightSwitch recognizes this relationship (it uses the original data and their existing structure) and represents it just as if it were added manually.

Attaching Additional Objects Using an Existing Connection

Figure 8-17 shows that the external database contains three tables (COMPANY, USER, and USER_CATEGORY), but the CUSTOMER table was not added to the project in the last exercise. That's because the exercise was merely intended to show you how you can utilize an existing connection to add more objects.

Typically, an external database has a lot of tables, and you may not know in advance which tables you need to attach. Later, as you progress with the implementation of your application, you might recognize that you need additional tables — or, more often, another kind of database object: a view.

The following exercise describes how you can manage additional objects for an existing connection.

TRY IT OUT   Adding the COMPANY Table Using the Existing Connection

In this exercise, you use a new script (`CreateCompanyView.sql`) to create a view based on the COMPANY table. You can download the script from this book's companion website (www.wrox.com). The script file is located in the `Chapter 08\ConsulArtCRM` folder.

To add the COMPANY table and vwCOMPANY view to the project, follow these steps:

1. Download and save the `CreateCompanyView.sql` file into a temporary folder. Note the name of this folder.

2. Start a command prompt by typing **cmd** in the Search Programs and Files box of the Start menu and pressing the Enter key (or start the command prompt in any other way you prefer).

3. Type the following line into the command window, replacing *<folder>* with the name of the folder that you noted in Step 1:

   ```
   sqlcmd -S .\SQLEXPRESS -i "<folder>\CreateCompanyView.sql"
   ```

   This script will add a new view named vwCOMPANY to the ConsulArtCRM database in a few seconds. When the new view is ready (the Changed database context to 'ConsulArtCRM' message appears), close the command prompt window.

4. In Solution Explorer, right-click the ConsulArtCRM node and run the Update Data Source command. LightSwitch starts the Attach Data Source Wizard. It knows the connection, and scans the database to collect its objects.

5. Expand the Tables and Views nodes. The wizard recognizes that the USER and USER_CATEGORY tables have already been added, so they are checked. Select the COMPANY table and the vwCOMPANY view by clicking their respective check boxes, as shown in Figure 8-19. Click Finish.

6. The warning shown in Figure 8-20 will appear. That's because the vwCOMPANY view does not contain any primary key, which is required in order to modify a table. Click Continue. LightSwitch will attach the vwCOMPANY view as a read-only table.

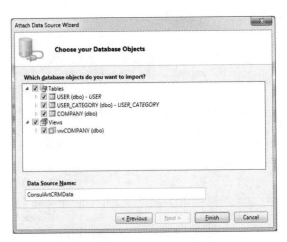

FIGURE 8-19: Refreshing the data source

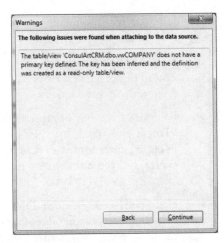

FIGURE 8-20: Displaying the warning about the vwCOMPANY view

7. As shown in Solution Explorer, both new database objects have been added to the data connection. Right-click `ConsulArtCRM` and run the Update Data Source command again.

8. In the Attach Data Source Wizard, expand the `Views` node and uncheck `vwCOMPANY`. Click Finish. LightSwitch will remove the `vwCOMPANY` object from Solution Explorer.

> **NOTE** *You may find the complete code to download for this exercise on this book's companion website at* www.wrox.com *in the folder* Chapter 08\ Sample 1 - Connecting to SQL Server.

How It Works

You added the `vwCOMPANY` view by running the script in Step 3. LightSwitch can attach to tables and views, which is why you could mark the `vwCOMPANY` view in Step 5. This view has no use in the `ProjectTrek` application; you added it only to learn about this feature. As demonstrated in Steps 7 and 8, you can remove an existing object from a connection.

> **NOTE** *Views are table-like objects in DBMSs that represent the results of queries. You can use them just like tables. When a view participates in a query, its name is substituted with its definition. The* vwCOMPANY *view is a query on the* COMPANY *table that omits the* cLONGNAME *and* cCOMMENT *fields from the table.*

CUSTOMIZING DATA IN EXISTING DATABASES

Legacy databases may use naming and programming conventions that are very different from the ones you would like to use. Here are a few examples:

> ➤ They may use unfriendly field names such as `CMR_ID` instead of `CustomerId`, or `SHADDR` instead of `ShippingAddress`. Working with unfriendly names can be frustrating, and diminish your productivity.

> ➤ Boolean values may be represented with characters. For example, "Y" stands for "Yes" or "True"; "N" stands for "No" or "False." In your programming logic, you cannot use simple Boolean expressions with field names, such as "If `Active` Then . . .". Instead of using this expression, you must write a more complicated and less intuitive expression, such as "If Active = "Y" Then . . .".

> ➤ Fields representing date and time values often store the date and the time parts in separate fields that accept either integers or characters. For example, the "12/31/2008 1:05PM" value can be stored as two integers, such as `20081231` and `130500`. It's difficult to work with these fields in their native representations.

You cannot change the structure of external databases, because doing so might break existing applications. However, with the help of LightSwitch, you can avoid these difficulties. You have a few tools you can use to tailor the external databases to the style you intend to work with — while keeping the original database structure intact.

Renaming Tables and Fields

ConsulArt updated its CRM system using a legacy system written in FoxPro. Developers migrated the FoxPro tables to SQL Server with original table and field names. The COMPANY, USER, and USER_CATEGORY tables inherit the names of their fields from the old FoxPro system.

These names do not conform to the naming conventions used at ConsulArt. The COMPANY name in the CRM system should be the Customer entity in ProjectTrek. Also, the original tables contain several fields that have no use in ProjectTrek.

With LightSwitch, you can easily change tables to meet these requirements, as you will learn in the subsequent exercises.

TRY IT OUT   Changing Table and Field Definitions

To change the newly added ConsulArtCRM tables, follow these steps:

1.   Double-click the COMPANies node in Solution Explorer to open the COMPANY table in the Designer. In the Properties window, change the Name property to Customer. The Plural Name property is automatically changed from COMPANies to Customers.

2.   Using Table 8-1 as a guide, change the field names of the Customer table. The left column lists the old field names; the right column defines the new ones.

TABLE 8-1: Field Names of the Customer Table

OLD NAME	NEW NAME
cSHORTNAME	Name
cLONGNAME	LongName
cADDRESS1	AddressLine1
cADDRESS2	AddressLine2
cCITY	City
cSTATE	State
cCOUNTRY	Country
cZIP	Zip
cCOMMENT	Comment

3. Save the changes by pressing Ctrl+S.

4. Use the same technique described in Step 1 to rename the USER table to Employee.

5. Using Table 8-2 as a guide, change the Employee field names, and then save the changes by pressing Ctrl+S.

TABLE 8-2: Field Names of the Employee Table

OLD NAME	NEW NAME
cLOGINNAME	LoginName
cDOMAINNAME	DomainName
cFIRSTNAME	FirstName
cMIDDLENAME	MiddleName
cLASTNAME	LastName
dCREATED	Created
dMODIFIED	Modified
fLOCKEDOUT	LockedOut
cFULLLOGINNAME	FullLoginName
cEMAILADDRESS	Email

6. Rename the USER_CATEGORY table to EmployeeCategory and use Table 8-3 as a guide to rename its fields. Save the changes.

TABLE 8-3: Field Names of the EmployeeCategory Table

OLD NAME	NEW NAME
cDISPLAYNAME	DisplayName
cDESCRIPTION	Description
mHOURLYFEE	HourlyFee
cSTATUS	Status
fFLAGS	Flags
USERs	Employees

How It Works

The changes you've made in the renaming steps leave the original tables (and all fields) intact. LightSwitch does not change the existing database because it could lead to unpredicted failures in the existing systems. Instead, LightSwitch creates mappings between the existing data tables (and all fields) and their representation within LightSwitch. These mappings are used with all database operations. For example, when you query the content of the EmployeeCategory table's Status field, LightSwitch takes care of using the cSTATUS name when communicating with the remote database.

 NOTE *As you may have recognized in this exercise, the primary key fields cannot be renamed. These fields are read-only, because LightSwitch handles all primary key fields as read-only ones. It is not a constraint of SQL Server, but rather a design pattern used in many enterprise applications, and LightSwitch designers opted to follow this pattern.*

The tables in the ConsulArtCRM database contain several fields that are useless in the ProjectTrek application. Such fields are Comment in Customer; FullLoginName and DomainName in Employee; or Flags in EmployeeCategory.

Although it might seem logical to simply delete these fields from table definitions, LightSwitch does not allow you to do that. While removing them from the definition would not cause any problem when querying data, inserting new data would be an issue. Even if a field is not used on the LightSwitch side, some data must be put into the database for required fields. LightSwitch handles this issue by not allowing the removal of fields.

Later, you will add screens using the attached tables. To avoid adding UI elements for the unused fields, you can uncheck their Is Visible On Screen property.

Mapping and Changing Field Types

LightSwitch automatically maps the storage types of fields (that is, the physical types used in SQL Server) to LightSwitch types. This mapping is summarized in Table 8-4. The first two columns show how a given SQL type is mapped. The SQL Server type in the first column is mapped to the LightSwitch type in the second column. There are types where either the maximum field length or field precision is used on the SQL Server side. These field attributes are mapped to LightSwitch field properties, as the third column of the table indicates. For example, the binary(128) SQL Server type is mapped to the Binary LightSwitch type so that its MaxLength property is set to 128.

TABLE 8-4: SQL Server Data Type Mapping

SQL TYPE	LIGHTSWITCH TYPE	FIELD PROPERTIES
binary(*n*)	Binary	MaxLength=*n*
image	Binary	MaxLength=Max
timestamp	Binary	MaxLength=8
varbinary(*n*)	Binary	MaxLength=*n*
bit	Boolean	
tinyint	Byte	
date	Date	
datetime	DateTime	
datetime2(*n*)	DateTime	
smalldatetime	DateTime	
decimal(*p*,*s*)	Decimal	Precision=*p* Scale=*s*
money	Decimal	Precision=19 Scale=4
numeric(*p*,*s*)	Decimal	Precision=*p* Scale=*s*
smallmoney	Decimal	Precision=10 Scale=4
float	Double	
uniqueidentifier	Guid	
smallint	Short Integer	
int	Integer	
bigint	Long Integer	
real	Single	
char(*n*)	String	MaxLength=*n*
nchar(*n*)	String	MaxLength=*n*
ntext	String	
nvarchar(*n*)	String	MaxLength=*n*
text	String	
varchar(*n*)	String	MaxLength=*n*
xml	String	MaxLength=Max
time(*n*)	TimeSpan	

The `Required` attribute of all fields is automatically mapped. If the specific field may contain a NULL value (in the SQL Server database), then `Required` is set to `False`; otherwise, it is set to `True`.

 WARNING *A few rarely used SQL Server types are not supported by LightSwitch, such as* `datetimeoffset`, `geography`, `geometry`, `hierarchyid`, *and* `sql_variant`. *If you attach tables containing fields with one of these types, LightSwitch excludes these fields from the attached tables.*

As you learned in Chapter 6, LightSwitch supports two types of fields:

➤ *Intrinsic types* — Sometimes known as *simple types*, these refer to physical storage types such as `Integer`, `String`, `Binary`, `Boolean`, and so on (refer to Table 8-4).

➤ *Business types* — Sometimes referred to as *semantic types*, these extend the behavior of intrinsic field types. They are wrappers around intrinsic types, and provide extra behavior such as predefined validation, specialized data entry, and data formatting.

When you attach an external table, LightSwitch maps SQL Server types to intrinsic types. You cannot change the type of a field to another intrinsic type. However, you can change it to a business type. In the following exercise you will learn how simple it is.

TRY IT OUT | **Changing Field Types of Attached Tables**

A few field types in the `ConsulArtCRM` tables are mapped to intrinsic types. However, there are business types that would better cover their semantics. Such fields are `HourlyFee` in `EmployeeCategory`, and `Email` in `Employee`.

To change the types of these fields, follow these steps:

1. Open the `EmployeeCategory` table in the Designer.

2. Select the `HourlyFee` field by clicking its row header. Click the drop-down arrow of the Type column and select `Money`, as shown in Figure 8-21.

FIGURE 8-21: Changing the HourlyFee type from Decimal to Money

3. Save the changes by pressing Ctrl+S.

4. Open the `Employee` table in the Designer.

5. Select the `Email` field by clicking its row header. Click the drop-down arrow of the Type column and select `Email Address` as the new type of the field.

6. Save the changes.

How It Works

Business types extend intrinsic (storage) types with behaviors such as input masking, output formatting, and validation. Each business type is based on a certain intrinsic type. You can change the field type from an intrinsic type to any business type based on the field's original type. Because Money is based on Decimal, you could change HourlyFee from Decimal to Money. This same concept applies to Email, so you can change it from String to EmailAddress.

Using Computed Properties to Extend Attached Tables

The ConsulArt's CRM application has a USER_CATEGORY table (renamed to Employee in the ProjectTrek application) with a field named cSTATUS (renamed to Status). This field is a one-character String, and is used as a Boolean value. Its "A" value ("A" stands for "Active") indicates that the record is active. The "D" ("Deleted") signals the inactive state of the record. Instead of using the unfriendly Status field, it would be better to use an Active field with a Boolean value — to follow the pattern used for the TimeCategory and ProjectRoleType tables in Chapter 6.

Computed properties in LightSwitch provide a great solution for this problem. At any time, you can add new computed properties to an attached table, as you will learn from the following exercise.

TRY IT OUT   Creating a New Computed Property for EmployeeCategory

The Status field is used to signal if an employee is active (Status contains an "A") or inactive (Status contains a "D"). To avoid using the unfriendly Status field, follow these steps to create a new Active computed Boolean property for the EmployeeCategory table:

1. Open the EmployeeCategory table in the Designer.

2. Select the Status field by clicking its row header, and uncheck the Display By Default check box in the Properties window.

3. Click the <Add Property> cell in the last row, and type **Active** to name the new property. Click Tab to change its type. As soon as the focus is moved to the Type column, a small calculator icon appears in the row header, indicating that this is a

FIGURE 8-22: The new Active computed property

computed property, as shown in Figure 8-22. Confirm that the Is Computed check box is set in the Properties window, and note that you're not allowed to change it.

4. Click the Edit Method task link in the Properties window to create the computing code for this property. The EmployeeCategory.vb (EmployeeCategory.cs) file is opened and the Active_Compute method's skeleton is shown as follows:

VB
```vb
Namespace ProjectTrek

    Public Class EmployeeCategory

        Private Sub Active_Compute(ByRef result As Boolean)
            ' Set result to the desired field value

        End Sub
    End Class

End Namespace
```

C#
```csharp
namespace LightSwitchApplication
{
    public partial class EmployeeCategory
    {
        partial void Active_Compute(ref bool result)
        {
            // Set result to the desired field value

        }
    }
}
```

5. Add the following boldfaced statement to the body of `Active_Compute`:

VB
```vb
        Private Sub Active_Compute(ByRef result As Boolean)
            ' Set result to the desired field value
            result = Me.Status.ToUpper = "A"
        End Sub
```

C#
```csharp
        partial void Active_Compute(ref bool result)
        {
            // Set result to the desired field value
            result = this.Status.ToUpper() == "A";
        }
```

6. Press Ctrl+Shift+S to save your changes.

> **NOTE** *You may find the complete code to download for this exercise on this book's companion website at* www.wrox.com *in the folder* Chapter 08\
> Sample 2 - Connecting to SQL Server.

How It Works

You can add computed properties to an entity representing an attached table, because computed properties are read-only, and therefore never written back to the database. When the `Active` property is accessed, its value is calculated by the `Active_Compute` method (with the statement you added in Step 5). Instead of using the `Status` field with "A" and "D" values (that do not tell what they mean), you can use the `Active` Boolean field, which is more natural and intuitive to use.

> **NOTE** You can use the `Active` property instead of `Status` only in read-only scenarios. If you had to write the `Active` value back to the database, this solution would not help, because `Active` is a read-only property. The `ProjectTrek` application uses the tables in the `ConsulArtCRM` database only for querying data. ConsulArt uses its own CRM system to change the content of these tables.

Server-Side Computed Fields

SQL Server tables can also have computed fields on the server side. (This is the same concept in SQL Server as computed properties in LightSwitch.) The `Employee` table has such a computed field, the `FullLoginName` field that is calculated from the `DomainName` and `LoginName` fields on the SQL Server side.

When attaching tables with server-side computed fields, LightSwitch exposes them as read-only fields, and uses this information when you create screens. For example, if you were to create a default edit screen for the `Employee` table, it would display the `FullLoginName` field with a `Label` control, indicating that it is read-only, as shown in Figure 8-23.

FIGURE 8-23: Server-side computed fields are read-only

MANAGING DATA RELATIONSHIPS

As you learned in Chapter 7, relationships are fundamental concepts in databases, and LightSwitch uses them to help you create master-detail screens.

When you use external databases, LightSwitch provides you with the same flexibility when working with relationships. It doesn't matter whether your tables and relationships are created in LightSwitch or come from external databases; you can use them in the same way.

Using Existing Relationships

Earlier, when you attached tables from the `ConsulArtCRM` database, you saw that LightSwitch recognized the one-to-many relationship between `USER_CATEGORY` (later renamed to `EmployeeCategory`) and `USER` (renamed to `Employee`), as shown in Figure 8-24.

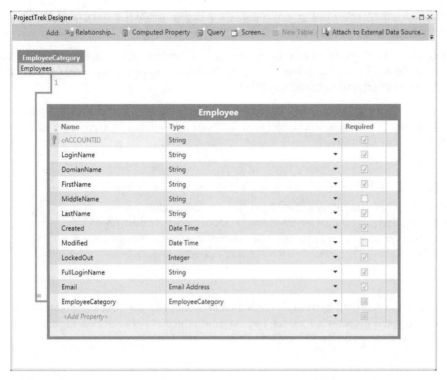

FIGURE 8-24: The relationship between EmployeeCategory and Employee, as recognized by LightSwitch

Because these relationships are managed by SQL Server, you have a very limited capability to edit the details. You cannot alter anything that would cause a change on the SQL Server side.

You can right-click on the line representing the relationship in the Designer and run the Edit Relationship command. This allows you to modify only the navigation property names. (These are not used on the SQL Server side, but only on the LightSwitch side.)

For the same reason, in the LightSwitch IDE you cannot delete relationships created (and managed) on the SQL Server side.

Creating New Relationships between a LightSwitch Table and an External Table

External tables can participate in new relationships created in LightSwitch. Because you are not allowed to alter any objects in the existing SQL Server database, you have only a limited number of options for creating a relationship between external tables and LightSwitch tables:

➤ You can create a one-to-many relationship if an existing SQL Server table is on the "one" side and a LightSwitch table is on the "many" side.

➤ A zero-or-one-to-many relationship is allowed when an existing SQL Server table is on the "zero-or-one" side and a LightSwitch table is on the "many" side.

➤ You can create a one-to-many or zero-or-one-to-many relationship if an existing SQL Server table is on the "many" side, and it has an existing field that can be used as a foreign key to the "one" side table created in LightSwitch.

➤ A one-to-zero-or-one relationship is allowed when an existing SQL Server table is on the "zero-or-one" side, and it has an existing field than can be used as a foreign key to the "one" side table created in LightSwitch.

NOTE *Any other options require creating a foreign field in the external database. Because this kind of modification is not allowed (it could break existing applications), you can use only the options mentioned here.*

When you select one of the accepted options, LightSwitch provides you with the same simplicity to create a relationship between LightSwitch tables and external tables as between two LightSwitch tables. The following exercise shows you how to do this.

TRY IT OUT   Creating Relationships between the ProjectTrek and ConsulArtCRM Tables

As shown in Figure 8-12, the `Project` and `ProjectRole` tables in the `ProjectTrek` database (created in LightSwitch) have relationships with the `Customer` and `Employee` tables (in `ConsulArtCRM`), respectively.

To establish these relationships, follow these steps:

1. In Solution Explorer, double-click the `Projects` node to open the `Project` table in the Designer. Click the Relationship button in the Designer's toolbar.

2. In the Add New Relationship dialog, `Project` is set as the source (as you can see in the From column and Name row). Select the `Customer` table as the destination (in the To column and Name row). At the bottom of the dialog, LightSwitch shows that it will automatically add a new foreign key field (named `Customer_iID`) to `Project` in order to implement the relationship, as shown in Figure 8-25. Click OK.

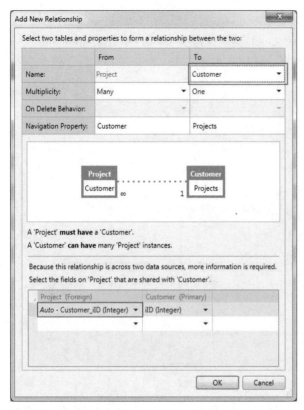

FIGURE 8-25: The Add New Relationship dialog shows the relationship between Project and Customer tables

3. The Designer depicts this new relationship between Project and Customer with a dashed line (as shown in Figure 8-26), whereas relationships created earlier are depicted with a solid line (as shown in Figure 8-24). Two new properties are added to the Project table. Customer represents the customer owning the project instance, and Customer_iID is the foreign key field to the Customer table.

4. Save the changes by pressing Ctrl+S.

5. Add a new table to ProjectTrek, and name it **ProjectRole**. This table will store information about team assignments, indicating which employees work on a specific project, and in what role. This table will hold only the default Id property and the relationships to the Project, ProjectRoleType, and Employee tables, but no other attributes.

6. Click the Relationship button. Then, in the Add New Relationship dialog, select Project in the To column and click OK.

FIGURE 8-26: The relationship is depicted with a dashed line, indicating that it is between separate data sources

7. Similarly, add a relationship to the `ProjectRoleType` table.

8. Add a new relationship to the `Employee` table. Simply select `Employee` in the To column and click OK. LightSwitch will add a new foreign key column (`Employee_cACCOUNTID`) to the table, as shown in Figure 8-27.

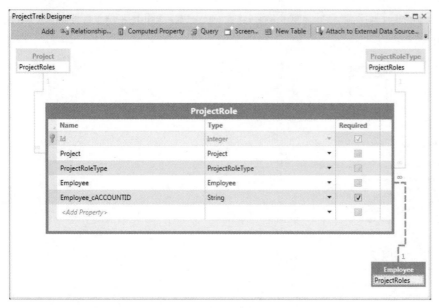

FIGURE 8-27: The ProjectRoleType table and its relationships

9. Save the changes by pressing Ctrl+S.

> **NOTE** *You may find the complete code to download for this exercise on this book's companion website at* www.wrox.com *in the folder* Chapter 08\
> Sample 3 - Managing Relationships.

How It Works

When you added a one-to-many relationship between a SQL Server table and a LightSwitch table (in Step 8), the Designer added two properties. The first represents the entity on the "one" side, and the other was created to store foreign key values to the SQL data tables.

As you learned in Chapter 7, LightSwitch creates foreign key values on the "many" side of relationships, even when you bind LightSwitch tables. However, in that case, these fields are not exposed. If the "one" side of the relationship is an external database, this foreign key is exposed. Without going into deep technical details, the reason is because this way, LightSwitch can use and cache the foreign key data internally without needing to access the external database. The SQL Server database is accessed only when data is about to be read from the Employee or Customer tables.

SUMMARY

Many applications use external databases to implement their functionality. Visual Studio LightSwitch allows accessing SQL Server databases, SharePoint 2010 lists, and external data sources through Windows Communication Foundation (WCF) Rich Internet Application (RIA) Services.

The Server Explorer window is a very useful tool for exploring existing data structures, including SQL Server databases or the LightSwitch database file.

You can easily connect to an existing SQL Server database and use table and view objects there just as if they were created within the LightSwitch projects. The IDE recognizes the existing relationships, and lets you rename external tables and fields. With computed properties, you can add virtual read-only data to external tables.

You can create relationships between LightSwitch tables and external tables (with a few constraints), and use them with the same simplicity as any other relationships.

EXERCISES

1. What type of data source can be used to access the SQL Server database created by LightSwitch?

2. Which utility program can be used from a command line to run scripts on your local SQL Express server?

3. Which command can be used to attach tables to a LightSwitch Project: Server Explorer ➪ Add Connection or Project ➪ Add Data Source?

4. How does LightSwitch handle relationships between tables within an external database when you add the tables to your project?

5. List a few limitations with regard to customizing external tables.

6. Explain how you can create a one-to-many relationship between a LightSwitch table and an external SQL Server table.

 NOTE *Answers to the Exercises can be found in the Appendix.*

▶ **WHAT YOU LEARNED IN THIS CHAPTER**

TOPIC	KEY CONCEPTS
Connecting to a SQL Server database from Server Explorer	Use the View ➪ Server Explorer command to display the Server Explorer tool window. Right-click the Data Connections node and run the Add Connection command. Specify the connection parameters in the Add Connection dialog and click OK.
Microsoft SQL Server data source type	This type of data source can be used to connect to an external (from the LightSwitch application's point of view) SQL Server database.
Microsoft SQL Server Database File data source type	This type of data source can be used to connect to the database that contains tables created in the LightSwitch IDE.
The `sqlcmd.exe` utility	With the help of this utility, you can run scripts on a SQL Server instance — assuming you have been granted the related permissions. In addition to other tasks, you can use this utility to create development-time copies of production databases.
Attaching tables in external databases	Select the Data Source node in Solution Explorer and run the Add Data Source command in its context menu. With the help of the Attach Data Source Wizard, specify the SQL Server connection, select the tables (or views) you want to attach, and click Finish.
Attaching or detaching external objects	Select the Data Source node in Solution Explorer and run the Refresh Data Source command in its context menu. In the Attach Data Source Wizard dialog, select the tables you want to attach and unselect the ones to detach. Click Finish.
Changing field types in external tables	You can change the type of an external table's field only to business types that are compatible with the storage type. A business type is compatible only with the storage type on which it is based. For example, `Decimal` and `Money` types are compatible, because `Money` is based on `Decimal`.
Adding new fields to external tables	You can add new fields to external tables but LightSwitch adds them as computed fields, so they are read-only. You cannot add read-write fields to an external table.
Managing existing relationships	LightSwitch recognizes existing relationships within an external database, and automatically creates them when you attach tables. You cannot edit the properties of these relationships, only the names of navigation properties.

TOPIC	KEY CONCEPTS
Creating a new relationship within an attached data source	LightSwitch does not allow creating a new relationship within an attached data source.
Creating a relationship between a LightSwitch table and an external table	You can create any kind of relationship that does not require creating a foreign key field in the external table. That table can be on the "one" side of relationships. It can also be on the "many" side of a relationship, assuming that it already has a field that can be used as the foreign key.

Building and Customizing Screens

WHAT YOU WILL LEARN IN THIS CHAPTER

➤ Understanding the role of data and layout items (the constituent parts of the UI)

➤ Working with layout containers and understanding how they provide elastic screen behavior

➤ Using data grids, lists, simple controls, and value pickers to build your screens

➤ Understanding the runtime customization feature of LightSwitch

➤ Creating methods and assigning them to buttons and links in the UI

➤ Changing the default screen navigation structure of your LightSwitch application

In Chapters 6 and 7, you created several screens and customized their layouts. The exercises there helped you try out simple layout manipulations. However, you have only scratched the surface of the features available in building LightSwitch screens.

In this chapter, you learn the most important concepts and the basic architecture of screens. You will go through many exercises to learn about each important element of building and customizing your screens.

UNDERSTANDING THE SCREEN LAYOUT STRUCTURE

By now, you have created several screens (including lists, search, and details screens) with the Add New Screen dialog. As you have already learned, LightSwitch uses a declarative approach to describe screen elements. Instead of positioning user interface (UI) controls with screen coordinates, LightSwitch uses a hierarchy to define the layout.

With many rapid application development (RAD) tools, a typical screen editor provides a WYSIWYG (What-You-See-Is-What-You-Get) approach. The editor shows the exact layout, and draws small adornments around controls to let the Designer move and resize them, as well as alter their visual properties. Most tools use a kind of data-binding mechanism to tie UI controls with the data they show.

LightSwitch has a totally different approach. Instead of supporting the WYSIWYG layout design, it uses two hierarchies to edit data items and layout items of a screen. Figure 9-1 shows the elements of the Screen Designer (the screenshot is grabbed from the `ListProjects` screen of the `ProjectTrek` project, and it reflects the completed state of the last exercise in Chapter 8).

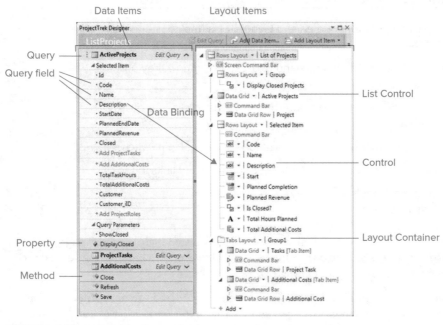

FIGURE 9-1: Elements of the Screen Designer

Let's take a closer look at some of those elements.

Data Items

The left panel of the Screen Designer shows the hierarchy of data items. A *data item* is a piece of information that can be shown in the screen. Of course, the majority of this information comes from a database, but you can use other kinds of data items, too, as you will learn soon.

Queries

Almost every screen includes a *query* that retrieves a set of items from the database, or (in the case of detail screens) exactly one item, assuming it can be found in the database. You can see three queries in Figure 9-1 — namely, ActiveProjects, ProjectTasks, and AdditionalCosts. You can easily recognize them by the Edit Query task links and the drop-menu indicators.

Queries can retrieve items not only from a database, but also from a container attached to an entity. In Figure 9-1, only ActiveProjects is bound directly to the database. The other two queries use the ProjectTasks and AdditionalCosts container properties of the selected ActiveProjects item (the source property names are the same as the query names).

Queries in LightSwitch are strongly typed, which means they retrieve one item or a collection of items that belong to a table type. For example, the ActiveProjects query retrieves a set of Project records.

The results of queries that retrieve a collection of items are generally displayed in lists or grids from which the user can select an item. This is represented by Selected Item, and it is a virtual container of entity properties. In Figure 9-1 you can see the properties such as Id, Code, Name, Description, and many others nested into Selected Item.

Screen Properties

You can work with data items that are not bound to tables. *Screen properties* (indicated with a small blue field icon) are such items. You can add local properties to the screens, which represent information used locally. For example, the DisplayClosed property in Figure 9-1 stores a flag signaling whether the list of closed projects should be displayed.

Although screen properties are intended to be used only within the screen declaring them, you can expose them to the environment by checking their Is Parameter property in the Properties window. If this flag is set, you can use the property to pass the parameter to the screen through the property. For example, if you created a screen for selecting an airport, you could use a Region property to pass the code of the region from which to select an airport. The property should have its Is Parameter property set.

The Is Required flag of a screen property (you find it in the Properties window) can be used to specify that the property must have a value. Unchecking this flag allows the property to have an empty value. For example, you could create a screen with a FocusProject parameter to automatically select the project with the Id passed in FocusProject. Check the Is Parameter property of FocusProject and uncheck its Is Required property. You can implement the screen's UI logic so that while FocusProject is empty, no project is selected; but when FocusProject has a value, you select the corresponding project.

Methods

You can add data items called *methods* to your screen. Methods are local screen operations that can be used in the screen either programmatically or by the user, assuming you provide a UI element that can trigger the method execution. For example, you could add a method to the `ListProjects` screen to calculate the backlog of the selected project, and show it in a separate screen. By default, methods do nothing until you add code that represents the operation to be executed by them.

Methods can be represented by a button or a task link (hyperlink) in the screen. You can also write code that tells the environment whether or not the method can be executed (that is, whether it should be displayed on the screen as enabled or disabled). For example, if no project is selected, the method calculating the project backlog should not be enabled.

Layout Items

The UI elements of the screen are represented by *layout items* that reserve the right panel of the Screen Designer, as shown in Figure 9-1. Layout items are organized into a hierarchy represented by a tree view. Every node in this tree represents an element in the UI, and nested nodes are all part of the UI element represented by their parent nodes. For example, the `Rows Layout` node represents a panel of the screen and all nested nodes (including `Command Bar`, `Code`, `Name`, and `Description` text boxes, as well as the other nested elements).

Displaying Layout Elements in the Screen Designer

All layout elements are displayed with four parts from left to right:

➤   A small icon depicting the type of the layout element.

➤   The type name of the layout element. (This is not always displayed.)

➤   The display name of the data item bound to the layout item. It can be empty, if the item is not bound to any data element.

➤   An optional display role that helps to indicate the relationship between the layout item and its parent element.

The type name and the display name are always separated by a vertical bar (|).

FIGURE 9-2: Layout element parts in the Screen Designer

The `Additional Costs Data Grid` uses all parts, as shown in Figure 9-2. In this case, the display role is set to [Tab Item], telling you that the `Additional Costs` element is placed on a separate tab within its parent `Tabs Layout` node.

The `Command Bar` layout element shown in Figure 9-3 does not have a data item bound to it, so the "Command Bar" text you see is its type name. The `Code` layout element in Figure 9-3 is a `Text Box`. It does not display a type name because the icon depicts clearly that it is a text box, so the type name would not add much value. The "Code" text is located to the right of the vertical bar, so it is the display name of the layout item bound to it.

FIGURE 9-3: The Command Bar and Text Box layout elements

Simple Controls

The leaves of the hierarchy tree are *controls* that represent UI elements to display or input data. Controls have a type, such as Text Box, Check Box, Label, Date Time Picker, Auto Complete Box, and so on. The type determines the basic appearance and behavior of a control. For example, a Label can display data but does not provide a means for input. An Auto Complete Box can be used to select an element from a drop-down list; a Text Box can be used to edit text, and so on.

Controls are the primitive UI elements that are generally bound to data items or screen properties to show and edit their values.

List Controls

Data is very often presented on the screen in tabular form using lists and grids. *List controls* provide the behavior that enables users to browse large amounts of data. LightSwitch comes with two list controls out-of-the-box: List and Data Grid. These controls manage a lot of tasks, including paging, sorting, selecting the current item, and so on.

List controls use their nested nodes to define the UI template of items to display. For example, the Data Grid list control in Figure 9-4 has two nested items: Command Bar defines buttons that are displayed in the toolbar of the grid, while Data Grid Row describes the template of one row by nesting UI elements bound to the properties. Figure 9-5 shows the result of this layout definition.

FIGURE 9-4: The layout definition of a Data Grid

FIGURE 9-5: The result of the layout definition in Figure 9-4

Layout Containers

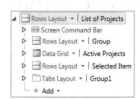

FIGURE 9-6: Layout containers in the UI definition

Layout containers are responsible for establishing the overall structure of a screen by rendering nested layout elements. For example, the root Rows Layout element in Figure 9-6 is a layout container that renders its nested items from top to bottom. The first nested element is rendered at the top, then the second beneath the first one, and so on. As you can see, it has three other nested layout containers, including two Rows Layout elements and a Tabs Layout element.

Layout containers can be nested into each other, which provides an opportunity to create very complex screen layouts, as you will learn later.

Data Binding

The simplicity and flexibility of LightSwitch screens are powered by *data binding*. This mechanism enables you to bind screen data items to layout elements — without writing any code. When the value of a data item changes, the new value is immediately shown in the UI. Conversely, when the user alters a value in the UI (for example, edits a Text Box, selects an item from an Auto Complete Box, and so on), the new value is stored back to the data item.

 NOTE *As you learned in Chapter 3, the presentation layer (the UI) of a LightSwitch application is implemented with Silverlight. Silverlight natively supports the data-binding mechanism, and LightSwitch utilizes it with all its powerful features.*

With LightSwitch, you can use the following types of data binding:

➤ *Data item to data item* — This type of one-way binding is generally used to bind query parameters to other data items (such as queries or screen properties). This is how master-detail screens are implemented — query parameters of detail queries are bound to the selected master instance's identifier. This kind of binding is also useful to bind custom filter or search parameters to queries.

➤ *Data item to layout item* — This is a two-way binding between a data item and a layout item. When either the data item's value or the UI element's value changes, it is automatically refreshed on the other side. This is the key to displaying data coming from the database, and this mechanism returns user input to a data item that stores it.

It's easy to determine which data item is bound to a layout element. The text of layout items contains the display name part to the right of the vertical bar (refer to Figure 9-2 and Figure 9-3). This text comes from the Display Name property of the data item bound to the layout item.

USING LAYOUT CONTAINERS

Visual Studio LightSwitch provides several layout containers out-of-the-box. A *layout container* is a UI element that (as its name suggests) embeds other UI elements. The container is responsible for rendering its child UI elements. For example, a Rows Layout element renders its children vertically, providing a separate row for each of them. This section describes the main layout containers and how to use them.

Understanding Layout Containers

An empty screen provides a great opportunity to have a look at layout containers. Although the Add New Screen dialog does not provide an option to create an empty screen, you can easily start with one. Simply use the Add Screen command with the New Data screen template type, and do not select any table or query in the Screen Data combo box. When you click the OK button, the Add New Screen creates an empty screen, as shown in Figure 9-7.

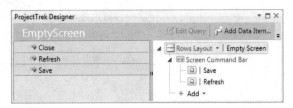

FIGURE 9-7: The layout of an empty screen

As you can see, an empty screen contains three methods (`Close`, `Refresh`, and `Save`), but no other data items. The root layout element is a layout container with a type of `Rows Layout`. This element has a nested `Screen Command Bar` with two `Shell Button` instances (`Save` and `Refresh`).

You can change the root layout container type by clicking the drop-down arrow to the right of the control type text and selecting another layout type from the drop-down list, as shown in Figure 9-8.

Table 9-1 summarizes the layout container types you can use in screens.

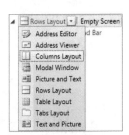

FIGURE 9-8: Changing the type of a layout container

TABLE 9-1: Layout Container Types

TYPE	DESCRIPTION
Address Editor	This layout type supports editing address information. It embeds the following placeholders: (STREET LINE 1), (STREET LINE 2), (CITY), (STATE), (ZIP CODE), and (COUNTRY).
Address Viewer	This layout type is the read-only version of the `Address Editor` layout type. It has the same placeholders, but you cannot edit the data in the controls assigned to placeholders.
Columns Layout	This layout type renders nested items from left to right. Each item has its own column. The first item is the leftmost one; the second is placed to the right of the first item, and so on.
Modal Window	If you select this layout type, you can define that the screen (or its part) can be used as a modal window (that is, a window that requires user interaction before the user can return to the parent application).
Picture and Text	This layout container divides its area into two vertical panels: a left-side panel with a picture, and a right-side panel with text describing the picture. The node has four placeholders: (PICTURE), (TITLE), (SUBTITLE), and (DESCRIPTION). (PICTURE) should be bound to a data item with the `Picture` type, and the other placeholders must be bound to `String` data items.

continues

TABLE 9-1 *(continued)*

TYPE	DESCRIPTION
Rows Layout	This layout type renders nested UI elements from top to bottom. Each item has its own row. The first item added will be placed at the top, the second item beneath the top item, the third item beneath the second, and so on.
Table Layout	This layout type allows creating a table-like layout with cells organized into rows and columns.
Tabs Layout	This type allows creating a tabbed view. Each nested node added to a `Tabs Layout` node represents a tab.
Text and Picture	This is similar to `Picture and Text`, but it places the picture in the right panel, while descriptive text items appear in the left panel.

As shown in Table 9-1, there are two kinds of layout containers that provide extensibility with nested layout elements:

➤ *Containers with placeholders* — These containers have predefined nested items (placeholders). You can't remove them or add new nested items directly to the container. For example, `Address Viewer`, and `Picture`, and `Text` are such containers. Use the Choose Content drop-down list to set their content, as shown in Figure 9-9.

➤ *Flexible containers* — You can add as many nested items to these as you want. The container can render them. To append an item to the container, select the layout container and use the Add drop-down list, as shown in Figure 9-10.

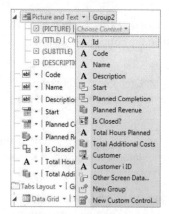

FIGURE 9-9: Use the Choose Content drop-down list to bind a placeholder with a data item

FIGURE 9-10: Use the Add drop-down list to extend a flexible container with a new nested element

Nesting Layout Containers

Layout containers can be nested into each other, a technique you can use to create very sophisticated layouts, as shown in Figure 9-11.

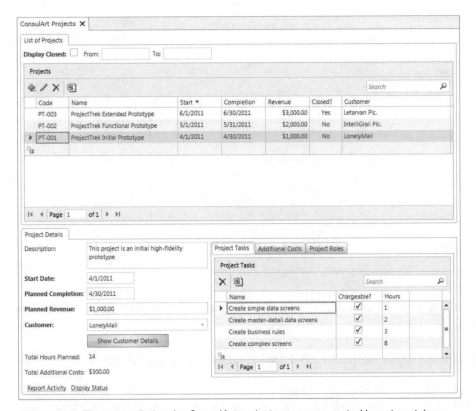

FIGURE 9-11: The screen listing the ConsulArt project uses many nested layout containers

You can implement this layout in many ways, with one possible solution shown in Figure 9-12. On the left, you can see the layout hierarchy of the UI; on the right, you see a portion of the screenshot shown in Figure 9-11. The lines between the layout elements and the screenshot show how the specific layout containers are displayed.

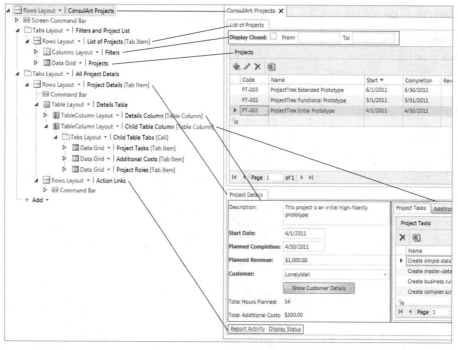

FIGURE 9-12: The connection between the layout hierarchy and the rendered screen

It is quite easy to establish this complex layout with the LightSwitch Designer, as you will learn in the next exercise.

TRY IT OUT Creating a Complex Screen with Nested Layout Containers

> **NOTE** *In this exercise, you continue the sample that you completed in Chapter 8. You can find the starting sample on this book's companion website at* www.wrox.com *in the folder* Chapter 09\Start.

To create the screen layout shown in Figure 9-11, follow these steps:

1. Start Visual Studio LightSwitch and open ProjectTrek.

2. Delete the ListProjects screen from the project.

3. Add a new screen using the Search Data template. Select Projects from the Screen Data combo box, type the **ListProjects** screen name, and click OK.

4. Change the Display Name property of the root Rows Layout item to **ConsulArt Projects**. From now on, when you are instructed to rename an item to *<new name>*, set its Display Name property to *<new name>*.

5. Delete the `Projects Data Grid`.

6. Add a New Group to the root node. Change its type to `Tabs Layout` and rename it **Filters and Project List**. The current layout is very simple, as shown in Figure 9-13.

FIGURE 9-13: The layout hierarchy after Step 6

7. Add a New Group to the `Tabs Layout` node, and rename it **List of Projects**.

8. Add a New Group to the new `Rows Layout` node created in the previous step. Change its type to `Columns Layout` and rename it **Filters**.

9. Select the root node and add another New Group to it. Change the new node's type to `Tabs Layout` and rename it **All Project Details**.

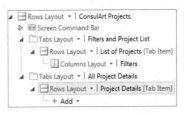

10. Add a New Group to this `Tabs Layout` node, and rename it **Project Details**. At this point, the layout is still simple, as shown in Figure 9-14.

FIGURE 9-14: The layout hierarchy after Step 10

11. Add a New Group to the `Rows Layout` node created in the previous step. Change the new node's type to `Table Layout` and rename it **Details Table**.

12. Add a New Group to the `Table Layout` node. You can see that it is added with the `TableColumn Layout` default type. Rename it **Details Column**.

13. Select the `Table Layout` node and add another New Group. Rename the new item **Child Table Column**.

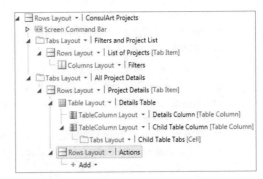

14. Add a New Group to this `TableColumn Layout` node. Change the new node's type to `Tabs Layout` and rename it **Child Table Tabs**.

15. Select the `Project Details Rows Layout` node and add a New Group. Rename the newly created node **Actions**. With this step, all your layout containers are created. Now it seems to be a bit more complex than at the beginning, as shown in Figure 9-15.

FIGURE 9-15: The completed layout hierarchy

16. Run the application by pressing F5. Open the ConsulArt Projects window, which displays an empty screen with a few tabs and placeholders. Resize the application screen and observe how the layout of the containers changes.

17. Close the application.

> **NOTE** You can find the complete code to download for this exercise on this book's companion website at www.wrox.com in the folder Chapter 09
> \Sample 1 - Layout Containers.

How It Works

Every time you added a New Group, a new layout container was added to the hierarchy. The type of the layout container was set according to its context. In most cases, Rows Layout was the default; but as you experienced, when you nested a new container into the Table Layout node in Step 12, its type was set to TableColumn Layout.

When you compare the layout you have created with Figure 9-12, you can see that Data Grid nodes are missing from your newly created screen. Data Grid nodes are not layout containers, although they contain nested items.

Layout Container Sizing

Layout containers provide elastic behavior in your screens. As you resize the screen, layout containers and their content (controls and nested layout containers) are rerendered accordingly. Using the sizing and alignment properties of layout containers, you can influence their elastic behavior. Figure 9-16 shows these properties.

You can set the width and height of the containers, as well as the horizontal and vertical alignment of their content. If you want to set a fixed pixel value as the height or width, select the appropriate Pixel option and specify the value in the text box beneath. In Figure 9-16, the Height property is specified as 120 pixels.

FIGURE 9-16: Sizing properties of layout containers

You can also set the height and width to be sized automatically. In this case, the size of the container will be calculated according to the size of its content and its parent, providing elastic behavior as the screen is resized, or the size of their content changes. Select the Auto option to use automatic sizing. You can optionally specify a minimum size and a maximum size (height and width) using pixel values. In Figure 9-16, the Width property is set automatically between 0 and 240 pixels.

Alignment properties define how the content should be aligned within the container. For Width, you can choose from the Left, Right, Center, and Stretch values. For Height, the Top, Bottom, Center, and Stretch options are available. Other than Stretch, these options are self-explanatory; their names indicate exactly what they do. For example, when you select Left and Top, the content will be aligned to the top-left corner of the container. Setting both horizontal and vertical alignment to Center will put the content exactly in the middle of the container.

The Stretch option works differently. When this option is set, the appropriate dimension of the content will be resized to fill the container. For example, if you have a button with a height of 20 pixels in an 80-pixel-high container, setting the vertical alignment to Stretch will resize the button's height to 80 pixels so that it fills its parent container.

Layout container nesting adds more complexity to sizing. You can nest layout containers in other layout containers to an arbitrary depth. In this case, you can use another kind of sizing, called *weighted sizing*. For example, the `Project Details Rows Layout` item in Figure 9-17 contains two directly nested layout containers, `Details Table` and `Actions`. When you select any of them, you will see the `Weighted Row Height` value beneath the `Stretch` option, as shown in Figure 9-18.

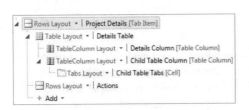

FIGURE 9-17: The Project Details layout container

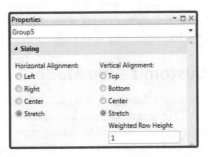

FIGURE 9-18: The Weighted Row Height property

This property can be used to make a weighted calculation that sets the dimensions of layout containers nested into another layout container. The current size is calculated so that the full size of a parent container is decreased by the combined size of its fixed-sized children. The remaining size is divided among the stretched child containers according to their weighted size.

To better understand this, let's take a look at an example. Assume the height of a container is 800 pixels, and it has four nested layout containers. The first is 100 pixels high; the other three are stretched vertically, and they have weighted row height values (height ratio values) of 4, 1, and 2. When the heights are calculated, the first container gets its fixed 100-pixel height. The remaining space is 700 pixels. The sum of weighted row height values is 7 (4+1+2), so one portion is 100 pixels (700 pixels/7). According to their weight, the remaining layout containers will be 400 pixels, 100 pixels, and 200 pixels high, respectively.

When looking only at the layout hierarchy, it is often very difficult to imagine how the rendered screen will look. The runtime customization feature built into LightSwitch applications makes it much easier to understand sizing and content alignment, and provides some great help for setting up these parameters.

RUNTIME SCREEN CUSTOMIZATION

Traditionally, you test screens by building and running your application. If you are not satisfied with the screen layout, you stop and close the application, alter a few parameters, then build and run the application again to test the effects of the changes. Often, this requires several cycles until you get the expected result. The overhead and time spent with screen tuning can be huge.

By utilizing the runtime customization feature of LightSwitch, you rid yourself of this overhead. When you run your application in Debug mode (that is, you start it with Debug ➪ Start Debugging, or press F5), you can use the Customization mode. In the top-right corner of your application's main screen is the Design Screen button, as shown in Figure 9-19, which enables you to change the layout of your screens during runtime.

FIGURE 9-19: The Design Screen button

Using Customization Mode

While a screen is displayed, you can click the Design Screen button and start Customization mode. While in this mode, you can alter the design of the screen by manipulating the layout hierarchy of the screen, and by setting item properties. When you finish, you can save the new layout and try the screen with the new design. The changes you make are saved to the integrated development environment (IDE). When you close the application and open the screen in the IDE, it will be displayed in the Designer with the layout you've saved in Customization mode.

In the following exercise, you will use Customization mode to change the sizing and alignment of a few layout containers in the ConsulArt Projects screen.

TRY IT OUT   Using Customization Mode to Change Layout Container Sizing

   NOTE *In this exercise, you start from a prepared sample. You can find the starting sample on this book's companion website at* www.wrox.com *in the* Chapter 09\ Sample 2 - Runtime Customization *folder.*

To alter the screen layout, follow these steps:

1.   Open ProjectTrek in the LightSwitch IDE, and press F5 to run the project in Debug mode.

2.   Open the ConsulArt Projects screen. Click the Design Screen button in the top-right corner of the application screen. If you can't see it, you launched the application with Debug ➪ Start Without Debugging (or pressed Ctrl+F5). In this mode, you cannot use the runtime customization. Stop the application and start it again by pressing F5.

3.   The Customization Mode screen appears, as shown in Figure 9-20. The header of this screen displays the name of the screen you're customizing.

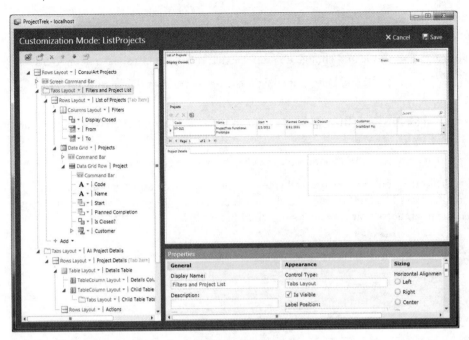

FIGURE 9-20: The ConsulArt Projects screen in Customization mode

On the right is the Cancel button, which exits Customization mode and ignores any changes you've made. The Save button also exits Customization mode but saves your changes back to the IDE.

The left panel of the screen shows the layout hierarchy. This panel's toolbar contains several buttons that help you change the hierarchy. Following are the buttons (from left to right):

➤ *Add Button* — Adds a new button to a command bar.

➤ *Add Group* — Creates a new group (layout container).

➤ *Delete* — Deletes the selected node and all its children.

➤ *Move Up* — Moves the selected node up in the layout hierarchy.

➤ *Move Down* — Moves the selected node down in the layout hierarchy.

➤ *Reset Items* — Resets all items that belong to the selected one. For example, if you're on a `Data Grid`, it automatically populates the columns of the grid according to the default settings.

The bottom panel displays the properties of the selected layout item. You can alter them, and changes are immediately reflected in the main window panel that contains a preview of the screen.

You probably noticed that there is a lot of unnecessary space between the filter fields and the grid beneath them, and the fields are not very well aligned. In the next few steps you are going to fix this.

4. Select the `Filters Columns Layout` node. You can see that its `Vertical Alignment` property is set to `Stretch`. Change it to `Top`.

5. Select the `Display Closed` node and change its `Horizontal Alignment` from `Stretch` to `Left`.

6. Select the `Projects Data Grid`, and change its height to `Auto-size`. Set the `MaxHeight` value to **240**.

7. Select the `Filters and Project List Tabs Layout` and change the `Vertical Alignment` from `Stretch` to `Top`.

8. Click Save to exit Customization mode and save the changes you've carried out.

9. The ConsulArt Projects layout immediately reflects the changes. Check and then uncheck the Display Closed filter box. The number of items in the list changes, and you can see that the List of Projects tab elastically reflects that change, as shown in Figure 9-21.

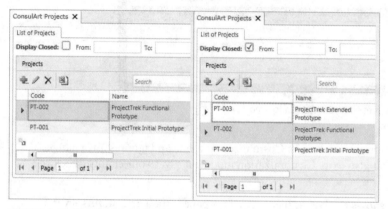

FIGURE 9-21: The height of the Projects grid elastically changes

10. Close the application.

11. In the LightSwitch IDE, open the `ListProjects` screen. Confirm that the layout item properties you've changed in the previous steps now have the values you set in Customization mode.

How It Works

Because you have started the `ProjectTrek` application in Debug mode, you can click the Design Screen button to enter Customization mode. When you changed the `Vertical Alignment` property of the `Filters` node in Step 4 to `Top`, you removed the unnecessary space consumed because of the `Stretch` setting. In Step 6, you set the height of the `Projects` node to automatically size with the `MaxHeight` property set to 240 pixels. The behavior of the data grid height in Figure 9-21 is caused by this change.

You exited Customization mode in Step 8 by selecting Save. This immediately saved the altered layout, which is why you see the same settings in the IDE.

Features and Restrictions in Customization Mode

Runtime customization is a powerful feature, as you experienced in the previous exercise. You can completely redesign the screen. However, you cannot do everything that you can do in the IDE.

The first very obvious thing that you cannot do is add new data items to the screen. LightSwitch uses objects to communicate through the layers. If you were to change the data items of a screen, it would imply a change in the structure of objects used to communicate between the presentation and Logic tier, and, of course, between the logic and the Data tier. This is not possible without rebuilding the application.

You are also not allowed to move controls out of their layout containers. A layout container can be bound to a specific data item — for example, to Selected Item — and controls within the container can be bound to properties within that data item. Moving a control out of the layout container would break this binding.

However, changing the layout hierarchy does not affect the objects used to communicate between tiers. It simply alters the rendering of the UI and data binding (that is, how data items are bound to visual controls of the screen). Because of the Silverlight technology used to implement the Presentation tier in LightSwitch, both rendering and data binding are dynamic features that do not require rebuilding the application.

The great thing with Customization mode is that these are the only restrictions! You can completely redesign the screen layout in Customization mode. If necessary, you can delete layout items and add new ones as well.

THE DATA GRID AND THE LIST CONTROLS

Most applications use many master-detail screens to display cohesive information (for example, a customer and his or her orders). The structure of master-detail screens requires the capability to display numerous records at the same time (numerous customers from which to select, or numerous orders that belong to the same customer). If the tables you want to display contain a massive amount of data, *paging* is a commonly used technique for managing this data. Your screen shows only a predefined chunk of data (a page) that is read from the database. You can move among the data in the visible page. When you need more data, you move to the next page. This operation reads the next chunk from the database, and displays it on your screen as a new page.

LightSwitch provides two out-of-the-box controls that enable you to display a set of records and navigate among them. These are the Data Grid and the List controls, samples of which are shown in Figure 9-22 and Figure 9-23, respectively.

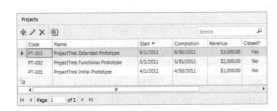

FIGURE 9-22: A Data Grid control displaying projects

FIGURE 9-23: A List control displaying projects

As you can see, these two controls share many things in common in terms of their visual appearance. Both have a title bar (Projects) and a toolbar beneath the title. By default, the toolbar displays several buttons and a search box that can be used to search for the specified text within the content of the control.

At the bottom is the paging bar. By clicking the icons of the First, Previous, Next, or Last buttons, you can select another page to be displayed. You can also specify a page number explicitly to go there directly.

The main difference between these two controls is the way they present their content — called a *data record*. Whereas a Data Grid can show several fields organized into columns, a List always displays one column.

Working with the Data Grid Control

The Data Grid control is both versatile and easy to work with. It supports the following operations:

➤ *Sorting* — If you can click the column headers, the content will be ordered by that column's content. When you click again, the sort order is reversed. The current sort order is indicated by small arrows to the right of the column name. You can include more columns to sort by pressing the Shift key while you click a new column.

➤ *Changing column order* — You can use drag-and-drop to change the order of the columns. Click on a column header and drag it with the mouse to a new position. When you release the mouse button, the columns will be reordered according to where you dropped the dragged column.

➤ *Resizing columns* — When you move the mouse to the boundary of two columns, the mouse pointer changes to a resize icon. Click the mouse button and resize the column to the left of the mouse pointer. Release the button when you reach the appropriate size.

In the following exercise, you will learn the basics of adding data grids to screens.

TRY IT OUT Working with Data Grid Controls

 NOTE *In this exercise, you will start from a prepared sample. You can find the starting sample on this book's companion website at* www.wrox.com *in the* Chapter 09\Sample 3 - Using Grids *folder.*

To add the new Data Grid controls, follow these steps:

1. Open the ProjectTrek project in the IDE. In Solution Explorer, double-click the ListProjects screen to open it in the Screen Designer. You will add three data grids to the Child Table Tabs node of the ConsulArt Projects screen, as shown in Figure 9-24.

2. Select the ProjectTasks data item (in the left panel of the Designer). Drag it to the layout hierarchy. When the mouse points to the Child Table Tabs node and a horizontal bar is shown beneath this item, release the mouse button. A new Data Grid named Project Tasks is

added to the hierarchy. Expand the `Command Bar` beneath the `Data Grid` node. The result is shown in Figure 9-25.

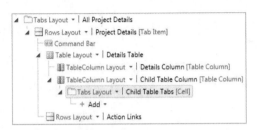

FIGURE 9-24: The Child Table Tabs node in the ConsulArt Projects screen layout hierarchy

FIGURE 9-25: The new Project Tasks Data Grid

As shown in Figure 9-25, the `Data Grid` contains a command bar (this is the toolbar of the grid) with three buttons added by default. The second child of the `Data Grid` node is a `Data Grid Row`. This node embeds the column definitions of the grid. As shown in Figure 9-25, the grid has four columns. The nodes representing grid columns were added according to the definition of the `Project Tasks` data element, and their control types have been set by the type of the underlying data. For example, the type of the `Chargeable?` field is `Boolean`, so its default control type is a check box.

3. From the `Command Bar` of the grid, delete the `Add ...` and `Edit ...` nodes (that is, click them and press Delete). These buttons are unnecessary there.

4. Select the `Project` node under the `Data Grid Row`, and delete it. This node is unnecessary because this data grid is shown as a detail of the project.

5. Select the `AdditionalCosts` data item in the Designer and drag it to the layout hierarchy. Move it so that the mouse points to the little triangle of the `Data Grid`, right beneath the `Tabs Layout` node. A vertical bar and a horizontal bar appear, as shown in Figure 9-26, indicating that the UI that represents the `AdditionalCosts` data item will be added as the next child of the `Tabs Layout` node. Release the mouse, and a new `Data Grid` is added to the layout hierarchy.

FIGURE 9-26: A vertical bar and a horizontal bar indicating the position of the data item being dragged to the layout hierarchy

6. Delete the `Add ...` and `Edit ...` buttons from the `Command Bar` of the new grid, and delete the `Projects` node under the `Data Grid Row` node.

7. Start the application by pressing F5, and open the ConsulArt Projects screen. Select the `PT-001` item in the `Projects` grid, and then click `Additional Costs` in the Project Details tab. Figure 9-27 shows how the layout established in Step 5 and Step 6 is rendered.

FIGURE 9-27: The Additional Costs grid

8. Close the application and return to the LightSwitch IDE.

9. Change the control type of the `Amount` node from `Money Editor` to `Label`, as shown in Figure 9-28. Use the drop-down arrow to the right of the icon indicating the control type. In the list showing the control types, only those that can handle the type of `Amount` (`Money`) are shown.

10. Run the application again, and check the `Additional Costs` grid of the `PT-001` project again. This time, the `Amount` column is displayed without the dollar currency symbol.

FIGURE 9-28: Changing the control type of the Amount node

11. Close the application.

12. In the Designer, change the control type of `Amount` back to `Money Editor`. Save the changes by pressing Ctrl+S.

13. Similar to what you did in Step 5, drag and append the `Project Roles` to the `Tabs Layout` node. Delete the Add . . . and Edit . . . buttons from the `Command Bar` of the `Data Grid` node. Delete the `Project` and `Employee c ACCOUNTID` nodes from the `Data Grid Row`.

> **NOTE** You can download the complete code for this exercise on this book's companion website at `www.wrox.com` in the folder `Chapter 09\Sample 4 - Using Lists`.

How It Works

Instead of adding a layout container and setting up its items one-by-one, you can drag a data item directly to the layout panel of the Designer, as you did it in Step 2 and Step 5. The data item is automatically converted into a layout item in these steps because you dropped two queries to the layout panel, they were converted to `Data Grid` controls by default, and the fields of queries were used to set up the columns of the grid.

By default, the `Data Grid` control has three buttons in its `Command Bar`. Because you can use the grid itself to edit the content of the grid, you do not need the default modal dialogs that add and edit records. That is why you deleted the Add... and Edit... buttons from all grids in Step 3, 6, and 13.

At any time, you can override the default control types. In Step 9, you changed the `Money Editor` of `Amount` to a `Label`, and in Step 12 you changed it back.

The Screen Designer always displays all control types that are available for a field. This information is determined by the type of the field, so that is why `Label`, `Money Editor`, `Money Viewer`, and `Text Box` are shown in Figure 9-28. A fifth control type, `Custom Control`, is also shown in this figure. You will learn a bit more about this control type later in this chapter.

Data Grid Properties

When working with a `Data Grid`, there are a few properties that influence the appearance and behavior of this control. Besides the standard appearance properties that you use in every UI control, `Data Grid` has a few extra ones:

➤ *Disable Export to Excel* — Check this property if you do not want to allow using the Excel export function of the grid. By default, it is unchecked, so a grid can be exported to Excel with a click of the toolbar button.

➤ *Show Add-new Row* — By default, a `Data Grid` shows an empty row (see, for example, Figure 9-27 or Figure 9-22) that represents the new record to add. When you edit this row's cells, you can add a new record. This behavior is controlled with "Show Add-new Row," which is checked by default. Uncheck it to disable adding new rows to a grid.

Often, you'll want to use a `Data Grid` in read-only mode, without allowing editing. You can change all control types of the `Data Grid Row` to their read-only equivalent — for example, a `Text Box` to a `Label`, a `Money Editor` to a `Money Viewer`, and so on. The "Use Read-only Controls" property of the `Data Grid Row` makes it easier. If you check this property, all control types belonging to the grid are automatically changed to their read-only versions. When you uncheck this property, the control types are reverted to the original ones. The `Data Grid Row` is smart enough to remember its original control set.

Working with the List Control

The `List` control provides a different view of data records than the `Data Grid` control. Instead of using a set of columns, a `List` control enables you to establish an item template. Although you can create `List` controls that enable data editing, they are primarily used to display data. In the following exercise, you will learn the basic customization features of a `List` control.

TRY IT OUT Using a List Control

To understand the customization features of a `List` control, follow these steps:

1. Open the `ListProjects` screen in the Designer and navigate to the `Project Tasks Data Grid` node.

2. Use the drop-down arrow of this node to change the layout type from `Data Grid` to `List`. The new `List` control contains a `Command Bar` node and a `Summary` node (named `Project Task`), as shown in Figure 9-29.

FIGURE 9-29: Changing the Project Tasks node to a List

3. Press F5 to start the application. When you open the ConsulArt Projects screen, you can see that a list is now used instead of a grid, as shown in Figure 9-30. This list does not allow editing project task details.

4. Close the application, and go back to the IDE. Select the `Project Task Summary` node (the node right beneath the `Command Bar` of the `Project Tasks List`) and, in the Properties windows, check its Show As Link property.

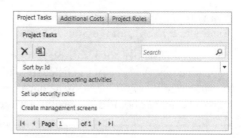

FIGURE 9-30: The project tasks are displayed in a List

5. Run the application again and open the ConsulArt Projects screen. Now you can click any of the project task items in the list to edit them in the default detail screen, as shown in Figure 9-31.

6. Close the application (by either discarding or saving changes), and go back to the Designer. Change the control type of the `Project Task` node from `Summary` to `Picture and Text`. By clicking the Choose Content list and selecting the appropriate item from the drop-down list, bind the `(TITLE)`, `(SUBTITLE)`, and `(DESCRIPTION)` placeholders to `Name`, `Hours`, and `Chargeable?` fields, respectively, as shown in Figure 9-32.

FIGURE 9-31: You can edit a project task in a detail screen

7. Run the application and open the ConsulArt Projects screen. The project task items are displayed with a new layout, as shown in Figure 9-33.

FIGURE 9-32: Using the Picture and Text layout as the Project Task list item template

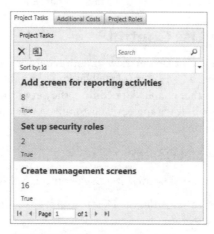

FIGURE 9-33: The Project Task list now has a new layout

8. Close the application.

9. Change the type of the `Project Tasks List` node back to `Data Grid` and save the changes by pressing Ctrl+S.

 NOTE *Although you have changed the layout of the ConsulArt Projects screen, after Step 9 the layout should be the same as in the beginning of the exercise. You can find the complete code to download for this exercise on this book's companion website at* `www.wrox.com` *in the folder* `Chapter 09\Sample 4 - Using Lists.`

How It Works

When you changed the layout type to a `List`, it automatically created a default list item template with a `Summary` control. The `Summary` control displays the field of its source table that is selected in the `Summary Field` property of the source table. For the `ProjectTask` record, it is the `Name` field, which is why this field was displayed in Figure 9-30.

In Step 6, you created a new layout template for a project task item using the `Picture and Text` layout template with predefined placeholders. Binding `ProjectTask` fields to the placeholders resulted in the layout shown in Figure 9-33.

You can change the default `Summary` control to many more layout containers, so you can establish quite complex list item templates. Because the original `Data Grid` provides the best editing experience for project tasks, in Step 9 you changed the list back to a grid, thus returning to the original screen layout.

A `List` control has the standard appearance properties that you can use with every UI control, and it provides the "Disable Export to Excel" flag to prevent users from exporting the content of the list to an Excel worksheet.

USING SIMPLE CONTROLS AND VALUE PICKERS

You already learned that the leaf nodes in the layout hierarchy are simple controls, such as a `Label`, `Text Box`, `Check Box`, and so on. When you add an existing data item into the layout hierarchy, the Designer automatically adds an appropriate control to display and edit the content of the item, according to the item's data type.

Table 9-2 summarizes the simple controls you can use in LightSwitch applications. The third column of this table shows the data types that can be used with the corresponding control.

TABLE 9-2: Simple Control Types

NAME	DESCRIPTION	TYPES SUPPORTED
Check Box	Allows you to edit Boolean values.	Boolean
Date Picker	A control that can be used to type or select a date from a calendar view.	Date
Date Time Picker	Allows editing a date and time value using a calendar view and a time drop-down list.	Date, Date Time
Date Time Viewer	Displays a date time value.	Date, Date Time
Date Viewer	Displays a date value.	Date
Email Address Editor	Allows editing of an e-mail address. Accepts only syntactically correct e-mail addresses.	Email
Email Address Viewer	Displays an e-mail address.	Email
Image Editor	Displays an image and allows selecting an image from a file.	Image
Image Viewer	Displays an image.	Image
Label	Displays the string representation of a value. Uses the default formatting, depending on the field type and the culture settings of the application.	Boolean, Date, Decimal, Double, Email Address, Integer, Long Integer, Money, Phone Number, Short Integer, String
Money Editor	Allows editing a monetary value.	Money
Money Viewer	Displays a monetary value.	Money
Phone Number Editor	Allows editing of a phone number.	Phone Number
Phone Number Viewer	Displays a phone number.	Phone Number
Text Box	Allows editing of a value. When storing back the value to the data item, the value is parsed according to the culture settings of the application.	Boolean, Date, Decimal, Double, Email Address, Integer, Long Integer, Money, Phone Number, Short Integer, String

NOTE In the General tab of the project properties (you can access it by double-clicking the `Properties` node in Solution Explorer), you can change the Culture setting of the project. The default is English (United States), but you can change it to another language. The controls in Table 9-2 (such as `Label` and `Text Box`) will use the settings (number, date, and currency format) according to the culture set in the General tab.

You can learn several things from Table 9-2. The `Label` and `Text Box` controls support almost all data types except `Binary` and `Image`. The `Binary` type is not supported directly by any built-in controls; you can use it only with user controls that understand the data behind a specific bit-flow represented by the `Binary` field.

The `Label` and all other viewer controls support only displaying the data; they do not allow editing them. All business data types have their own `Viewer` and `Editor` controls, and they also support controls that can handle the intrinsic data type the specific business type extends.

Besides the simple controls listed in Table 9-2, you can use custom controls, which you will learn more about later in this chapter.

Working with Simple Controls

It is very easy to use the simple controls, as you will learn in the next exercise. The ConsulArt Projects screen does not contain UI elements to edit the details of a project yet, so you will add them to the screen.

TRY IT OUT **Adding Simple Controls to Edit Project Details**

To allow users of `ProjectTrek` to edit project details in the ConsulArt Projects screen, follow these steps:

1. Open the `ListProjects` screen in the Designer and select the `Details Column TableColumn Layout` node in the layout hierarchy.

2. Use the Add button beneath this node to append the `Code` data item. It will be appended with the default `Text Box` control type, as shown in Figure 9-34.

FIGURE 9-34: The Code data item is added to the Details Column node

3. In the data item hierarchy, click the `Name` item and drag it to the layout hierarchy right beneath the `Code` node you added in the previous step. The `Name` data item is added to the `Details Column` node.

4. Use the Add button or drag the following data items to append them to the `Details Column` node: `Description`, `Start`, `Planned Completion`, `Planned Revenue`, `Is Closed?`, `Total Hours Planned`, and `Total Additional Costs`. The result you should see is shown in Figure 9-35. Note the default control types assigned to the UI elements.

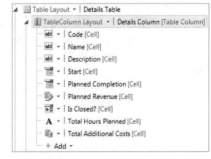

FIGURE 9-35: The Details Column node and its nested UI nodes

5. Set the height of the `Description` node to three lines.

6. Expand the `Child Table Column` node and select its only child, the `Child Table Tabs` node. In the Properties window, set the `Row Span` property value to 9.

7. Run the application by pressing F5, and then open the ConsulArt Projects screen. The project details are displayed in the screen, as shown in Figure 9-36.

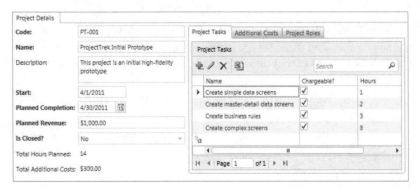

FIGURE 9-36: The project details are now displayed in the ConsulArt Projects screen

8. Close the application.

 NOTE *You can find the complete code to download for this exercise on this book's companion website at* www.wrox.com *in the folder* Chapter 09\Sample 5 - Simple Controls.

How It Works

In Step 3 and Step 4, you tried the two ways of adding simple controls to the layout — using the Add button, and dragging a data item to the layout hierarchy.

In Step 6, you changed the `Row Span` property of the `Child Table Tab` node to 9. This setting enables the project detail controls to be nicely aligned with the tab controls (refer to Figure 9-36). You added nine simple controls, and because they are children of a `TableColumn Layout` node (refer to Figure 9-35), each occupies a separate row. Setting the `Row Span` property to 9 enables the tab control to span all nine rows.

Control Sizing

Controls have the same sizing model as layout containers, as shown in Figure 9-37. You can set the width and height of a control, and set its content's alignment exactly as you do with layout containers.

When you work with controls that display or allow the editing of text, you have new options to set the width with the maximum number of characters, and the height with the number of rows, as highlighted in Figure 9-37. Of course, these settings do not prevent you from entering more characters or more lines of text than specified.

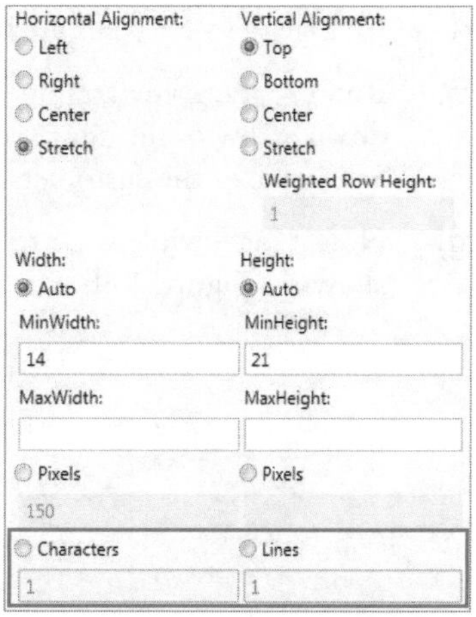

FIGURE 9-37: Control sizing options

Picking Up Values

In many situations, you will want to enable users to select a value from a list of predefined options. As you learned earlier, you can define choice lists for table fields, which allow users to pick one of the values in the list. When a table references a record in another table, you must also select the referenced record from a list. For example, when you need to assign a customer to a project, the best way is to select a customer from a list.

LightSwitch provides *value picker controls* for this purpose. When you add a data item to the layout hierarchy, the Designer is smart enough to automatically use a value picker control that has either a choice list defined at the field level, or references to a master table. Out-of-the-box, LightSwitch provides you with two value pickers: `Auto Complete Box` and `Modal Window Picker`.

Both value pickers display a list of values from which one can be selected. The `Auto Complete Box` provides a drop-down list that enables users to type in characters to narrow the list to items beginning with those characters. The `Modal Window Picker` (as its name suggests) pops up a modal window with a list of selectable items.

Using an Auto Complete Box

In the following exercise, you extend the ConsulArt Projects screen to allow specifying the customer to which the project belongs.

TRY IT OUT   Adding an Auto Complete Box to a Screen

To allow assigning a customer to a project, follow these steps:

1. Open the `ListProjects` screen in the Designer.

2. Select the `Details Column TableColumn Layout` node. With the Add button, append the `Customer` data item to this node. The new node is an `Auto Complete Box`.

3. Drag the new node to be the first nested node beneath `Details Column`, and then expand the `Customer` node. Your layout should be as shown in Figure 9-38.

FIGURE 9-38: The new Customer node uses an Auto Complete Box

4. Change the `Row Span` property of the `Child Table Tabs` node from 9 to 10.

5. Run `ProjectTrek` and open the ConsulArt Projects screen. Select a project, and click the drop-down arrow of the `Customer` list. The list displays the options to you, as shown in Figure 9-39. Select one of the customers, let's say IntelliGrail Plc.

6. Now, type **S** while you are in the `Customer` box. The list is filtered to items starting with "S," as shown in Figure 9-40. Select SoftwArt Ltd. and save the changes.

FIGURE 9-39: You can select a customer from the Auto Complete Box

FIGURE 9-40: The Auto Complete Box displays customers starting with "S"

7. Close the `ProjectTrek` application.

How It Works

When you added the `Customer` data item in Step 2, the Designer recognized that it is related to the `Customer` table, and assigned an `Auto Complete Box` control to this layout node by default. The default item template of this control contains a `Summary` control to the `Customer` table (as shown in Figure 9-38). The `Customer` table uses the `Name` field as its summary field, so the `Auto Complete Box` displays customer names, as shown in Figure 9-39 and Figure 9-40.

As its name suggests, an `Auto Complete Box` allows users to type the first few characters of a list item in order to automatically narrow the available options displayed (refer to Figure 9-40).

Using a Modal Window Picker

If you have many options, an `Auto Complete Box` may make it very difficult to find and select an item. In this case, a `Modal Window Picker` is a better choice.

TRY IT OUT Changing the Customer List to a Modal Window Picker

To use a `Modal Window Picker` control to assign a customer to a project, follow these steps:

1. Change the control type of the `Customer [Cell]` item from `Auto Complete Box` to `Modal Window Picker`.

2. Run the application. In the ConsulArt Projects screen, move the mouse over the `Customer` field. On the right side of the field, an ellipsis button appears, as shown in Figure 9-41. Click this button to pop up the list of customers.

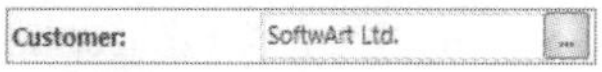

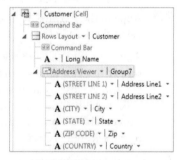

FIGURE 9-41: Click the ellipsis button to pop up the modal window with the list of customers

3. Select a customer from the list and click OK.

4. Save the changes and close the application.

The list shows only customer names, which may not be enough information to select a customer. You can change the item template of a customer to display more information.

5. Change the control type of the `Customer Summary` node (not the `Modal Window Picker`) to `Rows Layout`. Delete all automatically appended control nodes except `Long Name`.

6. Change the `Font Style` property of `Long Name` from `Normal` to `Heading1`.

7. Append a New Group to this `Rows Layout` node, and change its type to `Address Viewer`.

8. Use the Choose Content buttons of the `Address Viewer` placeholders to assign the appropriate customer fields, as shown in Figure 9-42.

FIGURE 9-42: Set up the placeholders of the Address Viewer

9. Change the `Width` property of the `(CITY)`, `(STATE)`, and `(ZIP)` placeholders to Auto.

10. Run the application. In the ConsulArt Projects screen, click the ellipsis button of the `Customer` field. The modal window that pops up now uses the new layout, as shown in Figure 9-43.

11. Close the `ProjectTrek` application.

How It Works

In Step 1, you changed the control type to a `Modal Window Picker`, and in Step 2, a new modal window was displayed in the application screen. In Step 5, you changed the default `Summary` layout to a `Rows Layout` to establish a more complex list item layout. In the subsequent steps, you created the new layout template containing an `Address Viewer`.

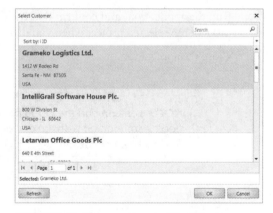

FIGURE 9-43: The new layout of the Select Customers modal window

Defining a Choice List

In the previous exercises, LightSwitch used all records in the `Customer` table to enable you to assign a customer to a project. Sometimes you need to filter the records displayed in the pick-up lists.

The `ProjectTask` table allows you to assign a parent task to each project task. For this purpose, the `ProjectTask` table contains a self-referencing relationship to itself. The current ConsulArt Projects screen does not allow selecting a parent task for any project task. You can easily add this simple functionality to the screen, as you will learn in the next exercise.

TRY IT OUT   **Assigning a Parent Task to a Project Task**

To assign a parent task to an existing project task, follow these steps:

1.   Open the `ProjectLists` screen in the Designer and select the `Project Task Data Grid Row`. (Figure 9-44 helps you to locate it.)

2.   Append the `Parent Task` data item to this node by using the Add button.

3.   Run `ProjectTrek` and select the ConsulArt Projects screen. Select a project. In the Project Tasks tab, you can use the last column of the grid to select a parent task from an `Auto Complete Box`. Notice how this list contains all project tasks, not only those defined in the selected project.

FIGURE 9-44: The Project Task node in the layout hierarchy

4.   Close the application.

5.   Select the `Parent Task` node you added to the layout hierarchy in Step 2. Locate the `Choices` property in the Properties window, and change its value from `Auto` to `ProjectTasks`.

6.   Run the application, and confirm that the ConsulArt Projects screen now shows only the project tasks of the selected project when you drop down the Parent Task list.

7.   Close the application.

> **NOTE** *You can find the complete code to download for this exercise on this book's companion website at* `www.wrox.com` *in the folder* `Chapter 09\Sample 6 - Value Pickers`.

How It Works

In Step 3, all `ProjectTask` records are displayed in the `Auto Complete Box`. The `ProjectTask` table has a self-referencing relationship to itself, which allows selecting any other `ProjectTask` record to be the parent of another `ProjectTask` record. If you have a task in Project A, you can set its parent to a task defined in Project B. However, it contradicts common sense and the logic of the `ProjectTrek` application.

LightSwitch allows you to filter records listed in the pick-up controls with a query. Often, you must create a custom query for this purpose and add it to the data items of a form. In this case, you need to display only those project tasks that belong to the selected project. The screen already contains such a query — namely, `ProjectTask`. In Step 5, you set the `Choice` property to this query; and in the next run, the screen worked as expected.

METHODS, BUTTONS, AND COMMAND BARS

As you learned earlier, you can add methods (which represent custom operations) to screens. To invoke a method, you must provide an appropriate control (for example, a button or a task link) in the UI. A method can be associated with one or more UI elements at the same time.

Here you will learn how to add buttons and task links to your screens that invoke operations implemented by a method.

Adding Methods and Buttons to a Screen

In the next exercise, you add three methods (with the UI controls activating the methods) to the ConsulArt Projects screen. These methods create a new project, close a project, and reopen a project.

TRY IT OUT   Adding Methods to the ConsulArt Projects Screen

NOTE In this exercise, you start from a prepared sample, which you can find on this book's companion website at `www.wrox.com` in the `Chapter 09\Sample 7 - Methods` folder. This sample slightly changes the layout of the ConsulArt Projects screen, and it does not allow editing the `Is Closed?` property of a project.

To add the methods to the ConsulArt Projects screen, follow these steps:

1.   Load the `ProjectTrek` project into the LightSwitch IDE, and open the `ListProjects` screen.

2.   In the Designer, locate the `Actions Rows Layout` node at the bottom of the layout hierarchy and select it.

3.   In the toolbar, drop down the Add Layout Item List and select Button. The Add Button dialog pops up, as shown in Figure 9-45. Select the New Method option and change the name to **CreateNewProject**. Click OK.

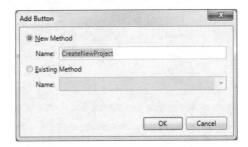
FIGURE 9-45: The Add Button dialog

The Designer creates two elements (both named `CreateNewProject`): a method (you can see it among the data items) and a `Button` beneath the `Command Bar` of the `Actions Rows Layout` node.

4. In the Data Items panel, select the `CreateNewProject` method, and click the Edit Execute Code task link in the Properties window. The `ListProjects.vb` (`ListProjects.cs`) file opens with an empty method named `CreateNewProject_Execute`. Add the following boldfaced code to the method body:

VB
```vb
Private Sub CreateNewProject_Execute()
    ' Write your code here.
    Me.Projects.AddNew()
    Me.FindControl("CodeControl").Focus()
End Sub
```

C#
```csharp
partial void CreateNewProject_Execute()
{
    // Write your code here.
    this.Projects.AddNew();
    this.FindControl("CodeControl").Focus();
}
```

5. Switch to the ProjectTrek Designer tab and, on the toolbar, click Add Data Item. When the Add Data Item dialog opens, select the Method option; and, at the bottom, type **CloseProject** in the Name field, as shown in Figure 9-46.

FIGURE 9-46: Add a new method with the Add Data Item dialog

6. In the Properties window, click the Edit Execute task link. Set the body of the `CloseProject_Execute` method according to the following boldfaced code:

VB
```vb
Private Sub CloseProject_Execute()
    ' Write your code here.
    Me.Projects.SelectedItem.Closed = True
End Sub
```

C#
```csharp
partial void CloseProject_Execute()
{
    // Write your code here.
    this.Projects.SelectedItem.Closed = true;
}
```

7. Switch to the ProjectTrek Designer tab and select the `Command Bar` of the `Actions Rows Layout`. Use the Add button beneath the `Command Bar` node to add a New Button. When the Add Button dialog appears, select the Existing Method option and choose `CloseProject` from the drop-down list, as shown in Figure 9-47. Click OK.

8. Change the control type of the `CloseProject` node to `Link`, as shown in Figure 9-48.

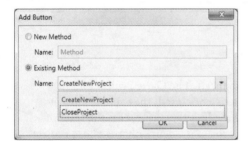

FIGURE 9-47: Assign an existing method to the CloseProject button

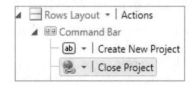

FIGURE 9-48: The control type of the CloseProject button is changed to Link

9. Repeat Steps 5 to 8, but this time name the method **ReopenProject,** and use the following boldfaced code to set up the `ReopenProject_Execute` method's body:

VB
```vb
Private Sub CloseProject_Execute()
    ' Write your code here.
    Me.Projects.SelectedItem.Closed = False
End Sub
```

C#
```csharp
partial void CloseProject_Execute()
{
    // Write your code here.
    this.Projects.SelectedItem.Closed = False;
}
```

10. Run the application and open the ConsulArt Projects screen. At the bottom of the screen is a button and two links, as shown in Figure 9-49. Click the Create New Project button. A new row is added to the Projects grid, and the details of the projects are also displayed. The focus is moved automatically to the Code field.

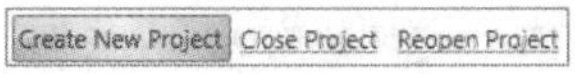

FIGURE 9-49: The buttons and links representing the three methods added

11. Click the Close Project link and then click the Reopen Project link. Notice that the Is Closed? flag changes to Yes and then to No, respectively.

12. Close the application and exit without saving.

How It Works

In Step 2, you created a new method and immediately assigned it to the Create New Project button. In Step 4, the code you inserted used the AddNew method of the Projects grid to create a new record. The FindControl method retrieved the object representing the Code field. In the starting sample, the control representing the Code field is named CodeControl, and this name is passed to FindControl. The invocation of the Focus method placed the focus on the Code field.

In Step 5 and Step 6, you set up a simple method to set the Closed field of the selected Project record to True. In Step 7, you added a new button and assigned it to the CloseProject method. In Step 8, you changed the type of this button to a link. In Step 9, you created a new method and a link that set the Closed field to False in order to reopen a closed project.

Enabling and Disabling Methods

There is one thing in the previous exercise that might be enhanced. The Close Project and Reopen Project buttons do not care whether the project is active or closed; they simply close it and reopen it. The UI would be much more intuitive if only the link that represents the state of the current project were enabled. In other words, when the project is open, only the Close Project link should be enabled; and when the current project is closed, only the Reopen Project operation could be executed.

Screen methods have two states: enabled or disabled. When a method is enabled, its associated controls (button or link) are also enabled on the screen. If the method is disabled, associated controls are also disabled, so they cannot be activated (clicked).

You can use the Edit CanExecute Code task link in the Properties window to write the code that sets the enabled or disabled state of a method. In the following exercise, you learn how to utilize this feature.

TRY IT OUT Enabling and Disabling Methods

To enable and disable the CloseProject and ReopenProject methods according to the state of the selected project, follow these steps:

1. Open the ListProject screen in the Designer. In the data items panel, select CloseProject. In the Properties window, click the Edit CanExecute Code task link. The CloseProject_CanExecute method is created with an empty body. Insert the following boldfaced code into the method body:

VB
```
Private Sub CloseProject_CanExecute(ByRef result As Boolean)
    ' Write your code here.
    result = Not Me.Projects.SelectedItem.Closed
End Sub
```

C#
```
partial void CloseProject_CanExecute(ref bool result)
{
    // Write your code here.
    result = !this.Projects.SelectedItem.Closed;
}
```

2. Switch to the ProjectTrek Designer tab. In the data items panel, select ReopenProject. In the Properties window, click the Edit CanExecute Code task link. The ReopenProject_CanExecute method is created. Change the method body according to the following boldfaced code:

VB
```
Private Sub ReopenProject_CanExecute(ByRef result As Boolean)
    ' Write your code here.
    result = Me.Projects.SelectedItem.Closed
End Sub
```

C#
```
partial void ReopenProject_CanExecute(ref bool result)
{
    // Write your code here.
    result = this.Projects.SelectedItem.Closed;
}
```

3. Run the application and open the ConsulArt Projects screen. Select an open project, and notice that the Close Project link is enabled, while the Reopen Project link is disabled, as shown in Figure 9-50.

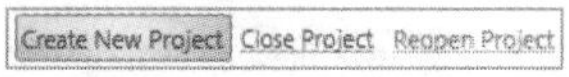

Create New Project | Close Project | Reopen Project

FIGURE 9-50: The Reopen Project link is disabled

4. Close the application and exit without saving.

NOTE *You can find the complete code to download for this exercise on the book's companion website at* www.wrox.com *in the folder* Chapter 09\Sample 8 - Buttons.

How It Works

The CanExecute methods set the result parameter to True (the method is enabled) or to False (the method is disabled), according to the status of the currently selected project. The application detects the event that the Project.SelectedItem.Closed property is changed when either the CloseProject_Execute or ReopenProject_Execute method is run, and automatically invokes both the CloseProject_CanExecute and ReopenProject_CanExecute methods.

These methods retrieve the result parameter, and the application enables or disables the corresponding methods accordingly. Changes in the state of the methods are automatically reflected in the visual state of the associated links.

Adding Buttons to the Screen's Command Bar

The LightSwitch application contains a Screen Command Bar that is a panel at the top of the application, similar to the Office ribbon. The buttons located here (such as the Save and Refresh buttons) provide application-wide functionality. You have already used these buttons a number of times throughout this book's exercises. You can also add your own buttons to the Screen Command Bar, as you will learn from the following exercise.

TRY IT OUT   Adding Buttons to the Screen Command Bar

 NOTE *In this exercise you start from a prepared sample. You can find the starting sample on this book's companion website at* www.wrox.com *in the* Chapter 09\Sample 9 - Screen Buttons *folder. This sample contains a new table (*ActivityEntries*) that stores project activities reported by employees. It also has two new screens.*

DisplayProjectActivities is a master-detail screen that lists projects and activities reported to that project. It accepts an optional ProjectId parameter. If it is set, it automatically selects the corresponding project when the screen is displayed.

ReportActivity is a screen used by employees (or project managers) to report project activities. The screen accepts two parameters: ProjectId and EmployeeId. When they are set, the activity entry will be automatically assigned to the specified project and employee.

To add a new button to the Screen Command Bar, follow these steps:

1. Open the ListProject screen in the Designer. Directly beneath the root layout node, expand and then select the Screen Command Bar node.

2. To append a button, click Add and select New Button from the drop-down list, as shown in Figure 9-51.

3. In the Add Button dialog, select New Method and name it **DisplayActivities**. Click OK.

FIGURE 9-51: Add a new button to the Screen Command Bar

4. In the layout hierarchy, select the newly added button; and in the Properties window, locate the Appearance category and click the Choose Image link. The Select Image dialog pops up, as shown in Figure 9-52.

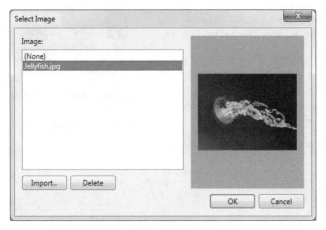

FIGURE 9-52: The Select Image dialog

This dialog contains a list of images you can use in your project. If you click the Import button, you can browse your folders for image files and add them to the list. If you click Delete, you can remove an image file already added to the list.

5. Use the Import button to append an image to the list (select any picture you like). Click OK.

> **WARNING** *The pictures you add to buttons become part of your application's executable file. If you add picture files that are large in size, your executable also will be large. Button images are displayed in a small size (generally, they are 32 by 32 pixels), so there is no real advantage to adding a high-resolution picture file to your project.*

6. In the data items panel, click the `DisplayActivities` method. In the Properties window, select the Edit Execute Code task link. Insert the following boldfaced code into the body of the `DisplayActivities_Execute` method:

VB
```
Private Sub DisplayActivities_Execute()
    ' Write your code here.
    Application.Current.ShowDisplayProjectActivities(Projects.SelectedItem.Id)
End Sub
```

C#
```
partial void DisplayActivities_Execute()
{
    // Write your code here.
    Application.Current.ShowDisplayProjectActivities(Projects.SelectedItem.Id);
}
```

7. Run the application and open the ConsulArt Projects screen. The Display Activities button is displayed in the Screen Command Bar, as shown in Figure 9-53.

8. Select the PT-002 project and click Display Activities. The screen with the project activities opens. Now, this new screen obtained the focus, and the Display Activities button disappeared from the Screen Command Bar.

FIGURE 9-53: The Display Activities button in the Screen Command Bar

9. Click the ConsulArt Projects tab. As this screen gets the focus, the Display Activities button is shown again.

10. Close the application.

How It Works

In Step 2 and Step 3, you added a new button, with its underlying method, to the Screen Command Bar in the same way you did in previous exercises. Unlike buttons added to simple command bars, Screen Command Bar buttons may have images. In Step 4, you assigned an image to the newly added button.

> **NOTE** *If you select a button added to the Screen Command Bar, in the Properties window you can see that this button has a* Shell Button *control type. The buttons and links you added in previous exercises had a control type of* Button *and* Link, *respectively.*

The Application.Current object used in Step 6 represents the running application. This object has an associated Show method for each screen defined in the project. The ShowDisplayActivities method is the one that launches the DisplayActivities screen and displays it in the application. The parameter passed to this method is the value of the optional ProjectId parameter accepted by the screen.

In Step 8 and Step 9, you saw that a Screen Command Bar button is shown only when the screen that defined it has the focus — the corresponding screen tab is selected in the application.

Adding Methods and Buttons to Controls

By now, you have learned that buttons can be added to the screen and to the Screen Command Bar. Many layout elements (such as data grids, lists, and summary controls) have a Command Bar node in the layout hierarchy. Buttons can be added not only to the controls that have a Command Bar node, but also to any control.

In the following exercise, you add a task link to a row of the Project Roles grid. This button will display the Report Activities screen so that the selected project member can report his or her project-related activities.

TRY IT OUT **Adding a Task Link to a Project Role Row**

To create and use a task link, follow these steps:

1. Open the `ListProjects` screen, and locate the `Project Roles Data Grid` node, as shown in Figure 9-54.

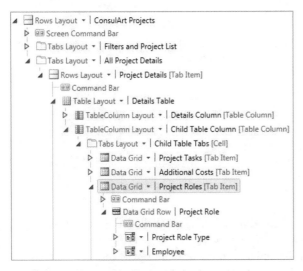

FIGURE 9-54: Locate the Project Roles layout node

2. Right-click the `Project Role Data Grid` node beneath `Project Roles` and select Add Button from the context menu. Set the New Method option in the Add Button dialog and name the method **ReportActivity**.

3. Set the control type of the new node to `Link`. The structure of the `Project Role` node should resemble Figure 9-55.

4. In the data items panel, click the `ReportActivity` method. In the Properties window, select the Edit Execute Code task link. Insert the following boldfaced code into the body of the `ReportActivity_Execute` method:

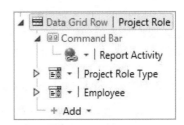

FIGURE 9-55: The Project Role node with the new link

VB
```vb
Private Sub ReportActivity_Execute()
    ' Write your code here.
    Application.Current.ShowReportActivity(Projects.SelectedItem.Id, _
        ProjectRoles.SelectedItem.Employee_cACCOUNTID)
End Sub
```

C#
```csharp
partial void ReportActivity_Execute()
{
    // Write your code here.
    Application.Current.ShowReportActivity(Projects.SelectedItem.Id,
        ProjectRoles.SelectedItem.Employee_cACCOUNTID);
}
```

5. Run the application and open the ConsulArt Projects screen. Select the PT-001 project. In the Project Roles tabs, you can see the Report Activity links for each project member, as shown in Figure 9-56. The Report Activity screen appears and shows the entries for the selected project member.

6. Close the application.

FIGURE 9-56: The Report Activity link is shown for each data grid row

 NOTE *You can find the complete code to download for this exercise on the book's companion website at* `www.wrox.com` *in the folder* `Chapter 09\Sample 10 - Control Buttons.`

How It Works

In this exercise, you used the same pattern used in the previous exercises to display the Report Activity screen. The button you added in Step 2 was appended to the `Command Bar` node of the `Project Role Data Grid Row`. During runtime, it is rendered in the last column of the grid (named `Commands`, as shown in Figure 9-56). When you click the link, the `ReportActivity_Execute` method calls the `ShowReportActivity` method of the current `Application` object, and passes the identifier of the selected project and the employee you clicked in the data grid.

Removing Buttons and Methods

You can remove buttons from the layout hierarchy just like any other nodes. Select them and press the Delete key. Alternatively, you can right-click the button and use the Delete command from the context menu. Always keep in mind that a button has a related method. It is easy to forget about it, especially when you use the Add Button dialog with the New Method option that automatically creates a method for the button.

If you delete a button, the method is still available, and you can locate it in the data items panel of the Designer. However, when you delete a method, all buttons and task links are also removed together with the method. The code belonging to methods (`Execute` and `CanExecute` procedures) is not removed. When you create a new method using the name of a removed method, the previously created `Execute` and `CanExecute` procedures are immediately associated with the new method.

In the preceding exercises, you always had to click the ConsulArt Projects screen to display it. In the following section, you will learn how to set up the screen navigation structure and select the startup screen.

TASKS AND NAVIGATION

When you create several screens and fail to establish an intuitive structure that helps users understand how to use them, your user will be lost in the application menu. Just as a restaurant menu contains logical groupings of items (such as appetizers, main dishes, desserts, and so on), your application must provide a navigational structure that users are familiar with.

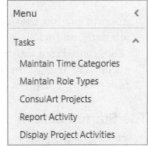

Your screens are placed in the Tasks menu in the order in which they were created within a project, as shown in Figure 9-57. You can see that the first two tasks (maintaining time categories and project role types) are less frequently used functions, but they are at the top because you created them first (in Chapter 6).

Generally, your users would like to see Task menu items in an appropriate order that reflects the natural order of tasks — instead of the order you created them in the underlying LightSwitch project. In the next section, you will learn about reorganizing the structure of the navigation structure.

FIGURE 9-57: The items in the Tasks menu follow the order of their creation in the project

Understanding the Screen Navigation Structure

The designers of LightSwitch made it very easy to customize the navigation structure to fit your needs. Use the project already open in the LightSwitch IDE, or load the project completed in the last exercise. In Solution Explorer, double-click the `Properties` node (or, alternatively, right-click the root project node and use the Properties command from the context menu). The Screen Navigation tab, shown in Figure 9-58, is where you can define this structure.

FIGURE 9-58: The Screen Navigation tab of the project properties in the Designer

Task Groups and Tasks

The navigation hierarchy contains two levels. The first level is a collection of task groups, which may contain an arbitrary number of tasks at the second level. Task groups are simple containers for your tasks.

You can add more task groups by clicking the Add Group command at the bottom of the window. Similarly, an Include Screen command with a drop-down arrow is displayed at the bottom of each task group. From the drop-down list, you can pick a screen to include it in the corresponding task group. The arrow buttons on the right side of the hierarchy enable you to move task items within task groups. However, you cannot move them from one task group to another.

The Startup Screen

The Maintain Time Categories task — which launches the screen with the same name — is displayed in bold. This indicates that this screen is the startup screen. When you launch the application, this screen will be automatically displayed just as if you manually clicked the task representing it. You can use the Set and Clear buttons to set the startup screen — which is also indicated by the label above these buttons.

Obviously, you cannot have more than one startup screen. When you select a new startup screen with the Set button, the previous one is retracted. Of course, you can use the Clear button to remove the current startup screen from being launched automatically. Your application may have no startup screen. In this case, no screen will be launched when the application loads. You should select the first screen manually from the Task menu.

Administrative Screens

In Figure 9-58, you can see a task group named Administration with two tasks, Roles and Users. These are real screens that are implicitly added to your application, but they are not displayed when you run the `ProjectTrek` application because, by default, you do not have permissions to use them. In Chapter 11, you will learn about setting up and checking permissions, and how you can display and use these screens. For now, assume they are not there.

Context Menus

You can right-click a specific task group or task to display its context menu. You can find the Delete and Rename commands in the context menus of both the tasks and task groups. If you click Rename, you can alter the name of the displayed group or tasks. It is important to know that when you rename a task here, the display name (title) of the related screen is also changed, and not just the title of the task. The Delete command removes the task or task group from the navigation hierarchy, but it does not delete the screen from your project.

The context menu of the task also contains an `Edit` *name*`_CanRun Code` command, where *name* is the name (and not the title) of your screen object in the project. This command navigates you to the Code Editor window where you can write a code snippet that checks whether the current user has the right to run this task. You will learn more about this feature in Chapter 11.

Changing the Navigation Structure of ProjectTrek

As you saw earlier, the current navigation structure of `ProjectTrek` is not very friendly. It would be much better if you set up another structure — for example, the one shown in Figure 9-59. In the next exercise, you implement this structure.

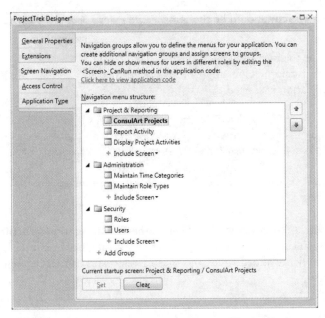

FIGURE 9-59: The new navigation structure of ProjectTrek

TRY IT OUT   **Building a New Navigation Structure for ProjectTrek**

1.   In Solution Explorer, double-click the `Properties` node to open project properties in the Designer. Select the Screen Navigation tab.

2.   Right-click the Administration group, and click the Rename command to change its name to **Security**.

3.   Click Add Group, and name the new group **Administration**.

4.   Click the up arrow on the right side of the hierarchy to move Administration group between Tasks and Security.

5.   Rename the Tasks group **Project & Reporting.** Now, all task groups have the expected names.

6.   Delete the Maintain Time Categories and Maintain Role Types tasks from the first task group (that is, select them and press Delete).

7. Click the Include Screen command of the Administration group and select the Maintain Time Categories screen. Press Enter to accept the screen name as it is. Repeat this step to add the Maintain Role Types screen to the Administration group.

8. Select the ConsulArt Projects task and click the Set button beneath the hierarchy. This will be the startup screen of the `ProjectTrek` application. At this point, your screen navigation hierarchy should be the same as the one shown in Figure 9-59.

9. Run the `ProjectTrek` application. Now the menu structure reflects the changes, as shown in Figure 9-60. This time, the ConsulArt Projects screen is automatically launched when the application is started.

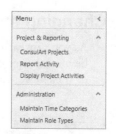

FIGURE 9-60: The new navigation structure of the Task menu

 NOTE *You can find the complete code to download for this exercise on the book's companion website at* `www.wrox.com` *in the folder* `Chapter 09\Sample 11 - Navigation.`

How It Works

The changes and their effects are really obvious. Your application displays the new navigation structure you established in Steps 1 through 8. Now you can see the Administration task group, because it contains your own screens. However, the implicitly added Roles and Users screens still cannot be seen, because you do not have the proper privileges.

EXTENDING THE UI WITH SHELLS, THEMES, AND CUSTOM CONTROLS

LightSwitch provides you a default UI design out-of-the-box. You can accept this design in most cases. However, there are situations when you must customize the UI (colors, fonts, styles, screen layout, and so on). You have several tools for changing it:

➤ *Shells* — You can change the shell (skin) of your application to use a different screen layout, menu appearance, screen layout, and design, instead of utilizing the default one.

➤ *Themes* — You can apply new themes to change colors and fonts, keeping the UI structure and behavior untouched.

➤ *Custom controls* — You do not have to content yourself with the set of controls provided by LightSwitch out-of-the-box. You can use custom controls that provide an extended functionality or user experience. For example, you may add a chart control to a screen in order to display a stacked bar chart — assuming, you installed a custom chart control.

In this section, you will learn about these options.

Applying Shells and Themes

In the project properties, the General Properties tab contains several items that influence the appearance of the application. Two of them, Shell and Theme, provide a drop-down list from which to choose, as shown in Figure 9-61.

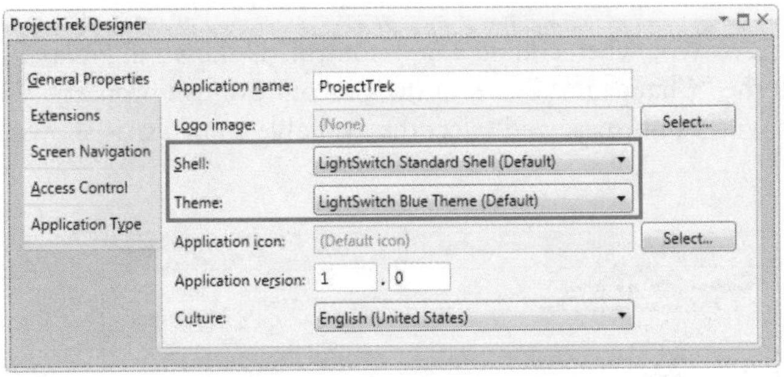

ProjectTrek Designer		▾ ☐ ✕
General Properties	Application name:	ProjectTrek
Extensions	Logo image:	(None) Select...
Screen Navigation	Shell:	LightSwitch Standard Shell (Default) ▾
Access Control	Theme:	LightSwitch Blue Theme (Default) ▾
Application Type	Application icon:	(Default icon) Select...
	Application version:	1 . 0
	Culture:	English (United States) ▾

FIGURE 9-61: The General tab of project properties

Applying a new Theme to your application changes the UI only slightly — it uses different colors and fonts. However, changing the Shell can clothe your application with not only totally new apparel, but also can change its behavior. For example, with a new shell, you can control a layout tailored especially for tablets.

Use the Shell and Theme drop-down list to change these settings. The next time you build and start your LightSwitch application, it will use the new settings.

> **NOTE** As of this writing, LightSwitch provides only one Shell and one Theme option out-of-the-box. However, third-party component developers and communities have already started working on creating new Shells and Themes. Use the Tools ➪ Extension Manager command. In the Extension Manager dialog, select the Online Gallery tab. You can browse the Visual Studio Gallery (www.visualstudiogallery.com) from whithin the LightSwitch IDE, and immediately install available extensions. You'll be able to find free and fee-based extensions, including Shells and Themes. After installing them, you'll be able to choose them in the project properties.

Custom Controls

In the previous exercises, you have changed the control types of layout items several times. When selecting a new control type, you often used the `Custom Control` type. As you will soon see, you can add custom controls to your LightSwitch projects in two ways:

➤ You can select a new custom control.

➤ You can install a custom control extension.

Selecting a Custom Control

In the Designer, select the `Custom Control` type when adding a new control, as shown in Figure 9-62. Go to the Properties window and click the "Change task" link of the Custom Control property. When the Add Custom Control dialog opens, you can browse and select the available controls, as shown in Figure 9-63.

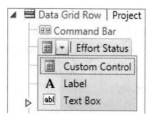

FIGURE 9-62: Selecting the Custom Control type

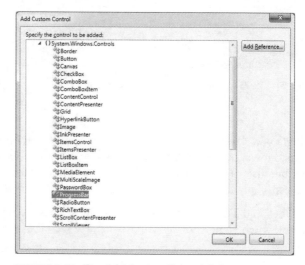

FIGURE 9-63: The Add Custom Control dialog

The controls you can add with this dialog do not know anything about LightSwitch, and cannot bind themselves to the data property you selected in the Designer. To use these controls, you must write explicit code (generally in the `Created` event-handling method of the screen) that sets up data binding. It's about a dozen lines of code, and requires a good understanding of Silverlight's data-binding mechanism.

Fortunately, there is an easier way.

Using a Custom Control Extension

You can install custom control extensions in LightSwitch. These extensions are integrated with the LightSwitch IDE, and do not require you to write any code in order to use them. In the following exercise, you will learn how to install and use a custom control extension.

TRY IT OUT: Installing and Using LightSwitch Custom Control Extensions

> **NOTE** *In this exercise, you start from a prepared sample, which you can find on this book's companion website at* www.wrox.com *in the* Chapter 09\Sample 12 - Custom Controls *folder. During this exercise, you will install a LightSwitch Extension, which you can find in the* Chapter 09\StatusControl *folder.*

1. If Visual Studio LightSwitch is open, close it.

2. Open Windows Explorer and navigate to the Chapter 9\StatusControl folder. There you will find the StatusControlSetup.vsix file. Run it by double-clicking the filename.

3. The Visual Studio Extension Installer starts, as shown in Figure 9-64. Click Install. The Status Control extension installs in a few seconds. When the installation completes, click Close.

The Status Control you've just installed can be bound to a Double property, and represents the double value with colors. Values greater than 0.0 and less then 0.8 are displayed in green. Values greater than 0.8 and less than 0.9 are marked with yellow. Values greater than 0.9 are marked with red. Negative and zero values are displayed in light blue.

FIGURE 9-64: The Visual Studio Extension Installer

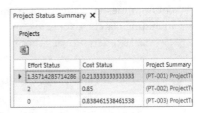

4. Start LightSwitch, and open the ProjectTrek project. Run the application and select the Project Status Summary screen from the Tasks menu. This screen contains a summary of the projects. The Effort Status and Cost Status columns show the ratio of used and planned project efforts and costs, respectively, as shown in Figure 9-65.

FIGURE 9-65: The Effort Status and Cost Status fields

5. Open the project properties and select the Extensions tab. In the list, locate the Status Control extension you installed in Step 2 and Step 3. Mark the check box before this extension item, as shown in Figure 9-66. Save the changes by pressing Ctrl+S.

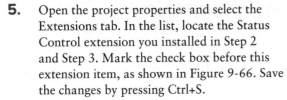
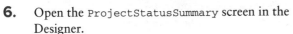

FIGURE 9-66: The newly installed Status Control extension

6. Open the ProjectStatusSummary screen in the Designer.

7. Select the Effort Status layout item and change its control type from `Label` to `Status Control`, as shown in Figure 9-67. In the Properties window, set the width and height of the Effort Status field to 40 pixels and 16 pixels, respectively. Set their horizontal and vertical alignment to `Center`.

8. Repeat Step 7 for the Cost Status layout item. Save changes by pressing Ctrl+S, and close the Designer.

9. Use the Build ➪ Rebuild ProjectTrek command. When the build succeeds, run the application and open the Project Status Summary screen. Now, you can see the Status Control instances displayed in the Effort Status and Cost Status columns, as shown in Figure 9-68.

10. Close the application.

FIGURE 9-67: Using Status Control

How It Works

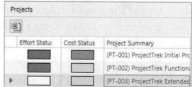

FIGURE 9-68: Displaying Status Control

In Step 2 and Step 3, you installed the Status Control extension. The new control type is immediately available in the Designer after you marked it in Step 5. In Step 7 and Step 8, you changed the default `Label` control type of Effort Status and Cost Status to `Status Control`. After buiding and running your application, this control provides a more useful view of the Project Status Summary screen than the default numeric representation.

The members of the Visual Studio Industry Partner program (third-party and Open Source communities) are already working on developing many custom control extensions for LightSwitch, including charts, data grids, picture viewers, and many more. Check the Visual Studio Gallery (www .visualstudiogallery.com) for new controls regularly.

> **NOTE** You can remove the StatusControl extension by deleting the content of the following folder from your computer: `C:\Users\<username>\AppData\Local\Microsoft\VisualStudio\10.0\Extensions\Istvan Novak`. Replace *<username>* with the username you use to log into Windows. If your system is on another drive (not on `C:`), change the drive letter accordingly as well.

SUMMARY

Unlike traditional RAD applications, LightSwitch has a totally different approach to representing and designing screens. Instead of supporting the WYSIWYG (What-You-See-Is-What-You-Get) layout design, it uses two hierarchies to edit screens: data items and layout items.

Layout containers (such as `Rows Layout`, `Tabs Layout`, `Table Layout`, and many more) provide elastic behavior when you resize your screen. They automatically take care of rendering their content, using the sizing model you defined through container properties. `Data Grid` and `List` controls provide a convenient way to display your tables in grids or lists, using customizable item templates.

You can work with many simple controls (such as Text Box, Check Box, Date Picker, and many more). Value picker controls (such as Auto Complete Box and Modal Window Picker) provide a sophisticated way to pick values or related records in your screens.

You can add methods to your screen that represent custom operations such as navigating to another screen or that process some information. These methods can be represented as buttons or links in the UI.

Although LightSwitch provides a default screen navigation structure, you can customize it to use your own tasks organized into task groups.

EXERCISES

1. Does LightSwitch allow you to bind data items to other data items?

2. What is the effect of setting the vertical alignment of a layout container to Stretch?

3. How must you start your LightSwitch application in order to use the runtime customization feature?

4. What is the role of a Data Grid Row node?

5. Name a typical situation when a Modal Window Picker is suitable.

6. What happens when you add a button to a screen using the New Method option of the Add Button dialog?

7. How can you set the startup screen of your application?

 NOTE *Answers to the Exercises can be found in the Appendix.*

▶ WHAT YOU LEARNED IN THIS CHAPTER

TOPIC	KEY CONCEPTS
Data item hierarchy	This is a hierarchy of elements (data items) that describe screen components that represent data — bound to either data in the database, or data used locally in the screen.
Screen property	A screen property is a data item that is not bound to any data coming from a data source. It represents information stored locally in the screen object. A screen property can be bound to layout elements or to query parameters, and can be used as an input parameter of the screen declaring it.
Method	A method is a local screen operation that can be used in the screen either programmatically or by the user, assuming you provide a UI element that can trigger the method execution.
Layout item hierarchy	This hierarchy describes the structure of layout items that are the constituent parts of the UI. Layout items can be bound to data items. At runtime, the layout hierarchy is rendered and shown as a screen.
Layout container	A layout container is a UI element that (as its name suggests) embeds other UI elements. The container is responsible for rendering its child UI elements. For example, a `Rows Layout` element renders its children vertically, providing a separate row for each of them.
Using the runtime screen customization	LightSwitch allows customizing application screens at runtime. Start the application by pressing F5 (or selecting Debug ⇨ Start With Debugging). Open the screen you intend to customize and click the Design Screen button in the top-right corner. This puts you in Customization mode, where you can change the design of the screen. After you have saved the altered screen layout and closed the application, design changes are available in the LightSwitch IDE.
`Data Grid` **control**	A `Data Grid` control provides a tabular view to display and edit your tables. It provides paging, column sorting, reordering, and resizing. You can use a nested `Data Grid Row` node to define the columns of the grid.
Adding a `Data Grid` **to a screen**	In the data item hierarchy of the Designer, select a query and drag it to the layout hierarchy. The query is immediately transformed into a `Data Grid`, and all visible query fields are added as default columns.
`List` **control**	A `List` control is functionally similar to a `Data Grid` control; it also can be used to display tables. Unlike `Data Grid`, `List` does not provide columns. It utilizes a list item template that can be customized with nested UI elements.

TOPIC	KEY CONCEPTS
Simple controls	The leaf nodes of the layout hierarchy are simple controls such as `Label`, `Text Box`, `Check Box`, and so on. When you add an existing data item to the layout hierarchy, the Designer automatically adds an appropriate control to display and edit the content of the item, according to the item's data type.
Value picker controls	Value picker controls (`Auto Complete Box`, `Modal Window Picker`) enable users to select a value from a choice list or from a table. The Designer is smart enough to assign the correct value picker in the layout hierarchy automatically when you add an appropriate data item.
Adding a method to a screen	You can add a method either by using the Add Data item command in the toolbar and selecting the Method option, or by using the Add New Button function and using the New Method option. In the latter case, a button is also added to the layout hierarchy, which is bound to the newly created method.
Changing the startup screen	Open the project properties in the Designer (double-click Properties in Solution Explorer) and select the Screen Navigation tab. In the task hierarchy, select the screen you intend to start automatically with your application, and click the Set button at the bottom of the page.

10

Validation and Business Rules

WHAT YOU WILL LEARN IN THIS CHAPTER

➤ Understanding the validation architecture of LightSwitch

➤ Using the Designer to create declarative validation rules

➤ Writing custom validation code for checking properties and entities

➤ Implementing business rules and intercepting the save pipeline

In the previous chapters, you built database tables, created simple and master-detail screens, and learned how to use a variety of methods to customize screens. However, you have not yet dealt with the consistency and integrity of data you typed in and saved to the database.

No line-of-business (LOB) application exists without accompanying rules that characterize the business. LightSwitch was designed with validation and business operations in mind. In this chapter, you will learn about the concept of data validation, and about the tools LightSwitch provides to create compound business operations.

 NOTE Compound business operations *consist of a set of steps to carry out a well-defined and consistent operation. They generally modify a set of related records in a database, generally in the form of an atomic transaction. For example, when you order a book that is not in stock, this operation may also generate a background order to fill up the stock and mark your purchase order to be continued when the book is in stock.*

VALIDATION AND BUSINESS LOGIC ARCHITECTURE OF LIGHTSWITCH

One of the most time-consuming and tedious development activities is writing the code that prevents users from entering invalid data in your application. You generally must check many things, including the format of the input typed in (for example, that an e-mail address is syntactically correct) and the semantics of the data (for example, whether the start date of an event is before its end). Even if the user provides valid data, your application may work with that data differently according to certain circumstances. For example, if the user enters a purchase order, your business logic should behave differently depending on whether the ordered product is in stock or must be ordered in the background from a supplier.

This situation can be more complex with multi-tier application architectures. If your application uses a web service with several clients (for example, separate clients for desktop computers and mobile devices), both client applications and the back-end web service should check whether the data entered by the user is correct. Although the client applications check the data, a web service must be "paranoid" (that is, it should not assume that only valid data is provided) and recheck the data received.

LightSwitch uses a clean validation architecture that helps you avoid issues that result from this kind of complexity. Here you will learn about this architecture.

Validation Steps

Each data entry or data modification operation starts in the LightSwitch client application where the user provides data in screens, and saves the information typed in. The data is persisted in the back-end database; and during its progression from the client to the database, there are several validation checks. These steps ensure that the result of the save operation is consistent with the expected business logic. Figure 10-1 shows a brief overview of these steps. In this section, you will learn about this process in detail.

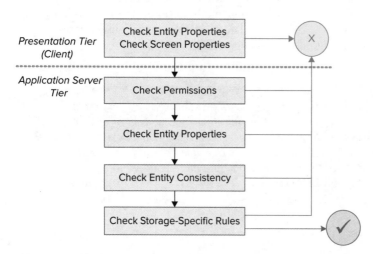

FIGURE 10-1: Validation steps carried out when LightSwitch saves data

Immediate Validation

As you type your data in LightSwitch screens and you move to another user interface (UI) control, LightSwitch immediately checks the content of the UI control you are about to leave. The data is checked to determine whether it can be parsed according to the data type represented by the control. For example, when an integer number is expected in a field, you cannot use letters, only digits. If a date is expected, that should be syntactically valid. When the UI controls provide valid data, those are copied into the data items bound to the control.

If the data you type in cannot be parsed, LightSwitch highlights the UI control and displays a message. Figure 10-2 shows an example that is the result of typing letters into a Date field. LightSwitch immediately reverts the invalid value to the original one. Only the message tells that the "aaa1" value was typed.

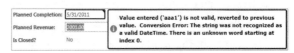

FIGURE 10-2: Invalid data is typed into a Date field

Validation on the Client Side

When you save a screen, the validation starts in the client application and contains the following step on the client side (as shown in Figure 10-1):

1. Each entity property (representing a table field) and each screen property is checked to ensure that its content is correct — in other words, that it contains only a value that fits into the expected value domain of the property. For example, if integer data must be non-negative, all negative values will be refused.

Validation on the Application Server Side

When Step 1 reveals that the data is valid, the entities to be saved are sent to the application server, which might run on a separate computer. The application server in LightSwitch exposes the available operations through web services using the Hypertext Transfer Protocol (HTTP) or Secure HTTP (HTTPS) protocol.

On the application server side, the validation continues with the following steps:

2. The application server checks to see whether the sender has the permission to call a certain operation. If not, the request is refused. In Chapter 11 you will learn the details of this check. For now, simply accept that it is done.

3. Now, Step 1 of the client-side validation step is repeated — with the exception that screen properties are not checked, because they do not exist on the application server side. Because the application server receives requests through web protocols, it cannot trust that the sender of the request is the client application, so it checks fields and entity consistency again.

4. Each entity is checked for consistency. Even if individual fields are valid, this does not guarantee that the entity is valid. For example, the Project entity in ProjectTrek must have a StartDate field with a date before its PlannedEndDate field. In this step, LightSwitch checks for all entity consistency rules.

5. The application server sends the appropriate data modification request to the database server — or, more generally, to the storage server.

6. The database server checks the storage-specific rules. For example, checking the Include in Unique Index property creates a unique index (an alternative primary key, often called a *candidate key*) in SQL Server. That rule is checked only by SQL Server behind the application. If you connect to existing databases, those also can have specific constraints and rules the LightSwitch IDE is not aware of. Before modifying the data, these constraints and rules are also checked.

Validation Failure Feedback

The operation is executed only if all the validation steps concluded that the data is valid for the corresponding operation. In this case, the operation is executed. Its result is retrieved and sent to the client.

Should any of the validation steps fail, the execution is interrupted, and the operation returns with an indication of failure (an error message), including details about validation issues found.

Defining Business Rules

LightSwitch was designed to make the development of this validation process in the IDE as easy as possible. Developers of a LightSwitch application do not need to deal with the details of creating the plumbing code to push the data through these steps.

The application developer's only task is to *define* the *validation rules* and *additional business logic activities*. The LightSwitch runtime — the engine that executes the application — takes care of all the other details. *Business rules* are a combination of validation logic and additional business activities that are part of the operation.

Defining Validation Rules

Developers have the following tools in the IDE to help them define validation rules:

➤   *Field validation properties* — In the Validation category of the Properties window, data fields have several properties that define their valid values. For example, numeric fields have `Minimum Value` and `Maximum Value` properties to define their valid range.

➤   *Custom field validation* — The Custom Validation task link in the Properties window provides a way to write a validation expression (or even longer validation code) to check a field's value. When you must express valid values in a way that cannot be simply described with validation properties, you can write validation code. For example, when all positive odd numbers are valid values for an integer field, you can only express this with code, because the `Minimum Value` and `Maximum Value` properties can define a range but cannot exclude even numbers.

➤   *Entity validation* — Similar to field validation, you can write a `Validate` method for each entity to check its consistency. (For example, the `Project` entity in `ProjectTrek` must have a `StartDate` field with a date before its `PlannedEndDate` field.) If you do not use a `Validate` method for an entity, its content is assumed to be valid unless an invalid field is found.

Intercepting Data Modification Operations

The business rules of an operation contain not only validation, but also other activities that should be carried out when modifying data. For example, there is a ConsulArt policy that says every new project should have a "Project Setup" additional cost category. You can either tell the users that they should manually create this cost category, or — and this is a more useful solution — automatically create this category when a new project is inserted. With the LightSwitch business logic model, you can intercept all data modification operations to add such logic.

However, this behavior introduces new questions! If you have already validated a record to be inserted, and then intercept the insert operation and add another record (probably into another table), how is this extra record validated? Is it validated at all? To resolve this issue, LightSwitch uses a mechanism called the *save pipeline*.

The Save Pipeline

LightSwitch uses a *data service* to manage the save operation for each data source. In the `ProjectTrek` application, two data services are used, one for the `ApplicationData` and another for the `ConsulArtCRMData` sources, as shown in Figure 10-3.

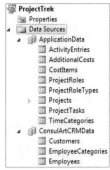

When you save a table, LightSwitch internally uses the `SaveChanges` operation of the appropriate data service. For example, when you modify a `Project` with the ConsulArt Projects screen, the `SaveChanges` method of `ApplicationData` is called — this data source defines the `Project` table. This method starts the save pipeline of the data source.

The save pipeline is executed in the application server tier, and it is responsible for processing the changes users have made in the screen. For example, you may save the ConsulArt Projects screen after you have changed a few project attributes, inserted a few new tasks, and deleted one of the project members. The data source keeps track of all these changes, and they are put into the save pipeline. The save operation persists all changes waiting in the pipeline.

FIGURE 10-3: Data sources in the ProjectTrek application

The pipeline starts a transaction and ensures that all changes in the queue are saved into the database. When everything is successful, the transaction is committed, and the changes — including modifications of the project attributes, the new tasks, and the deletion of the project member — are all in the database. If any kind of error occurs (for example, the business logic does not allow changing the project attributes), the transaction is rolled back as if the operation had never started.

This mechanism seems very simple, but it gets more complex as implicit changes are triggered. These changes can arrive from two sources:

➤ You intercept a change operation. For example, you create business logic that automatically inserts a "Project Setup" additional cost category when a new project is saved.

➤ You define a relationship with the "Cascade delete" behavior (as shown in Figure 10-4), and when a record is deleted that triggers this behavior.

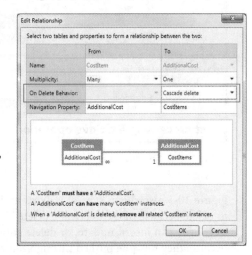

FIGURE 10-4: "Cascade delete" behavior defined for the AdditionalCost table

These new changes also must be processed, so they are placed into the save pipeline. Figure 10-5 summarizes the entire mechanism and its steps. The steps represented by a dark blue background are executed by the LightSwitch engine, and they cannot be changed. All steps with a pale blue background represent points where you can intercept the save mechanism; as you see, there are many of them. Later in this chapter, you will learn more about using these interception points.

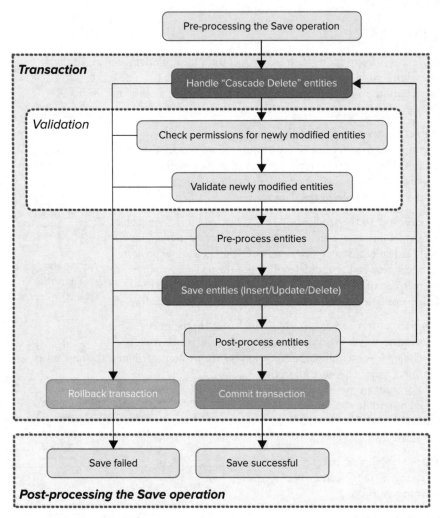

FIGURE 10-5: The save mechanism

Figure 10-5 also shows several important details. The mechanism checks whether there are entities to delete because of the "Cascade delete" behavior. In the pre-process entity and post-process entity steps, you can insert, update, or delete entities. These are entered again into the save pipeline, because they must be pushed through the validation again. The entry point of this change set is the "Handle 'Cascade Delete' entities" step.

Entities that are added to the save pipeline as a result of interceptions are validated again:

1. Permissions are checked (that is, whether the user is allowed to insert, update, or delete a record for a specific table).

2. Entity properties and entities are validated (as described earlier).

Any issues (such as validation errors, concurrency issues, or exceptions) terminate the save process, in which case the transaction started at the beginning of the save operation is rolled back. If all steps run successfully, the transaction is committed, and changes are persisted in the database.

> **NOTE** *The transaction started at the beginning of the save operation provides that either all modifications are successfully persisted to the database (committed) or none of them are (rolled back). The transaction prevents a situation in which some of the modifications are written to the database while others are not.*

By now, you should have a basic understanding of the validation process and the save pipeline mechanism. In the following section you will learn about some helpful tools provided by the LightSwitch IDE.

ADDING VALIDATION RULES

The `ProjectTrek` application does not contain explicit validation rules, so users can enter data that might violate the business logic (in other words, ConsulArt policies). In this section, you add several validation rules to prevent that:

➤ *Rule #1* — Negative planned revenue values are not accepted.

➤ *Rule #2* — According to policy, planned revenue value cannot exceed $100,000. (A large project that would exceed $100,000 in revenue should be divided into smaller projects.)

➤ *Rule #3* — The planned completion date cannot be earlier than the project start date.

➤ *Rule #4* — The total value of additional cost categories cannot exceed the planned revenue.

Declaring Simple Field Validation Rules

You can handle Rule #1 and Rule #2 declaratively using properties to describe them, as you will learn from the next exercise.

TRY IT OUT Adding Simple Field Validation Rules

> **NOTE** *In this exercise, you continue the sample from Chapter 9. You can find the starting sample on this book's companion website at* www.wrox.com *in the folder* Chapter 10\Start.

To implement Rule #1 and #2, follow these steps:

1. Start Visual Studio LightSwitch and open `ProjectTrek`.

2. Open the `Project` table in the Designer, and select the `PlannedRevenue` field.

3. In the Properties window, locate the Validation category. Set `Minimum Value` to **0**, and `Maximum Value` to **100000**, as shown in Figure 10-6.

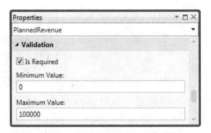

FIGURE 10-6: Minimum Value and Maximum Value properties of Planned Revenue

4. Run the application. In the ConsulArt Projects screen, try to modify the `Planned Revenue` value of an existing project to **-100**. As you leave the field, the `Planned Revenue` is highlighted with a red border that has a small triangle in its top-right corner. When you move the mouse over the triangle, the "Value must be 0 or greater" message indicates that you specified an invalid value, as shown in Figure 10-7. At the top of the screen, the ConsulArt Projects tab also signals this issue, and provides a validation summary, as shown in Figure 10-8. The validation summary has a drop-down arrow. Click it to see the summary details.

FIGURE 10-7: A validation message indicates that you specified an invalid Planned Revenue value

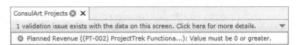

FIGURE 10-8: The validation summary at the top of the screen

5. Change the value of `Planned Revenue` to **120000**. When you leave the field, you'll be given a message (similar to Step 4) that says "Value must be 100000 or less."

6. Note that although your data is invalid, the Save button is enabled. Click Save to try to store the changes. You will get an error message: "Please correct data errors and try to save again." Click OK.

7. Close the application without saving.

How It Works

In Step 3, you defined a validation rule for the `Planned Revenue` field (its value must be between 0 and 100,000). When you entered an invalid value, as soon as you left the text box representing `Planned Revenue`, LightSwitch ran the validation rule and marked the field as invalid. The invalid state of the field was immediately indicated with the red border and the validation summary at the top of the screen.

Although the Save button is enabled when validation errors are present, LightSwitch does not allow you to save invalid changes, and pops up the message described in Step 6.

As shown in this exercise, declaring a simple field validation rule is quite easy. As you have already learned, all data fields have an `Is Required` property to declare that the field must have a value. Table 10-1 summarizes the other properties of data types that you can use for declaring simple field validation rules.

TABLE 10-1: Validation Properties of Data Types

DATA TYPE	VALIDATION PROPERTIES
Date, Date Time, Decimal, Double, Integer, Long Integer, Money, Short Integer	The Minimum Value and Maximum Value properties declare the range of valid values. Any values outside of this range are invalid. By default, these properties have no value, so the entire range of the corresponding data type is taken into account as valid data.
String	The Maximum Length property declares the maximum number of characters the String field can use. The default value is 255.
Email Address	In addition to the Maximum Length property, Email Address has a Require Email Domain property that (as its name suggests) declares whether the e-mail address must have an e-mail domain. If you do not require an e-mail domain, then you must specify a default value in the Default Email Domain property.
Phone Number	In addition to the Maximum Length property, Phone Number has a Phone Number Formats task link (located in the Appearance category). This task link opens the Phone Number Formats dialog, where you can specify how you want to validate and display phone numbers. You specify the format for the phone number using the letter "C" for country code, "A" for area or city code, and "N" for local number, with any symbols that are currently used to display phone numbers, such as +, -, (,), ., and spaces.
	The list allows you to add more than one format. When entering a phone number, LightSwitch first tries to validate against the first format in the list. If the digits match the format, then the phone number is displayed in that manner. Otherwise, LightSwitch tries to validate against the remaining formats in the list until a match is found.
Binary, Boolean, Image	These types do not have any other validation property except Is Required.

Declaring Custom Field Validation Rules

Rule #3 says that the planned completion date cannot be earlier than the project start date. This is a simple validation rule. However, you cannot declare it using the Minimum Value and Maximum Value properties of the Date type (the type of Start and Planned Completion). You can write a custom field validation rule to check whether this condition is met, as shown in the following exercise.

TRY IT OUT   **Declaring a Custom Field Validation Rule**

To implement Rule #3, follow these steps:

1.   Open the `Project` table in the Designer and select the `PlannedEndDate` field. (This is the field with the `Planned Completion` display name.)

2.   Click the Custom Validation task link in the Properties window. The `Project.vb` (`Project.cs`) file is shown with a new `PlannedEndDate_Validate` method, as follows:

VB
```vb
Private Sub PlannedEndDate_Validate(results As EntityValidationResultsBuilder)
    ' results.AddPropertyError("<Error-Message>")

End Sub
```

C#
```csharp
partial void PlannedEndDate_Validate(EntityValidationResultsBuilder results)
{
    // results.AddPropertyError("<Error-Message>");

}
```

3.   Remove the comment from the method body and replace it with the following boldfaced code snippet:

VB
```vb
Private Sub PlannedEndDate_Validate(results As EntityValidationResultsBuilder)
    If PlannedEndDate < StartDate Then
        results.AddPropertyError("Planned Completion cannot be before Start")
    End If
End Sub
```

C#
```csharp
partial void PlannedEndDate_Validate(EntityValidationResultsBuilder results)
{
    if (PlannedEndDate < StartDate)
    {
        results.AddPropertyError("Planned Completion cannot be before Start");
    }
}
```

4.   Run the application. In the ConsulArt Projects screen, modify the `Planned Completion` date of an existing project so that it is before its Start date. The expected validation message appears on the screen, as shown in Figure 10-9. The message also appears in the validation summary.

FIGURE 10-9: The expected validation message for Planned Completion

5.   Correct the `Planned Completion` field to a valid date, and modify `Start` to a date that occurs after `Planned Completion`. The same message is displayed again, and the `Planned Completion` date is marked as invalid.

6.   Close the application, and exit without saving.

How It Works

The key to the validation is the `PlannedEndDate_Validation` method. When the condition of Rule #3 is not satisfied, the `AddPropertyError` method of the `results` object is called. The `results` object is passed to the method as an input parameter, and it can be used to signal validation issues. The `AddPropertyError` method can be used to signal that a property has an invalid value. It accepts a message that is shown onscreen.

Although you defined the validation method for `PlannedEndDate`, when you modified the `StartDate` field in Step 5, it triggered the validation method, and the method recognized that Rule #3 was violated. The LightSwitch engine recognized that the `StartDate` field was changed, and knew that the validation method used `StartDate` in its condition, so it automatically invoked `PlannedEndDate_Validate`.

In this exercise, although you created a field validation rule, if you analyze Rule #3 a bit more, you can see that it is actually not really about the `Planned Completion` or `Start` fields. Rather, it is a rule about the `Project` entity. You could attach this rule to the `StartDate` field instead of `PlannedEndDate` as well, and it would work properly — but in that case it would signal that the `StartDate` field is invalid. Later in this chapter, you will return to this issue and learn how you can handle it by validating the `Project` entity.

Validation through Navigation Properties

Rule #4 says that the total value of additional cost categories cannot exceed the planned revenue. The `Project` entity has a navigation property, `AdditionalCosts`, which is a collection of `AdditionalCost` items that belong to a `Project` instance. An `AdditionalCost` instance has a `Project` navigation property pointing to the project to which the additional cost category belongs. You can write validation code for a navigation property as well, as you will learn in the next exercise, and it is a good opportunity to implement Rule #4.

TRY IT OUT Validating a Navigation Property

To implement Rule #4, follow these steps:

1. Open the `AdditionalCost` table in the Designer and select the `Project` navigation property.

2. In the Designer's toolbar, click the drop-down arrow of Write Code, and select the `Project_Validate` item, as shown in Figure 10-10. This method is where you can write the custom validation method for the `Project` navigation property.

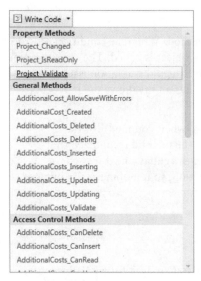

FIGURE 10-10: Selecting the Project_Validate method

3. Insert the following boldfaced code into the body of the `Project_Validate` method:

VB
```
Private Sub Project_Validate(results As EntityValidationResultsBuilder)
    If Project IsNot Nothing Then
        Dim total = Me.Project.AdditionalCosts.Sum(Function(c) c.Amount)
        If Me.Project.PlannedRevenue < total Then
            results.AddPropertyError("The total of additional costs " +
                                     "cannot exceed the planned revenue.")
        End If
    End If
End Sub
```

C#
```
partial void Project_Validate(EntityValidationResultsBuilder results)
{
    if (Project != null)
    {
        var total = Project.AdditionalCosts.Sum(c => c.Amount);
        if (Project.PlannedRevenue < total)
        {
            results.AddPropertyError("The total of additional costs " +
                                     "cannot exceed the planned revenue.");
        }
    }
}
```

4. Run the application. In the ConsulArt Projects screen, select the PT-001 project. In the Additional Costs tab, change the Amount value of the Books item from 200 to 1100. As soon as you leave the Amount field, the validation is carried out, and the summary at the top of the screen indicates that

the additional costs exceed the planned revenue, as shown in Figure 10-11.

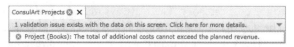

However, this time the red border indicating an invalid value is missing from the Amount field. That's because you validated

FIGURE 10-11: Changing the Amount field to cause a validation error

the Project property, which is a navigation property, so it is not directly bound to a specific UI control. You are going to fix this behavior in the next steps.

5. Close the application, and exit without saving.

6. Open the AdditionalCost table in the Designer. Select the Amount field; and in the Properties window, click the Custom Validation task link.

7. Cut the body of the Project_Validate method (by pressing Shift+Delete) and paste it into the body of the Amount_Validate method (by pressing Ctrl+V).

8. Remove the declaration of the Project_Validate method.

9. Run the application, and verify that changing the Amount value of the Books item from 200 to 1100 in project PT-001 works as expected. Now, not only does the validation summary indicate the invalid value, but the Amount field is marked as invalid, as shown in Figure 10-12.

FIGURE 10-12: The Amount field in now marked as invalid

10. Close the application, and exit without saving.

 NOTE *You can find the complete code to download for this exercise on the book's companion website at* www.wrox.com *in the folder* Chapter 10\ Sample 1 - Property Validation.

How It Works

The validation method uses the Project navigation property to access the Project instance owning the AdditionalCost item. The first condition in the method body checks whether any project is bound to the cost category. There always must be such a `Project` instance, but it is a good practice to check it. The `Sum` operation invoked on `Project.AdditionalCosts` calculates the total cost of these categories, and this value is compared with the planned revenue of the project. If this value violates Rule #4, then the `result.AddPropertyError` method is used to signal the issue.

In Steps 6 through 8, you moved this code into the `Amount_Validate` method, which provided the benefit of not only displaying the issue in the validation summary, but also marking the `Amount` field with the red border.

As you learned in this exercise, navigation properties can also be used for validation. However, because a navigation property is not bound explicitly with any UI control, the validation issues are displayed only in the validation summary, but no UI control is marked invalid.

A navigation property does not have a Custom Validation task link, so you had to use the Write Code button in Step 2.

Validating Entities

In the earlier exercises for this chapter, you learned about declaring field validation properties and writing custom field validation code. Even if it is not instantly obvious, these validations ran on the client application side only, but not at the server side. The server side is activated only when you click the Save button, but in these exercises you didn't save the changes.

Multi-User Issues

Client-side validation is useful because you do not send values to the server side — and therefore save server resources — unless the data is valid. However, in many situations, client-side validation cannot check everything. In particular, it cannot handle situations in which multiple users are concurrently accessing the application. For example, when more than one user can edit the additional cost categories of the same project, Rule #4 can result in those users thinking the business logic is faulty.

Assume that the PT-001 project is opened by two separate users on two separate computers. The planned revenue of this project is $1,000, and $300 in total additional costs are already added to the project. Each user attempts to add a new cost category item with a value of $500, separately from the other. The client application can initiate saving the PT-001 project information on the application server for both user requests, because the client-side validation calculates $800 total additional costs, which is less than $1,000.

The user who first saves PT-001 can do it successfully. However, the second user will fail and receive the "Please correct data entry errors and try to save again" message, and the validation summary will indicate that additional costs exceeded the planned revenue. The second user won't understand this behavior, because the screen displays $800 in the `Total Additional Costs` field, and the user will probably curse the application or its developer.

The explanation of this phenomenon is the validation mechanism. As you have learned, the client-side validations are also executed on the application server side. The first user ran both the client-side and server-side validations successfully. The second user went through the client-side validation successfully, because `ProjectTrek` used the data already read by the client (it did not include the new cost item added by the first user), and it was valid. However, when the `Amount_Validate` method ran on the server side, it used the data read from the database at the moment of validation. At this point, the cost item inserted by the first user was in the database, so when the second user added another new cost item, the total value at the server side was $1,300; a value that violated Rule #4.

 NOTE *You can experiment with your own multi-user access scenarios. By pressing Ctrl+F5, you can start not only one, but multiple application instances. After the first application has started, return to the LightSwitch IDE and press Ctrl+F5 again. Because each open application represents a separate user, you can emulate the scenario described here or create another.*

Validation Steps Revisited

To help you better understand and assess the effects of the validation steps, Table 10-2 summarizes them from a different perspective: This table shows where and when the validation steps run.

TABLE 10-2: Running Validation Rules

VALIDATION STEP	RUNS AT	WHEN DATA CHANGES ON CLIENT	SAVE, ON THE CLIENT	SAVE, ON THE SERVER
Screen Property Validation	Client	Yes	Yes	No
Entity Property (Field) Validation	Client, server	Yes	Yes	Yes
Entity Validation	Server	No	No	Yes

This table confirms that the validation rules you created in the previous exercises run both on the client side and on the server side.

Using Entity Validation

As shown in Table 10-2, entity validation is executed only on the server side. If you had implemented Rule #4 as an entity validation rule running on the application server, you would avoid the multi-user issue described earlier. Of course, it would not provide immediate feedback in the UI when you edit the `Amount` value of an additional cost entry. However, it would recognize that the operation is invalid as soon as you saved the project.

Implementing Rule #4 as an entity validation rule would also reveal a flaw in the current client-side implementation. Currently, if you modify the planned revenue of a project (for example, set it to zero), but do not touch any additional cost item, the validation logic does not recognize that Rule #4 is violated! That's because the Amount_Validation method runs — on both the client side and the server side — only when there is an AdditionalCost entry with a changed Amount field, because a validation rule assigned to a field runs only when the value of the field changes.

 NOTE *In theory, LightSwitch could validate all field properties independently whether the field value changed or not. Generally, users change only a few fields when editing a large set of information. Checking each field would result in an unnecessary waste of resources and loss of performance. Although it would not be an issue on the client side, it definitely would be on the application server. Therefore, the designers of LightSwitch — keeping resources and performance in mind — decided to validate only changed properties.*

In the next exercise, you will implement Rule #4 with entity validation.

TRY IT OUT **Using Entity Validation**

To implement Rule #4 with entity validation, follow these steps:

1. Open the Project table in the Designer. Select the table (if it is not already selected) by clicking the table header.

2. In the toolbar, use the Write Code drop-down list to select the Projects_Validate method — it is the last item in the General category. The ApplicationDataService.vb (ApplicationDataService.cs) file opens, and the Projects_Validate method is created with an empty body. Copy the following boldfaced code into the method body:

VB
```vb
Private Sub Projects_Validate(entity As Project,
    results As EntitySetValidationResultsBuilder)
    If entity IsNot Nothing Then
        Dim total = entity.AdditionalCosts.Sum(Function(c) c.Amount)
        If entity.PlannedRevenue < total Then
            results.AddEntityError(
                String.Format("The total of additional costs ({0}) " +
                "cannot exceed the planned revenue ({1}).",
                total, entity.PlannedRevenue))
        End If
    End If
End Sub
```

C#
```csharp
partial void Projects_Validate(Project entity,
    EntitySetValidationResultsBuilder results)
{
```

```
    if (entity != null)
    {
        var total = entity.AdditionalCosts.Sum(c => c.Amount);
        if (entity.PlannedRevenue < total)
        {
            results.AddEntityError(
                String.Format("The total of additional costs ({0}) " +
                "cannot exceed the planned revenue ({1}).",
                total, entity.PlannedRevenue));
        }
    }
}
```

3. Open the `AdditionalCost` table in the Designer. Click the Write Code button, and delete the `Amount_Validate` method from the code.

4. Run the application. In the ConsulArt Projects screen, select the `PT-001` project. Change the `Planned Revenue` value to **300**. Although Rule #4 would currently invalidate the project, the validation has not yet been executed.

5. Click the Save button. A pop-up message appears, indicating that the application was unable to save the data. Click OK to close the message. The validation summary at the top of the screen indicates that an error was returned from the server (violation of Rule #4), as shown in Figure 10-13.

FIGURE 10-13: The validation summary shows an error retrieved from the application server

6. Close the application, and exit without saving.

 NOTE *You can find the complete code to download for this exercise on the book's companion website at* www.wrox.com *in the folder* Chapter 10\ Sample 2 - Entity Validation.

How It Works

When you selected the `Projects_Validate` method in Step 2, it was created in the `ApplicationDataService` object that runs only on the server side. This method accepts two parameters: the `entity` that is an instance of `Project`, and a `results` parameter used to signal validation error information. The method works the same way as you already learned in the previous exercise. Here, the `AddEntityError` method of `results` was used, and it indicated that the validation error belongs to the entity.

The validation summary shown in Figure 10-13 explicitly indicated that the error was retrieved from the application server side. This enables you to differentiate between client-side issues and server-side validation failures.

Validation Messages in the UI

As you saw in the previous exercises, validation errors are shown on the screen so that users can find and fix them. When a property validation issue occurs and the specified property is bound to a visible UI control, the control is marked with a validation adornment, as shown in Figure 10-14. This adornment is always visible, regardless of whether the UI control has the focus.

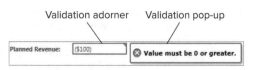

FIGURE 10-14: UI control with validation error

All validation errors that belong to a screen are displayed in the validation summary shown at the top of the screen. This summary contains both client-side and server-side errors, as shown in Figure 10-15. Unlike client-side validation messages, server messages are not removed until the next save operation.

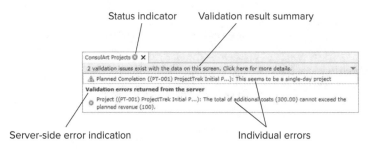

FIGURE 10-15: Structure of the validation summary

You can create your validation methods so that they provide the best messages to the user in a certain validation context. In the previous exercises, you saw that validation methods have special signatures, and they accept a `results` parameter. Client-side validation methods are passed an `EntityValidationResultsBuilder` instance, while server-side validation methods use an `EntitySetValidationResultsBuilder` instance. These objects are provided so that the validation methods can provide feedback regarding the result of the validation process.

Both object types (as their names suggest) are helper objects for building a list of validation messages. The validation process collects all messages returned from the validation steps and uses them to display any issues in the UI.

EntityValidationResultsBuilder Methods

The client-side validation methods can use an `EntityValidationResultsBuilder` instance to signal validation issues. Table 10-3 summarizes the methods you can use to create validation messages.

TABLE 10-3: EntityValidationResultsBuilder Methods

METHOD	DESCRIPTION
AddEntityError	Adds a new entity error with the message string passed to the method.
AddPropertyError	Adds a new property error with the message string passed. This method has an overload that accepts a property parameter. Invoking this method can be used to add an error found in a specific property while another property or an entity was validated.
AddEntityResult	With this method, you can add an entity validation message and select its severity. The method accepts a message string parameter and a severity parameter that takes its value from the Microsoft .LightSwitch.ValidationSeverity enumeration. These values can be Error, Warning, and Informational.
AddPropertyResult	Similar to the AddEntityResult method, you can add a property validation message, passing a message sting and a severity enumeration. This method also has an overload that accepts a property parameter, which is used as described for the AddPropertyError method.

EntityValidationResultsBuilder Methods

The builder class (EntityValidationResultsBuilder) on the application server side uses the same methods listed in Table 10-3. Although the names of the methods and their semantics are the same, there a few slight differences. The AddPropertyError and AddPropertyResult methods always request a property parameter that identifies the property.

Passing Property Parameters

The AddProperty and AddPropertyResult methods can accept a property parameter to identify the property that belongs to a validation message. Through the Details collection of a property, you can access these identifiers, as the following code snippets show:

VB
```
' Client-side access to the StartDate property of Project
results.AddPropertyResult("This is a warning", ValidationSeverity.Warning,
    Details.Properties.StartDate)

' Server-side access to the identifier of the PlannedRevenue property
results.AddPropertyResult("This is a property error", ValidationSeverity.Error,
    entity.Details.Properties.PlannedRevenue)
```

C#
```
// Client-side access to the StartDate property of Project
results.AddPropertyResult("This is a warning", ValidationSeverity.Warning,
    Details.Properties.StartDate);
```

```
// Server-side access to the identifier of the PlannedRevenue property
results.AddPropertyResult("This is a property error", ValidationSeverity.Error,
    entity.Details.Properties.PlannedRevenue);
```

At this point, you have learned how to use property and entity validation, and you should understand the differences between client-side and server-side validation. In the next section you'll learn about writing business rules that not only validate entities when you save them, but also add special actions as a part of the operation.

IMPLEMENTING BUSINESS RULES

In a LOB system, real *business rules* have two ingredients:

➤ *Validation rules* specify how to maintain coherence among the entities of the system, and define either valid scenarios (that is, when consistency is preserved) or invalid scenarios (that is, when system integrity is somehow violated).

➤ *Business transactions* describe how entities should cooperate and be changed together to implement a compound operation.

In the previous exercises you implemented only validation rules; you have not yet created any business transactions.

Intercepting the Save Pipeline

ConsulArt has a policy that states every project must have an additional cost category named "Project Setup" with an initial amount of 2 percent of the expected project revenue, but at least $100. This category is reserved for the costs of establishing the minimum environment of a project. This policy is not yet implemented.

In many applications, developers would implement this business transaction by creating an operation that creates a `Project` record and a related `AdditionalCost` record in a database transaction.

You could implement it with LightSwitch in this way if you wanted, but it would require writing code manually to insert both the `Project` and the related `AdditionalCost` records. LightSwitch uses a different approach. You can intercept the save pipeline and define additional operations, as you will learn in the next exercise.

TRY IT OUT   **Intercepting the Save Pipeline**

Here, you will change the operation that inserts a new `Project` so that it adds the `Project Setup` cost category by intercepting the save pipeline. To implement this simple business rule, follow these steps:

1.   Open `ProjectTrek` in the LightSwitch IDE.

2.   Open the `Project` table in the Designer. Click the drop-down arrow of the Write Code toolbar button and select the `Project_Inserting` method. Copy the following boldfaced code into the method body:

```vb
VB   Private Sub Projects_Inserting(entity As Project)
         Dim costValue = entity.PlannedRevenue * 2 / 100
         Dim setupCost = New AdditionalCost()
         setupCost.Name = "Project Setup"
         setupCost.Description = "Initial project setup costs"
         setupCost.Amount = If(costValue < 100, 100, costValue)
         entity.AdditionalCosts.Add(setupCost)
     End Sub
```

```csharp
C#   partial void Projects_Inserting(Project entity)
     {
         var costValue = entity.PlannedRevenue * 2 / 100;
         var setupCost = new AdditionalCost();
         setupCost.Name = "Project Setup";
         setupCost.Description = "Initial project setup costs";
         setupCost.Amount = costValue < 100 ? 100 : costValue;
         entity.AdditionalCosts.Add(setupCost);
     }
```

3.   Run the application. In the ConsulArt Projects screen, click the Create New Project button and fill in the attributes of the new project as shown in Figure 10-16.

4.   Click Save. When the save operation has finished, click Refresh. Select the PT-004 project from the Projects grid. Select the Additional Costs tab. Here you can see the new Project Setup cost item, as shown in Figure 10-17.

FIGURE 10-16: Attributes of the PT-004 project

FIGURE 10-17: The newly created Project Setup additional cost category

5.   Click the Create New Project button. Fill in the attributes of the new project as shown in Figure 10-18.

FIGURE 10-18: Attributes of the PT-005 project

6. Click Save. This time, the new `Project` record is not saved, and you are given an error message. When you click OK and close the pop-up message, the validation summary shows an issue, as shown in Figure 10-19.

FIGURE 10-19: The PT-005 project cannot be saved

7. Click the Additional Costs tab. As you can see, there are no cost category entries at all.

8. Close the application, and exit without saving.

> **NOTE** *You can find the complete code to download for this exercise on the book's companion website at* www.wrox.com *in the folder* Chapter 10\Sample 3 - Interception.

How It Works

In Step 2, the `Projects_Inserted` method (which intercepted the save operation) was executed just before the new `Project` record was about to be inserted into the database. The code created a new `AdditionalCost` instance and set its attributes with initial values, then used the `Add` operation to add it to the `project.AdditionalCost` collection. When the screen was saved, after being refreshed in Step 4, you confirmed that the `Project Setup` cost category was added as expected.

The save pipeline recognized that the newly inserted `Project` instance was modified (a new `AdditionalCost` instance was added to it), and validated the `Project` instance again. The validation error message shown in Figure 10-19 is clear evidence of this fact. The PT-005 project had a `Planned Revenue` of $0, but the `Project Setup` cost category has an `Amount` value of $100, which is why the validation message was returned.

However, a drawback of the solution is that you do not see the newly added `AdditionalCost` instance unless you refresh the screen.

Save Pipeline Event-Handling Methods

In the previous exercise, you saw only the `Projects_Inserting` method that intercepted the save pipeline. LightSwitch defines many other event-handling methods that can intercept the save pipeline, and the `Inserting` method is just one of them. Figure 10-5, shown earlier, depicts the data flow of the save pipeline. Another view is shown in Figure 10-20, which indicates the event-handling methods executed at the specific phases of the save process.

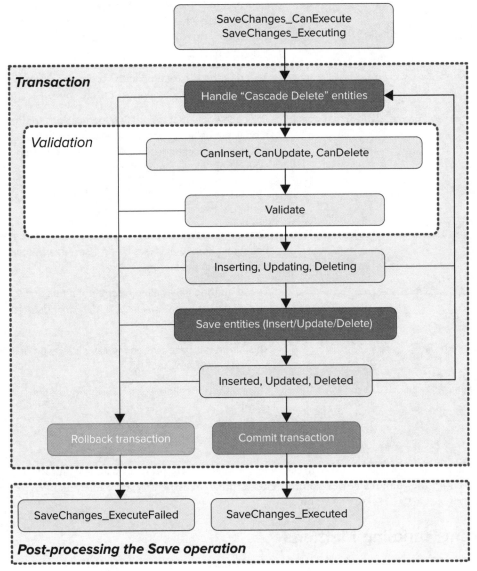

FIGURE 10-20: Save pipeline event-handling methods

Table 10-4 provides a brief explanation of these methods.

TABLE 10-4: Save Pipeline Event-Handling Methods

EVENT METHOD	DESCRIPTION
SaveChanges_CanExecute	This method is executed in the pre-process phase to determine whether the save operation can be executed. You will learn more about this method in Chapter 11.
SaveChanges_Executing	This method is executed in the pre-process phase before the save operation is started.
CanInsert, CanUpdate, CanDelete	For each entity that is modified, permissions for the modifications are checked to determine whether the requested changes are allowed. You will learn more about these methods in Chapter 11.
Validate	This method is called for each modified entity, as you learned earlier.
Inserting, Updating, Deleting	These methods are called just before the entities are being modified (that is, are being inserted, updated, or deleted) in the storage.
Inserted, Updated, Deleted	These methods are called after the entities are modified (that is, are inserted, updated, or deleted) in the storage.
SaveChanges_Executed	This method is called when the save operation has successfully completed.
SaveChanges_ExcutedFailed	This method is called when the save operation failed.

All method names (except the ones starting with SaveChanges) are prefixed with the pluralized name of the entity they handle. For example, events of the Project entity are named like Projects_Inserted, Projects_Validate, and so on.

Query Event-Handling Methods

Just as you can utilize event methods that change the save operation, you also can declare event methods to intercept the process of data query. Table 10-5 summarizes the query event-handling methods. All methods listed in this table run on the application server, and they are prefixed with the plural name of the entity they handle.

TABLE 10-5: Query Event-Handling Methods

EVENT METHOD	DESCRIPTION
query_PreprocessQuery	This method runs before the query runs, and therefore allows query customization. For example, you can customize the query so that only specific records are retrieved, depending on the current user.
query_Executing	This method is called just before the query is being executed.
query_Executed	This method is called right after the query has been successfully executed.
query_ExecuteFailed	When the query execution fails, this method is invoked.

LightSwitch defines three types of queries; query is replaced with these names, as summarized in Table 10-6.

TABLE 10-6: Query Types in LightSwitch

QUERY TYPE	DESCRIPTION
All	Retrieves all instances of an entity from the storage.
Single	Returns a single entity from the storage, using the primary key passed as the parameter of the query. If the specified entity cannot be found in the database, an exception is raised.
SingeOrDefault	The same as Single, but if the entity cannot be found, it retrieves a null value in C# (Nothing in Visual Basic).

Using this naming scheme, if you want to handle the event when a query that is retrieving a single Project entity is prepared, define the Projects_Single_PreprocessQuery method.

Auditing Data Modifications

The previous exercise used the Projects_Inserting method to intercept the save pipeline. It did the expected job. However, from the user's point, it is not really ideal. Without refreshing the ConsulArt Projects screen, the user would not know that the Project Setup cost category was inserted.

A typical use for save pipeline event-handling methods is adding audit entries to your database. For example, when you want to follow the modifications carried out with projects, you can intercept the save pipeline. You can catch the moment when a new project is inserted, or when an existing one is modified or deleted.

NOTE *You can download the complete code that implements this audit function on this book's companion website at* www.wrox.com *in the folder* Chapter 10\ Sample 4 - Audit. *This sample uses a new table,* AuditLog, *shown in Figure 10-21. It also changes the code that creates the* Project Setup *cost category.*

AuditLog		
Name	Type	Required
🔑 Id	Integer ▾	☑
TableName	String ▾	☑
TimeStamp	Date Time ▾	☑
Operation	String ▾	☑
Field	String ▾	☐
OldValue	String ▾	☐
NewValue	String ▾	☐
<Add Property>	▾	☐

FIGURE 10-21: Structure of the AuditLog table

When you load this project in the LightSwitch IDE and open the Project table in the Designer, you can find the core elements of the solution. Use the Write Code toolbar button to navigate to the Project_Created method. This method is called when a new entity instance is created. The following boldfaced code creates the Project Setup cost category:

VB
```vb
Private Sub Project_Created()
    Code = "PT-"
    Closed = False
    StartDate = Date.Now
    PlannedEndDate = Date.Now.AddMonths(1)
    PlannedRevenue = 1000
    Dim setupCost = New AdditionalCost()
    setupCost.Name = "Project Setup"
    setupCost.Description = "Initial project setup costs"
    setupCost.Amount = 100
    AdditionalCosts.Add(setupCost)
End Sub
```

C#
```csharp
partial void Project_Created()
{
    Code = "PT-";
    Closed = false;
    StartDate = DateTime.Now;
    PlannedEndDate = DateTime.Now.AddMonths(1);
    var setupCost = new AdditionalCost();
    setupCost.Name = "Project Setup";
    setupCost.Description = "Initial project setup costs";
    setupCost.Amount = 100;
    AdditionalCosts.Add(setupCost);
}
```

Go back to the Designer. Use the Write Code button to navigate to the `Projects_Inserted` method. As the following code extract shows, this method creates a new audit trail record:

VB
```vb
Private Sub Projects_Inserted(entity As Project)
    Dim audit = DataWorkspace.ApplicationData.AuditLogs.AddNew()
    audit.TableName = "Project"
    audit.TimeStamp = Date.Now
    audit.Operation = "Insert"
End Sub
```

C#
```csharp
partial void Projects_Inserted(Project entity)
{
    var audit = DataWorkspace.ApplicationData.AuditLogs.AddNew();
    audit.TableName = "Project";
    audit.TimeStamp = DateTime.Now;
    audit.Operation = "Insert";
}
```

You can access the set of `AuditLog` entities through the `DataWorkspace.ApplicationData.AuditLogs` collection, and use the `AddNew` method to create a new instance. The `AddNew` method ensures that the new `AuditLog` record is tracked by the save pipeline so it will be written to the database. The method body simply sets the attributes of this instance.

When you navigate to the `Projects_Deleted` method, you can see that it uses the same logic as `Projects_Inserted`. Of course, it sets the `Operation` property to `Delete`.

The `Projects_Updating` method is more interesting, as the following code extract shows:

VB
```vb
Private Sub Projects_Updating(entity As Project)
    Dim auditTimestamp = Date.Now
    If entity.Details.Properties.Code.IsChanged Then
        Dim audit = DataWorkspace.ApplicationData.AuditLogs.AddNew()
        audit.TableName = "Project"
        audit.TimeStamp = auditTimestamp
        audit.Operation = "Update"
        audit.Field = "Code"
        audit.OldValue = entity.Details.Properties.Code.OriginalValue
        audit.NewValue = entity.Code
    End If
    ' A part of the code is omitted for brevity
    If entity.Details.Properties.Closed.IsChanged Then
        Dim audit = DataWorkspace.ApplicationData.AuditLogs.AddNew()
        audit.TableName = "Project"
        audit.TimeStamp = auditTimestamp
        audit.Operation = "Update"
        audit.Field = "Closed"
        audit.OldValue = entity.Details.Properties.Closed.OriginalValue()
        audit.NewValue = entity.Closed
    End If
End Sub
```

C#
```csharp
partial void Projects_Updating(Project entity)
{
    var auditTimestamp = DateTime.Now;
```

```
if (entity.Details.Properties.Code.IsChanged)
{
    var audit = DataWorkspace.ApplicationData.AuditLogs.AddNew();
    audit.TableName = "Project";
    audit.TimeStamp = auditTimestamp;
    audit.Operation = "Update";
    audit.Field = "Code";
    audit.OldValue = entity.Details.Properties.Code.OriginalValue;
    audit.NewValue = entity.Code;
}
// A part of the code is omitted for brevity
if (entity.Details.Properties.Closed.IsChanged)
{
    var audit = DataWorkspace.ApplicationData.AuditLogs.AddNew();
    audit.TableName = "Project";
    audit.TimeStamp = auditTimestamp;
    audit.Operation = "Update";
    audit.Field = "Closed";
    audit.OldValue = entity.Details.Properties.Closed.OriginalValue.ToString();
    audit.NewValue = entity.Closed.ToString();
}
}
```

The `Properties` collection that can be accessed through `Details` contains a property for each table field. For example, the `Code` field can be accessed as `Details.Properties.Code`. You can use the `IsChanged` property to check whether a specific property has been changed. The `OriginalValue` property can be used to access the value of the property before the change. The sample code checks a few more properties than what is shown in the preceding code extract. It uses the same pattern for each property.

The sample code uses the `Projects_Updating` method to catch changes in the entity instance passed as a method argument. If you used the `Projects_Updated` method, you would not be able to check for changes. The `Projects_Updated` method is passed an `entity` instance read from the database right after it was written there. For example, it would contain the `Id` field value automatically generated at the database side. `Projects_Updated`, `IsChanged` would be `False` for each property.

When you run the sample application, the Project Audit Log screen displays the audit trail, as shown in Figure 10-22.

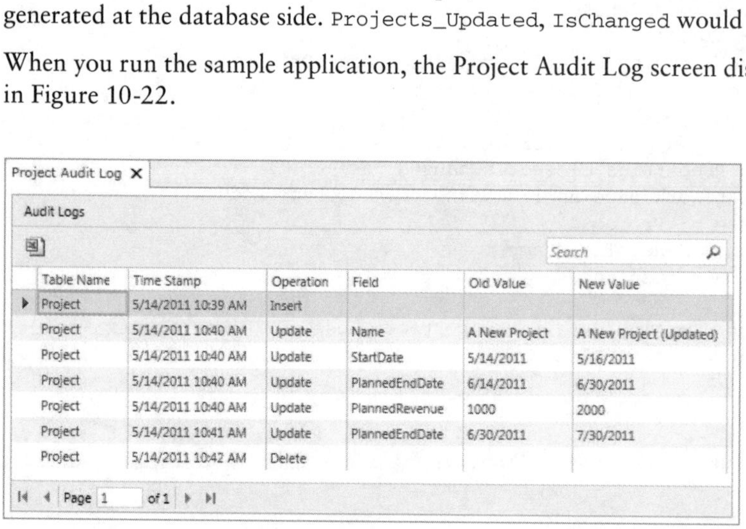

Table Name	Time Stamp	Operation	Field	Old Value	New Value
▶ Project	5/14/2011 10:39 AM	Insert			
Project	5/14/2011 10:40 AM	Update	Name	A New Project	A New Project (Updated)
Project	5/14/2011 10:40 AM	Update	StartDate	5/14/2011	5/16/2011
Project	5/14/2011 10:40 AM	Update	PlannedEndDate	6/14/2011	6/30/2011
Project	5/14/2011 10:40 AM	Update	PlannedRevenue	1000	2000
Project	5/14/2011 10:41 AM	Update	PlannedEndDate	6/30/2011	7/30/2011
Project	5/14/2011 10:42 AM	Delete			

FIGURE 10-22: The Project Audit Log screen

SUMMARY

LightSwitch implements a clear validation logic that checks all data in the screens before passing them to the application server to save. All entity properties and screen properties are checked for syntactic correctness (for example, where numbers are expected, only appropriate characters are typed in) and semantic correctness (for example, if a number must be positive, it really is). The application server checks for user permissions, and validates entity properties and entity coherence before writing it to the database.

Developers can declare property validation by setting a few properties (such as `Minimum Value` and `Maximum Value` for numeric properties), or write their own custom property validation code. Entities are validated only on the application server side, according to the `Validate` method you write to check them. The validation methods use builder objects to define validation messages to be displayed in application screens.

When you save data, you can define additional operations that should be carried out together with the save operation. For example, you can insert audit records into the database. To handle the complexity that may result from this mechanism, LightSwitch uses the save pipeline, which can be intercepted with several event-handling methods. By defining the appropriate event-handling methods, you can implement compound business operations.

EXERCISES

1. How many times are entity properties checked during a save operation?

2. Where is entity validation (that is, checking the internal coherence of an entity) carried out?

3. Which methods of the `results` parameter passed to the `Validate` method can be used to signal validation issues?

4. Which event-handling method is called by the save pipeline when a `Project` entity is about to be deleted?

5. How can you check in the `Projects_Updated` method whether a certain property of a `Project` instance was modified?

 NOTE *Answers to the exercises can be found in the Appendix.*

▶ **WHAT YOU LEARNED IN THIS CHAPTER**

TOPIC	KEY CONCEPTS
Property (field) validation	Each property of an entity is checked as to whether its content is correct — in other words, it has a value that fits into the expected value domain of the property.
Entity validation	Even if individual properties (fields) are valid, this provides no guarantee that the entity is valid. Entity validation checks the internal coherence of an entity. For example, it can confirm that a start date within an entity does not exceed the end date.
Storage-specific rules	The database server behind the application may check storage-specific rules. For example, checking the `Include in Unique Index` flag of an entity property creates a unique index (an alternative primary key, often called a *candidate key*) in SQL Server. That rule is checked only in SQL Server when you modify the value of the property.
Business rule	A business rule is a combination of validation logic (that describes the coherence among the entities defined by a system) and additional business activities that are part of a business transaction.
Declaring a custom property validation	In the Designer, open the table and select the property for which you want to write the custom validation. In the Properties window, click the Custom Validation task link. In the Code Editor, define the validation method body. Use the `results` parameter's methods to signal validation issues.
Declaring entity validation	In the Designer, open the table representing the entity. Use the Write Code toolbar button to select the `Validate` method. In the Code Editor, define the method body. Use the `results` parameter's methods to signal validation issues.
Multi-user validation issues	Because client-side validation steps work with the data already read by the client, changes in the back-end are not recognized unless the data is refreshed. In a multi-user environment, this could lead to validation problems, because the client application uses different data than the back-end. Use server-side (entity) validation whenever issues resulting from a multi-user environment are likely.
Save pipeline	LightSwitch uses a save pipeline mechanism to provide a consistent way to save changes. You can write custom code that intercepts the save process — for example, to add an audit trail to the application. The save pipeline handles all changes that result from interceptions. It uses a transaction to provide integrity for the entire save operation. In case of validation or operation errors, this transaction is rolled back. If all operations are successfully carried out, the transaction commits all changes.
Event-handling methods	The save pipeline and query operations can be intercepted by event-handling methods. These methods are listed in Table 10-4 and Table 10-5.

11

Authentication and Access Control

WHAT YOU WILL LEARN IN THIS CHAPTER

➤ Grasping the concept of authentication and access control in LightSwitch applications

➤ Understanding the role and implementation of access control methods

➤ Using the Windows authentication and Forms authentication models

➤ Managing users and roles in a published LightSwitch application

No real line-of-business (LOB) applications can succeed without authenticating users and restricting their access to only those functions they are permitted by their position in the organizational structure of the company (or by some other kind of project or job assignment). Every company works with sensitive business information that is important to conceal not only from competing companies, but also from the eyes of non-privileged employees, partners, or suppliers.

By now, the ProjectTrek application you have built has ignored this important requirement for the sake of keeping the focus on building data, screens, and functionality. In this chapter, you learn about the authentication and access control concepts of LightSwitch, and, of course, how to apply them in your applications.

AUTHENTICATION AND ACCESS CONTROL CONCEPTS

The designers of LightSwitch created the application architecture and the tools available in the IDE so that security is not an afterthought, but rather part of the standard development process. Many business application development projects suffer from a lack of thorough authentication and access control design. At the beginning of a project, these issues are often handled with a "we'll solve it later, it shouldn't be too difficult" attitude. Unfortunately, this is often the source of significant extra effort and overtime as the project enters into the end-game phase.

When you create LightSwitch applications, the architecture and the IDE enable you to painlessly add security features. You do not have to refactor your LightSwitch application because you failed to handle authentication or access control issues earlier. However, you mustn't omit a few important design steps:

1. Your application's functionality must be established with the different roles that users can have. For example, you may need to create different screens for users with fewer privileges, and for business administrators of the application.

2. You must carefully consider data access issues, and clarify who can use a certain kind of data with a certain set of privileges.

3. You must determine whether you want to create an audit log of your application; and if so, what kind of events this log should contain. (An audit log is used to record user activities, such as invoking important operations or changing particular data, for audit purposes.)

Step 1 is the most important when designing LightSwitch applications. If you omit this step, later in the implementation phase, you may need to re-create screens — and that might take a long time. This extra work typically requires designing a new screen — in terms of usability — not technically building it.

ConsulArt has already carried out Step 1, when Mary designed the functionality of `ProjectTrek` (which you learned about in Chapter 5). She summarized the roles of users as shown in Table 11-1.

TABLE 11-1: Actors in the ProjectTrek System

ACTOR	ROLE
Resource manager	This person is responsible for keeping track of projects and related resources within ConsulArt. Responsibilities include creating a new project and identifying its most important attributes (deadlines, planned revenues, project members, and so on).
Project manager	Each project is led by a project manager who is responsible for planning the tasks and additional costs of the project, and keeping track of the project's status.
CEO	The CEO wants an overview of each project's overall status.
Project member	Project members report their daily activities so that the project manager can follow that project's resource usage. Project members send invoices, bills, and notes of cost items (books, photocopying, and other expenses) to the project manager, who administers those items.
`ProjectTrek` administrator	This person is responsible for setting up user rights for `ProjectTrek` and administering dictionary tables (for example, time categories) in the system.

When you were guided through the implementation of `ProjectTrek`, the list of roles summarized in Table 11-1 were taken into account — even if you didn't realize it.

Before implementing the security aspects in `ProjectTrek`, let's be sure you understand the concepts of authentication and access control.

Authentication

Authentication is the process used to identify the user of the application. In terms of security, this is the most important task; otherwise, user privileges cannot be checked. When you create a new application project in LightSwitch, the default setting in the Access Control tab of the project properties does not enable authentication, as shown in Figure 11-1.

FIGURE 11-1: Authentication is not enabled in a new LightSwitch project by default

Any other options enable authentication. The identity of the user is considered in every layer of the application, as shown in Figure 11-2.

When authentication is enabled, the Presentation tier asks the user to provide authentication data (such as username or password), and the application checks the identity of the user according to this information. During this process, the Presentation tier uses the business Logic tier and the data to carry out the authentication. This action has been omitted from Figure 11-2 for the sake of simplicity. Alternatively, if your application uses Windows authentication, the Presentation tier accepts the user identity information that was created when the user logged on to the computer.

The result of the authentication is a *user token* that is just like a driver's license — it identifies the user to the application. This token contains the username, but not the user's password, and the system handles it as evidence that the user is who he or she claims to be. When you use Windows authentication, the Presentation tier gets this user token from the computer.

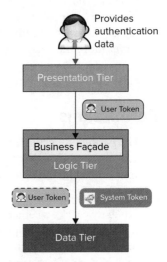

FIGURE 11-2: User identity is considered in every application layer

 NOTE *Of course, a complete discussion of authentication is beyond the scope of this book. For more information, see Imar Spaanjaar's* Beginning ASP.NET 4 in C# and VB *(Indianapolis: Wiley, 2010), which explains complex authentication topics such that you do not need to be a security expert to understand them.*

Access Control

Access control is the process that uses the identity of the user to check whether he or she can carry out a certain operation — such as opening a screen, reading data from a specific table, modifying the content of a table, and so on. The LightSwitch application adds permission information to the user token (refer to Figure 11-2) — a list of rights the user is granted in the application.

The Presentation tier uses this permission information to display the screens to which you have the proper rights to open and use. When your rights tell the presentation layer that you are not permitted access to a specific screen, the Presentation tier hides the task link of that screen, so you won't be able to open it.

When a screen queries information from the application server, or saves data, this user token is passed to the business Logic tier through a *business façade*. The façade checks the permissions listed in the user token to determine whether the user is allowed to carry out the requested operation. If he or she is not allowed, the request will be refused.

When the business logic talks with the Data tier, the user token is also passed with the request. Very often, this user token is changed to a *system token*. This change has a very important effect from a security perspective. Instead of managing dozens (or even more) separate user rights in the database server (or in the back-end system providing data), only the rights of a single system token should be managed. As you can imagine, this is a much easier task, and results in fewer potential security holes than user-based rights management.

Permissions

The *permission* is the smallest unit of rights that you can have. A permission object has a name, and you can check whether the user has the permission with the specified name. Your application's users are assigned permissions (according to the user database) when they are logged into the application.

LightSwitch utilizes only a single predefined permission (named Security Administration) that explicitly checks whether the current user has access to user administration screens. You can define your own application-specific permissions. Utilizing them, you can explicitly implement access control checks in a LightSwitch application so that you tell the combination of permissions the user must have to access certain functions.

For example, if you have a permission named `Wizard` and another named `Hobbit`, you can specify that a user can read data from the `Magic` table only when he or she possesses either the `Wizard` or the `Hobbit` permission. Of course, if they have both, it implies that they can read the `Magic` table.

NOTE The `Wizard` and `Hobbit` *names were intentionally used instead of something like* `CanReadMagicTable` *to demonstrate that permissions do not imply anything by their name. Of course, in your application, you should use permission names that suggest their usage.*

Roles and Users

Users are not directly assigned permissions in a LightSwitch application, but rather roles. It is the role that is associated with a set of permissions, not the individual user. The idea behind this concept is very simple. Generally, you manage a few dozen permissions in a typical business application. You also may have, let's say, 10 to 100 users. Although these users are not totally different from one another, you can divide them into logical groups according to what they do with the system. These groups are called *roles*.

If you had to manage users directly by assigning them permissions, it would be a tedious and error-prone task because of the large number of users and permissions. Roles simplify this task in the following ways:

➤ You group permissions required for a specific task into a role. You can group zero, one, or more permissions into a role.

➤ You assign zero, one, or more roles to a user.

➤ The set of permissions held by a user is calculated as the union of permissions from every role assigned to that user.

Later in this chapter, you'll learn how to manage users, roles, and permissions.

Access Control Methods

You could implement access control with a large grid whereby rows would define users, and columns would reflect the operations that users are allowed or not allowed to perform (for example, adding a new record to a table). In other words, grid cells would indicate whether the user represented by a row is allowed to execute the operation represented by a column.

Instead of managing such a large grid, LightSwitch uses a different approach. It defines a set of access control methods you can use to calculate a Boolean value indicating whether the user is allowed to access the operation. In Chapter 10, you learned about the save pipeline and event-handling methods. Well, access control methods are event-handling methods. They respond to the event when the LightSwitch engine is about to execute an operation, and check whether the current user has the right to carry out that operation. The CanInsert, CanUpdate, and CanDelete methods introduced in Chapter 10 are such methods.

By default, if you do not handle an access control method, LightSwitch responds as if you explicitly enabled the operation. If you want more control, you must define the method body. For example, the following access control method checks whether the ProjectAuditLog screen can be run by the current user:

VB
```vb
Private Sub ProjectAuditLog_CanRun(ByRef result As Boolean)
    result = User.HasPermission(Permissions.SecurityAdministration)
End Sub
```

C#
```csharp
partial void ProjectAuditLog_CanRun(ref bool result)
{
    result = User.HasPermission(Permissions.SecurityAdministration);
}
```

The `result` parameter is used to enable or disable the operation guarded by the access control method. By default, it is set to `True`. The boldfaced code does exactly as it reads — it checks whether the current user has the `SecurityAdministration` permission.

Now that you have learned the most important concepts of authentication and access control in LightSwitch, it's time to use them in the `ProjectTrek` application.

USING ACCESS CONTROL IN LIGHTSWITCH APPLICATIONS

You have seen that to use the access control features of LightSwitch, users must first be authenticated. To help you develop an application, the LightSwitch IDE authenticates you differently when you start the application from the IDE. It does not require your user information (your roles and permissions) to be stored in the application database. Instead, it allows you to specify the permissions you want to use to test the application during the development phase. Therefore, the following sections describe how to define and check permissions.

Defining and Checking Permissions

There are a few screens in the `ProjectTrek` application that allow changing business parameters — for example, maintaining the dictionary table of time categories and project role types. In the following exercise, you set up a permission to control access to these screens, and implement the appropriate check for this new permission.

> **TRY IT OUT** Defining and Checking a New Permission

 NOTE *In this exercise, you continue the sample that you worked with in Chapter 9. You can find the starting sample on this book's companion website at* www.wrox .com *in the folder* Chapter 11\Start.

1. Start Visual Studio LightSwitch and open the `ProjectTrek` project.

2. In Solution Explorer, double-click the `Properties` node to display the project properties in the Designer. Select the Access Control tab.

3. Set the "Use Windows authentication" option, and then the "Allow only users specified in the Users screen of your application" option beneath it.

4. Click the <Add New Permissions> cell in the table at the bottom of the Access Control tab, and type **BusinessAdministration**. This will be the name of the new permission you are about to create.

5. Click Tab, and then type **Business Administration** to set the display name of the new permission. Click Tab again and specify "Allows administering dictionary tables" as the text description of the permission.

6. Click Tab and press the spacebar to set the "Granted for debug" check box (or check it with the mouse). The Access Control tab should look like Figure 11-3.

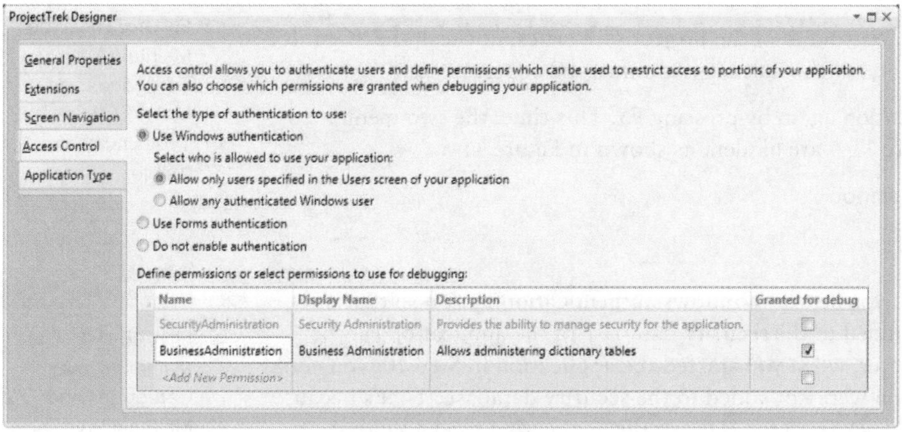

FIGURE 11-3: An example of users, roles, and permissions

7. Click the Screen Navigation tab. In the navigation menu structure hierarchy, right-click the Maintain Time Categories item beneath the Administration group. Select "Edit EditableTimeCategoriesGrid_CanRun code" from the context menu.

8. Insert the following boldfaced code into the body of the `EditableTimeCategoriesGrid_CanRun` method:

```vb
Private Sub EditableTimeCategoriesGrid_CanRun
    (ByRef result As Boolean)
        result = User.HasPermission
            (Permissions.BusinessAdministration)
End Sub
```

```csharp
partial void EditableTimeCategoriesGrid_CanRun(ref bool result)
{
    result = User.HasPermission
        (Permissions.BusinessAdministration);
}
```

9. Repeat Step 7 and Step 8, but this time select the Maintain Role Types screen with the "Edit EditableProjectRoleTypesGrid_CanRun code" command in its context menu. Insert exactly the same code line into the empty `EditableProjectRoleTypesGrid_CanRun` method body as in Step 8.

10. Run the application by pressing F5 and then expand the Administration menu. You can see that it displays both the Maintain Time Categories and the Maintain Role Types items, as shown in Figure 11-4.

11. Close the application.

12. In the Access Control tab of the project properties, uncheck the "Granted for debug" check box of the Business Administration permission.

13. Run the application again by pressing F5. This time, the two menu items visible in Figure 11-4 are hidden, as shown in Figure 11-5.

14. Close the application.

FIGURE 11-4: The Maintain Time Categories and Maintain Role Types items are visible

FIGURE 11-5: The Maintain Time Categories and Maintain Role Types items are hidden

How It Works

In Step 2 and Step 3, you set the Windows authentication option so that only the users manually added to the security database of the application can be authenticated. However, when you started the application in Step 10, you could use it even though you were not added to the security database. That's because you started `ProjectTrek` from the IDE, so the application used a kind of authentication that treats you as if you were in the database.

In Step 4 and Step 5, you created a new permission. In Step 8 and Step 9, you defined the body of access control methods guarding the two screens maintaining time categories and project role types, respectively. The expression that sets the `result` parameter value used the `HasPermission` method of the `User` object.

The `User` object represents the user token of the current user, and its `HasPermission` method checks whether the specified permission is assigned to this token. The `Permissions` class contains strings representing the names of permissions defined in the Access Control project property tab. As a result of the code, the screens are allowed (and their corresponding menu items are shown) only when the current user has the Business Administration permission.

In Step 10, because you started the application with the "Granted for debug" flag of the Business Administration permission set, the screens were available to the user (refer to Figure 11-3). After unchecking the "Granted for debug" flag (running the application in Step 13), the screens were unavailable. When you set the flag, the permission was added to the user token.

Available Access Control Methods

There are many access control methods you can define in a LightSwitch application. These belong to one of the following categories:

➤ Data tables you create in the LightSwitch IDE

➤ Data tables defined in external data sources

➤ Queries implicitly defined by LightSwitch

> ➤ Queries explicitly defined by developers

> ➤ Screens

> ➤ Methods

> ➤ Save pipeline

In this section, you learn more about working with access control methods.

Access Control Method Names

The names of access control methods have two constituent parts following the `<object name>_<privilege name>` pattern. The `<object name>` tag is the name of the data set (table or query), or the screen guarded by the access control method. The `<privilege name>` tag identifies the elementary permission checked on the guarded object.

For example, the name of the access control method that checks whether you can update the `Project` table is `Projects_CanUpdate`. Because not only one `Project` record is guarded by the access control method, but rather the whole data set represented by the `Project` table, the plural `Projects` name is used as a convention.

Access Control Method Semantics

Every access control method has a single Boolean parameter, as shown by the following definitions:

VB
```
Private Sub <object name>_<privilege name>(ByRef result As Boolean)
```

C#
```
partial void <object name>_<privilege name>(ref bool result);
```

Access control methods retrieve the result of the check in their `result` Boolean parameter. They do not have a return value. If you did not define an access control method, or you left the body empty, it is the same as if you were returning `result` with a `True` value, and the requested operation would be granted. You should set the `result` parameter to `False` if you want to disallow the guarded operation.

Editing an Access Control Method

To define the body of an access control method, you must open the related object (table, query or screen) in the Designer. Using the Write Code button, these access control methods are available in the Access Control Methods category, as shown in Figure 11-6, and in the Query Access Control Methods category.

Select the appropriate method from the list, and, in the Code Editor window, implement the method body.

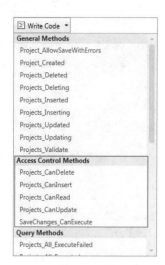

FIGURE 11-6: Access Control Methods in the Write Code drop-down list

Available Access Control Methods

You can define access to a data table (either defined in LightSwitch or in an external data source) with a few access control methods, as summarized in Table 11-2. The Method column of the table contains only the `<privilege name>` part of the method's name.

TABLE 11-2: Data Table Access Control Methods

METHOD	DESCRIPTION
CanDelete	Checks whether the user is allowed to delete a record from a table
CanInsert	Checks whether the user is allowed to insert a new record into a table
CanRead	Checks whether the user is allowed to read records from a table
CanUpdate	Checks whether the user is allowed to modify existing records in a table

Explicit queries (for example, the `Active Projects` query belonging to the `Project` table) have only a single access control method, `CanExecute`, to define whether the current user is allowed to execute the query.

Implicit queries are automatically defined by LightSwitch for each table added to the project, or attached to it from an external data source. Table 11-3 summarizes the access control methods available for implicit queries.

TABLE 11-3: Implicit Query Access Control Methods

METHOD	DESCRIPTION
All_CanExecute	Checks whether the user is allowed to execute the query that retrieves all entities from the specified table.
Single_CanExecute	The `Single` query of a table retrieves a single record from the underlying table, addressed by the record identifier. The `Single` query raises an exception when the record cannot be found. This method checks whether the user is allowed to execute the `Single` query.
SingleOrDefault_CanExecute	The `SingleOrDefault` query of a table retrieves a single record from the underlying table, addressed by the record identifier. The `SingleOrDefault` query retrieves a `null` value in C# (`Nothing` in Visual Basic) when the record cannot be found. This method checks whether the user is allowed to execute the `SingleOrDefault` query.

Screens have only a single `CanRun` access control method — the one you used in the last exercise. `CanRun` determines whether the current user can open the specified screen. When a screen is allowed to run, it is displayed in the application's task menu; otherwise, it is not shown there. Methods assigned to screens have a `CanExecute` method. You can use `CanExecute` to define the access control condition of a method.

The save pipeline also has an access control method, named `SaveChanges_CanExecute`. This method is called on the application server side right before a save operation is about to start. If it returns the `result` parameter with a `False` value, the user cannot save any modifications to the database.

Writing Access Control Methods

You can write arbitrary code into the body of an access control method that calculates the value of the `result` parameter. Here you can use any kind of test to set this value (including astronomical calculations) using data stored in your application. The application does not care how this calculation is done. The only thing that matters is the value of `result`. If it is `True`, the user is granted permission for the guarded operation. If it is `False`, the operation is not allowed.

Although you can use arbitrary code and calculations, the best practice is to use the `User` object and its `HasPermission` method, and set the result parameter according to the permissions of the current user. Of course, you can combine conditions by checking user permissions with other conditions.

FILTER OPERATIONS

In advanced security scenarios, you may want to use separate queries or tighten the results of a query according to the permissions of the current user. For example, you might want to allow a sales agent to view only the orders belonging to him or her. Access control methods are not for this purpose, and you cannot use them for filtering.

You can carry out such operations in LightSwitch by utilizing the `All_PreprocessQuery` and the `All_Executed` event-handling methods that belong to a specific table you want to filter. This is an advanced topic that requires a good understanding of LINQ. Search MSDN with the `All_PreprocessQuery` keyword to find more information and samples for this topic.

You can find a sample application on this book's companion website at `www.wrox.com` in the `Chapter 11\Sample 1 - Permissions` folder that demonstrates writing a few access control methods. This sample uses the set of permissions shown in Figure 11-7.

Name	Display Name	Description	Granted for debug
SecurityAdministration	Security Administration	Provides the ability to manage security for the application.	☑
BusinessAdministration	Business Administration	Allows administering dictionary tables	☑
CanCreateProject	Can Create a Project	Allows creating a new project	☑
CanEditProject	Can Edit a Project	Allows editing a project	☑
CanDeleteProject	Can Delete a Project	Allows deleting a project	☑
CanEditTasks	Can Edit Project Tasks	Allows editing project tasks	☑
CanEditCosts	Can Edit Project Costs	Allows editing project costs	☑
CanViewStatistics	Can View Statistics	Allows viewing project-related statistics	☑
CanReportActivity	Can Report Activity	Allows reporting any user's project activity	☑
CanViewAuditLog	Can View Audit Log	Allows viewing the audit log	☑
<Add New Permission>			☐

FIGURE 11-7: Permissions implemented in ProjectTrek

Table 11-4 identifies which access control methods are used in this sample application. Load the sample into the LightSwitch IDE and take a closer look at how these access control methods are implemented.

TABLE 11-4: Access Control Methods Used in the Sample Application

OBJECT	ACCESS CONTROL METHODS
`Project` table	`Projects_CanInsert`, `Projects_CanUpdate`, `Projects_CanDelete`
`ProjectTask` table	`ProjectTasks_CanInsert`, `ProjectTasks_CanUpdate`, `ProjectTasks_CanDelete`
`AdditionalCost` table	`AdditionalCosts_CanInsert`, `AdditionalCosts_CanUpdate`, `AdditionalCosts_CanDelete`
`CostItem` table	`CostItems_CanInsert`, `CostItems_CanUpdate`, `CostItems_CanDelete`
`DisplayProjectActivities` screen	`DisplayProjectActivities_CanRun`
`ListProjects` screen	`CreateNewProject_CanExecute`, `CloseProject_CanExecute`, `ReopenProject_CanExecute`, `ReportActivity_CanExecute`, `ReportCosts_CanExecute`
`ProjectAuditLog` screen	`ProjectAuditLog_CanRun`
`ProjectStatusSummary` screen	`ProjectStatusSummary_CanRun`
`ReportActivity` screen	`ReportActivity_CanRun`

By now, you have learned about the roles of users and permissions. You also know how to implement access control methods. However, you do not know how to create and manage users. It's time to learn how to do that.

MANAGING USERS, ROLES, AND PERMISSIONS

The LightSwitch IDE does not require you to manage users and roles while you develop an application. In the Access Control tab of project properties, you can mark permissions with the "Granted for debug" flag. When you start the application from within the IDE, LightSwitch assigns you the permissions you marked.

When your application is completed and tested, you can deploy it to users. After deployment, however, you must manage users, roles, and permissions; otherwise, no user can work with the application. Before going into this further, a brief look at authentication options would be useful.

Authentication in LightSwitch

You can select from three options for authentication in a LightSwitch application:

➤ *Windows authentication* — You are logged into your computer or into the Windows domain your computer belongs to (generally to your company's domain) with a user account. LightSwitch uses the token of this authenticated account, and attaches the user information, roles, and permissions to it. This means that you are automatically authenticated in the LightSwitch application when it is launched.

➤ *Forms authentication* — When you start the LightSwitch application, you must log in with a username and a password. If you log in successfully, your user information, roles, and permissions are assigned to you according to the application's database.

➤ *No authentication* — You are not authenticated in LightSwitch, and you have not been assigned any permissions. The LightSwitch application uses a default user token, and you can access all operations that do not require any special permission.

 NOTE *Using the "no authentication" mode does not mean that you cannot define access control methods. You can still implement access control methods and program the logic that determines whether an operation is enabled. However, you must allow or disable access based on some other information than permissions. For example, you may use the system date to disallow certain operations outside of the official working hours.*

Using Windows Authentication

The easiest authentication method is to use the Windows authentication option with a LightSwitch application, as you will learn from the next exercise. To see how authentication works, you must publish and install your application. When you start it from the IDE, LightSwitch automatically provides you with a default account that uses the permissions marked with the "Granted for debug" flag. Deployment details won't be explained here; you will learn the important details in Chapter 13. For now, simply follow the steps in the exercise.

TRY IT OUT Using Windows Authentication

To use Windows authentication, follow these steps:

 NOTE *In this exercise, you will start from a prepared sample. You can find the starting sample on this book's companion website at* www.wrox.com *in the* Chapter 11\Sample 1 - Permissions *folder.*

1. Open ProjectTrek in the LightSwitch IDE.

2. In Solution Explorer, double-click the Properties node to display the project properties in the Designer. Select the Access Control tab.

3. Set the "Use Windows authentication" option, and then the "Allow only users specified in the Users screen of your application" option beneath, as shown in Figure 11-8.

FIGURE 11-8: Selecting the Windows authentication option

4. Select the Application Type tab, and set the Client and Application Server options shown in Figure 11-9. Click Publish.

5. The LightSwitch Publish Application Wizard appears. Select the Authentication item on the left. Select the "Yes, create the Application Administrator at this time" radio button and provide your full Windows login name — including the name of your computer or Windows domain — as shown in Figure 11-10. Click Publish.

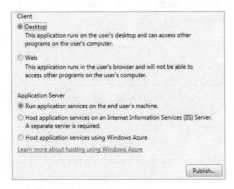

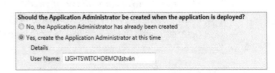

FIGURE 11-9: Selecting the Client and Application server options

FIGURE 11-10: Providing the full Windows login name

6. The IDE creates an installation set for `ProjectTrek`. It takes about two to five minutes, depending on your computer's performance. When it is ready, in Windows, open the `ProjectTrek` solution folder and navigate to the `ProjectTrek\Publish` folder. Locate the `ProjectTrek` file (its type is Click Once Application Deployment Manifest), and double-click it.

7. In a few seconds, the "Application Install - Security Warning" dialog pops up. Select Install. In a short time, `ProjectTrek` is installed and started. Your Windows login name appears in the bottom-right corner of the application, as shown in Figure 11-11, indicating that you're logged in.

FIGURE 11-11: The current user's name is displayed

8. Expand the Security task group and click Users. Select the first row in the Users grid, which represents the account you specified in Step 5. This user has the Administrator role, as shown in Figure 11-12.

FIGURE 11-12: The User screen with the default user

9. Close the application without saving.

How It Works

In Step 3, you selected authentication. In Step 5, you provided the login name for the Application Administrator — specifying your own login name. During the deployment, LightSwitch created an installation kit for `ProjectTrek`, and prepared its database. This database was initialized with your login information, and you were assigned to the Administrator role.

When you launched the application, `ProjectTrek` recognized your Windows login and created your user token accordingly. Because of your permissions, you had the right to manage users, roles, and permissions.

Windows authentication cannot be used everywhere — for example, in applications that run on a Mac, or where the application is deployed to Windows Azure. However, LightSwitch supports Forms authentication, which can be used as an alternative to Windows authentication.

Using Forms Authentication

When you use a LightSwitch application with Forms authentication, the application asks for a username and a password. If the information you provide matches the user data stored in the database, the application lets you log in. It assigns you the appropriate permissions according to the user account you've specified.

You can repeat the steps of the previous exercise to try Forms authentication. In the Access Control project property page, select the "Use Forms authentication" option. When running the LightSwitch Publish Application Wizard, in the Authentication page, provide the Administrator user account with username, full name, and password, as shown in Figure 11-13.

After the application is published and installed, you will be asked for the user account information when you start it, as shown in Figure 11-14. When you successfully log in, the application assigns administrative permissions to you.

FIGURE 11-13: Specifying the Administrator user account

FIGURE 11-14: Forms authentication in action

Managing Roles and Permissions

The Administrator user account — independent of the authentication mode — is granted the Security Administration permission. A security administrator can access two screens under the Security task group, Users and Roles, which can be used only with this privilege.

Earlier in this chapter, you learned that permissions are grouped into roles, and users can be assigned to one or more roles. The resultant permissions are calculated as the union of permissions with the roles the user is assigned to. The Roles screen is where the security administrator can manage roles that group permissions. The Users screen is the one where users can be managed and assigned to roles.

> **NOTE** *You do not have to specify an Administrator account on the Authentication page when you publish the application. The installation kit contains an* Install .html *document that describes how to use the* SecurityAdmin.exe *utility to create an Administrator account.*

The Roles screens can be used intuitively to create roles that group permissions. For example, creating a Project Manager role takes only a few steps (the result is shown in Figure 11-15):

1. Add a new role named **Project Manager** to the Roles panel.

2. When Project Manager is selected in the Roles panel, add the following items to the Permissions panel (use the Permission column's drop-down list):

   ➤ Can Create a Project

   ➤ Can Edit a Project

   ➤ Can Delete a Project

   ➤ Can Edit Project Tasks

   ➤ Can Edit Project Costs

   ➤ Can View Statistics

3. Save the changes.

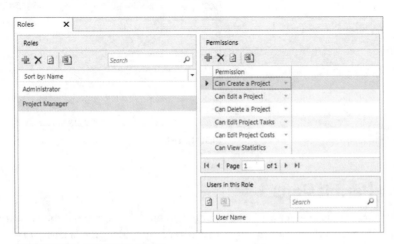

FIGURE 11-15: The Roles screen

The "Users in this Role" panel displays those users who are assigned to this role.

Managing Users

With the Users screen, you can manage application users by adding new accounts, modifying accounts, or removing existing ones. As shown in Figure 11-16, you can add users and specify the roles assigned to the users. The user Scott Douglas, assigned to the Project Manager role, has the permissions shown in Figure 11-15.

FIGURE 11-16: The Users screen

When you restart the application and use Scott's account to log in, only those screens that are allowed appear in the task list, according to the permissions belonging to Scott through the Project Manager role, as shown in Figure 11-17. Because Scott does not have access to any screens in the Administration and Security task groups, these groups are not displayed.

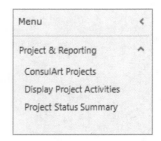

FIGURE 11-17: Screens available with Scott's account

SUMMARY

The security settings in LightSwitch applications are managed through the concept of permissions. A permission object is an elementary unit of right that can be granted to users. Permissions can be grouped into roles, and users assigned to zero, one, or more roles. When users log in, the set of permissions they are granted is determined by the roles to which they belong.

Permissions can be checked in access control methods that guard operations. Before executing an operation, LightSwitch invokes the corresponding access control methods to check whether the current user has the necessary rights.

LightSwitch supports running an application without explicit authentication, and using either Windows authentication or Forms authentication. When publishing an application, you can create an initial administrative account. This account can be used to manage users and roles.

In Chapter 12, you will learn about the Office integration features of LightSwitch, and have a closer look at a few samples that use Microsoft Excel and Word.

EXERCISES

1. What is a permission? How is it related to access control?

2. What is an access control method, and how is it used by LightSwitch?

3. Which access control methods of the `CostItem` table should be defined if you want to allow or disallow any kind of modifications of this table?

4. In which page of the LightSwitch Publish Application Wizard can you set the initial Administrator account?

 NOTE *Answers to the Exercises can be found in the Appendix.*

▶ **WHAT YOU LEARNED IN THIS CHAPTER**

TOPIC	KEY CONCEPTS
Authentication	Authentication is the process used to identify the user of the application.
Access control	Access control is the process that uses the identity of the user to check whether he or she can carry out a certain operation, such as opening a screen, reading data from a specific table, modifying the content of a table, and so on.
Permission	A permission is the smallest unit of right you can have. A permission object has only a name, and you can check whether the user has the permission with the specified name.
Role	A role is a container that groups permissions. Users are assigned to roles. This concept makes user and permission management easier and less error-prone than assigning permissions directly to users.
Access control method	Access control methods are event-handling methods used to guard a certain operation. When LightSwitch is about to execute a guarded operation, first the corresponding access control method is invoked. When the method disallows the operation, LightSwitch refuses to execute it.
Defining an access control method	Open the appropriate object (table, query, or screen) in the Designer, and select the appropriate access control method with the Write Code toolbar button. Write the method body so that it sets the `result` parameter to `True` or `False`, stating the operation is allowed or disallowed, respectively.
Windows authentication	The user is logged into the LightSwitch application with his or her already authenticated Windows account. The application won't ask for any username or password.
Forms authentication	When the user starts the LightSwitch application, he or she must provide a user name and a password. If the specified user information matches what is stored in the database, the user is logged in to the application; otherwise, he or she is refused.
Setting up the initial Administrator account	When publishing an application, you can provide the initial Administrator account in the Authentication page of the LightSwitch Publish Application Wizard. When you use Windows authentication, you need to set only the Windows logon name. In the case of Forms authentication, you must provide a username, full name, and password.

12

Microsoft Office Integration

WHAT YOU WILL LEARN IN THIS CHAPTER

➤ Exporting your application's data to a Microsoft Excel worksheet

➤ Understanding Office automation

➤ Creating LightSwitch methods that use Office automation

➤ Discovering the automation object model with macros

Visual Studio LightSwitch has been designed with Microsoft Office integration in mind. That means you can export your lists and tables to an Excel worksheet without writing any code. The automation features of Office applications make it easy to use Word, Excel, Outlook, or even PowerPoint from LightSwitch, but these tasks require writing code.

In this chapter you will learn how to use these integration features.

EXPORTING DATA TO MICROSOFT EXCEL

LightSwitch makes it extremely easy to utilize Microsoft Excel. With a simple click, you can export data to an Excel worksheet, as you will learn from the following exercise.

TRY IT OUT Exporting Data to Microsoft Excel

> **NOTE** *In this exercise, you continue the sample that you completed in Chapter 11. You can find the starting sample on this book's companion website at* www.wrox.com *in the folder* Chapter 12\Start.

To export a list of projects to Microsoft Excel, follow these steps:

1. Open Visual Studio LightSwitch and load the `ProjectTrek` solution.

2. Run the application by pressing Ctrl+F5. After it is launched, open the ConsulArt Projects screen.

3. In the Projects grid, select the `PT-001` link to display this project's details.

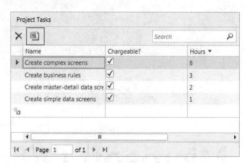

4. In the bottom part of the screen, select the Project Tasks tab and click the Hours column header twice to order the grid rows descending by this column's value.

5. Click the Export to Excel button in the toolbar of the Project Tasks grid, as shown in Figure 12-1.

FIGURE 12-1: The Project Tasks grid with the Export to Excel button

The `ProjectTrek` application opens Microsoft Excel and creates a new worksheet with the project task information exported from the grid. As shown in Figure 12-2, the list of tasks is added to the Excel worksheet in the same order as they are displayed in the Project Tasks grid. You can continue working using the Excel worksheet just as if you typed in the data manually.

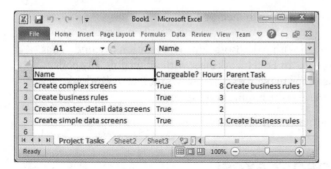

FIGURE 12-2: Project task data exported to an Excel worksheet

How It Works

The `ProjectTrek` application uses Microsoft Excel automation objects to carry out the exporting process. It starts Excel, and sends commands to it, such as creating a new worksheet, renaming it, copying data to cells, and so on. These commands work just as if you used the Excel menu commands and the keyboard to create and fill the worksheet manually.

As shown in Figure 12-2, LightSwitch not only exports the data, but also uses the existing property names in your application to name the worksheet and the column headers.

You can control whether you want to allow this built-in feature to export to Excel. The `DataGrid` and `List` elements provide the "Disable exporting data to Excel" property, as shown in Figure 12-3. Check this box for each UI control for which you intend to forbid Excel export. Doing so will remove the "Export to Excel" button from the toolbars of those controls.

FIGURE 12-3: The "Disable exporting data to Excel" property

 WARNING *If your application contains sensitive data, it can be easily downloaded by a user if you enable exporting your grids and tables to Excel. (Of course, it also can be taken without exporting, but it is more laborious.) In any case, disabling export to Excel does not solve the basic problem. You must ensure that you employ appropriate security and permissions.*

UNDERSTANDING AND USING OFFICE AUTOMATION

The Microsoft Office products have been designed with extensibility and programmability in mind. As an Office user, you can create and run macros in all core Office applications — including Word, Excel, PowerPoint, and Outlook. Macros can automate tasks that you would otherwise manually perform.

Microsoft Office products implement and exploit an object model that can be used externally to drive the application to carry out tasks. This object model is called the *automation model,* and it is accessible from a number of tools, including Windows scripts, Office macros, and Visual Studio applications.

The objects in the automation model form a hierarchy that reflects the natural relationship of objects within an Office application. For example, the root object of Excel is `Excel.Application`. This object exploits a `Workbooks` property that represents a collection of workbooks open in Excel. The `Cells` collection represents a two-dimensional array of spreadsheet cells.

The automation model contains a vast number of objects that cover the full range of Office functionality.

NOTE *Microsoft Office applications are not the only ones that exploit the automation model. Many other applications provide Common Object Model (COM) interfaces, such as Windows Media Player, Adobe Acrobat, Windows Live, Apple QuickTime Player, Visual Studio, Zune, and many more. You can also access them from your LightSwitch applications. You can obtain more information about general Office development topics, as well as about the Office Automation Model, at* `http://msdn.microsoft.com/en-us/office`.

Using the Microsoft Office Automation Model from LightSwitch Applications

As you learned in Chapter 3, the UI of a LightSwitch application is implemented with the Silverlight technology. The presentation layer (what the user perceives as the UI) of an application can be hosted in the browser or in a desktop application, with restricted rights to access the underlying operating system resources (including files, operations, and so on).

By default — as you have seen throughout the exercises thus far in this book — LightSwitch starts applications in the *out-of-browser (OOB) elevated trust* mode. Out-of-browser mode means that your application runs in its own desktop window — not in the browser, as most Silverlight applications run by default. Elevated trust means that the application has more access to system resources than it does with normal mode — for example, it can use automation objects. The OOB elevated trust mode is what made it possible for the Export to Excel command to work in the previous exercise.

However, you can deploy your application so that the UI runs in a browser. In that case, you won't be able to use the automation model.

 NOTE *Chapter 13 contains detailed information about deployment. After reading that chapter, you'll be able to evaluate the potential advantages and disadvantages of a specific deployment model.*

Exporting to Excel Using the Automation Model

Earlier in this chapter, you learned that it is very easy to export the content of a List or DataGrid element to an Excel worksheet. You can do it without writing a single line of code. However, many screens may contain master-detail relationships with more than one grid or list. You cannot export the content of the screen with one click — unless you develop this functionality.

In the next exercise, you will create code that exports the selected project in the ListProjects screen with all project properties, including related tasks, additional costs, and project members (see Figure 12-4).

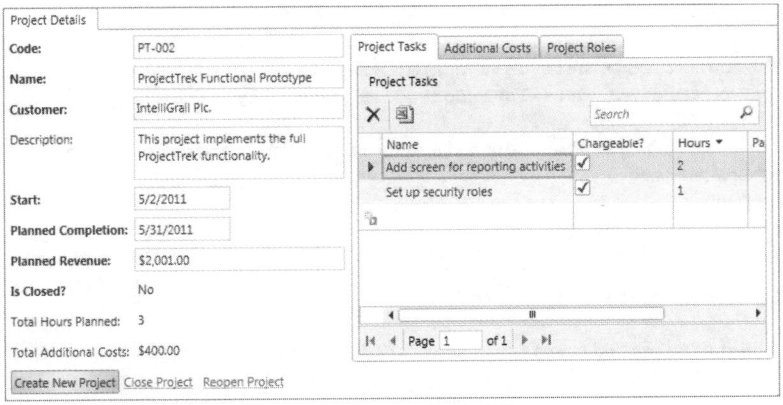

FIGURE 12-4: The part of the ListProjects screen to export

TRY IT OUT   Starting Excel from a LightSwitch Application

To start Microsoft Excel from `ProjectTrek` using the automation features, follow these steps:

1. Open the `ListProjects` screen in the Designer.

2. Select the `Screen Command Bar` node, and add a new button to it. In the Add Button dialog, use the New Method option and name the method **ExportDetails**. Click OK.

3. In the data item panel, select the `ExportDetails` method. While this item is selected, click the Edit Execute Code task link in the Properties window.

4. Add the following code line to the top of the file open in the Code Editor:

VB
```
Imports System.Runtime.InteropServices.Automation
```

C#
```
using System.Runtime.InteropServices.Automation;
```

5. Change the body of the `ExportDetails_Execute` method by adding the `ExportToExcel` method, as the following boldfaced code shows:

VB
```
Private Sub ExportDetails_Execute()
    ExportToExcel(Projects.SelectedItem)
End Sub

Private Sub ExportToExcel(ByVal project As Project)
    Try
        ' --- Before exporting, check whether Office automation is available
        If Not AutomationFactory.IsAvailable Then
            Throw New InvalidOperationException("Office automation
                is not available.")
        End If

        ' --- Create an Excel application and display it immediately
        Dim excel As Object = AutomationFactory.CreateObject("Excel.Application")
```

```vbnet
                excel.Visible = True

                ' --- You will insert code here in the next exercise
                Me.ShowMessageBox("Project details exported successfully.")
        Catch ex As Exception
                Dim message As String = "Project details export failed: " & ex.Message
                Me.ShowMessageBox(message)
        End Try
End Sub
```

C#
```csharp
partial void ExportDetails_Execute()
{
    ExportToExcel(Projects.SelectedItem);
}

private void ExportToExcel(Project project)
{
    try
    {
        // --- Before exporting, check whether Office automation is available
        if (!AutomationFactory.IsAvailable)
        {
            throw new InvalidOperationException("Office automation
                is not available.");
        }

        // --- Create an Excel application and display it immediately
        var excel = AutomationFactory.CreateObject("Excel.Application");
        excel.Visible = true;

        // --- You will insert code here in the next exercise
        this.ShowMessageBox("Project details exported successfully.");
    }
    catch (Exception ex)
    {
        var message = "Project details export failed: " + ex.Message;
        this.ShowMessageBox(message);
    }
}
```

6. Save your changes by pressing Ctrl+S.

7. Run the application by pressing Ctrl+F5. After it is launched, click the Export Details button in the Screen Command Bar.

8. A new instance of Microsoft Excel is started without any open document — assuming you have installed Excel on your computer. The task is done, as confirmed by the "Project details exported successfully" message. Click OK.

9. Close the application.

How It Works

With the first three steps in this exercise, you created and set up the screen's command bar button to initiate the export command from the application. The automation objects can be found in the System .Runtime.InteropServices.Automation namespace of the Silverlight runtime, so you imported it in Step 4 to refer to its objects (for example, AutomationFactory) with simple names.

The ExportToExcel method you added in Step 5 receives a Project instance to export. It uses a Try...Catch block to handle exceptions. Before trying to access Excel, the code checks the AutomationFactory.IsAvailable property. The True value of this property indicates that the application runs in a context where Office automation is enabled (in out-of-browser mode with elevated trust). The False value indicates that you cannot use automation features (perhaps your application runs within a browser).

The AutomationFactory.CreateObject method is responsible for instantiating an object supporting automation — in this case, the type of this object is Excel.Application. This call starts Excel running invisibly in the background. By setting its Visible property to True, the main window of Excel is displayed.

The ShowMessage method is a useful utility to pop-up modal messages.

Although you launched Microsoft Excel in this exercise, it still does not export project information. You must add more code to use the automation model, as demonstrated in the next exercise.

TRY IT OUT Using Excel Automation

In this exercise, you insert four chunks of code. You must insert them into the ExportToExcel method, right before the ShowMessage method of the Try block.

To export all project details, follow these steps:

1. Insert the following code into the ExportToExcel method:

VB

```
' --- Create a new workbook
excel.Workbooks.Add()

' --- Export project properties
excel.Cells(1, 1).Value = "Code"
excel.Cells(1, 2).Value = project.Code
excel.Cells(2, 1).Value = "Name"
excel.Cells(2, 2).Value = project.Name
excel.Cells(3, 1).Value = "Description"
excel.Cells(3, 2).Value = project.Description
excel.Cells(4, 1).Value = "Customer"
excel.Cells(4, 2).Value = project.Customer.Name
excel.Cells(5, 1).Value = "Start Date"
excel.Cells(5, 2).Value = project.StartDate
excel.Cells(6, 1).Value = "Planned Completion"
excel.Cells(6, 2).Value = project.PlannedEndDate
```

```
excel.Cells(7, 1).Value = "Planned Revenue"
excel.Cells(7, 2).Value = project.PlannedRevenue
excel.Cells(8, 1).Value = "Work Planned"
excel.Cells(8, 2).Value = project.TotalTaskHours
excel.Cells(9, 1).Value = "Additional Costs Planned"
excel.Cells(9, 2).Value = project.TotalAdditionalCosts
excel.Cells(10, 1).Value = "Closed?"
excel.Cells(10, 2).Value = IIf(project.Closed, "Yes", "No")
```

C#
```
// --- Create a new workbook
excel.Workbooks.Add();

// --- Export project properties
excel.Cells(1, 1).Value = "Code";
excel.Cells(1, 2).Value = project.Code;
excel.Cells(2, 1).Value = "Name";
excel.Cells(2, 2).Value = project.Name;
excel.Cells(3, 1).Value = "Description";
excel.Cells(3, 2).Value = project.Description;
excel.Cells(4, 1).Value = "Customer";
excel.Cells(4, 2).Value = project.Customer.Name;
excel.Cells(5, 1).Value = "Start Date";
excel.Cells(5, 2).Value = project.StartDate;
excel.Cells(6, 1).Value = "Planned Completion";
excel.Cells(6, 2).Value = project.PlannedEndDate;
excel.Cells(7, 1).Value = "Planned Revenue";
excel.Cells(7, 2).Value = project.PlannedRevenue;
excel.Cells(8, 1).Value = "Work Planned";
excel.Cells(8, 2).Value = project.TotalTaskHours;
excel.Cells(9, 1).Value = "Additional Costs Planned";
excel.Cells(9, 2).Value = project.TotalAdditionalCosts;
excel.Cells(10, 1).Value = "Closed?";
excel.Cells(10, 2).Value = project.Closed ? "Yes" : "No";
```

In the previous exercise you started Microsoft Excel from the `ProjectTrek` application, but it did not open any workbook. The `Add` method of the `Workbooks` collection in the first code line creates a new empty workbook. All subsequent operations are carried out on this new workbook.

The majority of the code creates a two-column table, with a label and the related `project` property value. The `Cells` property is used to explicitly set the value of a single workbook cell. The indices specify the row and column positions (starting from 1), respectively.

2. Insert the following code:

VB
```
' --- Export project task details
excel.Cells(12, 1).Value = "Project Tasks:"
excel.Cells(13, 1).Value = "Name"
excel.Cells(13, 2).Value = "Chargeable?"
excel.Cells(13, 3).Value = "Hours"
excel.Cells(13, 4).Value = "Parent task"
Dim rowCount As Integer = 14
For Each task As ProjectTask In project.ProjectTasks
    excel.Cells(rowCount, 1).Value = task.Name
```

```vb
        excel.Cells(rowCount, 2).Value = IIf(task.Chargeable, "Yes", "No")
        excel.Cells(rowCount, 3).Value = task.EstimatedHours
        If Not task.ParentTask Is Nothing Then
            excel.Cells(rowCount, 4).Value = task.ParentTask.Name
        End If
        rowCount = rowCount + 1
    Next
    rowCount = rowCount + 1
```

C#
```csharp
// --- Export project task details
excel.Cells(12, 1).Value = "Project Tasks:";
excel.Cells(13, 1).Value = "Name";
excel.Cells(13, 2).Value = "Chargeable?";
excel.Cells(13, 3).Value = "Hours";
excel.Cells(13, 4).Value = "Parent task";
var rowCount = 14;
foreach(var task in project.ProjectTasks)
{
    excel.Cells(rowCount, 1).Value = task.Name;
    excel.Cells(rowCount, 2).Value = task.Chargeable ? "Yes" : "No";
    excel.Cells(rowCount, 3).Value = task.EstimatedHours;
    if (task.ParentTask != null)
    {
        excel.Cells(rowCount, 4).Value = task.ParentTask.Name;
    }
    rowCount++;
}
rowCount++;
```

This code creates a four-column table and appends a separate table row for each project task. The For Each construct uses the `project.ProjectTasks` collection, which contains the tasks related to the `project` instance. The `rowCount` variable is used to keep track of row positions.

3. Append the following code snippet to the `ExportToExcel` method:

VB
```vb
' --- Export additional cost details
excel.Cells(rowCount, 1).Value = "Additional Costs:"
rowCount = rowCount + 1
excel.Cells(rowCount, 1).Value = "Name"
excel.Cells(rowCount, 2).Value = "Description"
excel.Cells(rowCount, 3).Value = "Amount"
rowCount = rowCount + 1
    For Each cost As AdditionalCost In project.AdditionalCosts
        excel.Cells(rowCount, 1).Value = cost.Name
        excel.Cells(rowCount, 2).Value = cost.Description
        excel.Cells(rowCount, 3).Value = cost.Amount
        rowCount = rowCount + 1
    Next
rowCount = rowCount + 1
```

C#
```csharp
// --- Export additional cost details
excel.Cells(rowCount, 1).Value = "Additional Costs:";
rowCount++;
```

```
excel.Cells(rowCount, 1).Value = "Name";
excel.Cells(rowCount, 2).Value = "Description";
excel.Cells(rowCount, 3).Value = "Amount";
rowCount++;
foreach(var cost in project.AdditionalCosts)
{
    excel.Cells(rowCount, 1).Value = cost.Name;
    excel.Cells(rowCount, 2).Value = cost.Description;
    excel.Cells(rowCount, 3).Value = cost.Amount;
    rowCount++;
}
rowCount++;
```

This code works similarly to the code you appended in the previous step, but it uses the `project.`
`AdditionalCosts` collection to export cost details related to the `project` instance.

4. Append the last piece of code to export project members:

VB
```
' --- Export project members
excel.Cells(rowCount, 1).Value = "Project Members:"
rowCount = rowCount + 1
excel.Cells(rowCount, 1).Value = "Role"
excel.Cells(rowCount, 2).Value = "Member"
rowCount = rowCount + 1
For Each member As ProjectRole In project.ProjectRoles
    excel.Cells(rowCount, 1).Value = member.ProjectRoleType.DisplayName
    excel.Cells(rowCount, 2).Value = member.Employee.FullNameWithCategory
    rowCount = rowCount + 1
Next
rowCount = rowCount + 1
```

C#
```
// --- Export project members
excel.Cells(rowCount, 1).Value = "Project Members:";
rowCount++;
excel.Cells(rowCount, 1).Value = "Role";
excel.Cells(rowCount, 2).Value = "Member";
rowCount++;
foreach (var member in project.ProjectRoles)
{
    excel.Cells(rowCount, 1).Value = member.ProjectRoleType.DisplayName;
    excel.Cells(rowCount, 2).Value = member.Employee.FullNameWithCategory;
    rowCount++;
}
rowCount++;
```

5. Save the code by pressing Ctrl+S.

6. Start `ProjectTrek` by pressing Ctrl+F5. Click the Export Details button. The application starts Microsoft Excel and exports the project information, as shown in Figure 12-5.

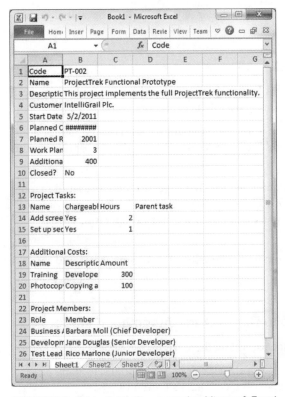

FIGURE 12-5: Project details exported to Microsoft Excel

7. Click OK to close the confirmation message, and then close the ProjectTrek application.

> **NOTE** You can find the complete code to download for this exercise on the book's companion website at www.wrox.com in the folder Chapter 12\ Sample 1 - Exporting Details.

How It Works

The project instance passed to the ExportToExcel method holds all details related to the specific project. The preceding code can access all project properties and related tasks, costs, and members through the ProjectTasks, AdditionalCosts, and ProjectMembers containers, respectively. This information is directly put into the worksheet cells through the Cells array.

Despite the fact that all project detail attributes are added to the Excel worksheet, as shown in Figure 12-5, this information is not really nicely formed. The previous exercise does not contain code to format this sheet. Perhaps it is not a good idea to put all details in the same worksheet! A more useful approach would be to divide the project detail information into four worksheets, such as `Project Details`, `Tasks`, `Costs`, and `Members`. Later in this chapter, you will alter the `ExportToExcel` method accordingly.

Exploring the Automation Model

The Microsoft Office automation model supports hundreds of objects with thousands of properties and operations, so how do you know which object to use for a certain operation?

Starting with a search of the Web for the specific information might sound like a good idea at first, but it isn't easy to quickly find the right reference documentation topics or the appropriate forum entry. Fortunately, there is an easier solution!

The Excel and Word applications can record macros, which enable you to bundle a set of manual operations into one step. The macros use the Office automation model. By looking at the recorded code, you can discover the object model and understand how your manual operations are automated.

In the following exercise, you learn how to automate the creation of new worksheets and the resizing of columns.

TRY IT OUT   **Recording an Excel Macro to Discover the Automation Model**

To learn how to automate a couple of Excel operations, follow these steps:

1. Start the `ProjectTrek` application. Open the ConsulArt Projects screen and select any project from the grid to view its details. Click the Export Project Details button in the application's command bar. `ProjectTrek` exports the project details into an Excel workbook.

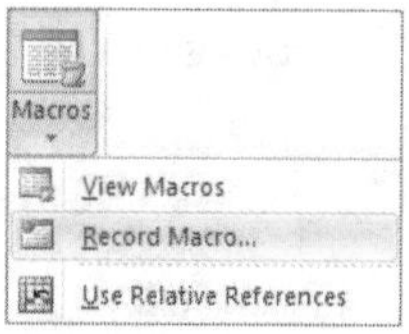

2. Switch to Excel. (For example, you can click its window title with the mouse, or press the Alt+Tab keys.)

3. Click the View tab. The rightmost button is Macros. Use its drop-down arrow to list related commands and select Record Macro, as shown in Figure 12-6. Excel pops up the Record Macro dialog.

FIGURE 12-6: The Record Macro command in Excel

4. Change the macro name from `Macro1` to `MyNewMacro` and click OK. Now Excel will continue to record your activities until you stop recording.

5. Move the mouse pointer between the A and B column headers of the worksheet. When the pointer changes to the resize shape, double-click with the mouse. Column A will be resized to fit its content.

6. At the bottom of the worksheet, click `Sheet2` and press Shift+F11. A new worksheet is created and named `Sheet4`.

7. Right-click `Sheet4` and select Rename from the context menu. Change the name of `Sheet4` to **My New Sheet** and press Enter.

8. In the View tab, select the Stop Recording command from the Macros drop-down. Now, your manual operations have been recorded into a macro.

9. Select the View Macros command from the Macros drop-down. The Macro dialog opens with `MyNewMacro` selected in its list. Click Edit to open the macro. Microsoft Visual Basic for Applications (VBA) opens and displays the freshly recorded macro, as shown here:

```
Sub MyNewMacro()
'
' MyNewMacro Macro
'

'
    Columns("A:A").EntireColumn.AutoFit
    Sheets("Sheet2").Select
    Sheets.Add
    Sheets("Sheet4").Select
    Sheets("Sheet4").Name = "My New Sheet"
End Sub
```

10. Click in the macro and place the cursor after the letter "A" of `Sheets.Add`. Press F1 to display Help. Excel Help opens and shows details about the `Sheets.Add` method, as shown in Figure 12-7.

11. Close the Help window, close VBA, close Excel (without saving the document), and close the `ProjectTrek` application. To learn how you can add these operations to the `ExportToExcel` macro, examine the simple macro code.

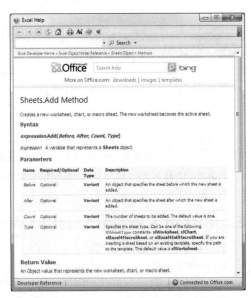

FIGURE 12-7: Context-sensitive help information about Sheets.Add

How It Works

The recorded `MyNewMacro` contains five operations. The first one is as follows:

```
Columns("A:A").EntireColumn.AutoFit
```

This operation resizes the first column's width so that it is adjusted automatically to fit the content. As you may guess from the code, the `Sheets("name")` expression retrieves the worksheet specified by *name*. The `Add` operation creates a new worksheet, and the `Select` operation makes the specified sheet active. Setting the `Name` property, you can alter the name of a worksheet.

You can repeat the steps of this exercise and use Excel Help to learn more about the properties and operations mentioned previously.

> **NOTE** Using what you've learned in this exercise, it is easy to modify the `ExportToExcel` method. You can find the complete code to download for this exercise on the book's companion website at `www.wrox.com` in the folder `Chapter 12\Sample 2 - Polishing`.

When you modify the `ExportToExcel` method and run the `ProjectTrek` application, you can see the changes. Now the project details are divided into four worksheets (`Project Details`, `Tasks`, `Costs`, and `Members`), as shown toward the bottom of Figure 12-8.

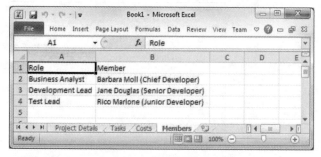

FIGURE 12-8: Project details are now divided into separate worksheets

Exporting a Project List to Word

You can easily use other Microsoft Office programs in your LightSwitch application. In the following example, you export the list of ConsulArt projects to Microsoft Word. This example is very similar to the functionality described earlier to export the project details to Excel.

Add a command screen button to the `ProjectList` screen (as described previously in this chapter) using a method named `ExportToWord`. Listing 12-1 shows the implementation of the `ExportToWord_Execute` method.

LISTING 12-1: The ExportToWord_Execute method

VB

```vb
Private Sub ExportToWord_Execute()
    Try
        ' --- Before exporting, check whether Office automation is available
        If Not AutomationFactory.IsAvailable Then
            Throw New InvalidOperationException("Office automation
                is not available.")
        End If
        ' --- Create a Word application and display it immediately
        Dim word As Object = AutomationFactory.CreateObject("Word.Application")
        word.Visible = True
        word.Documents.Add()
        With word.Selection
            .TypeText("List of Projects")
            .Style = "Heading 1"
            .TypeParagraph()
            .TypeText("Start date filter: " & If(FilterFrom.HasValue,
                FilterFrom.Value, "not specified"))
            .TypeParagraph()
            .TypeText("End date filter: " & If(FilterTo.HasValue,
                FilterTo.Value, "not specified"))
            .TypeParagraph()
            For Each project In Me.Projects
```

```vb
                            .TypeText(project.Code & " - " & project.Name)
                            .Style = "Heading 2"
                            .TypeParagraph()
                            ' --- Add automation code to display project attributes

                    Next
                End With

                Me.ShowMessageBox("Project list exported successfully.")
            Catch ex As Exception
                Dim message As String = "Project list export failed: " & ex.Message
                Me.ShowMessageBox(message)
            End Try
        End Sub
```

```csharp
        partial void ExportToWord_Execute()
        {
            try
            {
                // --- Before exporting, check whether Office automation is available
                if (!AutomationFactory.IsAvailable)
                {
                    throw new InvalidOperationException("Office automation
                        is not available.");
                }

                // --- Create a Word application and display it immediately
                var word = AutomationFactory.CreateObject("Word.Application");
                word.Visible = true;
                word.Documents.Add();
                var sel = word.Selection;
                sel.TypeText("List of Projects");
                sel.Style = "Heading 1";
                sel.TypeParagraph();
                sel.TypeText("Start date filter: " + (FilterFrom.HasValue
                    ? FilterFrom.Value.ToString() : "not specified"));
                sel.TypeParagraph();
                sel.TypeText("End date filter: " + (FilterTo.HasValue
                    ? FilterTo.Value.ToString() : "not specified"));
                sel.TypeParagraph();
                foreach(var project in Projects)
                {
                    sel.TypeText(project.Code + " - " + project.Name);
                    sel.Style = "Heading 2";
                    sel.TypeParagraph();
                    // --- Add automation code to display project attributes

                }
                this.ShowMessageBox("Project list exported successfully.");
            }
            catch (Exception ex)
            {
                var message = "Project list export failed: " + ex.Message;
                this.ShowMessageBox(message);
            }
        }
```

The method body has the same structure you learned about earlier in this chapter. This time, the AutomationFactory's CreateObject method instantiates a Word.Application object to access Word automation.

The method intensively uses the TypeText and TypeParagraph operations, which are utilized to insert text and new paragraphs into the Word document, respectively. You can apply a formatting style by setting the value of the Style property to a string that refers to the appropriate name (such as "Heading 1" and "Heading 2" in Listing 12-1).

Figure 12-9 shows the result of running the ExportToWord_Execute method.

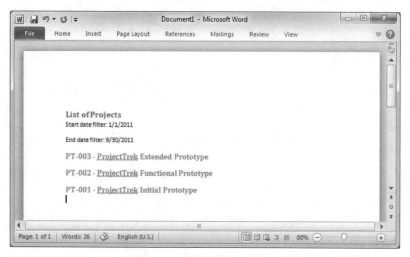

FIGURE 12-9: List of projects exported to Microsoft Word

The body of the method is left open — marked with the comment — so that you can exercise your own coding skills to display project attributes.

SUMMARY

Lists and data grids in LightSwitch natively support the export of tabular content into Microsoft Excel worksheets. The toolbar of these controls has an "Export to Excel" button that, when clicked, instantly launches Excel and creates a workbook with a table reflecting the content of the control.

Your application can use the automation model of Office applications. With the AutomationFactory object that can be found in the System.Runtime.InteropServices .Automation namespace, your LightSwitch application can create objects to utilize the existing objects in the Office automation model. Through these objects, you can programmatically carry out all the tasks that you would otherwise manually perform with Office applications.

The Office automation model is extensive, with hundreds of objects and thousands of methods. Using the macro recording features of Word and Excel, you can discover this object model and use it in your LightSwitch applications.

EXERCISES

1. How can you enable or disable exporting lists to Microsoft Excel?

2. What is out-of-browser elevated mode, and how it is related to the "Export to Excel" feature?

3. How can you check programmatically whether automation is available in your LightSwitch application?

4. How can macro recording help you discover the Office automation model?

 NOTE *Answers to the Exercises can be found in the Appendix.*

▶ **WHAT YOU LEARNED IN THIS CHAPTER**

TOPIC	KEY CONCEPTS
"Export to Excel" button	Each list and data grid control in a LightSwitch application has an "Export to Excel" button in its toolbar. Click this button to export the content of the control into an Excel worksheet.
"Disable exporting to excel" property	By default, all lists and data grids enable exporting. You can disable this feature by checking the "Disable exporting to Excel" property of the appropriate control.
Automation model	Many applications (including those of Microsoft Office) exploit an object model that can be used externally to drive the application to carry out tasks. This object model is called the *automation model*.
Out-of-browser (OOB) mode	LightSwitch applications use the Silverlight technology for implementing the UI. Silverlight can run either within a browser or in a separate desktop window. The latter mode is called *out-of-browser (OOB)* mode.
Elevated trust mode	Silverlight applications running in OOB mode can be used in elevated trust mode. In this case, they have more access to system resources than in normal mode. LightSwitch applications use elevated trust mode when they run in OOB mode.
AutomationFactory	You can use the `AutomationFactory` object to integrate your LightSwitch application with automation object models. This object is declared in the `System.Runtime.InteropServices.Automation` namespace.
Checking availability of automation	You can use the `IsAvailable` method of the `AutomationFactory` object to check whether automation can be used in your application. It retrieves `True` if your application runs in OOB mode (with elevated trust), which is a prerequisite for using automation models.
Creating automation objects	Use the `CreateObject` method of the `AutomationFactory` object to instantiate an automation object. You can pass the name of the object as the argument of `CreateObject`. For example, you can start Excel or Word applications by using `Excel.Application` or `Word.Application`, respectively.

PART III
Advanced LightSwitch Application Development

13

Deploying LightSwitch Applications

WHAT YOU WILL LEARN IN THIS CHAPTER

➤ Understanding the LightSwitch application deployment options

➤ Deploying an application as a thick client with no separate application server

➤ Three-tier application deployment with Internet Information Services (IIS)

➤ Deploying LightSwitch applications to the Windows Azure platform

After you create an application with LightSwitch, it's great when it works as expected. However, you must deploy it before the real end-users can use it. In general, application deployment is easy, but occasionally it can be a nightmare. In most cases, you must create setup kits and installation manuals so that either the end-users or your company's system administrators can deploy the application components.

With LightSwitch, the whole process is straightforward. The IDE was designed with easy and powerful application deployment in mind. In this chapter, you learn about the options provided by the LightSwitch IDE, and you'll be guided through several deployment types.

DEPLOYMENT OPTIONS

As you learned in Chapter 3, LightSwitch applications use the three-tier application architecture pattern. The presentation, logic, and Data tiers are separated from each other so that each application layer can be put on a separate machine.

This architecture provides versatile deployment models, which LightSwitch fully leverages. If you created a simple application to manage your personal home CD library, for example, a single-machine installation could be perfect. If you created this application for your family, you might have another model in mind, one in which your loved ones could access the same library database from different computers in your home.

If you work for a larger company, an application you develop with LightSwitch (such as an expense sheet) should be accessible to all employees, either through the company's intranet or maybe from the Internet. If you create a useful application for thousands of users, you can deliver it with the Software-as-a-Service (SaaS) model.

Thin Client and Thick Client

Even if an application contains several architectural layers (tiers), end-users working with the application interact with the presentation layer (the user interface), perceiving it as the *client* of the system. With LightSwitch, you can use both *thin client* and *thick client* applications. Although these terms are frequently used, there is sometimes confusion about what exactly they mean. This confusion stems from the fact that the terms "thin client" and "rich client" can refer to either how an application is architected or how it's deployed.

You can use the following terms from the deployment perspective:

➤ *Thick client* — You must install a component (or several) on the end-user's machine so that he or she can run your application.

➤ *Thin client* — There is no need to install any component on end-users' computers. They can run the application in a web browser. You only need to provide a URL (such as `http://MyCompany.com/MyApplication`) in order for the end-user to access it.

From an architectural point of view, a different definition of these terms emerges:

➤ *Thick client* — The client application encapsulates both the business logic of the system and the presentation layer (UI). Only the data is stored outside of the application (for example, in a remote database server). The application knows how to access this database server.

➤ *Thin client* — The client application entails only the presentation layer (UI). It uses a network protocol to communicate with an application component that provides the business logic. This logic conceals how the database is accessed. The client only knows how to access the business layer.

You can see the architectural differences between thin and thick client from the structures shown in Figure 13-1.

With LightSwitch, you can handle thin and thick clients from both the architectural and deployment points of view.

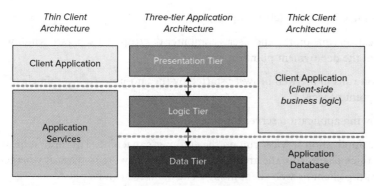

FIGURE 13-1: Comparing the thin and thick client architectures

Client and Application Server Topologies

In LightSwitch, you can choose from five deployment methods that can be defined through two groups of options:

➤ You can select the *type of the client* you intend to use (thick or thin client from the deployment point of view).

➤ You can choose the *type of the application server* (thick or thin client from the architectural point of view).

In LightSwitch, these option groups are referred to as the *client topology* and *application server topology*, respectively. You can access them through the loaded project's properties. In Solution Explorer, select the project node and press Alt+Enter, or, alternatively, double-click the Properties node. When the project properties are displayed in the Designer, select the Application Type tab, as shown in Figure 13-2.

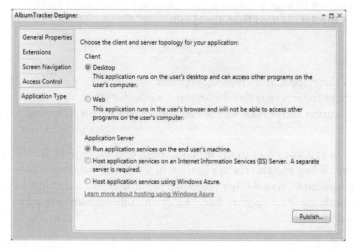

FIGURE 13-2: The Application Types tab of project properties

You can select from the following client types (client topologies):

➤ *Desktop* — The application runs on the end-user's computer desktop in a separate window. (It is a thick client from the deployment point of view.)

➤ *Web* — The application runs in the web browser started by the end-user. (It is a thin client from the deployment point of view.)

You can choose from the following application server topology options:

➤ *Client machine* — The application services run on the end-user's machine. This option means that you implement a thick client from the architectural point of view, regardless of whether you have chosen a desktop client or web client model. The database can be put on any remote computer in the network, including the client machine.

➤ *Internet Information Services (IIS)* — The application services (the server-side components of a LightSwitch application) run on a separate server machine, hosted in IIS. The database can be put on any remote computer in the network, including the application server machine.

➤ *Windows Azure* — The application services and the database are hosted in the Windows Azure platform (that is, in the cloud).

With the last two options, you deploy a thin client from the architectural point of view. The application server topology options provide you some freedom as to where your databases are located.

With the Windows Azure option, your database is hosted in the cloud using a SQL Azure database, and this is your only choice. The first two options provide you with more flexibility, as your database server can be anywhere in the network.

Note that you can still store your database in SQL Azure when you select one of the first two application server options. The SQL Server instance working in your intranet uses exactly the same protocol to communicate with client applications as SQL Azure. You can change the database connection information in your client (or in your business logic hosted in IIS) so that it points to a SQL Azure database, in which case the data is used from the cloud.

Restrictions

You have two client topologies and three application topology options that altogether provide six combinations. However, LightSwitch supports only five deployment methods. When you select the web client, you cannot put the application server logic on the client machine; it must be hosted either in IIS or Windows Azure.

You can run your clients in a desktop application or in the browser. Both options require Silverlight to be installed on the client machine. When you run the application in a desktop window, it uses elevated trust that allows your application to access other programs running on the client machine. For example, with this option, you can use the Export to Excel function and communicate with other Microsoft Office applications.

Running the client in the web browser uses a normal trust level that does not allow communicating with any other applications or services on the same machine. In this case, you cannot export your data to Excel directly.

At this point, you should be familiar with your deployment options. In the next section, you'll take a closer look at how to use these options to deploy an application.

THICK CLIENT DEPLOYMENT

In the previous chapters of this book, you used the F5 (Debug ⇨ Start Debugging) or Ctrl+F5 (Debug ⇨ Start Without Debugging) commands frequently. These commands deployed the application on your development machine, even if you did not ask the IDE explicitly to do so. If your application has only a few users (for example, only during the user acceptance test period), *thick client deployment* is the best option to choose.

As you learned earlier, a thick client — from an architectural point of view — combines the presentation layer and the business logic layer into a single client application. With LightSwitch, you have two options for deploying a thick client, as shown in Figure 13-3:

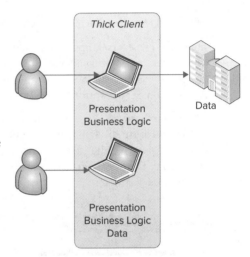

FIGURE 13-3: Comparing the thick client deployment choices in LightSwitch

> You can move your database to a server in your company's network — as shown in the upper part of the figure.

> You can put the database on each user's computer — as shown in the lower part. In this case, you may install SQL Express on the end-user's computer.

When you're ready to deploy your application, the LightSwitch Publish Application Wizard guides you through the steps of creating and optionally running the installation kit. You can start this wizard in a couple of different ways:

> In Solution Explorer, right-click the root node (the project node) and select Publish from the context menu.

> Double-click the Properties node in Solution Explorer, or press Alt+Enter while the project node is selected. With the Application Type tab selected, click the Publish button.

Creating a Desktop Client Installation Kit

Using the LightSwitch Publish Application Wizard, you can create installation kits for all the five options described earlier in the section, "Client and Application Server Topologies." In the following activity, you learn how easy it is to create an installation kit for a desktop client with LightSwitch.

TRY IT OUT Creating a Desktop Client Installation Kit

 NOTE *In this exercise, you start from a prepared sample, which you can find on this book's companion website at* `www.wrox.com` *in the* `Chapter 13\ToDeploy` *folder.*

To create a desktop client installation kit, follow these steps:

1. Open the ProjectTrek application located in the `ToDeploy` folder. Double-click the Properties node in Solution Explorer to display the project properties, and then select the Application Type tab. Select the Desktop client option and the "Run application services on the end-user's machine" Application Server option. Click Publish.

The Wizard opens. Click the Client Configuration tab. The Welcome page is displayed, as shown in Figure 13-4. The left side of the screen lists the pages of the wizard, with the currently displayed page highlighted. You can select a page by clicking it directly in the list, but you should go through them by using the Next button (and occasionally the Back button) while you specify all required settings.

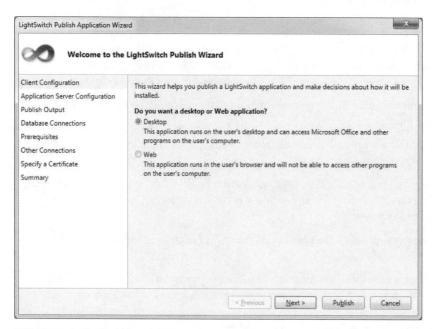

FIGURE 13-4: The LightSwitch Publish Application Wizard lets you select the client configuration

This first page enables you to choose the client topology. It is set to Desktop by default, which is shown in the Application Type tab of the project properties. You can change this selection here if you want.

NOTE *Figure 13-4 shows a screenshot of the entire LightSwitch Publish Application Wizard. To conserve space, henceforth only the content of wizard pages are shown in the figures in this chapter, cropped from a screenshot of the entire dialog.*

2. Leave the Desktop options selected for a thick client installation, and click Next. The Application Server Configuration page is displayed (see Figure 13-5), showing the Local option selected — the option you selected in Step 1. Click Next.

3. From the Publish Output page that appears, select the folder where all application files and installation utilities should be placed. By default, this is the `Publish` folder under your project directory. Leave this as it is. This page also enables you to specify how you want to publish the default database (the tables you create in your project). You can let the wizard create the database (by selecting the "Publish directly to the database now" option as shown in Figure 13-6), or you can create an installation script and run them separately.

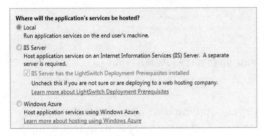

FIGURE 13-5: The Application Server Configuration page

FIGURE 13-6: The Publish Output page

Generally, you can use the first option on the machines that are under your control, and use the second option when you need to have your system administrators create the database. Leave the first option selected, and click Next.

4. In the Database Connections page shown in Figure 13-7, you can specify the information for an administrator and a user SQL connection. The administrator connection is used by the wizard to create your application's database structure during deployment. The user connection is used by the installed application to access the database while your application runs.

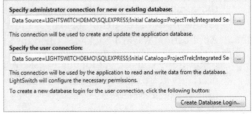

FIGURE 13-7: The Database Connections page

By default, the SQL Express instance running on your computer is defined with both SQL connections. Accept the default settings.

NOTE *If you need to change the connection information, click the ellipsis button to the right of the administrator connection. When the Connection Properties dialog opens, specify the elements of the connection information as discussed in Chapter 8. The administrator connection is automatically copied to the user connection, but you can change it separately by clicking the related ellipsis button. You can click the Create Database Login button to add a new user account to the destination database. When you do so, this new account will be set up for your user connection.*

5. Click Next. In the Prerequisites page, you can define additional components on which your application depends, as shown in Figure 13-8.

Your LightSwitch application needs a few components (LightSwitch runtime libraries) that are automatically included in the installation kit. If you select the "No, only install the prerequisites" option, no other dependencies will be added to the installation kit. However, in many cases, you might want to add other dependencies to the setup kit. If so, select the "Yes, I need to specify additional prerequisites" option, and check the appropriate components in the list.

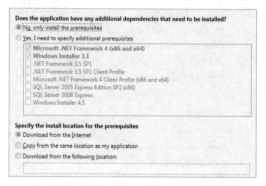

FIGURE 13-8: The Prerequisites page

For example, if you want to deploy the database with your application, you may decide to deploy SQL Server 2008 as well. You may include libraries in your LightSwitch application that require other components using .NET Framework 3.5 SP1.

Beneath the "Specify the install location for the prerequisites" entry, you can choose from three options. These tell the wizard the location from which the installation packages of other selected components can be obtained. Selecting the first option will download those components from the Internet during setup time. Selecting the third option also causes the additional components to be searched during setup time, but instead of the Internet, the specified location is used to download the components (typically from an install folder in your company's network). If you choose the second option, the install packages must be copied to your machine. The LightSwitch Publish Application Wizard packages them into the install kit.

Right now, you are deploying a desktop client application, so you do not need any additional prerequisites packed into the installation kit, and you can keep the option "No, only install the prerequisites" selected.

6. Click Next. The Other Connections page, shown in Figure 13-9, is displayed. Here you can set up the connection information for the existing data connections, such as SQL Server databases, SharePoint 2010 lists, or Windows Communication Foundation (WCF) data sources. In `ProjectTrek`, you connect to the `ConsulArtCRM` database; and in this page you can set up that connection. The wizard automatically uses the connection information you specified during development. If you need to use another database in the production environment, you can set it here. Accept the default settings, and click Next.

7. In the "Specify a Certificate" page, you can provide a certificate to sign the `.XAP` file representing the UI layer of your application, as shown in Figure 13-10. With this certificate, you assure users that the publisher (that's you) is reliable and that the code has not been tampered with.

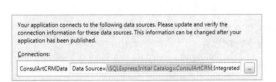

FIGURE 13-9: The Other Connections page   **FIGURE 13-10:** The "Specify a Certificate" page

In this case, you are deploying a desktop client application, without signing the `.XAP` file. Leave the "Specify a certificate" option unchecked, and click Next.

 NOTE *As you learned in Chapter 3, the client application uses Silverlight technology to implement the UI. When the IDE compiles a Silverlight component, it is put into a `.XAP` file. This `.XAP` file is loaded into the browser or into your desktop application, and then started by the Silverlight runtime.*

8. As shown in Figure 13-11, the Summary page of the wizard provides a brief overview of the deployment options and settings selected in the previous steps. You can click the Previous button to return to previous settings, or you can click a page directly to instantly access that page and change the settings there.

FIGURE 13-11: The Summary page

9. Click Publish. The IDE builds your application and creates the setup kit. It may take a few minutes. When the process completes, you can see the "Publish succeeded" message in the status bar at the bottom of the IDE.

10. Using Windows Explorer, navigate to your project directory (the one used to open the project), and select the `ProjectTrek\ Publish` folder. Here you can find the output of the process, as shown in Figure 13-12.

FIGURE 13-12: The result of the process in the Publish folder

How It Works

The LightSwitch Publish Application Wizard collects the settings according to your selected client and application server topology. When you click Publish, it starts the build process and parameterizes it according to your settings. The build process creates the setup components and places them in the `Application Files` folder (refer to Figure 13-12). It also prepares the schema of the destination database.

During the build, a setup kit (`Setup.exe`) is created. In the `Publish` folder is an `Install.html` file with more instructions for deploying the application. You can also find a ClickOnce Application Manifest file (`ProjectTrek.application`). This file can be used to put your setup kit into a web folder and install it through a URL.

> **NOTE** *It is beyond the scope of this book to teach you ClickOnce deployment. However, if you are interested, you can start learning about it by visiting the web page at* `http://msdn.microsoft.com/en-us/library/t71a733d.aspx`.

Using the Installation Kit

The LightSwitch Publish Application Wizard creates the installation kit for you but it does not start the installation process. As shown in the next activity, however, the installation kit is easy to use on your own computer.

TRY IT OUT   Installing ProjectTrek on Your Own Development Machine

To install the `ProjectTrek` application on your computer, follow these steps:

1. Start Windows Explorer and navigate to the project folder of the `ProjectTrek` sample you used in the previous activity. From the `ProjectTrek\Publish` folder, start the `Setup` program by double-clicking it.

    The Launching Application window appears, as shown in Figure 13-13. It checks whether all prerequisites required by `ProjectTrek` are already installed on your machine. Because those are already there, this pop-up disappears in a few seconds — so fast that you probably won't be able to read its title.

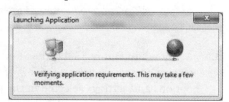

FIGURE 13-13: The Launching Application pop-up

2. The Application Install dialog appears with a security warning telling you that your application's publisher cannot be verified (see Figure 13-14). At this point, you could refuse the installation by clicking the Don't Install button. However, *you are the publisher* of this application, so click Install.

3. In a few seconds, `ProjectTrek` installation completes, and the application is automatically started. Looking at any screen (for example, the List of Projects screen), you can see that the application's database is empty.

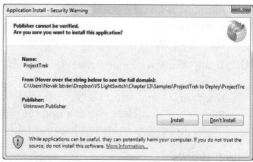

FIGURE 13-14: The Application Install dialog with security warning

4. Close the application. Double-click the `Setup` program again. The Launching Application pop-up appears for an instant and then the `ProjectTrek` application starts again. Close `ProjectTrek`.

How It Works

When you start `Setup`, it checks the application prerequisites and verifies that the newest version is installed on your computer — this is how ClickOnce works. The LightSwitch Publish Application Wizard has already created the `ProjectTrek` database on your computer's SQL Express instance, but it left it empty; and your application starts with an empty database. In Step 4, you restarted `Setup`, and it found the application to be up-to-date, so rather than install it, it simply started it.

Removing the Desktop Client

You can easily remove the desktop client from your computer — or from any other computer on which you've installed it. LightSwitch applications are deployed with ClickOnce, so you can remove them using the Control Panel, just like any other Windows application. When you start the Control Panel, select Programs and Features (if you're using either the Small icons or the Large icons view), or click "Uninstall a program" (if you're using the Category view).

You can find `ProjectTrek` in the list of installed programs, as shown in Figure 13-15. Select the `ProjectTrek` item and click Uninstall/Change in the header to remove it. Alternately, you can right-click `ProjectTrek` and select Uninstall/Change from its context menu. In a few seconds, the application is uninstalled and removed from the list.

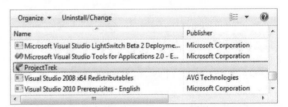

FIGURE 13-15: ProjectTrek in the list of installed programs

You have learned how to create the installation kit for your application, and how to use this kit to install the clients. However, you very rarely start a freshly installed application with an empty database — as it was set up in the previous exercise. Now, you will learn how to initialize your application's database.

MANAGING THE DATABASE DEPLOYMENT

When the LightSwitch Publish Application Wizard creates the database for you (that is, you have selected the "Publish directly to the database now" option, as shown in Figure 13-6), you get an empty database. In many cases, that's OK, but generally you want to deploy an application with several tables filled with data. For example, end-users cannot use `ProjectTrek` without time categories or project role types, so you must put initial data into the corresponding tables.

If you cannot start with an empty database, you must take care of initializing the database. In the following activity, you learn how to manage this process.

TRY IT OUT   Initializing the ProjectTrek Database

In this exercise, you initialize the `ProjectTrek2` database on your computer, as though it were a remote database server on your company's network. To carry out this task, follow these steps:

1. Open the LightSwitch IDE and load the `ProjectTrek` solution you used in the earlier exercise "Creating a Desktop Client Installation Kit."

2. In Solution Explorer, double-click the Properties node and select the Application Type tab. The client topology option should be set to Desktop, and the Application Server option set to "Run application services on the end-user's machine." If your settings are different, you probably loaded a wrong `ProjectTrek` solution.

3. Click Publish. The LightSwitch Publish Application Wizard starts and displays the Summary page. Click Publish Output on the left to show the related page. Select the "Create a script file to install and configure the database" option, as shown in Figure 13-16.

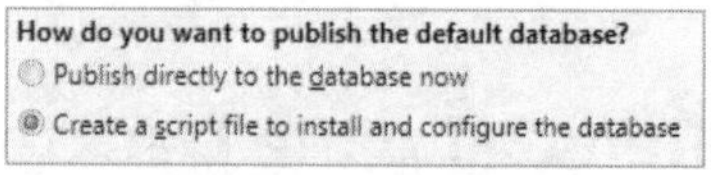

> **How do you want to publish the default database?**
> ○ Publish directly to the database now
> ● Create a script file to install and configure the database

FIGURE 13-16: Using the create script option

4. Select the Database Configuration page, and change the name of the database to generate to `ProjectTrek2`, as shown in Figure 13-17.

> **How will you want to deploy your database?**
> ● Generate a new database called:
>   ProjectTrek2

FIGURE 13-17: Change the name of the database to create

5. Click Publish. In a few minutes, the wizard compiles the new installation kit. It does not create the `ProjectTrek2` database for you. Instead, it prepares SQL scripts to run on your database server. When the publish process completes, the `ProjectTrek\Publish` folder will contain two new files, `ProjectTrek.sql` and `CreateUser.sql`.

The `CreateUser.sql` file enables your system administrator to create new SQL user accounts to have read and write permissions to your database. In this exercise, you won't use this script. The `ProjectTrek.sql` script contains all necessary SQL statements to create the `ProjectTrek2` database structure.

6. Start a command prompt (for example, type **cmd** in the Search Programs and Files box of the Windows Start menu, and press the Enter key).

7. Type the following line into the command window, replacing `<folder>` with the full name of the `ProjectTrek\Publish` folder:

```
sqlcmd -S .\SQLEXPRESS -i "<folder>\ProjectTrek.sql"
```

8. When the script completes (the "Completed execution of InstallRoles.SQL" message appears), keep the command prompt window open.

9. In the sample code folder that belongs to this chapter, you can find an `InitProjectTrek` folder containing an `InitProjectTrek.sql` script file. Note the full path of this folder.

10. Type the following line into the command window, replacing *<folder>* with the folder name you noted in the previous step:

```
sqlcmd -S .\SQLEXPRESS -i "<folder>\InitProjectTrek.sql"
```

11. When the script completes (that is, the "Changed database context to 'ProjectTrek2'" message appears), close the command prompt window.

How It Works

It is very common for an application's database to be put on a central server within a company. Because of the related security policies, handling a central database is a totally different task than managing a development database in a local computer.

When you select the "Create script file to install and configure the database" option in Step 3, that instructs the LightSwitch Publish Application Wizard to create installation script files for the database. The `ProjectTrek.sql` and `CreateUser.sql` files can be handed to system administrators, who can then install the central database with the help of these scripts.

In the steps starting with Step 6, you played the role of a system administrator (using your local database server). You extended the database installation process by running the `InitProjectTrek.sql` script to fill your database with initial information.

> **NOTE** *You can test whether the database installation script works as you expect. Use Server Explorer and connect to the freshly deployed database in order to check its contents.*

At this point, both the installation kit and the application database are prepared. However, the installation kit still points to the `ProjectTrek` database, not to `ProjectTrek2`, because you didn't change the Database Connection information when setting up the wizard. This step was intentionally omitted so you can learn how to change a database connection in the setup kit.

TRY IT OUT | **Redirecting the Database Connection in the Application Configuration File**

To change the configuration file of the `ProjectTrek` installation kit to use the `ProjectTrek2` database, follow these steps:

1. Open the `web.config` file under the `ProjectTrek\Publish\Application Files` folder with LightSwitch (that is, right-click the file and select Open from the context menu).

2. The `web.config` file is an XML file that contains configuration information used by the application. Search for the `<connectionStrings>` section, which looks like the following code snippet:

```
<connectionStrings>
  <add name="_IntrinsicData" connectionString="..." />
  <add name="ConsulArtCRMData" connectionString="..." />
</connectionStrings>
```

The ellipses represent the connection string information. The highlighted connection with the _IntrinsicData name points to the database containing the tables you created in LightSwitch. The ConsulArtCRMData connection describes the access to the ConsulArt CRM system's database, which is an external database from the ProjectTrek application's point of view.

3. You must change the connectionSting attribute of _IntrinsicData. Find the Initial Catalog=ProjectTrek part of the attribute and alter ProjectTrek to ProjectTrek2. Save the file by pressing Ctrl+S.

4. Start the Setup.exe file in the ProjectTrek\Publish folder to install ProjectTrek (as shown in the previous exercise). The setup will automatically launch ProjectTrek.

5. From the Tasks menu, open the Maintain Time Categories screen. This list contains a few predefined time category entries. You can also confirm that the Maintain Role Types screen lists several entries. All this information has been put into the database in the previous exercise by running the InitProjectTrek.sql script.

6. Close the application.

How It Works

In Step 3, you changed the connection string information in the web.config file so that it points to the ProjectTrek2 database. When you run the setup kit, it installs the application with the updated configuration file, so the ProjectTrek client uses the ProjectTrek2 database. This database contains initial data that can be seen immediately after the first launch.

By now, you have learned about all the important tasks related to deploying a LightSwitch application as a thick client. It is time to learn about three-tier deployment options.

DEPLOYING WITH IIS

Mission-critical applications — and related databases — are operated in IT environments with a high level of security, fault-tolerance, and scalability expectations. The desktop client deployment model you learned about thus far is not suitable for such environments for a couple of reasons:

> The client can directly access the database (that is, the database connection string is put into the application configuration file), resulting in a security weakness.

> The business logic is deployed together with the client. If the business logic changes, every client installation should be upgraded at the same time. Otherwise, only new clients will use the updated business logic, while old clients still use the obsolete one.

Three-Tier Deployment

Using three-tier deployment with IIS provides a solution that addresses the weaknesses of a desktop client installation. This deployment model separates the business layer by putting it on a web server running IIS that is physically separated from both the clients and from the database server, as shown in Figure 13-18.

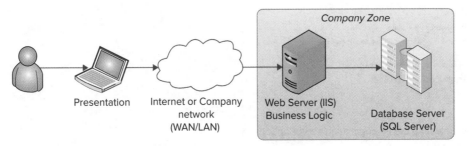

FIGURE 13-18: Three-tier deployment with IIS

The web server and the database are located on the company network, which can be secured against malicious attacks from the Internet with appropriately configured network equipment (such as routers and firewalls). Also, well-defined security policies can prevent intrusions into the company zone.

The business logic is deployed on the web server. If business processes and rules change, the business logic components deployed to the web server can be changed all at once — even without reinstalling all clients. Client applications do not know where the database is located. They know only the connection to the web server, as their configuration contains only the URL of the web server. The database connection information is available only for the components deployed to the web server, which are concealed from clients.

The web server can be established as a set of servers constituting a web farm that provides fault tolerance (if one web server is broken, the others can still serve users) and scalability (separate user requests are served by different web servers in the farm).

LightSwitch and Three-Tier Deployment

The LightSwitch Publish Application Wizard can create installation packages targeting three-tier deployments. Two application server options support the three-tier deployment model: You can host application services on an IIS server or use Windows Azure. Later in this chapter, you will learn about Windows Azure deployment. In this section, you'll learn the most important things about using IIS.

 WARNING *If you want to install the application server on IIS, you must be familiar with a lot of infrastructure and security information related to configuring IIS and the operating system behind it. This kind of configuration is an advanced topic that is far beyond the scope of this book. In this discussion, you will learn the basics of the deployment process; not covered here are step-by-step instructions to guide you through the process. To deploy your application in a real-world environment, seek the assistance of your system administrators.*

To use the three-tier deployment with IIS, select the "Host application services on an Internet Information Services (IIS) Server" option, as shown in Figure 13-19.

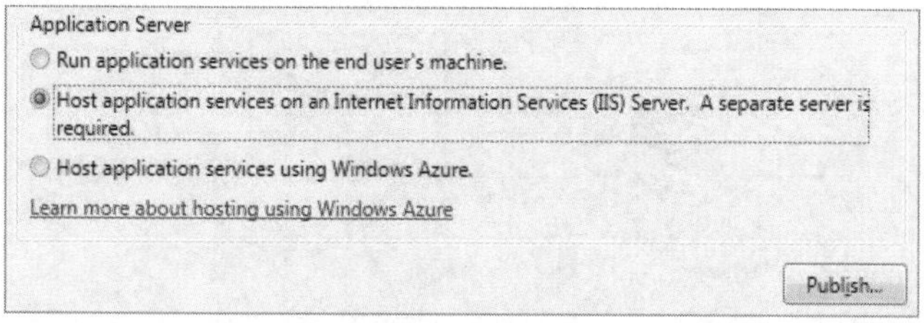

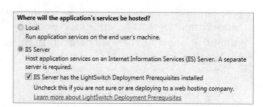

FIGURE 13-19: Selecting the IIS application server option

Publishing the Application Server to IIS

To publish a LightSwitch application using IIS as the application server, you must prepare the web server. This preparation entails the following tasks:

➤ Install LightSwitch prerequisites to the web server machine.

➤ Verify IIS settings and set up IIS features and services.

➤ To enable your website to access the database server, you must configure the SQL Server client network access on the web server computer.

 NOTE *These preparation tasks require an understanding of the web server's operation, and experience with its configuration. You can find more information at* http://blogs.msdn.com/b/bethmassi/archive/2011/03/23/ deployment-guide-how-to-configure-a-web-server-to-host-lightswitch- applications.aspx.

You can run the LightSwitch Publish Application Wizard as you did with a thick client installation. The Application Configuration page of the wizard (see Figure 13-20) provides the "IIS Server has the LightSwitch Deployment Prerequisites installed" option, which you enable to indicate that you've done the installation.

FIGURE 13-20: The Application Configuration page

In the Publish Output page, you can select whether you would like to create a deployment package, or let the wizard remotely publish the application server, as shown in Figure 13-21.

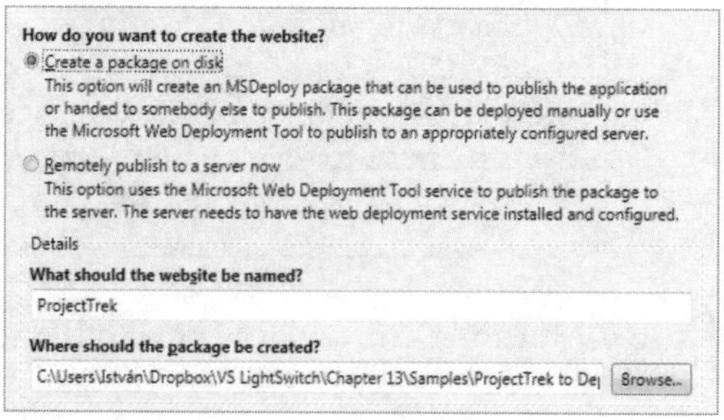

When you select the "Remotely publish to a server now" option, you must specify the Service URL of the application server with IIS, and you must also have a web server account with the appropriate permissions.

FIGURE 13-21: The Publish Output page

After you have set all the information to publish the application, click the Publish button. In addition to the files you learned about earlier in this chapter, the `Publish` folder in your application now contains a new zip file, `ProjectTrek.zip` (see Figure 13-22), that can be used for installation on IIS with the MSDeploy tool (a web deployment utility for IIS). This file contains all the components and the configuration of your application server.

Name	Type	Size
Application Files	File folder	
CreateUser	Microsoft SQL Server Query File	1 KB
Install	HTML Document	6 KB
ProjectTrek	ClickOnce Application Deployment Manifest	2 KB
ProjectTrek	Microsoft SQL Server Query File	151 KB
ProjectTrek	Compressed (zipped) Folder	9,003 KB
setup	Application	418 KB

FIGURE 13-22: The content of the Publish folder

Publishing a LightSwitch application to IIS is a tough task because of the complexity of security settings. However, you can still go through all the tasks of a three-tier deployment another way, as you will learn in the next section.

WINDOWS AZURE DEPLOYMENT

One of the LightSwitch's greatest features is that it supports application deployment to the Windows Azure platform. This deployment option also enables you to use a three-tier deployment. It is easier to use than the three-tier deployment with IIS, because the LightSwitch Publish Application Wizard undertakes the configuration of the web server running in Windows Azure.

Figure 13-23 shows the architecture of a LightSwitch application deployed to the Windows Azure platform. The presentation layer still runs on the client computer. The business logic and the website that hosts the client application run in Windows Azure, and the database is deployed to a SQL Azure database.

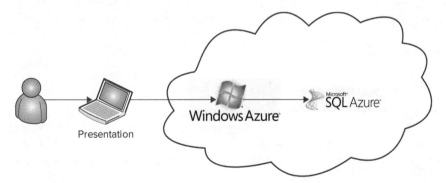

FIGURE 13-23: Three-tier deployment with the Windows Azure platform

To use this deployment option, select the "Host application services using Windows Azure" option in the Application Server section of the Application Type tab of your project's properties, as shown in Figure 13-24.

In Chapter 3, you learned that Windows Azure is a great alternative to using your own infrastructure and software

FIGURE 13-24: Using the Windows Azure application server option

licenses when the computing resources required for your system change over time. In many cases, it's difficult to guess in advance what the maximum or average load will be later. If you underestimate your resources or allocate them for average use, users will suffer during peak usage. In the worst-case scenario, your system will collapse — and you'll lose business. If you allocate many more resources than you actually need, users will be happy, but you are throwing money out of the window.

Using Windows Azure, you can dynamically adjust computing resources to fit your needs. You can start with resources appropriate to your current requirements. As your system is used, you can monitor it and dynamically adjust the computing resources according to usage patterns. If you anticipate additional users or significant changes in system usage over time, Windows Azure deployment is a great option.

Prerequisites for Windows Azure Deployment

To deploy applications to Windows Azure, you must meet the following prerequisites:

➤   You must have a Windows Azure subscription.

➤   You must learn the basics of creating hosted service and storage accounts, as well as SQL Azure databases using your subscription.

> **NOTE** *If you are new to Windows Azure, visit the* `http://azure.com` *web page to learn the basics and create a subscription. Generally, you must pay to use Windows Azure, but several inexpensive or free options are available to help you learn and try the basics. You will find related information in the Windows Azure home page. It is beyond the scope of this book to teach you the basics of using Windows Azure.*

Before the deployment, you must complete the following options:

➤   *Create a Hosted Service* — Name your hosted service **MyTodoList**. You must also create a unique URL prefix to access this service through the Internet. Use the `MyTodoList` name with a random suffix to ensure that it will be unique (such as `MyTodoList2654323` or `MyTodoList-xqedhr`). Select the region (data center where your solution is hosted) that is closest to you (for example, "Anywhere in US").

➤   *Create a Storage Account* — Select a unique URL prefix for your storage account. (You can select the same prefix you used for the hosted service.) Select the same region used by the hosted service.

➤   *Create a SQL Azure database* — Choose the Web edition with 1GB maximum data size. Name it `MyTodoListData`. Be sure to set SQL Azure Server's firewall rules so that your client can access the server!

NOTE *Start the Windows Azure Management Portal (*`http://windows.azure`
`.com`*). After you have logged in with your Live ID, the home screen displays a
collection of links beneath the How to Perform Common Tasks heading. Here
you can find step-by-step instructions for creating an account and database.
During the deployment, you also need the administrative account to access SQL
Azure. If you don't remember the password for this account (the username is
displayed in the portal), you can reset it and note it.*

Using the Publish Application Wizard for Windows Azure Deployment

In this section you will deploy an application named `MyTodoList` to Windows Azure. After you
have downloaded the source code from `www.wrox.com`, you find this project under the `Chapter 13\`
`MyTodoList` folder. To keep the required deployment steps as simple as possible, whereas the
`ProjectTrek` sample uses two databases (the one created by the application and the already existing
`ConsulArtCRM` database), `MyTodoList` contains only a single database — which should make it
easier to learn Windows Azure deployment.

After you have set up the hosted service, the storage account, and the SQL Azure database as
described previously, you are ready to start deploying the `MyTodoList` application to Windows
Azure. You are going to deploy this application using a web client (browser), and with Forms
Authentication.

TRY IT OUT Setting Up the Publish Application Wizard for Windows Azure Deployment

To deploy the `MyTodoList` application to Windows Azure, follow these steps:

1. Start LightSwitch and open the `MyTodoList` project. In Solution Explorer, double-click the
   Properties node. In the Designer, select the Access control tab and choose the Use Forms
   Authentication option.

2. Select the Application Type tab. Set the Web option for the client, and the "Host application
   services using Windows Azure" option for the application server topology. Click the Publish
   button to start deployment.

3. The LightSwitch Publish Application Wizard starts and displays the Client Configuration page.
   The Web option is selected. Click Next.

4. In the Application Server Configuration page, the Windows Azure option is selected.
   Click Next.

5. The Connect to Windows Azure page is displayed. Here you must provide the information
   required to connect to Windows Azure: the identifier of your subscription and a management
   certificate (see Figure 13-25).

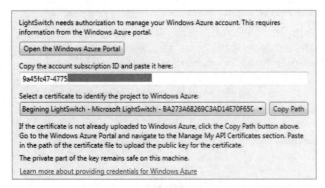

FIGURE 13-25: The Connect to Windows Azure page

The subscription ID can be found in the management portal. You can click the "Open the Windows Azure portal" button to immediately navigate to the management portal. There — when you display either the Hosted Services or the Storage Account information — you can view your Subscription ID in the Properties panel. Select the ID with your mouse, and copy it by pressing Ctrl+C. Go to the Wizard page and paste it by pressing Ctrl+V.

For security purposes, you must provide a management certificate with your connection request. This certificate must be uploaded to Windows Azure. In the Connect to Windows Azure page, select this certificate from the drop-down list (refer to Figure 13-25).

6. The first time you use the wizard, you can create an appropriate certification. Use the arrow of the drop-down list and select the <Create new self-signed certificate ... > item. In the New Management Certificate dialog that appears, shown in Figure 13-26, you can provide a friendly name for the certificate. This name is added to the list so that later you can select the newly created certificate again.

FIGURE 13-26: The New Management Certificate dialog

The IDE creates a certificate and saves it to a location under your user profile in Windows. Click the Copy Path button (refer to Figure 13-25) to copy the full path of the newly generated certificate to the clipboard.

7. Return to the management portal and select the Management Certificates tab. Click the Add Certificate button in the toolbar to display the Add New Management Certificate dialog, shown in Figure 13-27.

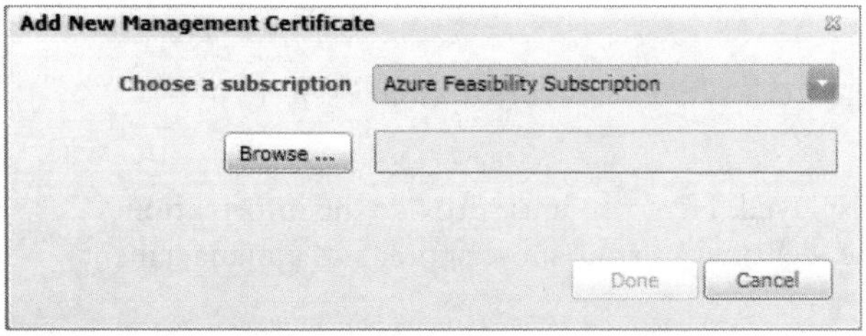

FIGURE 13-27: The Add New Management Certificate dialog in the portal

8. In this dialog, click the Browse button. When the Open dialog appears, press Ctrl+V to paste the full path information (copied to the clipboard in Step 6) into the File Name text box. Click Open. Then, in the Add New Management Certificate dialog, click Done. The certificate is immediately uploaded to Windows Azure. Go back to LightSwitch and click Next in the wizard dialog.

9. In the Azure Service Configuration page, you can set the Service and Storage account information. Use the drop-down arrows of the Service and Storage lists to display their content, and select the appropriate accounts, as shown in Figure 13-28. You can specify whether you want to deploy the MyTodoList application to the staging or production environment. Select the Staging item from the Environment list because in this activity, you test the application in the staging environment before releasing it to production. Click Next.

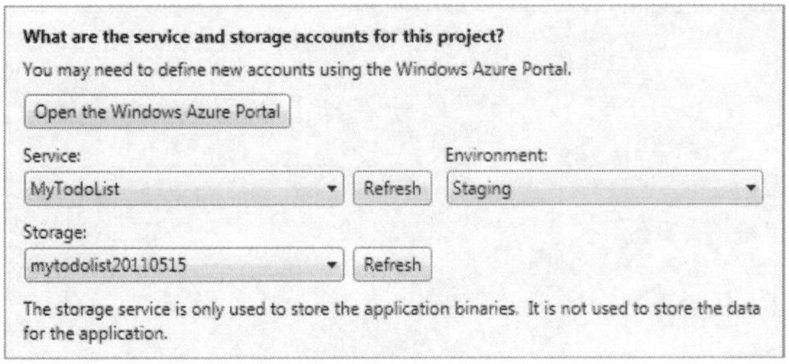

What are the service and storage accounts for this project?
You may need to define new accounts using the Windows Azure Portal.

Open the Windows Azure Portal

Service: Environment:
MyTodoList   ▼ | Refresh   Staging   ▼

Storage:
mytodolist20110515   ▼ | Refresh

The storage service is only used to store the application binaries. It is not used to store the data for the application.

FIGURE 13-28: The Azure Service Configuration page

10. You will use Forms Authentication with MyTodoList. The application will ask for your username and password, and sends this information to the server using secure HTTPS communication. HTTPS requires a certificate that the client and the server use in the communication. In the Security Settings page, you can select this certificate from the existing ones (as shown in Figure 13-29) or create a new one.

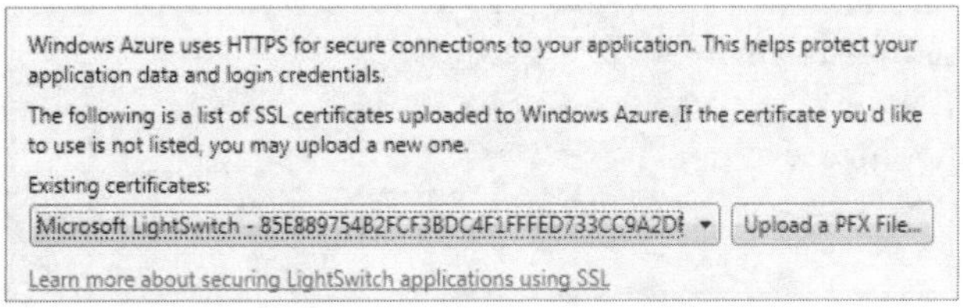

Windows Azure uses HTTPS for secure connections to your application. This helps protect your application data and login credentials.

The following is a list of SSL certificates uploaded to Windows Azure. If the certificate you'd like to use is not listed, you may upload a new one.

Existing certificates:

Microsoft LightSwitch - 85E889754B2FCF3BDC4F1FFFED733CC9A2Df ▼ | Upload a PFX File...

Learn more about securing LightSwitch applications using SSL

FIGURE 13-29: The Azure Service Configuration page

11. If you do not have such a certificate, use the arrow of the drop-down list and select <Create new self-signed certificate ... >. A new dialog opens, as shown in Figure 13-30, asking for the name and path of the new certificate. It will be encrypted with a password, so you must provide one and confirm it in this dialog. Click OK to create the certificate file. Click the Upload a PFX

File button to select the newly created certificate file. In the Upload PFX File dialog, you must select the same file and specify the same password used to create the file. Click OK to upload the certificate. In the wizard, click Next.

12. In the Database Connections page shown in Figure 13-31, you can specify the SQL connection information for an administrator connection and a user connection. The administrator connection is used by this wizard to create the `MyTodoList` application's database tables during deployment. The user connection is used by the application server to access the database while your application runs.

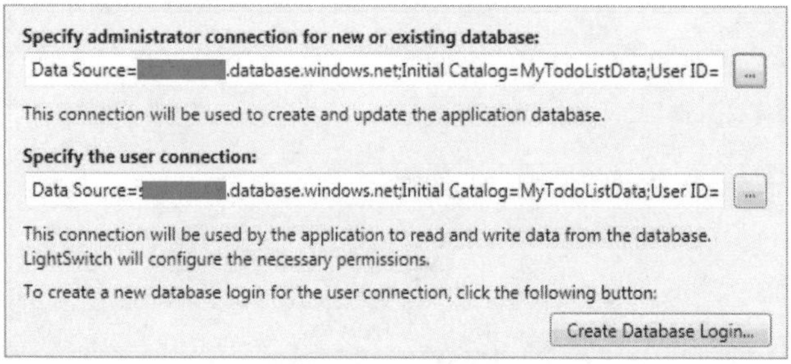

FIGURE 13-30: The New Self-Signed Certificate dialog

FIGURE 13-31: The Database Connections page

13. Click the ellipsis button to the right of the administrator connection. When the Connection Properties dialog, shown in Figure 13-32, opens, set the name of your SQL Azure server. (You can copy this name from the management portal.) For the Use SQL Server Authentication option, enter the administrator username and password you used to create your SQL Azure server instance. Type **MyTodoListData** (or the appropriate name, if you have used a different one) in the "Select or enter a database name" text box, and click OK.

14. The information specified for the administration connection is automatically copied to the user connection info. For now, leave it as it is. When you deploy a real application, you can use the Create Database Login button to create a separate account for a user connection. Click Next.

FIGURE 13-32: The Connection Properties dialog

15. In the Authentication page, you can set up an initial administrative account used by the `MyTodoList` application, as shown in Figure 13-33. Enter your username and password. When you start `MyTodoList` the first time, log in with this account to create users and set up their permissions. Click Next.

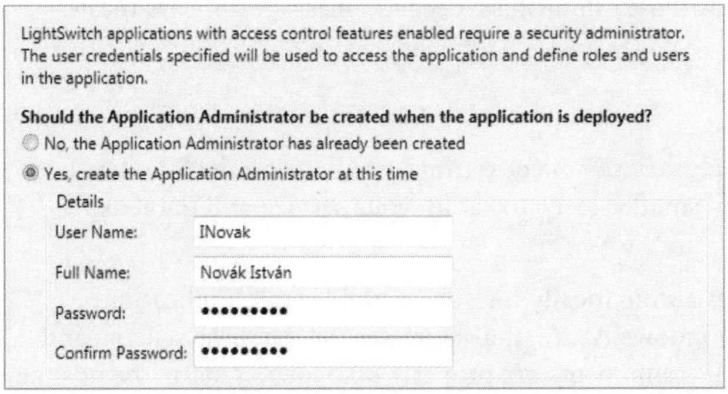

FIGURE 13-33: The Application Administrator page

16. In the Specify a Certificate page you can provide a certificate to sign the `.XAP` file representing the UI layer of `MyTodoList`, as shown in Figure 13-34. With this certificate, you assure `MyTodoList` users that the publisher (the service hosted in Windows Azure) is reliable and the code has not been tampered with. Without this certificate, a malicious publisher would be able to provide tampered code that can be used to extract sensible information — for example, user password or credit card data — while your client is communicating with the server. Although you can uncheck the "Specify a certificate" flag, a signed `.XAP` file is required for an application hosted on Windows Azure, so leave this option checked.

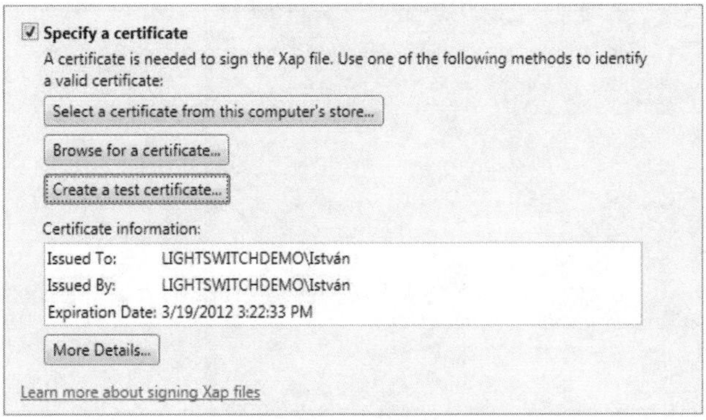

FIGURE 13-34: The Specify a Certificate page

17. You can select an existing certificate from your computer store, or select a certificate file by browsing your computer. Clicking the "Create a test certificate button" enables you to create a new one. Click this button. The Create Test Certificate dialog opens, asking for a password to encrypt the certificate file. Enter and confirm the password. Click OK to create the new certificate.

18. Click Publish to start Windows Azure deployment. The wizard compiles your application and starts publishing it. The entire process takes about 10 to 20 minutes. While it is in progress, a modal dialog appears in the IDE with the "Publishing project 'MyTodoList'" message. When the process completes, the dialog disappears and the "Publish succeeded" message appears in the status bar of the IDE.

How It Works

The wizard guides you through all the steps necessary to collect settings used during the Windows Azure deployment. It asks you to perform many smaller tasks to set up your service and database environment.

Behind the scenes, the wizard does a lot of things automatically for you. It builds your application and creates a package that can be deployed to Windows Azure. It also creates the database schema and deploys it to your SQL Azure database. When all components are properly uploaded, it starts the hosting service, making your application ready to use.

Starting the Application in Windows Azure

When the LightSwitch Publish Application Wizard completes the publish process, your application server is deployed to Windows Azure and is already started. However, starting a new deployment in Windows Azure takes a few minutes. During this time, a new virtual machine that runs your application server components is created and started. Switch to the Windows Azure Management portal and you can see this machine starting, as shown in Figure 13-35.

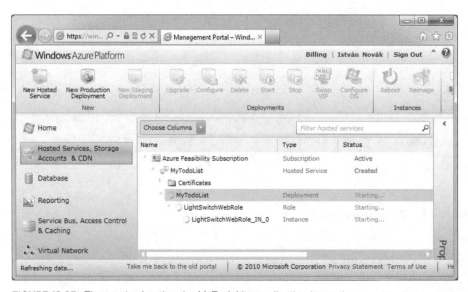

FIGURE 13-35: The service hosting the MyTodoList application is starting

The `LightSwitchWebRole` beneath `MyTodoList` represents the web role component of `MyTodoList` that hosts your application. A service can run one or more instances. In Figure 13-35, you can see that the `LightSwitchWebRole` component runs a single instance named `LightSwitchWebRole_IN_0`.

When the status of `MyTodoList` is "Started" (in the figure, it is "Starting…"), the application is ready to use. Expand the Properties panel on the right, and click the link in the DNS name property. This is a link to your application deployed into the staging environment.

In a few seconds, a message appears in your browser, as shown in Figure 13-36, indicating that there is a problem with the website's security certificate. That's because in Step 17 of the previous exercise, you created a certificate that does not come from a trusted authority (it was created by your own computer). Ignore the message and click the "Continue to this website (not recommended)" link to run `MyTodoList`.

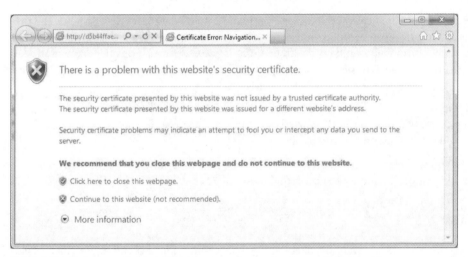

FIGURE 13-36: Starting MyTodoList raises a message about a certificate problem

The Silverlight client of `MyTodoList` starts in the browser and asks for the login information, as shown in Figure 13-37. In Step 15 of the previous exercise, you specified the administrative account to be used by `MyTodoList`. Enter this account information here and you can log into the application with administrative privilege. Now you can set up your application's users and security roles, as described in Chapter 11.

FIGURE 13-37: The Login screen of MyTodoList

SUMMARY

After your application is implemented and tested, you must deploy it so end-users can access it. LightSwitch helps you with application deployment. It can create an installation kit for your application, and deploy the application's server components and database.

Your deployment model is based on the client and application server topology of your choice. LightSwitch enables you to create either a desktop client or a browser client. Your application server components can run on the local machine, in a separate server hosting IIS, or you can even deploy them to Windows Azure.

If you are creating applications only for yourself and a small group of people, the desktop client option with locally installed application server components — whereby your client contains both the presentation and the business logic layers — is a great option. Your database can be deployed to all client computers as well, or hosted somewhere else on your network.

If you create a company application that accesses mission-critical databases and systems, the three-tier deployment with IIS-hosted application server components may be the best solution. In this case, you need help from your company's system administrators, because this deployment model requires many preparation steps on the server hosting IIS. It also requires administrative privileges.

When your application has a large number of users and its expected computing resources change over time, Windows Azure is the best deployment option. This method of three-tier deployment is much easier to carry out than the IIS-hosted one, but you must obtain a Windows Azure subscription and learn Windows Azure basics.

In Chapter 14 you will learn about SharePoint 2010 lists, including how to use them to create LightSwitch applications, and how to access and manipulate the data in these lists.

EXERCISES

1. What is the difference between a thin client and a thick client from an architectural point of view?

2. What kinds of client deployment topologies are supported by LightSwitch?

3. What kinds of application server deployment topologies are supported by LightSwitch?

4. List the tasks that are required to prepare an IIS server for LightSwitch application deployment.

5. What are the prerequisites for a Windows Azure deployment?

6. What information do you specify on the Azure Service Configuration page of the LightSwitch Publish Application Wizard?

 NOTE *Answers to the Exercises can be found in the Appendix.*

▶ **WHAT YOU LEARNED IN THIS CHAPTER**

TOPIC	KEY CONCEPTS
Desktop client	The application runs on the end-user's computer desktop in a separate window.
Web client	The application runs in the web browser started by the end-user.
Locally hosted application services	The application services run on the end-user's machine. This option means that you implement a thick client from the architectural point of view.
Application services hosted in IIS	The application services run on a separate server machine, hosted in IIS.
Windows Azure deployment	The application services and the database are hosted on the Windows Azure platform.
LightSwitch Publish Application Wizard	You can start this wizard from the project Properties window by selecting the Application Type tab and clicking the Publish button. Alternatively, in Solution Explorer, you can select the Publish command from the project node's context menu. This wizard guides you through the steps of publishing a LightSwitch application.
Publish folder	When you create an installation kit for your LightSwitch application, the output of the process (client installation kit, application server installation kit, database initialization scripts) is put into this folder. You can select this folder's location in the Publish Output page of the wizard.
Using the client installation kit	Double-click the `Setup.exe` program in the `Publish` folder. The Launching Application pop-up checks whether all prerequisites are installed on your machine, and then starts the Application Install dialog that guides you through the client installation steps.
Removing the client application from your desktop	Access the Programs and Features applet of the Control Panel on your machine. In the list of installed programs, right-click the name of the client application and select Uninstall.
Signing the `.XAP` file	You can sign the `.XAP` file representing the UI layer of your application with a certificate. This certificate assures your application's users that the publisher (you or your company) is reliable, and that the code has not been tampered with.

14

Using SharePoint 2010 Lists

WHAT YOU WILL LEARN IN THIS CHAPTER

➤ Creating SharePoint 2010 custom lists

➤ Using LightSwitch to attach to built-in and custom SharePoint lists

➤ Understanding how SharePoint lists are mapped to LightSwitch tables

➤ Creating and using relationships between SharePoint lists and LightSwitch tables

The information assets of an enterprise include all information related to the business — not only traditional databases, but also any other kind of information that has a value from the business perspective. In addition to data coming from applications and back-end systems, information workers use documents and data stored in Enterprise Content Management (ECM) systems. Many enterprises have deployed Microsoft SharePoint, and use it as an ECM to store a large amount of unstructured information as a valuable part of their IT assets.

Visual Studio LightSwitch was designed to support not only developers, but also business analysts and other information workers in their everyday activities. LightSwitch can manage both new and existing SQL Server databases seamlessly.

It also enables you to utilize the information stored in SharePoint 2010. In this chapter, you learn how to access SharePoint 2010 lists and use them in your application — with the same ease that you experience while building SQL Server-based solutions.

 NOTE *Visual Studio LightSwitch supports only SharePoint 2010. You cannot connect to SharePoint data created in older (2007 or 2003) versions.*

CREATING A SAMPLE SHAREPOINT SITE

To go through the examples in this chapter, you need access to an existing SharePoint 2010 Server installation, and permissions to create a sample site. Whereas in Chapter 8 it was easy to create a sample SQL Server database (because LightSwitch installs SQL Server 2008 Express on your local machine), the situation is a bit more difficult with SharePoint. Although SharePoint 2010 has a lightweight version named SharePoint Foundation 2010, it is not installed with LightSwitch, and its install kit is not a part of the LightSwitch setup pack.

You have two options to prepare the SharePoint site required for this chapter:

➤ Ask your system administrator to prepare a SharePoint 2010 site for you.

➤ Install SharePoint Foundation 2010 (or SharePoint 2010 Server) on your development machine.

Let's take a closer look at these options.

Using Your Company's SharePoint Server

If your company already has a SharePoint 2010 Server instance, you can easily have your system administrators prepare a site for you. Show them this section and ask them to help you! To provide you with an empty site required to complete the exercises in this chapter, the SharePoint administrator should follow these steps:

1. Create a new SharePoint site named `ProjectTrekKB` (or, if your company's policy requires some other name, that name can also be used). This site should be created with the Blank Site template.

2. Grant the user (you) administrative permissions (full control) to this site (and only to this site).

3. Provide the user (you) with a URL pointing to this new site. Generally, this is something like `http://yourcompanyserver/ProjectTrekKB`. Depending on your company policy, `https://` may be used, or the `ProjectTrekKB` site (or equivalent) may be deeper in the site hierarchy and not directly in the root of `yourcompanyserver`.

When you get the URL, open a web browser on your development machine where LightSwitch is installed, and try to access the newly created site. Refer to your system administrator if you have any access permission problems.

Installing SharePoint Foundation 2010

As an alternative, you can install SharePoint Foundation 2010 on your development machine. To do so, you must be logged in with administrative privileges on your computer. Follow these steps:

1. Open your web browser and navigate to the Microsoft Download Center (`www.microsoft.com/downloads`).

2. Type **SharePoint Foundation 2010** in the Search box and press Enter. The first row (or one of the first rows) in the result list will point to the download page (Microsoft SharePoint Foundation 2010). Click it.

3. On the download page, click the Download button and save the installation kit to your hard drive. The size of the kit is about 170 MB.

In production environments, you generally deploy SharePoint Foundation to a Windows Server 2008 or Windows Server 2008 R2 installation. However, it can also be installed to Windows 7. While the installation kit is being downloaded, scroll down the download page to the System Requirements heading and navigate to the "Setting Up the Development Environment for SharePoint 2010 on Windows Vista, Windows 7, and Windows Server 2008" link. The page to which the link points contains very detailed instructions on the installation process.

You must follow those steps correctly; otherwise, the installation will fail. If the installation steps seem too complex, you can seek help from your company's system administrator or from a friend who has experience with SharePoint.

> **NOTE** Installing SharePoint Foundation 2010 on a virtual machine or a virtual server is a great option to avoid issues resulting from a failed installation. If your developer machine has enough capacity to assign at least 2GB of RAM to a virtual machine, it is worth creating one. Otherwise, you can ask your company's system administrator to provide you with a virtual server.

To create the `ProjectTrekKB` site on the newly installed SharePoint instance, follow these steps:

1. Start your web browser and navigate to the root site of the newly installed SharePoint instance. If you do not know its URL, use the Windows Start menu to launch the All Programs ➪ Microsoft SharePoint 2010 Products ➪ SharePoint 2010 Central Administration application. When it has started, select the Manage Web Applications task link beneath Application Management. It displays the URL of the SharePoint root, as shown in Figure 14-1.

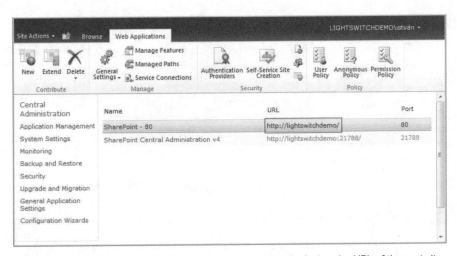

FIGURE 14-1: The SharePoint Central Administration utility displaying the URL of the root site

2. Depending on your settings, SharePoint may authenticate you. In this case, provide your username and password in the authentication dialog.

3. The SharePoint site appears (it's named `Team Site`). In the top-left corner, you'll find the Site Settings drop-down list. Click it and select the New Site command, as shown in Figure 14-2. If you cannot find the Site Settings drop-down, or you do not see the New Site command in the list, your administrative permissions are missing. (You probably used a non-administrative account in Step 2 to log into the site.)

4. A pop-up page appears in the middle of the screen. Select the Blank Site template and specify `ProjectTrekKB` for both the site name and URL, as shown in Figure 14-3. If your company policy requires another name, use that one.

FIGURE 14-2: Selecting the New Site command

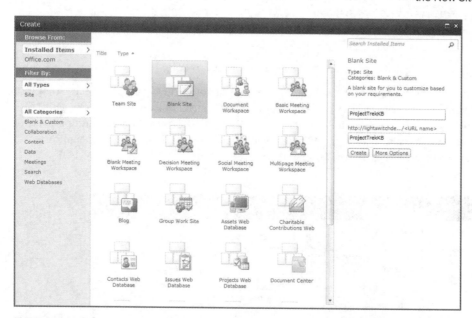

FIGURE 14-3: Setting the site template and name parameters

5. Click Create. In a few seconds, the site is created. Its home page is displayed in your browser.

Preparing a Custom SharePoint List

At this point, you should have a functional SharePoint site — either created by you or set up by a system administrator. SharePoint uses the concept of a *list* as a kind of mechanism for storing structured information. In order to understand this concept and prepare the site for the exercises in this chapter, you must create a custom list. You will access this custom list from the LightSwitch IDE later.

TRY IT OUT   Creating a Custom SharePoint List

In this chapter, you learn the SharePoint-related features of LightSwitch with the help of a custom SharePoint list that contains questions and answers (Q&A). The Q&A entries have columns for a title, a description, an answer, and a status, and they can be attached to projects. To create the custom list, follow these steps:

1. Start the web browser and navigate to the `ProjectTrekKB` site. In the menu on the left, click Lists, and then click Create. A new pop-up window opens in the middle of the screen.

2. This dialog enables you to create new site elements. Select List beneath the Filter By category and then the Custom List type, as shown in Figure 14-4. Set the name of the list to Q&A and click Create.

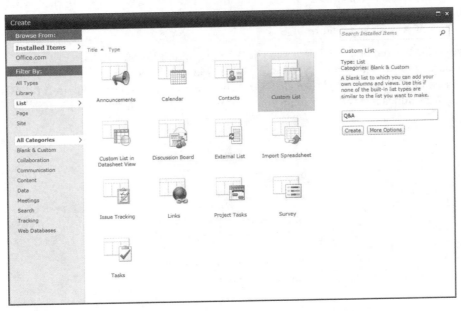

FIGURE 14-4: Creating a new custom list

3. The new custom list is created, and a few predefined fields are automatically added. One of them is Title, which is displayed in the default view of the list, as shown in Figure 14-5. You will use this field to specify a short title for Q&A items in the list.

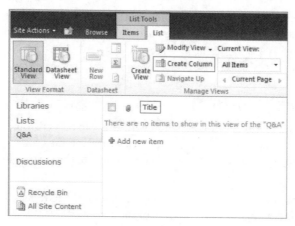

FIGURE 14-5: The newly created, and empty, custom list

4. You now need to add new columns to the Q&A list. In the List tab, there is a Create Column link (as highlighted in Figure 14-5). Click it to add a column. A new dialog pops up with the Create Column title. Set the name of the new column to **Description** and select the "Multiple lines of text" radio button, as shown in Figure 14-6.

5. Scroll down to the bottom of the window and click the Yes option for the "Require that this column contains information" property. Also, click the "Plain text" option for the "Specify the type of text to allow" property, and then click OK. These settings are shown in Figure 14-7. With these steps, you've added a mandatory multi-line text property that contains plain text.

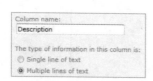

FIGURE 14-6: Setting the name and the type of the new column

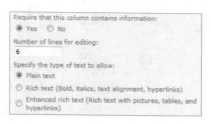

FIGURE 14-7: Setting properties of the new Description column

6. Repeat Step 4 and Step 5 to add a new Answer column, but this time select the No option for the "Require that this column contains information" property.

7. Create a new column. Name it **State**, and select the "Choice (menu to choose from)" option as the type of the field. Scroll down to the bottom of the window and set the properties as shown in Figure 14-8. Click OK. With these settings, you've added a column that enables you to select a state (New, Answered, Accepted, or Refused) from a drop-down box.

8. Create a Project Code column to store the code of the project to which this Q&A item belongs. Set its type to "Single line of text," and use the properties shown in Figure 14-9 to set up this column. Click OK.

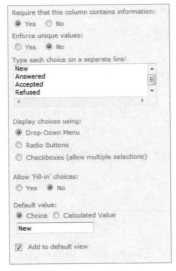

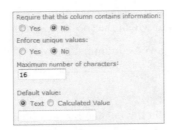

FIGURE 14-8: Properties of the Status column

FIGURE 14-9: Properties of the Project Code column

9. All columns of the Q&A list are created. Since the list is empty, click the "Add new item" link beneath the column headers to create a new item. A new dialog opens with the columns you have just added, as shown in Figure 14-10. Type some text into the required fields (marked with an asterisk) and click Save.

FIGURE 14-10: Adding a new Q&A item to the list

10. Add several new Q&A items to the list. The items are listed in SharePoint, as shown in Figure 14-11. Close the browser.

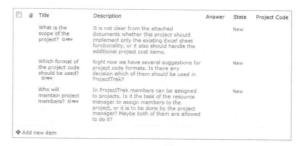

How It Works

With SharePoint 2010, you can create custom lists in a few steps. First, you must create a new list on your site with the custom list template. Then you can add columns to your list by specifying the name and field type of the new column, and setting column properties. This process is very similar to creating a new table in LightSwitch.

FIGURE 14-11: A few items in the Q&A item list

In this example, you added the `Project Code` column to this list, which can be used to store information about the project to which the specific Q&A item belongs.

When the custom list is created, you can immediately fill it with data.

Now you have a custom list in the `ProjectTrekKB` SharePoint site that can be easily maintained. The structure of this list is very similar to a LightSwitch table. Whereas the table is composed from fields, the list is composed from columns. Both fields and columns have types and properties describing their behavior.

In the next section, you will learn how to access this custom list from a LightSwitch application.

USING SHAREPOINT 2010 LISTS

Integrating the `ProjectTrek` application with the `ProjectTrekKB` SharePoint site has a great value. ConsulArt employees can pose questions in the `ProjectTrek` application, and let the targeted employees or customers answer them through the `ProjectTrekKB` site. Customers of ConsulArt do not have the `ProjectTrek` application installed on their machines, because it is an internal application. However, customers can access the `ProjectTrekKB` site, and use it to read and answer questions.

You will integrate the Q&A SharePoint list into the `ProjectTrek` application. A SharePoint list is an object that stores structured information in SharePoint, just as SQL Server stores structured information in a database table.

Attaching to SharePoint Lists

With LightSwitch, you can attach to external SharePoint 2010 lists with the same ease as you can attach to external SQL Server tables. With this feature, it is easy to integrate the `ProjectTrekKB` site into the `ProjectTrek` application, as you will learn from the next exercise.

TRY IT OUT   Attaching to the Q&A List

 NOTE *In this exercise, you continue the sample that you completed in Chapter 12. You can find the starting sample on this book's companion website at* www .wrox.com *in the folder* Chapter 14\Start.

To attach to the Q&A custom list you created in the previous exercise, follow these steps:

1. Start LightSwitch and open the
    ProjectTrek project.

2. In Solution Explorer, right-click the
    Data Sources node and select Add Data
    Source from the context menu. The Attach
    Data Source wizard will appear on the screen.

3. In the Choose Data Source Type page,
    select SharePoint, as shown in Figure 14-12.
    Click Next.

4. In the Enter Connection Information page,
    specify the URL to access your SharePoint
    site, as shown in Figure 14-13. This must
    be the URL of the ProjectTrekKB site
    (or the site prepared for you by your
    company's system administrator). If you
    use the SharePoint server on your own
    (company) network, you can use your

FIGURE 14-12: Selecting SharePoint from the Choose Data Source Type page of the Attach Data Source wizard

Windows Credentials to access the site. However, if you must access an external site with a specific account, click the Other Credentials option and specify your username and password information. Click Next.

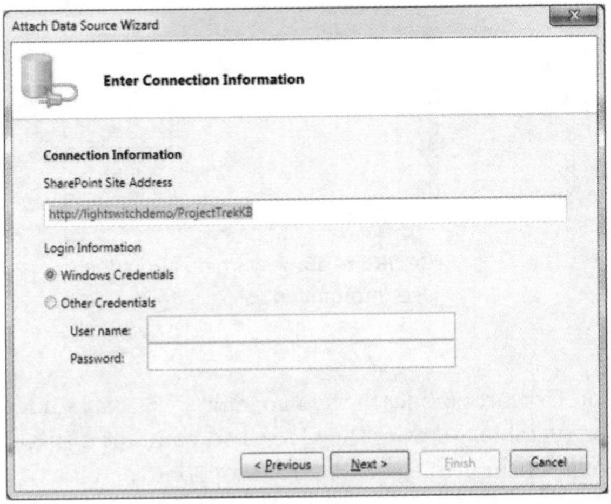

FIGURE 14-13: Specifying the SharePoint site address

> **WARNING** *It's common to specify the SharePoint site address by copying the appropriate URL from your web browser's address bar. Be sure to copy the site address only, not the URL of the list you want to attach to. If you specify the URL of the Q&A list instead of the* `ProjectTrekKB` *site, the Attach Data Source wizard will return an error message — "<your URL> does not appear to be a valid site. SharePoint 2010 (or later) with an installation of WCF Data Services is required."*

5. In the Choose Your SharePoint Items page, expand the `Lists` node and select `QA` and `QAState`. Uncheck `UserInformationList`, as shown in Figure 14-14. The selected lists point to the Q&A list (`Q&A`) you created in the previous activity and the menu options of the `State` column of the Q&A list (`QAState`). The Data Source name is set to `ProjectTrekKBData`, so leave it as it is. Click Finish.

6. The wizard pops up a warning message, as shown in Figure 14-15. This message tells you that the wizard will also import the `UserInformationList` object because it has a relationship with the lists you've selected in the previous step. The Q&A list has two predefined columns named `Created By` and `Modified By`, which contain the ID of the user adding (`Created By`) and modifying (`Modified By`) the item to the Q&A list. These columns have references to the `UserInformationList` object. Click Continue.

FIGURE 14-14: Selecting the lists to attach to

FIGURE 14-15: A warning about the UserInformationList

7. The newly attached lists are added to Solution Explorer (beneath the `ProjectTrekKBData` node), as shown in Figure 14-16. As you can see, the `QA` table (items of the Q&A list) contains a single relationship to the `QAState` table, and two relationships to the `UserInformationList` table.

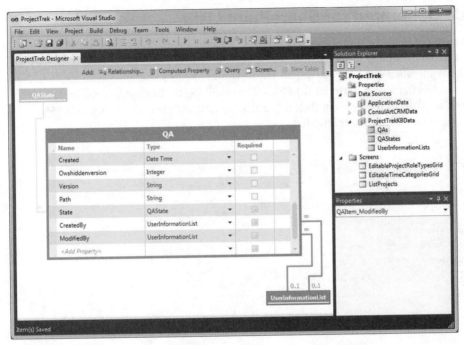

FIGURE 14-16: Attached SharePoint lists in Solution Explorer and the Designer

How It Works

The Attach Data Source wizard works in the same way as if you were attached to external SQL Server tables. However, this time you must specify a SharePoint 2010 site with a URL, and select lists. The wizard also checks for other lists that have relationships with the ones you've selected — in this exercise, the `UserInformationList` was also attached to preserve consistency. Without retaining these relationships, you might attempt to enter data that does not conform to the relationship between lists, and those changes would be refused by SharePoint.

The type of original list columns is automatically converted to the appropriate LightSwitch field types.

One important difference here is that unlike SQL Server table relationships, you have navigation properties from the Q&A list (`QA` table) to the other lists (`QAState` and `UserInformationList`), but not vice versa. The reason behind this behavior is that SharePoint does not contain a mechanism (SQL Server does) that allows easy navigation from a list on the "zero-or-one" side of the list to the "many" side of a zero-or-one-to-many relationship.

Later, you can use the data source node created during the import to add or remove SharePoint lists. Right-click the data source node and select the Update Data Source command. The Attach Data Source wizard pops up and lets you modify the selection of lists. You can select new lists to add, or uncheck already imported lists to remove them from your data source.

Table Fields Generated for SharePoint Lists

If you take a closer look at the QA table, you can see that there are many fields in addition to the ones you have explicitly added to the custom list after its creation. These fields were automatically added by SharePoint when you created the list. If you would like to know their content, you can create a List and Details screen with the Add New Screen dialog to display the QA table, as you already learned it. Most of the fields in the table are automatically created, as shown in Figure 14-17. The custom fields you added are highlighted.

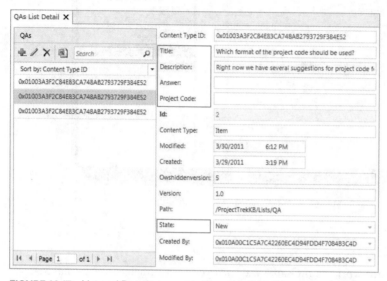

FIGURE 14-17: List and Details screen built on the QA table

NOTE *By now, you have learned that creating a List Detail screen is very easy, so you are not guided through the steps required to implement it. Because Figure 14-17 is used only for illustration, the downloaded source code does not contain this screen.*

Table 14-1 provides a short overview of the list columns (fields in LightSwitch) managed by SharePoint.

TABLE 14-1: List Columns Managed by SharePoint

COLUMN NAME	DESCRIPTION
Content Type	Each object in SharePoint (lists, items, and so on) has a *content type*. This column is the name of the content type, and its value is always Item for a custom list item.
Content Type ID	Unique identifier of the content type.
Id	Unique identifier of the list item, generated when the item is added to the list.
Created	Date and time information indicating when the item was added to the list.
Modified	Date and time information indicating when the item was last modified.
Owshiddenversion	Object versions in SharePoint can be preserved. This column points to an internal identifier indicating the current version in the list item's version history.
Version	Version label of the item.
Path	Path of the list containing the item, relative to the site owning the list.
Created By	Identifies the user who created this item. It references to UserListInfo.
Modified By	Identifies the user who last modified this item. It references to UserListInfo.

All fields except Id are technically writable, so you can modify their value either in the UI or programmatically. However, when you save them, their values will be overridden by SharePoint.

Using SharePoint Data

Your tables attached to SharePoint lists are as easy to use as any other tables in LightSwitch. In the following exercise, you create a List and Detail form to maintain the Q&A list.

TRY IT OUT Creating and Using a Screen with Q&A Data

To create a new screen in order to maintain the Q&A list, follow these steps:

1. Using the Add New Screen dialog, create a new List and Details Screen based on the QA table (select ProjectTrekKBData.QAs in the Add New Screen dialog), and name it **ListQandA**. When it is opened in the Designer, change its Display Name property to **List Q&A**. Alter the root node's type from Columns Layout to Rows Layout.

2. Remove the following layout elements from the QA Details Rows Layout node: Content Type ID, Id, Content Type, Owshiddenversion, Version, Path, Created By, and Modified By. Alter the type of the Created and Modified controls' type from Date Time Picker to Date Time Viewer.

3. Change the height of the Description and Answer text boxes to three lines.

4. Change the layout of the QAs node from List to Data Grid. Remove all elements from the QA Data Grid Row node except Title, Modified, and State. Alter the Modified control's type from Date Time Picker to Date Time Viewer.

FIGURE 14-18: A modified entry in the List Q&A screen

5. Press F5 to run the application. When ProjectTrek is started, open the List Q&A screen. You will see the data of the list items you added earlier through the ProjectTrekKB SharePoint site.

6. Modify one of the list items. For example, type an answer and set the Status to Answered. Click the Save button. The item is saved back to SharePoint, and the Modified field's value is changed accordingly, as shown in Figure 14-18. Notice that you could select the State value from a drop-down list, just as you could earlier in SharePoint.

7. Return to the ProjectTrekKB site (start your web browser and navigate there), and check the content of the Q&A list. Move your mouse over the title of the item you edited in Step 6 and click the drop-down arrow, as shown in Figure 14-19. Select the View Item command from the menu to view all item details.

FIGURE 14-19: Accessing the View Item command

8. You can see that the changes you saved in Step 6 are saved to the SharePoint list. As shown in Figure 14-20, the Answer and State columns are changed, as well as the modification time.

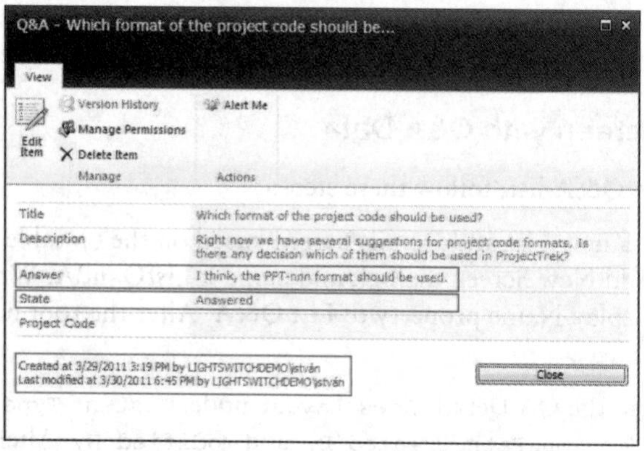

FIGURE 14-20: The modified list item in SharePoint

9. Close the web browser and the `ProjectTrek` application.

 NOTE *You can find the complete code to download for this exercise on this book's companion website at* www.wrox.com *in the folder* Chapter 14\Sample 1 - Attached List.

How It Works

You created a screen based on the `QA` tables exactly as you previously learned. When you ran the application and saved the modified data, it was directed to the `ProjectTrekKBData` source. Instead of sending SQL instructions to a database, this data source sent HTTP requests — using the OData protocol — to the SharePoint server. The server processed the request and saved the data.

After the data was saved, the `ProjectTrek` application refreshed the saved data — by sending another OData request to the SharePoint server — and that is how the new modification time was displayed in Figure 14-18.

The `State` field gets its values from the `QAStates` table (which also comes from SharePoint). When you generated the screen, an Auto Complete Box was generated to represent the `State` UI, so you could use a drop-down list to change its value.

As this exercise demonstrated, there is nothing different about working with SharePoint data than working with SQL Server data. All the mechanisms built into LightSwitch — such as validation, business rules, permissions — function independently of the data source.

However, SharePoint can also have business rules on the server side. For example, if you defined a workflow that does not allow arbitrary changes of the `State` field — only according to the workflow — any violating changes would be rejected by SharePoint. Workflows are just one example of server-side rules that may prevent you from saving changes. LightSwitch will handle them just as any other server-side validation issues during save operations.

Data Type Mapping between SharePoint and LightSwitch

LightSwitch and SharePoint use different data types to represent similar concepts. When you attach to a SharePoint list, the column data types are automatically mapped to LightSwitch types. Table 14-2 summarizes these mappings.

TABLE 14-2: Mappings between SharePoint and LightSwitch Types

SHAREPOINT TYPE	LIGHTSWITCH TYPE	NOTES
Attachment	N/A	In SharePoint, each list item may have an attachment. However, LightSwitch does not support them, so attachment columns are not imported when you attach to a SharePoint list.
Choice Menu	String	LightSwitch imports the menu option values specified in SharePoint as a separate table. In the previous exercise, the QAStates table was a result of this import.
Currency	Double	
Date	DateTime	A Date column stored in SharePoint is imported as a DateTime. You can change the LightSwitch type from DateTime to Date.
Date and Time	DateTime	
Hyperlink	String	The value is a URL. There is no built-in Hyperlink control in LightSwitch to display it as a clickable URL.
Id	Integer	This column is the identifier of the item at the SharePoint site. It is used in LightSwitch as the unique key of the table. Id is read-only.
Multiple Lines of Text	String	This kind of text may contain rich text data. However, there is no built-in control in LightSwitch (such as a rich text or HTML editor) that can be used to display and edit rich text data.
Number	Double	Even if the number set in the SharePoint list is an integer (that is, it has zero digits after the decimal point), the number is represented in LightSwitch as a Double.
Picture	String	A Picture is represented with a URL pointing to the picture source, and the value of a Picture field stores this URL. There is no built-in control to display the picture available at the specified URL.
Single Line of Text	String	If the maximum length of the SharePoint column is defined, LightSwitch imports it and sets the MaxLength property of the imported field accordingly.
Yes/No	Boolean	

Customizing List Data

You can change fields and field properties of the table imported from a SharePoint list, as summarized in the following points:

➤ The name of the table and its fields can be changed to any new name that conforms to the naming rules, as discussed in Chapter 6.

➤ You can change the table and field properties that belong to the Appearance category in the Properties window — namely, the Description, Display Name, and Display by Default properties.

Following are some restrictions on customizing tables imported from SharePoint:

➤ You cannot delete existing table fields.

➤ You can change the field type from an intrinsic type to any business type based on the field's original type. For example, Email Address is based on String, so you can change a Single Line Text or Multiple Line Text SharePoint list column (that is represented in LightSwitch as a String) to Email Address.

➤ You can extend the imported table only with computed properties.

The changes you make in LightSwitch tables leave the original SharePoint lists and their columns intact. LightSwitch does not change them, because that could lead to unpredicted failures in the existing systems. Instead, LightSwitch creates mappings between the existing lists (and all columns) and their representation within LightSwitch. These mappings are used with all list operations. For example, when you retrieve the contents of a list's column, LightSwitch takes care of using the original column name when communicating with SharePoint.

In addition to customizing lists, you can also create relationships between attached SharePoint 2010 lists and LightSwitch tables, as you will learn in the next section.

CREATING RELATIONSHIPS WITH SHAREPOINT 2010 LISTS

You have already learned that the Attach Data Source wizard recognizes the internal relationships within a SharePoint site. You have also learned that when you attach to lists, related lists are also imported, conserving the relationship between tables. This is how the relationships between the Q&A list and the UserInformationList object were preserved. You cannot add new relationships between tables representing SharePoint lists.

Editing Existing SharePoint Relationships

You cannot change the structure of an existing relationship between SharePoint tables. The only thing you can alter is the names of navigation properties.

For example, if you open the QA table in the LightSwitch IDE (double-click the QAs node in Solution Explorer), you'll see two relationships between the QA and UserListInfo tables (as shown earlier in Figure 14-16). Click the `QAItem_ModifiedBy` relationship, and then click the Edit relationship properties task link in the Properties window. (You can also see the name of the relationship in the Properties window.) The Edit Relationships dialog appears, as shown in Figure 14-21. Here you can edit only the names of navigation properties.

Creating Relationships between SharePoint Lists and LightSwitch Tables

Although you are not allowed to change the structure of existing relationships between tables connecting to a SharePoint data source, you have some freedom when creating new relationships between an existing LightSwitch table and an imported SharePoint list. You can create any kind of relationship that does not require changing the structure of the SharePoint list.

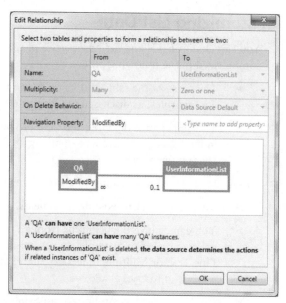

FIGURE 14-21: The Edit Relationships dialog allows only navigation property name editing

Creating such a relationship is an easy task, as you will learn in the following exercise.

TRY IT OUT Creating a Relationship between the QA and Project Tables

The items in the Q&A SharePoint list can be associated with a project record. To assign a Q&A item to a project in the `ProjectTrek` application, you must establish a relationship between the `QA` and `Project` tables. To create this relationship, follow these steps:

1. In the LightSwitch IDE, open the `QA` table in the Designer, and click Add Relationship.

2. When the Add New Relationship dialog appears, `QA` is put on the "many" side of the relationship, as shown in Figure 14-22. This is because, by definition, zero, one, or more `QA` items can be assigned to a `Project`.

3. Select `Project` in the `To` column of the `Name` row as the other side of the relationship. Its multiplicity is set to One by default. Because

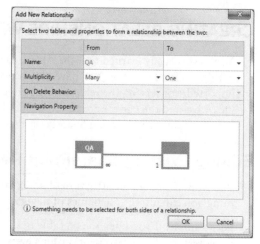

FIGURE 14-22: The QA table is on the "many" side of the new relationship

there may be general Q&A items that do not belong to any concrete project, change the `Project` Multiplicity to Zero or One. Although you specified the role of the tables in this new relationship, you must still find the fields that bind the tables together. The dialog signifies this task with the "A shared property must be selected on both items" message at the bottom, as shown in Figure 14-23.

4. The dialog offers the `Id (Integer)` field of the `Project` table as the primary key at the "zero-or-one" side of the relationship, because this field is the primary key of `Project`. However, there is no integer field in the QA table that matches `Id`. The Q&A list has a `Project Code` column that can be matched with the `Code` column of `Project`. Select `ProjectCode (String)` on the `QA (Foreign)` side, and `Code (String)` on the `Project (Primary)` side, as shown in Figure 14-24.

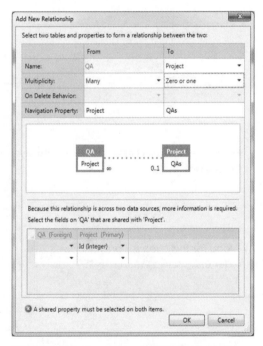

FIGURE 14-23: You must select the fields binding the two tables

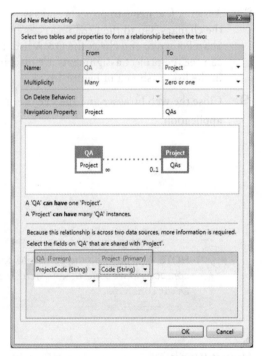

FIGURE 14-24: Project Code and Code are the binding fields of the relationship

5. Click OK. The Designer establishes the relationship between the `QA` and `Project` tables. Save the changes by pressing Ctrl+S.

6. Open the `ListQandA` screen in the Designer. Select the QA `Data Grid Row` and add the `Project` property to this layout item.

7. Start the Application by pressing F5. When `ProjectTrek` is started, open the List Q&A screen. You can assign Q&A items to projects, as shown in Figure 14-25.

FIGURE 14-25: You can assign Q&A items to projects

8. Assign a few items to projects and save the changes. Go to the `ProjectTrekKB` SharePoint site and check the Q&A list. You can see the project assignments are displayed in the list, as shown in Figure 14-26.

9. Close the web browser and the `ProjectTrek` application.

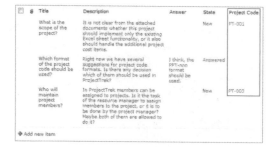

FIGURE 14-26: Project assignments are displayed in the Q&A list

> **NOTE** *You can find the complete code to download for this exercise on this book's companion website at* `www.wrox.com` *in the folder* `Chapter 14\Sample 2 - Relationships`.

How It Works

The Add New Relationship dialog works exactly the same way as you learned earlier. Because `QA` is on the "many" side of the relationship, it needs a foreign key that can be bound with a primary key field in `Project`. However, `QA` represents the Q&A list imported from SharePoint, so it cannot be extended with a new foreign key column. Only the existing columns can be used for this purpose. That is why the `Project Code` column was added to the Q&A list when you created it. On the `Project` side, the `Code` field is the one that semantically matches with `Project Code`, so it is used.

A natural question is why was the `Project Code` column added to the Q&A list when it was created? Why not a `Project Id` column with a `Number` type? As shown in Table 14-2, a `Number` column in SharePoint is mapped to a `Double` field in LightSwitch. If you had created a `Project Id` column, it would have had to be bound with the `Id` field of `Project`. However, `Id` is an `Integer` and it could not be bound to a `Double` field. The `Code` in `Project` is a required field that is included in a unique index, so it also uniquely identifies a `Project` record, just like the `Id` field. Therefore, binding the `Project Code` column with the `Code` field is a workable solution.

There is one small issue with the List Q&A screen. You can easily assign a Q&A item to a project, but you cannot detach an item already bound to a project. It is very easy to add a Detach button that does this job. Using what you learned in Chapter 9, you can do this by yourself. The `Sample 3 - Polishing` folder of the downloaded code contains the solution for this issue.

SUMMARY

LightSwitch applications can be integrated with SharePoint 2010 sites because the IDE can attach to SharePoint lists. With the help of the Attach Data Source wizard, you can select lists from a SharePoint site. These lists are imported into LightSwitch, where you can use them in your screens and business logic exactly as you do in other tables. When you modify data in an imported table, changes are saved back to the SharePoint list.

When the columns of a SharePoint list are imported, their original field types are mapped to LightSwitch field types. You can rename these imported fields by adhering to syntax rules, but you can only change their type from an intrinsic type to any business type based on the field's original type.

The Attach Data Source wizard recognizes the existing relationships among SharePoint lists, and represents them as relationships between the imported tables. You can create new relationships between LightSwitch tables and those imported from SharePoint lists. This feature provides great integration opportunities for SharePoint sites with other data managed in your LightSwitch application.

EXERCISES

1. What version of SharePoint can be used to integrate lists with LightSwitch applications?

2. What URL should you provide to SharePoint when using the Attach Data Source wizard? Should it be the URL of the SharePoint site or the URL of the list you want to attach?

3. When you import a SharePoint list column with a `Number` type, what will be the type of the imported field?

4. What are the restrictions of editing a relationship between two SharePoint lists within the LightSwitch IDE?

 NOTE *Answers to the Exercises can be found in the Appendix.*

▶ **WHAT YOU LEARNED IN THIS CHAPTER**

TOPIC	KEY CONCEPTS
SharePoint list	SharePoint uses the concept of a list as a mechanism for storing structured information. With SharePoint, you can create lists that comprise columns. These columns have types and other properties. The list and its columns are analogous with a database table and its fields.
Attaching to SharePoint lists	In Solution Explorer, right-click the `Data Sources` node and select Add Data Source from the context menu. When the Attach Data Source wizard starts, select the SharePoint data source type, then specify the URL to access the SharePoint site containing the lists. The wizard lets you select the lists to import.
Updating the collection of imported SharePoint lists	Right-click the data source node representing your SharePoint site, and select the Update Data Source command. The Attach Data Source wizard pops up and lets you modify the selection of lists. You can select new lists to add them, or uncheck already imported lists to remove them from your data source.
Data type mappings	When SharePoint lists are imported with the Attach Data Source wizard, columns are imported as fields. The SharePoint column data types are mapped to LightSwitch field types, as summarized in Table 14-2.
Adding a new relationship between a LightSwitch table and a SharePoint list	Open either the LightSwitch table or the imported SharePoint list in the Designer. Click the Add Relationship button, and set the other table of the relationship in the `To` column of the `Name` row. Set up the multiplicity properties, and then define the primary key and foreign key fields. While a foreign key field can be automatically created at the LightSwitch table side, you can only choose from existing columns on the SharePoint table side.

PART IV
Appendix

▶ **APPENDIX:** Answers to Exercises

Answers to Exercises

This appendix provides the answers to Exercises found at the conclusions of each chapter.

CHAPTER 1 EXERCISE ANSWERS

Following are the answers to the Exercises in Chapter 1.

Answer to Question 1

These challenges originate from the fact that people working on a LOB application development project have different mindsets.

➤ The requirements of a LOB application should be carefully collected and communicated within the project to ensure that the right application is being developed.

➤ Key users must be provided with feedback about how you understand their expectations, and you need their feedback about the pieces of your application to check if you are constructing the software they really need.

➤ You must find the optimal feedback frequency to gain the most from the communication surrounding the construction phases. For example, you need to obtain feedback about UI imaginations more often (for example, twice a week) than about results of slight implementation changes (for example, twice a month).

Answer to Question 2

A wireframe is a prototype that depicts the layout of the fundamental elements in the user interface (UI). It contains only a simple graphical design, because its aim is to focus on the structure and content elements. Neglecting the detailed graphical design allows key users to grab the structural details.

Answer to Question 3

A proof-of-concept model is a prototype that proves the feasibility of certain ideas. It is a working model that can be used to demonstrate that the imagined works. Having a proof-of-concept model can not only underpin that the idea is feasible, it can even warn you that you're headed in the wrong direction.

Answer to Question 4

Rapid application development (RAD) emphasizes minimal planning and rapid prototyping against thorough application design and waterfall-like models. This approach is very useful, because it allows software to be developed much faster — while makes it easier to accommodate to the continuously changing project environment.

Answer to Question 5

Here are a few methodologies based on the rapid application development (RAD) principle:

➤   Scrum

➤   Extreme Programming (XP)

➤   Lean Software Development (LD)

➤   Joint Application Development (JAD)

CHAPTER 2 EXERCISE ANSWERS

Following are the answers to the Exercises in Chapter 2.

Answer to Question 1

Visual Studio 2010 is an integrated development environment (IDE) from Microsoft that can be used to develop applications for all Microsoft platforms, including Windows, .NET Framework, Windows Mobile, Windows Phone, Silverlight, and Azure. It has several editions targeting both professional software developers and hobbyists.

Visual Studio LightSwitch is a new member of the Visual Studio family. It is a rapid application development (RAD) tool to aid in writing data-centric line-of-business (LOB) applications.

While LightSwitch enables prototyping with as little explicit coding as possible, Visual Studio provides flexibility and freedom for those who want to develop complex LOB applications.

Answer to Question 2

➤   A business application is currently implemented as a set of Excel sheets and you need to create a more sophisticated UI.

➤ You must create an application working on a small amount of data with a relatively simple structure (simple according to your experience). Most operations create, edit, remove, and list data.

➤ You have an existing application for which you must create a few new functions for a set of users (for example, administering data dictionaries of a large system).

Answer to Question 3

➤ Your project handles a massive amount of data (for example, millions of entries), and, in your experience, the same data has already proven to be a challenge in other projects.

➤ You already have a database and you must primarily create listings and reports. This is not the functionality LightSwitch is tuned for.

➤ You have some technology requirements that cannot be matched with LightSwitch.

Answer to Question 4

You can use the Visual Basic or Visual C# programming languages to develop LightSwitch applications. You can select your preferred programming language when creating a new project.

Answer to Question 5

When you edit a table, you should provide the following information for each field:

➤ *Name* — A unique name that is used in the IDE to identify the field and to refer it.

➤ *Type* — The type of data stored in the field.

➤ *Required* — This flag indicates that the field must contain data. It cannot be left empty when inserting a new record or modifying an existing one.

Answer to Question 6

LightSwitch does not create a screen with WYSIWYG (what-you-see-is-what-you-get) layout whereby each UI element representing your data is exactly positioned. LightSwitch creates a hierarchical layout of the screen elements, which are rendered at runtime.

Answer to Question 7

You can customize a screen in Debug mode within the running application using the Customization Mode dialog. This enables you to modify screens and see how they look without leaving the application. All changes you make are saved back to the development environment.

CHAPTER 3 EXERCISE ANSWERS

Following are the answers to the exercises in Chapter 3.

Answer to Question 1

➤ *Presentation* — This tier is responsible for translating user interactions to tasks that can be sent to the Logic layer, and presenting the results returned from the Logic layer.

➤ *Logic (Business Logic)* — This tier is responsible for executing tasks (business functions) of the application by using the Data tier, and sending the operation results to the Presentation layer.

➤ *Data* — This tier is responsible for storing and retrieving information used by the application — created and consumed by the Logic tier.

Answer to Question 2

The Microsoft .NET Framework is a runtime environment that sits between the operating system and the applications. Its main role is to provide access to all services of the underlying operating system in a managed way that enables developers to be productive. It is the backbone of a LightSwitch application. All related technologies are based on the .NET Framework.

Answer to Question 3

The Base Class Library (BCL) provides objects — several thousands of them — that make complex tasks quite simple and intuitive by utilizing the operating system's API.

Answer to Question 4

Silverlight employs a very flexible layout system. Using it, you can easily create layouts that automatically adapt to the following factors:

➤ Available screen size

➤ Number of items displayed

➤ Size of the displayed elements

➤ Magnification factor

The layout system allows nesting UI elements into other user interface elements (called content controls), and it has layout controls that can automatically position their child elements.

Answer to Question 5

Data binding connects elements of the UI to data or other UI elements — declaratively. This mechanism is especially useful in LOB applications, because information coming from the database and processed by the Logic tier can be declaratively bound (that is, without writing code) to the user interface elements.

Answer to Question 6

The Server Explorer tool window can be used to look at SQL Server data. It can be accessed with the View ⇨ Server Explorer command.

Answer to Question 7

LightSwitch can access lists stored in SharePoint 2010 and use the elements of a list similarly to records in a database table.

Answer to Question 8

Windows Azure is an application platform in the cloud. When you deploy your application to Azure, you can easily upsize and downsize the virtual infrastructure behind your application in minutes through simple configuration.

CHAPTER 4 EXERCISE ANSWERS

Following are the answers to the Exercises in Chapter 4.

Answer to Question 1

This is the SQLCMD utility. This utility is installed on your computer together with Visual Studio LightSwitch.

Answer to Question 2

The original table is left intact. You perceive that LightSwitch uses the new names when you access the external table, but, in the background, the runtime engine maps the new names to the ones that exist in the external table.

Answer to Question 3

Yes, you can. This feature makes LightSwitch very useful and productive.

Answer to Question 4

Open the screen in the Designer and change its layout. You can change the template of screen elements (for example, from a grid to a list), and alter their order. You can also modify their visual appearance and behavior.

Answer to Question 5

No, you don't need to. Define a one-to-many relationship between the table to pick up the items from, and the table having the field that takes its value from the other table. When you create an editable screen, a Modal Window Picker is provided for the field to choose its value from the pick-up table.

Answer to Question 6

➤ Defining default values for table fields

➤ Creating business rules (by intercepting data-modification operations)

➤ Validating the content of entities

➤ Defining code that authorizes the current user against data-modification operations

➤ Defining events to influence the behavior of UI

CHAPTER 5 EXERCISE ANSWERS

Following are the answers to the exercises in Chapter 5.

Answer to Question 1

The use case diagram depicts the users (called *actors*) working with the `ProjectTrek` system, as well as the most important functions (called *use cases*) they deal with. Knowing who the users of `ProjectTrek` are and what functions they use in the application helps facilitate understanding of the application's functional scope.

Answer to Question 2

Each `Project` contains a list of planned additional cost item categories stored in `AdditionalCost`. (It is one of the most important requests of ConsulArt's management.) During the project's lifetime, concrete instances of `CostItem` are assigned to the related `AdditionalCost` item. For example, if a project contains an additional cost category for books, cost items (invoices) for the books *Why Software Sucks* and *Professional Visual Studio 2010* are added to this category.

Answer to Question 3

Yes, definitely. The LightSwitch approach helps you to create simple working application prototypes in a very short time. You can check whether this prototype conforms to the business requirements, and refine it in a few iterations while it is being accepted — either as a high-quality prototype or as the go-live form of the business application.

Answer to Question 4

Visual Studio 2010 can help you extend LightSwitch applications in two ways:

➤ You can load your LightSwitch project in Visual Studio 2010 and add extra projects to the solution (for example, additional code libraries).

➤ You can use Visual Studio 2010 to create extension components for LightSwitch (for example, new themes or custom controls), and integrate them with the LightSwitch IDE.

CHAPTER 6 EXERCISE ANSWERS

Following are the answers to the Exercises in Chapter 6.

Answer to Question 1

➤ Use the "Create new table" task shown in the application Designer right after you create a new project.

➤ Right-click the `Data Sources` node in Solution Explorer and select Add Table from the context menu that pops up on the screen.

➤ When any table is open in the Designer, use the New Table button in the Designer's toolbar.

Answer to Question 2

It is the Maximum Length property. The field will be defined in the database so that it stores up to the number of characters specified in this property.

Answer to Question 3

Intrinsic types represent physical storage types (such as `Integer`, `String`, or `Date`). In contrast, business types extend an intrinsic type with extra behavior (such as validation and formatting).

Answer to Question 4

It is the New Data Screen. All other screens display data coming from the database, so they have a query behind them.

Answer to Question 5

In the table Designer, assign a choice list to the corresponding field, and set it up using pairs of associated values and display names. If you use the default control type for the field in the screen layout, a drop-down list will be provided in the UI, allowing the user to pick a value.

CHAPTER 7 EXERCISE ANSWERS

Following are the answers to the exercises in Chapter 7.

Answer to Question 1

This kind of relationship means that the entity instance at the "one" side has zero, one, or more related instances at the "many" side, while any instance at the "many" side has exactly one instance at the "one" side.

Answer to Question 2

When you select the screen template and specify the table or query to be used as screen data, the dialog provides you with all the tables that can serve as details to your selected table. These are represented with check boxes in the dialog beneath the Additional Data to Include label. Select the ones you want to include in the screen and click OK.

Answer to Question 3

When you create a screen and select a table or a query as the screen data, LightSwitch uses it as an implicit query for the screen. You can add filter conditions, sort order declarations, and parameters to this query, which are used only by the screen.

When you intend to use a query with parameters, filters, and sort orders in more than one screen, you can create an explicit query and save it. When you create new screens, you can select your saved query as the screen data source.

Answer to Question 4

You can do it in two ways:

➤   *Programmatically* — You have to write code to pass parameters to a query and run it explicitly.

➤   *With data binding* — You bind the Parameter Value property of the parameter to a screen data item.

Answer to Question 5

A computed property is a read-only property that is calculated during runtime. For example, if a `Customer` entity has a `FirstName` and a `LastName` property, you can create a `FullName` computed property composed of the first name and last name. Computed properties are not stored in the database.

Answer to Question 6

The following steps show you how to create the `TaskCount` property:

1. Open the `Project` table in the Designer.
2. Click the Computed Property button in the toolbar.
3. Name the new property **TaskCount**, and set its type to `Int32`.
4. While this new property is selected in the Designer, click the Edit Method link in the Properties window.
5. Add the following boldfaced code to the compute method:

```
Private Sub TaskCount_Compute(ByRef result As Integer)
    ' Set result to the desired field value
    result = Me.ProjectTasks.Count
End Sub
```

CHAPTER 8 EXERCISE ANSWERS

Following are the answers to the exercises in Chapter 8.

Answer to Question 1

It is the Microsoft SQL Server Database File data source type. You can connect to a LightSwitch database only by selecting this data source type. The Microsoft SQL Server data source type is useful when you access external SQL Server databases.

Answer to Question 2

This is the `sqlcmd.exe` utility that was installed with SQL Server Express when you ran the setup kit of Visual Studio LightSwitch.

Answer to Question 3

It is the Project ⇨ Add Data Source command. The Server Explorer ⇨ Add Connection command can be used to add a data connection to the Server Explorer tool window, but this connection won't be the part of your project.

Answer to Question 4

LightSwitch recognizes the existing relationships, and automatically creates them. Later, you cannot alter or remove them. You are allowed to modify only the navigation properties of such a relationship.

Answer to Question 5

The golden rule is that you cannot make any modification that would alter the table structure in the external database. As a consequence of this rule, you cannot do the following:

➤ Change the type of a field.

➤ Remove a field from the table.

➤ Add a read-write property to the table (because you can add only computed properties).

Because LightSwitch uses mappings between entities and their underlying tables, you can change table and field names.

Answer to Question 6

You can create a one-to-many relationship between a LightSwitch table on the "one" side and an external SQL Server table on the "many" side, but with restrictions. Because you are not allowed to alter the SQL Server database, you must manually select an existing field of the SQL Server table to function as a foreign key.

If the SQL Server table does not have such a field, you cannot create this kind of relationship.

CHAPTER 9 EXERCISE ANSWERS

Following are the answers to the exercises in Chapter 9.

Answer to Question 1

Yes. LightSwitch not only allows you to bind a data item to another data item, but also uses it as a fundamental technique. For example, this is how screen properties are bound to query parameters. As the screen properties are altered, query parameters automatically follow that change.

Answer to Question 2

If you set the vertical alignment of a layout container to `Stretch`, its height will be stretched to the height of its parent container, and its child controls (including nested layout containers) also will be resized according to their vertical alignment. If the size of the parent container changes (for example, the screen is resized by the user), the layout container follows that change.

Answer to Question 3

The runtime customization works only when you start the application with debugging (by pressing F5 or selecting the Debug ➪ Start Debugging command). In this case, you can see the Design Screen button in the top-right corner of the application. If you can't see this button, you run the application with Ctrl+F5 (Debug ➪ Start Without Debugging).

Answer to Question 4

The `Data Grid Row` node is a container for child elements that defines the columns of the data grid. Each element you add to this node defines a column. They are displayed in the order from left to right as they are nested into the `Data Grid Row`, and their properties determine how the columns are rendered in the grid.

Answer to Question 5

A `Modal Window Picker` can be used to select values from a list shown in a pop-up modal window. It is based on a list that supports paging, search, and sorting, so it is very useful for picking a value from a set with numerous options. For example, when you have many (let's say, several hundred) customers, a `Modal Window Picker` control is a good choice for selecting a customer from the big list.

Answer to Question 6

When you use the Add Button dialog with the New Method option, you add two items to the screen. A method is added to the data item hierarchy, and a button is added to the layout hierarchy. The button is bound to the method, so when it is clicked, the method is executed.

Answer to Question 7

In Solution Explorer, double-click the `Properties` node and select the Screen Navigation tab in the Designer. This tab shows the navigation structure. Select the screen you intend to launch automatically when your application is started, and click the Set button beneath the task hierarchy. The startup screen will be displayed in boldface.

CHAPTER 10 EXERCISE ANSWERS

Following are the answers to the exercises in Chapter 10.

Answer to Question 1

In a normal case, the entity properties are checked twice. First they are validated on the client side. When all client-side checks show that the entity is valid, they are sent to the application server. There they are checked again, because the application server does not trust that its clients have already checked entity properties.

If the save pipeline is intercepted, and somewhere in this logic the entity is modified, all the modified properties are checked again before the data is stored.

Answer to Question 2

Entity validation is always executed on the application server side, after you click the Save button.

Answer to Question 3

You can use the `results` parameter of the `Validate` method to signal validation issues related to a specific entity or an entity property. The `AddPropertyError` and `AddEntityError` methods can be used to signal error messages. The `AddPropertyResult` and `AddEntityResult` methods can be used to add other kinds of messages, such as warnings and informational messages.

Answer to Question 4

It is the `Projects_Deleting` method. The `Projects_Deleted` method is called right after the `Project` instance has been deleted.

Answer to Question 5

In the `Projects_Updated` method, you cannot check it. For this purpose, you must use the `Project_Updating` method, and use the `Details.Properties` collection to access the property to check. Test the value of `IsChanged` to determine whether the property was modified. For example, to check whether the `Code` property was modified, test the `Details.Properties.Code .IsChanged` value.

CHAPTER 11 EXERCISE ANSWERS

Following are the answers to the Exercises in Chapter 11.

Answer to Question 1

Permission is the smallest unit of right an application user can have. You can check the existence of a permission in an access control method. Thus, a permission can be used to control whether you have access to a certain application function.

Answer to Question 2

LightSwitch uses access control methods to check whether certain operations in the application are enabled for the current user. When LightSwitch must check whether an operation is allowed, it invokes the related access control method. You can define the body of access control methods to retrieve a Boolean value in the `result` parameter, which determines whether the operation can be executed. If you do not define an access control method for a guarded operation, it is enabled, by default.

Answer to Question 3

You must define the `CostItems_Insert`, `CostItems_Update`, and `CostItems_Delete` access control methods. You must set the `result` parameter of these methods to `True` when modification is allowed; otherwise, it must be set to `False`.

Answer to Question 4

You can use the Authentication page of the LightSwitch Publish Application Wizard to set up the initial Administrator account. When you use Windows authentication, you need to set only the Windows logon name. In the case of Forms authentication, you must provide a username, full name, and password.

CHAPTER 12 EXERCISE ANSWERS

Following are the answers to the exercises in Chapter 12.

Answer to Question 1

Select the list in the layout item hierarchy and check or uncheck its "Disable exporting data to Excel" property. When it is checked, the "Export to Excel" button is not available in the toolbar of the related control (a `List` or a `DataGrid`).

Answer to Question 2

The UI of LightSwitch applications use Silverlight. A Silverlight application can run either in the browser or out-of-browser (OOB) in its own desktop window. *Elevated trust* means that the application running out-of-browser has more access to system resources than with normal mode — for example, it can use automation objects. The "Export to Excel" command is available only when the LightSwitch application uses the OOB elevated trust mode.

Answer to Question 3

You must check the `AutomationFactory.IsAvailable` property. It retrieves a `True` value if you can use automation; otherwise, it returns `False`. The `AutomationFactory` object is declared in the `System.Runtime.InteropServices.Automation` namespace.

Answer to Question 4

Macro recording, available in Microsoft Word and Excel, is very useful when you do not know exactly which object and method to use for a certain operation. Turn on macro recording and carry out the required operation manually. After you stop recording, you can have a look at the macro and associate code lines with your manual operations. You can use the context-sensitive help (F1) to obtain more information.

CHAPTER 13 EXERCISE ANSWERS

Following are the answers to the exercises in Chapter 13.

Answer to Question 1

The thin client application involves only the presentation layer (UI). It uses a network protocol to communicate with an application component that provides the business logic.

The thick client application encapsulates the business logic of the system, not just the presentation layer (UI). Only the data is stored outside of the application (for example, in a remote database server).

Answer to Question 2

You can select from the desktop or web client types. When you choose a desktop client, the application runs on the end-user's desktop in a separate application window. A web client runs in the browser started by the user.

Answer to Question 3

You can choose from three application server topology options:

➤ *Client machine* — The application services run on the end-user's machine in the same client as the presentation layer. This option can be paired only with the desktop client topology.

➤ *Internet Information Services (IIS)* — The application services run on a separate server machine, hosted in Internet Information Services (IIS).

➤ *Windows Azure* — The application services and the database are hosted in the Windows Azure platform.

Answer to Question 4

In order for your IIS server to be properly prepared for deploying LightSwitch application server components, you must carry out the following tasks:

- ➤ Install LightSwitch prerequisites to the web server machine.
- ➤ Verify IIS settings and set up IIS features and services.
- ➤ Configure the SQL Server client network access on the IIS server computer.

Answer to Question 5

To prepare for deploying to the Windows Azure platform, you must meet the following prerequisites:

- ➤ Obtain a Windows Azure subscription.
- ➤ Learn the basics of creating hosted services, storage accounts, and SQL Azure databases.
- ➤ Create a hosted service and a storage account for your LightSwitch application.
- ➤ Create a SQL Azure database to hold your application's data.

Answer to Question 6

In the Azure Service Configuration page you can set the Service and Storage account information used by your application. This is also where you specify whether you want to deploy the application to the staging environment or the production environment.

CHAPTER 14 EXERCISE ANSWERS

Following are the answers to the exercises in Chapter 14.

Answer to Question 1

You must use SharePoint 2010 or later. Earlier versions (such as SharePoint 2003 and 2007) cannot integrate with LightSwitch.

Answer to Question 2

The Attach Data Source wizard expects the URL of the SharePoint site. According to this URL, it retrieves the collection of available site lists so that you can select the ones you want to attach. If you specify a list URL, the wizard will give you an error message stating that the URL you provided is invalid.

Answer to Question 3

If you import a SharePoint list column with the Number type, it is always imported as a Double field, even if the Number column is declared semantically as an integer value with no digits after the decimal point. This means that you cannot create a column in a SharePoint list to be used as a foreign key to an `Integer` LightSwitch field.

Answer to Question 4

The relationship between two SharePoint lists appears as a relationship between the imported tables. You cannot edit the structure of this relationship (that is, change tables or multiplicities). The only thing you can do is change navigation property names.

INDEX

W

X

Y